Individual Differences and Instructe

Language Learning and Language Teaching

The *LL&LT* monograph series publishes monographs as well as edited volumes on applied and methodological issues in the field of language pedagogy. The focus of the series is on subjects such as classroom discourse and interaction; language diversity in educational settings; bilingual education; language testing and language assessment; teaching methods and teaching performance; learning trajectories in second language acquisition; and written language learning in educational settings.

Series editors

Birgit Harley
Ontario Institute for Studies in Education, University of Toronto

Jan H. Hulstijn
Department of Second Language Acquisition, University of Amsterdam

Volume 2

Individual Differences and Instructed Language Learning
Edited by Peter Robinson

Individual Differences and Instructed Language Learning

Edited by

Peter Robinson

Aoyama Gakuin University

John Benjamins Publishing Company
Amsterdam/Philadelphia

™ The paper used in this publication meets the minimum requirements of American National Standard for Information Sciences – Permanence of Paper for Printed Library Materials, ANSI Z39.48-1984.

Library of Congress Cataloging-in-Publication Data

Individual Differences and Instructed Language Learning / edited by Peter Robinson.
  p. cm. (Language Learning and Language Teaching, ISSN 1569–9471 ; v. 2)
 Includes bibliographical references and indexes.
  1. Language and languages--Study and teaching. 2. Individual differences. I. Robinson, Peter, 1956- II. Series.

P53.446 I53 2002
418 .0071-dc21   2002074622
ISBN 90 272 1693 2 (Eur.) / 1 58811 230 6 (US) (Hb; alk. paper)
ISBN 90 272 1694 0 (Eur.) / 1 58811 231 4 (US) (Pb; alk. paper)

John Benjamins Publishing Co. · P.O. Box 36224 · 1020 ME Amsterdam · The Netherlands
John Benjamins North America · P.O. Box 27519 · Philadelphia PA 19118-0519 · USA

Contributors

Zoltán Dörnyei, University of Nottingham, U. K.

Takako Egi, Georgetown University, U. S. A.

Akiko Fujii, Georgetown University, U. S. A.

Elena L. Grigorenko, Yale University, U. S. A., and Moscow State University, Russia.

Birgit Harley, Ontario Institute for Studies in Education, University of Toronto, Canada.

Doug Hart, Ontario Institute for Studies in Education, University of Toronto, Canada.

Peter D. MacIntyre, University College of Cape Breton, Canada.

Alison Mackey, Georgetown University, U. S. A.

Jenefer Philp, University of Tasmania, Australia.

Leila Ranta, University of Alberta, Canada.

Peter Robinson, Aoyama Gakuin University, Japan.

Steven Ross, Kwansei Gakuin University, Japan.

Miyuki Sasaki, Nagoya Gakuin University, Japan.

Peter Skehan, King's College, University of London, U. K.

Robert J. Sternberg, Yale University, U. S. A.

Tomoaki Tatsumi, Georgetown University, U. S. A.

Naoko Yoshinaga, Hirosaki Gakuin College, Japan.

Contents

Preface ix

1. Introduction: Researching individual differences and instructed
   learning 1
   Peter Robinson

Section I Theoretical Issues

2. The theory of successful intelligence and its implications
   for language aptitude testing 13
   Robert J. Sternberg

3. Motivation, anxiety and emotion in second language acquisition 45
   Peter D. MacIntyre

4. Theorising and updating aptitude 69
   Peter Skehan

5. Foreign language acquisition and language-based learning
   disabilities 95
   Elena L. Grigorenko

6. Learning conditions, aptitude complexes and SLA: A framework 113
   for research and pedagogy
   Peter Robinson

Section II   Empirical Studies

Classroom studies

7. The motivational basis of language learning tasks   137
    Zoltán Dörnyei

8. The role of learners' language analytic ability in the
    communicative classroom   159
    Leila Ranta

Experimental studies

9. Individual differences in working memory, noticing of
    interactional feedback and L2 development   181
    *Alison Mackey, Jenefer Philp, Takako Egi, Akiko Fujii,
    and Tomoaki Tatsumi*

10. Effects of individual differences in intelligence, aptitude and
    working memory on adult incidental SLA: A replication and
    extension of Reber, Walkenfield and Hernstadt (1991)   211
    Peter Robinson

Instructed versus naturalistic exposure studies

11. Aptitude-exposure interaction effects on Wh-movement violation
    detection by pre-and-post-critical period Japanese bilinguals   267
    Steven Ross, Naoko Yoshinaga, and Miyuki Sasaki

12. Age, aptitude and second language learning on a bilingual
    exchange   301
    Birgit Harley and Doug Hart

References   331

Index   373

Preface

Learners differ in how successfully they adapt to, and profit from instruction. This book aims to show that this fact cannot be explained by research into individual differences (IDs) in such areas as aptitude, anxiety and motivation *alone*, or by debates over the merits of one form of pedagogic intervention versus another *alone*. Rather, learning (and relative success) is a result of the *interaction* between learner characteristics, and learning contexts. Describing, and explaining these patterns of ID-intervention interactions is fundamentally important to theories of instructed second language acquisition (SLA), and for effective pedagogy.

Researching such interactions, while therefore necessary, is both theoretically, and empirically challenging. Research into IDs, and their effects on learning, is a huge field of study, with an academic journal (often multiple journals) dedicated to reporting findings about almost every ID variable one could name (*Intelligence*; *Journal of Personality and Social Psychology*; *Motivation and Emotion*, etc.). Debate about the optimal conditions for instructed language learning, often drawing on findings from SLA research, also fills the pages of many major journals each month (*Language Learning*; *Studies in Second Language Acquisition*; *TESOL Quarterly*, etc). This book brings these two areas of research *together*, providing an up-to-date perspective, from leading researchers interested in both, on how individual differences affect second language learning in a variety of contemporary instructional contexts and settings. The first section, 'Theoretical Issues', contains chapters summarizing relevant recent research into the roles of intelligence, language learning aptitude, and motivation, anxiety and emotion during SLA, and contains a number of programmatic proposals for future research in these areas. In the second section, issues raised in earlier chapters are further explored in empirical studies of the effects of these ID variables on language learning in classroom (task-based, immersion and communicative), naturalistic, and experimental settings.

Many people provided the theoretical input, and practical help that led to this book. My own interest in this area was kindled by a finding from my Ph.D research, supervised by Dick Schmidt (and reported in chapters by Skehan, and Robinson, this volume) that L2 learning in an incidental, processing for meaning, condition, showed no significant relationship to two traditional subtests of aptitude, in contrast to learning in an instructed, and rule-search condition, and even an implicit condition, where learners memorized examples. I thought then that this result was found because the measures of aptitude were insensitive to the processing requirements of incidental learning (Robinson, 1997a), but that other measures may be sensitive to these — an issue I explore in detail in Chapter 10. At the same time I had begun to examine ways in which pedagogic tasks could be sequenced for learners on the basis of intrinsic differences in the processing demands contributing to their relative cognitive complexity, and the implications of this for syllabus design (see Long & Crookes, 1992; Robinson, 1995a). But I was also interested in how differences *between* learners (in say aptitude, or anxiety) contributing to their perceptions of the 'difficulty' of any one task type would affect learning and performance, as well as how such differences would affect uptake of focus on form (Long, 1991), delivered via various techniques during on-task interventions. These two lines of research, then, are fairly typical examples of aptitude (individual differences) — treatment (task or processing condition) interaction research, as described by Richard Snow (1994), and also in the work of Robert Sternberg, and Peter Skehan (see their chapters, this volume).

The idea for this book led first to a conference, *Individual differences in foreign language learning: Effects of aptitude, intelligence and motivation*, held at Aoyama Gakuin University in March, 1999. I am very grateful to all those English Department members, faculty and students who made that conference possible, and successful; in particular, Tamae Yoshino and Kasumi Kohno, Ben Saito and Greg Strong, and two graduate students, Yukiko Niwa and Yuki Yoshimura, all helped considerably. Thanks are also due to the many paper presenters and other attendees who contributed to the discussions, to Steve Cornwell for helping edit the proceedings, and to the plenary speakers, Elena Grigorenko, Peter MacIntyre, Peter Skehan and Robert Sternberg for travelling to Tokyo, and for subsequently agreeing to write their chapters for the first section of this book. Following the conference contributors to the second section agreed to submit complementary data-based studies, and I am extremely grateful for their subsequent hard work and e-mail cooperation in preparing and revising their chapters. I thank also the blind, external reviewers of those chapters, Robert DeKeyser, Robert Gardner, Michael Harrington, and Mark Sawyer, for their prompt, critical, and helpful reviews. Larry

Selinker, and above all Peter Skehan, have been very supportive of this project as it approached publication, and I thank them warmly for that. Finally, my thanks go to the series editors, Jan Hulstijn and Birgit Harley, and to Kees Vaes at John Benjamins for all they have done, and for their commitment to seeing this project to completion.

Peter Robinson, January, 2002

CHAPTER 1

Introduction

Researching individual differences and instructed learning

Peter Robinson
Aoyama Gakuin University

The broad aim of this book is to present recent theoretical thinking about, and empirical research into, the fit between person (second language learner) and situation (learning condition) in second language (L2) classrooms. As such the chapters in this book are concerned with what has been called aptitude-treatment interaction research and theory (see Corno, Cronbach, Kupermintz, Lohman, Mandinach, Porteus & Talbert, 2002; Cronbach & Snow, 1977), as it applies to L2 learners in instructed settings.

The studies presented in the second section of this book illustrate three complementary, contexts for conducting such research. The approach, illustrated by Dörnyei, and Ranta, in their chapters, is to use *intact classes* to examine the interaction of individual difference variables with learning over extended periods of time in classrooms following different instructional programs (task-based, and communicative instructional programs respectively). The chapters by Mackey, Philp, Egi, Fujii and Tatsumi, and by Robinson adopt *experimental* designs, and random selection, and allocation of participants to learning conditions with the aim of investigating the interaction of individual difference variables with specific learning processes, such as (in Mackey et al.'s case) noticing and uptake of recasts, or (in Robinson's case) incidental learning during processing for meaning. Finally, since one aim of recent communicative and task-based approaches to classroom instruction is to accommodate as far as possible — while 'speeding up' — naturalistic processes (Long, 1988), a third option is to examine aptitude-learning relationships both *within* as well as *outside* classrooms in order to examine areas of difference, and similarity between them (see the chapters by Harley & Hart, and Ross,

Yoshinaga & Sasaki on learning during study abroad programs, and the effects of early, naturalistic, versus late, instructed exposure on learning).

Person variables can be broadly classified as cognitive and affective/conative, where cognitive abilities (such as intelligence, language learning aptitude, or working memory capacity and speed) are distinguished from affective/conative factors (such as anxiety, motivation, and emotion). The five chapters in the first section of this collection describe recent theoretical developments in thinking about cognitive abilities and affective/conative variables, and their relationship to instructed language learning, in a variety of contexts. As Snow (1987) and others (see e.g., Sternberg & Wagner, 1994) have pointed out, it is only in establishing and researching the interaction of each of these kinds of person variables with the learning context that the nature of the optimal 'fit' between learning and instruction can be identified. In the domain of L2 learning in instructed settings there is considerable need for renewed research effort into establishing this optimal fit. There are four main reasons for this.

The differentiation of cognitive abilities, intelligences, and aptitudes

Firstly, theoretical perspectives on the nature of the relevant cognitive abilities for language learning, and their structure, have progressed considerably in recent years. It is now widely argued, for example, that intelligence, and language learning aptitude, are not monolithic and general, but differentiated concepts, and that there are likely multiple intelligences, as well as multiple aptitudes for language learning. This is the theme of the chapters by Sternberg, Grigorenko, and Robinson, in the first section of this book. Sternberg (1985a, 1990) has long challenged the traditional, psychometric notion of intelligence as an overarching, general ability or 'g' (see Gustaffson, 1988; Jensen, 1998 for review), in favor of a model that proposes three types of intellectual competence; *analytic* abilities used in analyzing, judging and comparing and contrasting; *creative* abilities used in creating, inventing and discovering; and *practical* abilities used to apply, implement or use knowledge. Individual differences in each of these abilities need to be considered in matching learners to appropriate instructional methods, and in his chapter Sternberg describes research into how this can be — and has been — done, and its implications for language aptitude testing, in particular the design of the CANAL-F aptitude test (Grigorenko, Sternberg & Ehrman, 2000).

Sternberg therefore strongly argues that the abilities necessary for suc-

cessful learning must be more than those memory and analytic abilities largely measured by traditional intelligence tests such as the Wechsler Adult
Intelligence Scale (Wechsler, 1939, 1997), or language learning aptitude tests
such as the Modern Language Aptitude Test (MLAT, Carroll & Sapon, 1959).
While traditional measures of memory and analytic abilities are still important predictors of instructed L2 learning, as Skehan (1998a, this volume) has
argued, and as some of the studies in the second section of this volume show
(e.g., Ranta, and Harley & Hart), other studies lend support to Sternberg's
claim that there is a need to supplement traditional ways of measuring these
(see Mackey et al., and Robinson), and to motivate a broader range of component aptitude processes and abilities which can be matched to specific
instructional options. This is an area for much needed future research.

In her chapter Grigorenko provides a detailed summary of research into
individual differences in cognitive abilities — and at the lower tail of their distribution in populations, what can be called deficits or 'disabilities' — across
a variety of language learning contexts and skill domains. One issue she
explores is the extent to which native language (NL) disabilities, as manifest,
for example, in specific language impairment, or dyslexia, are related to poor
aptitude for foreign language learning, proposing a number of explanations
for why this may be so. Grigorenko's review of NL deficiencies in speech perception, and how they might be related to phonological working memory
provides an interesting link to the later chapter in the second section of this
volume by Mackey et al. who explore L2 differences in phonological working
memory capacity as it affects 'noticing' (Schmidt, 1990, 2001), and uptake of
'focus on form' (Long, 1991) prompted via recasts. Grigorenko's review of NL
abilities and disabilities in phonological, morphological and syntactic awareness, also has implications for many other focus on form techniques for
prompting 'noticing' (see Doughty & Williams, 1998), and the extent to
which the success of each may be facilitated, or inhibited, in L2 classrooms by
the residue of NL abilities possibly contributing to L2 aptitude — an issue
Robinson takes up in his chapter.

Robinson, adopting the interactionist framework of Snow (1987, 1994)
identifies a number of 'aptitude-complexes' or combinations of cognitive abilities that he argues are differentially related to processing under different conditions of instructional exposure to L2 input, and therefore that strengths in
one or another of these complexes of abilities can be expected to be important
to learning from one instructional technique, or under one condition, versus
another. Sternberg, in his chapter comments on his own attempts to learn

three different languages — with very different degrees of success — that '...my aptitude was not internal to me, but in the interaction between my abilities and the way I was being taught'. Robinson's framework is an attempt to specify the information processing details of this observation, and to relate them to current issues in SLA theory and pedagogy. Robinson also argues, as Grigorenko illustrates, that some learners may have more clearly differentiated abilities than others — and it is particularly important to match these learners to instructional conditions which favor their strengths in aptitude complexes, in contrast to other learners who may have less differentiated abilities, and equivalent strengths, and aptitudes for learning under a variety of conditions of exposure.

Evidence of second language acquisition processes and constraints

It is also clear that the last two decades of second language acquisition (SLA) research have added considerably to our knowledge of the cognitive processes, and constraints, implicated in instructed SLA. We know not only considerably more about the course of L2 morphological and syntactic development, and stages of acquisition (e.g., Andersen, 1991; Li & Shirai, 2000; Meisel, Clahsen & Pienemann, 1981; Perdue, 1993), but more about such processes as L2 automatization and restructuring (DeKeyser, 2001; McLaughlin & Heredia, 1996; Segalowitz, in press); lexical access and retrieval in a second language (Kroll & de Groot, 1997; Pienemann, 1998); differences in the processes underlying, and the scope of, implicit, incidental and explicit L2 learning (de Graaff, 1997b; N.Ellis, 1994; Hulstijn, 2001, in press; Robinson, 1996a); form-function mappings in L2 development (Becker & Carroll, 1997; Sato, 1990; Slobin, 1993); and the extent to which interaction can facilitate these and other L2 learning processes (Doughty, 2001; Gass, 1997; Gass, Mackey & Pica, 1998; Long, 1996; Mackey, 1999; Pica, Young & Doughty, 1987; Sato, 1990).

We also have much more evidence for the existence of a critical period for L2 learning, and the extent of its effects on language development in such areas as phonological, lexical, and syntactic development (Birdsong, 1999; DeKeyser, 2000; Long, 1990; Skehan, 1998a, this volume). Critical period effects have often been considered important to the debate over whether, and to what extent, adult L2 learners have 'access' to the innate knowledge and mechanisms described in theories of, or programs for investigating, Universal

Grammar (Chomsky, 1986, 1995) which some argue guide L1 acquisition (see e.g., Gregg, 2001; Schachter, 1996; Schwartz & Sprouse, 2000; White & Genesee, 1996). But they also imply (in the absence of convincing evidence that such access is obligatory, and automatic — see Carroll, [2001]) that age of onset of L2 acquisition (before versus following the critical period) might be expected to draw on *different clusters* of cognitive abilities — an interaction illustrated by Ross, Yoshinaga, and Sasaki, and Harley and Hart in their studies in the second section of this volume, and a finding of considerable consequence for both SLA theory and pedagogy.

As Skehan points out in his chapter, the information summarized briefly above was not available to researchers investigating the structure of foreign language learning aptitude in the 1960s and 1970s. Consequently, some reconceptualisation of language learning aptitude is currently necessary, in order to bring conventional measures more closely into line with what we now know of language learning processes, and mechanisms, and Skehan (1998a, this volume) makes a number of suggestions about how this could best be done. The core of Skehan's proposal in his chapter is that aptitude measures need to be differentiated according to the SLA processing stage they correspond to, and he identifies four broad stages; *noticing* the input; *patterning* the input to facilitate further analysis and generalization; *controlling* the analyzed knowledge in production; and *lexicalising*, or variegating the patterns learned to suit different communicative, and situational contexts.

This sequential, processing stage approach to identifying the components of aptitude is similar in conception to one approach adopted by MacIntyre and Gardner (1994a; MacIntyre, this volume; Onwuegbuzie, Bailey, & Daley, 2000) to measuring the effects of anxiety on L2 learning and use at the input, central processing, and output stages (the Input, Processing, Output Anxiety Scale, IPOAS), and it is an interesting question whether aptitude and anxiety at these different stages are related, such that, for example, poor aptitude for noticing input leads to greater input anxiety. If so, then this would be evidence in support of Sparks and Ganschow's claim (1991, 1993a, 1993b; see Grigorenko's review, this volume), that anxiety is largely an epiphenomenon (not a cause) of poor L2 performance, and further that poor aptitude for L2 learning (which does cause poor performance) may also be related to deficits in L1 encoding abilities (an issue which Skehan also addresses). However, reviewing the evidence in this area, MacIntyre (this volume) argues that while there is some support for the anxiety-as-epiphenomenon claim made by Sparks and Ganschow, other research has shown anxiety to directly influence

L2 learning and performance (both positively and negatively), independently of learners' current level of L2 ability, or level of aptitude.

Robinson and Skehan's frameworks, while ultimately complementary, therefore address the issue of reconceptualising aptitude (urged by Sternberg, this volume) from different directions. Robinson, following Snow (1987), attempts to describe aptitude as it is relevant to learning under different conditions of exposure to input. Starting from a description of different *learning conditions* (see Robinson, 1996a, 1997b; Robinson & Ha, 1993, for studies) he then attempts to match them to aptitude complexes which complement the information processing abilities they draw on. In contrast, Skehan takes as his starting point the *information processing operations* implicated in learning under *any* condition of exposure (see also Skehan, 1998a for discussion) and attempts to match stages in global information processing to aptitude characteristics and potential subtests. These different emphases, and frameworks, also point to different potential applications of aptitude tests — Robinson's to *matching* of learners to optimum learning conditions based on strengths in aptitude complexes — Skehan's to *diagnosing* (and subsequently supporting) poor aptitude at one or another processing stage.

Skehan's and Robinson's introductory chapters, dealing directly as they do with issues in current SLA research, such as the nature of automatization in access to L2 knowledge, and control of L2 production (DeKeyser, 2001; Hulstijn, 2001; Segalowitz, in press); the nature of implicit versus explicit SLA processes (de Graaff, 1997b; DeKeyser, in press; N. Ellis, 1994; Hulstijn, in press); the putative necessity of 'noticing' for L2 learning (Schmidt, 1990, 1993, 2001; Tomlin & Villa, 1994), and effective options for delivering 'focus on form' during communicative interaction which aim to facilitate it (Doughty & Williams, 1998; Long, 1991; Long & Robinson, 1998), therefore lead in naturally to the issues addressed in the second section of this book, where empirical studies of learning inside and outside classrooms are reported.

The changing nature of second language instructional practices

Second language instructional practices have also changed and diversified over the last twenty years. While measures of ability for language learning such as the MLAT were found to have predictive validity as measures of learning in predominantly audiolingual classrooms in the 1960s (see the chapter by Skehan for historical review) there is likely a need to revise them in line with the very different '*macro' level* processing, and practice demands of instruction in *immersion* (see Harley & Hart, this volume); *communicative* (see Ranta, this volume); and *task-based* classrooms (see Dörnyei, this volume), as well as with more '*micro' level* analyses of the interaction of cognitive abilities with different instructional techniques for focus on form (see Doughty & Williams, 1998), such as *recasting* (Mackey et al. this volume), *input flooding* (White, 1998), or *input processing* instruction (Van Patten, 1996) as they occur in each of these contemporary instructional settings.

The well known response of Krashen (1981) to the fact that traditional measures of language learning aptitude seemed heavily biased towards predicting the effects of instruction in audiolingual, and grammar-focussed instructional settings was to argue that aptitude only predicted 'learning', not 'acquisition' as it occurred in classrooms which prioritized the provision of comprehensible input and eschewed any systematic attempts at focus on form. Each of the authors of the studies in the second section of this book take issue with the facts of, or the reasoning behind, such a simple dismissal of the relevance of aptitude to classroom learning. In some cases they show that the *fact* itself is not true (components of traditional aptitude tests *do* predict differential learning in immersion, and communicative classrooms; see the chapters by Harley & Hart, and Ranta) or take issue with the *reasoning* behind the claim that, in principle, individual differences in aptitude do not predict differences in natural acquisition processes (e.g., by showing that individual differences in, for example, working memory capacity *can* be shown to predict uptake of focus on form provided by recasts, see Mackey et al., or incidental learning during processing for meaning, see Robinson). Taken together, the results of these studies show that traditional measures of aptitude need not be abandoned, but do need to be modified in order to be optimally predictive in contemporary classroom settings.

Rethinking connections between motivation, anxiety, emotion and classroom variables

Finally, while conceptions of aptitude are currently under revision, to bring them into line with findings from SLA research and innovations in the conditions of SL pedagogy — and the information processing demands they implicate — there has also been considerable reconceptualization of the affective variables thought to contribute to differential instructed L2 learning success. While aptitude and intelligence are to a large extent fixed cognitive attributes of the learner (though Sternberg and Grigorenko, this volume, argue these are, to some extent, both trainable and learnable — another area of needed future research), motivation and anxiety can clearly often be changed and shaped through teacher intervention in learning. Gardner's model of motivation (1985), distinguishing between *attitudes* towards a target culture's speakers; *integrative motivation* (to learn the language in order to acculturate to, or integrate with the target language community); and *instrumental motivation* (to learn the L2 for some external reward), has been the basis of by far the largest part of sustained SLA research into the roles of attitudes and motivation in SLA to date. However, this model is currently being expanded, incorporating new concepts from psychology and learning theory (Crookes & Schmidt, 1991; Dörnyei, 2001, this volume; MacIntyre, this volume; Tremblay & Gardner, 1995).

In his chapter MacIntyre argues strongly for the continuing importance of the measure of attitudes and motivation put forward by Gardner (the Attitudes and Motivation Test Battery — AMTB — Gardner, 1985) and of his socio-educational model. This model was based on initial research (Gardner & Lambert, 1959) into school-age, Anglophone, learning of French in Canada, which subsequently carefully explored the predictive validity of the factors it distinguished across a variety of other learning and cultural contexts, e.g., learning English in India (Lukmani, 1972), and in the Philippines (Gardner & Lambert, 1972). Since then the AMTB has been widely adapted and translated, allowing cross-cultural research into the roles of attitudes and motivation to proceed programmatically (see e.g., Brown, Robson & Rosenkjar, 1996; Yamashiro & McLaughlin, 2000). However, MacIntyre cautions, care is always necessary in adapting specific items in the questionnaire instrument itself to different social-cultural contexts. To take one example, 'attitudes' to the target culture (a key construct in Gardner's theory) in the original version of the AMTB necessarily operationalizes French-L1-culture in Canada as the attitudinal target of interest. But in adapting the AMTB to language learners in different social-cultural contexts, such as, for example, learners of English in Japan where attitudes to the English-L1-culture of preference are naturally more diversified (including English speakers from Australia, Canada, New Zealand, the UK, the USA, etc.), the items assessing attitudes themselves also need to be diversified in order to accommodate such a range of target cultures, and so to properly assess 'attitudes' to them (see Suzuki, 2002, for discussion).

Leaving aside issues of the cultural validity of translated *adaptations* of the AMTB (issues, of course, relevant to the cross-cultural adaptation of many other measures of individual differences, see Ceci, 1990; Dörnyei & Schmidt, 2001; Gardner, Smythe & Lalonde, 1984; Oxford, 1997; Sternberg & Wagner, 1994; Sternberg, this volume), MacIntyre also suggests that anxiety, and in particular the role of emotion in L2 learning are deserving of more attention than they have received in individual differences research into instructed L2 learning to date (see Schumann, 1998, for an extensive treatment of the neural correlates of emotion, and their possible relation to SLA processes). For example, describing a common finding of studies adopting the AMTB, i.e., that reported high integrative and instrumental 'orientations' alone do not often correlate highly with higher levels of L2 proficiency, MacIntyre argues that '...a better understanding of emotion has the capacity to explain cases where students endorse orientations but might not be energized to take action, and also cases where action is prevented by emotional arousal, either present or anticipated'.

In addition, as MacIntyre further explains in his chapter, recent research in motivation and anxiety has also become increasingly concerned with measuring the effects of specific *classroom variables*, such as *task type* (Holthouse, 1995; Jacob, 1996; Julkunen, 1989, 2001; Niwa, 2000; Robinson, 2001a; Skehan, 1998a, 1998b) and *grouping options* (Crookes & Schmidt, 1991; Dörnyei, 2001; Dörnyei & Malderez, 1997; Oxford & Shearin, 1994) on motivation and anxiety, and the mediating effects of these factors on instructed L2 learning and performance. Zoltán Dörnyei has, as MacIntyre notes, been at the forefront of attempts to theorize, and operationalize classroom-centered models of motivation (see Dörnyei, 2001; Dörnyei & Otto, 1998), and Dörnyei, in his chapter in the second section of this volume, proposes a 'process' model of motivation suitable for measuring these effects — pointing out where it is complementary to, and different from, previous models of L2 motivation — and assesses its relationship to measures of classroom (task-based) L2 language change.

SLA processes, transitions, and L2 pedagogy

Given all of these recent changes and advances — in conceptions of the nature of intelligence, aptitude, motivation, and the roles of anxiety and emotion in language learning, as well as in the recommendations for effective classroom instruction, following recent findings from SLA research — the time is clearly right for a book which brings together contemporary theoretical insight into, and empirical studies of, the role of individual differences in L2 learning. This book therefore moves from a survey of theoretical issues in the study of individual differences in Section 1–containing a number of programmatic proposals for how current measurement instruments might be further adapted, or new ones developed and implemented — to rigorous empirical studies of the effects of individual differences on instructed and naturalistic learning in Section 2; themselves adding to our knowledge of how individual differences in person variables interact with the conditions of instructed language exposure. Such research is doubly necessary, as the sections and chapters which follow show, not only for the light it casts on the cognitive correlates of SLA *processes*, and thereby on the cognitive architecture within which *transitions* in L2 knowledge states occur, but also on the design of effective instructional *practice* which aims to facilitate them.

Theoretical Issues

The theory of successful intelligence and its implications for language-aptitude testing

Robert J. Sternberg
Yale University

Introduction

When I studied Latin, I was a good student. My teachers gave me good grades, and, from time to time, complimented me on my performance. When next I studied French, I was a humdrum student at best. One of my teachers commented that it was obvious that I was doing as well as I was — which was nothing great — only because of my general abilities: I certainly lacked language-aptitude skills. At that point I decided never to take another course in a foreign language. Why bother if I had no talent for it?

As a faculty member just entering my early thirties, an occasion arose that forced me to study a foreign language again, this time, Spanish. I had been asked to develop a program to help improve the thinking skills of Venezuelan undergraduate university students. As the program would be in Spanish in a Spanish-speaking country, I was able to use the general abilities on which my French teacher had complimented me to figure out that I had better learn some Spanish. I did, and had the greatest success of all. My tutor repeatedly commented on how fast and how well I was learning.

So I learned three different languages, with three very different language-learning experiences. My teachers of each language had very different ideas about what my language aptitude was. Did I actually have a different level of language aptitude for each language I studied? Possibly, but not probably. Rather, a very different mechanism much more likely was at work. I was being taught in different ways and responding differently to each of these ways. My aptitude was not internal to me, but in the interaction between my abilities and the way I was being taught.

In fact, the Latin courses relied very heavily on analytical kinds of thinking — analyzing, evaluating, comparing, and contrasting. We frequently were analyzing texts and trying to figure out what they meant. The French courses relied very heavily on memory skills — recalling, recognizing, and discriminating. We memorized long lists of paired associates and had to repeat them back on tests. The Spanish instruction was much more creative and at the same time more practical. I was creating dialogues and having real conversations. My tutor and I talked in Spanish about what my experiences in Venezuela would be like. I was very focused on learning Spanish so that I actually could use it. Later I would go to teach in Mexico, in Spanish, and once again I started lessons with a very creative and practical focus.

These experiences suggest that language aptitude is not some single fixed quantity but involves multiple aspects (see also Carroll & Sapon, 1959; Home 1971; Parry & Child, 1990; Petersen & Al-Haik, 1976; Pimsleur, 1966a). Rather, it may vary as a function of the way a language will be taught and progress assessed. These experiences are consistent with the common-sense notion that there is more to language aptitude than IQ or some general factor of intelligence (Carroll, 1981; Lett & O'Mara, 1990; Robinson, 1997a, this volume; Sasaki, 1996; Sawyer & Ranta, 2001; Skehan, 1989, 1998a, this volume), and they also are consistent with the theory of successful intelligence (Sternberg, 1997), the theory I describe in this chapter.

Many psychometric researchers studying intelligence believe there is overwhelming evidence for a conventional psychometric view, positing a general ability, or g, at the top of a hierarchy and then successively more narrow abilities below that. The thesis of this chapter is that conventional notions of intelligence are incomplete and in most instances wrong and hence inadequate. I argue further that a construct of successful intelligence better captures the fundamental nature of human abilities. If we take this new construct into account in the laboratory, the schools, and the workplace, not only will, science benefit, but so will individuals, organizations, and society — both in the short-term and the long-term. And if we take it into account in assessing foreign-language aptitude as well as teaching and assessing achievement in foreign languages, many students who now are not doing particularly well will be shown to have the potential to do much better.

Although many different definitions of intelligence have been proposed over the years (see, e.g., "Intelligence and its measurement", 1921; Sternberg & Detterman, 1986), the conventional notion of intelligence is built around a loosely consensual definition of intelligence in terms of generalized adaptation to the environment. Theories of intelligence extend this definition by suggesting that there is a general factor of intelligence, often labeled g, that underlies all adaptive behavior. As mentioned above, in many theories, including the theories most widely accepted today (e.g., Carroll, 1993; Gustafsson, 1999; Horn, 1994), other mental abilities are hierarchically nested under this general factor at successively greater levels of specificity. For example, Carroll suggested that three levels could nicely capture the hierarchy of abilities, whereas Cattell (1971) and Vernon (1971) suggested two levels were especially important. In the case of Cattell, nested under general ability are fluid abilities of the kind needed to solve abstract reasoning problems such as figural matrices or series completions and crystallized abilities of the kind needed to solve problems of vocabulary and general information. In the case of Vernon, the two levels corresponded to verbal: educational and practical: mechanical abilities. These theories and others like them are called into question in this chapter.

The notion of intelligence as adaptation to the environment and as operationalized in narrowly based intelligence tests is inadequate. In contrast, the notion of successful intelligence takes into account the ability to achieve success in life, given one's personal standards, within one's sociocultural context. One's ability to achieve success depends on one's capitalizing on one's strengths and correcting or compensating for one's weaknesses through a balance of analytical, creative, and practical abilities in order to adapt to, shape, and select environments. People have different patterns of abilities, and they will learn a language successfully when the way they are taught fits their ability patterns.

The remainder of this chapter is divided into four main parts. First I argue that conventional (and some other) notions of intelligence are, at best, incomplete, and, at worst, wrong. Second I suggest an alternative notion of successful intelligence that expands upon conventional notions of intelligence. The formulation presented here goes beyond that in previous work (Sternberg, 1997). Third I discuss how we have gotten to the point in psychology and society in which we draw heavily on theories and tests that are inadequate. Finally I draw some conclusions about the nature of intelligence.

Notions of intelligence that are inadequate

Conventional notions

In this section I argue that conventional notions of intelligence are inadequate and that certain modern ones (e.g., Gardner, 1983) also do not pass muster. I explain that intelligence is not a unitary construct and so theories based on notions of general intelligence, dating back to Spearman (1904) and up to the present (e.g., Brand, 1996; Carroll, 1993; Jensen, 1998), cannot be correct either.

There now has accumulated a substantial body of evidence suggesting that, contrary to conventional notions, intelligence is not a unitary construct. This evidence is of a variety of different kinds, most of which suggest that the positive manifold (pattern of positive correlations) among ability tests is not a function of some inherent structure of intellect. Rather, it reflects limitations in the interaction among the kinds of individuals tested, the kinds of tests used in the testing, and the situations in which the individuals are tested.

One kind of evidence suggests the power of situational contexts in testing (see also Ceci, 1996; Gardner, 1983; Lave, 1988; Nunes, Schliemann, & Carraher, 1993). For example, Carraher, Schliemann, and Carraher (1987) (see also Ceci & Roazzi, 1994; Nunes, 1994) studied a group of children that is especially relevant for assessing intelligence as adaptation to the environment. The group was of Brazilian street children. Brazilian street children are under great contextual pressure to form a successful street business. If they do not, they risk death at the hands of so-called "death squads," which may murder children who, unable to earn money, resort to robbing stores (or who are suspected of resorting to robbing stores). The researchers found that the same children who are able to do the mathematics needed to run their street business are often little able or unable to do school mathematics. In fact, the more abstract and removed from real-world contexts the problems are in their form of presentation, the worse the children do on the problems. These results suggest that differences in context can have a powerful effect on performance.

Such differences are not limited to Brazilian street children. Lave (1988) showed that Berkeley housewives who successfully could do the mathematics needed for comparison shopping in the supermarket were unable to do the same mathematics when they were placed in a classroom and given isomorphic problems presented in an abstract form. In other words, their problem was not at the level of mental processes but at the level of applying the processes in specific environmental contexts. Although these studies were in mathematics, they apply in any area. Many of us have seen students who can get A's in foreign-language courses but seem clueless, when they are thrown on the street in a country where people speak the language the students suppos-edly have learned. Other students may not ace their foreign-language courses, but are effective communicators when they are thrown into an environment in which the language they have learned is spoken. There are many reasons for the discrepancy. One is desire or willingness to use language skills (see MacIntyre, and Dornyei, this volume): The student with the A who is afraid to communicate in the language he or she has learned will not be in a good position to show his or her learning. Another reason is the difference in vocabulary and grammar skills needed. Some students may be able to com-municate effectively orally, which may be all they need to get on in a foreign country, but may not have done well on the written tests required for an A in a language course. Or other students may have an excellent command of the basic street vocabulary of the language without having learned the higher level vocabulary needed to perform well in a course. Or a course may emphasize lit-erary analysis skills, which are of little use in the typical train-station encounter. Whatever the reasons, though, actual language skills in use may not be predicted well by performance in a foreign-language classroom. In our own research, we have found results consistent with those described above. These results have emanated from studies both in the U.S. and in other coun-tries. I describe here our international studies because I believe they especial-ly call into question the straightforward interpretation of results from con-ventional tests of intelligence that suggest the existence of a general factor.

In a study in Usenge, Kenya, near the town of Kisumu, we were interested in school-age children's ability to adapt to their indigenous environment. In one collaborative study, I was involved in devising a test of indigenous intelli-gence for adaptation to the environment (see Sternberg & Grigorenko, 1997; Sternberg, Nokes, Geissler, Prince, Okatcha, Bundy & Grigorenko, 2001). The test measured children's informal tacit knowledge for natural herbal medi-cines that the villagers believe can be used to fight various types of infections. This is knowledge, that, like language skills picked up when one is thrown into an environment are learned informally rather than formally. We measured the children's ability to identify the medicines, what they are used for, and how they are dosed. Based on work we had done elsewhere, we expected that scores on this test would not correlate with scores on conventional tests of intelli-gence. In order to test this hypothesis, we also administered to the children the

Raven Coloured Progressive Matrices Test, which is a measure of fluid or abstract-reasoning-based abilities, as well as the Mill Hill Vocabulary Scale, which is a measure of crystallized or formal-knowledge-based abilities. In addition, we gave the children a comparable test of vocabulary in their own Dholuo, language. The Dholuo language is spoken in the home, English in the schools.

We did indeed find no correlation between the test of indigenous tacit knowledge and scores on the fluid-ability tests. But to our surprise, we found statistically significant correlations of the tacit-knowledge tests with the tests of crystallized abilities. The correlations, however, were negative. In other words, the higher the children scored on the test of tacit knowledge, the lower they scored, on average, on the tests of crystallized abilities. This surprising result can be interpreted in various ways, but based on the ethnographic observations of the cultural anthropologists on our team, Geissler and Prince, we concluded that a plausible scenario takes into account the expectations of families for their children.

Most families in the village do not particularly value formal Western schooling. There is no reason they should, as their children will for the most part spend their lives farming or engaged in other occupations that make little or no use of Western schooling. These families emphasize teaching their children the indigenous, informal knowledge that will lead to successful adaptation in the environments in which they will really live. At the same time, there are some (perhaps not many) families in the village that have different expectations for their children. They hope that their children eventually may be able to leave the village and to go to a university, perhaps the University of Nairobi. These families tend to emphasize the value of Western education and to devalue indigenous informal knowledge. Thus the families typically value and emphasize one or the other kind of knowledge but not both. From the standpoint of most students, investing a lot of time in the development of the academic skills needed for success in school and on tests is a poor investment, because these skills do not seem to be ones that will serve them particularly well later on. Rather, they see the learning of informal knowledge relevant to their everyday adaptation as a better use of their time.

The Kenya study suggests that the identification of a general factor of human intelligence may tell us more about patterns of schooling and especially Western patterns of schooling than it does about the structure of human abilities. In Western schooling, children typically study a variety of subject matters from an early age and thus develop skills in a variety of skill areas.

This kind of schooling prepares the children to take a test of intelligence, which typically measures skills in a variety of areas. Often intelligence tests measure skills that children were expected to acquire a few years before taking the intelligence test. But as Rogoff (1990) and others have noted, this pattern of schooling is not universal and has not even been common for much of the history of humankind. Throughout history and in many places still, schooling, especially for boys, takes the form of apprenticeships in which children learn a craft from an early age. They learn what they will need to know in order to succeed in a trade, but not a lot more. They are not simultaneously engaged in tasks that require the development of the particular blend of skills measured by conventional intelligence tests. Hence it is less likely that one would observe a general factor in their scores, much as we discovered in Kenya. Some years back, Vernon (1971) pointed out that the axes of a factor analysis do not necessarily reveal a latent structure of the mind but rather represent a convenient way of characterizing the organization of mental abilities. Vernon believed that there was no one "right" orientation of axes, and indeed, mathematically, an infinite number of orientations of axes can be fit to any solution in an exploratory factor analysis. Vernon's point seems perhaps to have been forgotten or at least ignored by later theorists.

These results may help us learn why everyone learns a first language but so many people have trouble learning a second. Everyone needs a first language and virtually everyone is placed in an environment that facilitates his or her learning of a first language. A second language, however, may or may not be viewed as valuable. Much of what appears to be foreign-language learning aptitude may reflect a valuing process. In Belgium, those who learn Flemish as a first language are much more likely to learn a second and even a third language than are those who learn French as a first language. Why? Can anyone seriously believe that the difference is one of language-learning aptitude? Probably not. Rather, the difference is that of the perceived need for additional languages. There is a practical need for additional languages, and the languages are taught with this practical use in mind.

The developing world provides a particularly interesting laboratory for testing theories of intelligence because many of the assumptions that are held as dear in the developed world simply do not apply. A study we have done in Tanzania (see Sternberg & Grigorenko, 1997) points out the risks of giving tests, scoring them, and interpreting the results as measures of some latent intellectual ability or abilities. We administered to young school children in Bagamoyo, Tanzania, tests such as a form-board test and a Twenty Questions

Test, which measure the kinds of skills required on conventional tests of intelligence. Of course, we obtained scores that we could analyze and evaluate, ranking the children in terms of their supposed general or other abilities. However, we administered the tests dynamically rather than statically (Feuerstein, 1979; Grigorenko & Sternberg, 1998; Vygotsky, 1978). Dynamic testing is like conventional static testing in that individuals are tested and inferences about their abilities made. But dynamic tests differ in that children are given some kind of feedback in order to help them improve their scores. Vygotsky (1978) suggested that the children's ability to profit from the guided instruction the children received during the testing session could serve as a measure of children's zone of proximal development (ZPD), or the difference between their developed abilities and their latent capacities. In other words, testing and instruction are treated as being of one piece rather than as being distinct processes.

In our assessments, children first were given the ability tests. Then they were given a brief period of instruction in which they were able to learn skills that potentially would enable them to improve their scores. Then they were tested again. Because the instruction for each test lasted only about 15 minutes, one would not expect dramatic gains. Yet, on average, the gains were statistically significant. More importantly, scores on the pretest showed only weak although significant correlations with scores on the post-test. These correlations, at about the $r=.3$ level, suggested that when tests are administered statically to children in developing countries, they may be rather unstable and easily subject to influences of training. The reason, of course, is that the children are not accustomed to taking Western-style tests, and so profit quickly even from small amounts of instruction as to what is expected from them. Of course, the more important question is not whether the scores changed or even correlated with each other, but rather how they correlated with other cognitive measures. In other words, which test was a better predictor of transfer to other cognitive performance, the pretest score or the post-test score? We found the post-test score to be the better predictor, by a factor of 4. In other words, any general-factor score, or really, any other factor score obtained from the pretest, which was equivalent to a typical statically administered test, would be of substantially lower validity than would be a gain score measuring learning at the time of test as obtained from a dynamically-administered test.

We also have done work on dynamic testing of foreign-language aptitude (Grigorenko, Sternberg, & Ehrman, 2000), finding that a dynamic test of foreign-language learning ability that takes into account the kinds of skills discussed in this chapter provides impressive prediction of foreign-language learning and performance skills. Other work also shows that general ability is either not general or not particularly important. In a study in Russia (Grigorenko & Sternberg, 2001; Sternberg & Grigorenko, 1997), we gave Russian mothers tests of conventional abilities and also a measure of practical intelligence. We also tested them for their mental and physical health, measuring mental health in terms of standard psychometric measures of anxiety and depression and physical health in terms of a questionnaire. We found that practical intelligence better predicted mental and physical health than did academic intelligence.

Modern notions

Recognizing problems with general-ability theories, Gardner (1983, 1999) has proposed a model of multiple intelligences, according to which intelligence is viewed as comprising originally seven, and now eight multiple intelligences: linguistic, logical-mathematical, spatial, musical, bodily-kinesthetic, interpersonal, intrapersonal, and now naturalistic. Gardner also has speculated that there may be existential and spiritual intelligences, which he has referred to as candidate intelligences. This theory has received widespread recognition and has been adopted in many schools (see Gardner, 1993).

This theory could be applied to the issue of foreign language aptitude. Presumably, linguistic intelligence would be involved in the learning of any foreign language. Languages such as Chinese and Japanese, with their particular kinds of characters, also might involve a degree of spatial intelligence that is higher than that in alphabetic languages such as English and French. All languages might require some measure of logical-mathematical intelligence, and especially a language such as Latin, which seems to involve an especially high degree of analysis.

This theory has made a valuable contribution to the literature on intelligence by breaking away from g theory. At the same time, the theory is problematical in a number of ways. First, although the theory was proposed roughly 20 years ago, there has not been, to my knowledge, even one study designed to collect empirical predictive rather than armchair retrospective evidence in favor of this particular collection of intelligences. I speak here not of evidence that could be interpreted in retrospect as consistent with the theory but of evidence that specifically tests the existence of this particular set of intelligences as opposed to some other. Neither Gardner nor anyone else has even suggested how such a study might be designed, as Gardner has dismissed past evidence inconsistent with his theory as not worthy of consideration. Moreover, it seems at least doubtful that empirical operations ever could be designed to test for the existence of intelligences, such as existential or spiritual intelligence, but again, the proof is in the testing, and the testing has not occurred. Second, the evidence in favor of intercorrelations among at least some of the abilities in the theory (e.g., spatial and logical-mathematical) is so overwhelming that Gardner is able to deal with it only by labeling paper-and-pencil tests as trivial. They may be trivial from his point of view, but the fact that they predict so many things (Jensen, 1998; Sternberg, 2002) suggests that they cannot be dismissed so casually. It is just too easy to label as trivial or uninteresting any data that one cannot account for. If Gardner or anyone else could collect data showing that this particular set of intelligences is largely independent when assessed by a set of reliable measures, then the issue would be resolved in his favor. But no such data have been collected.

Third, the criteria Gardner uses to identify intelligences perhaps need some reexamination, especially in light of his recent suggestion of the existence of existential and spiritual candidate intelligences. The criteria Gardner (1983) has proposed are used so loosely in his book that it is not clear that they even support the original seven. Some criteria are used for some intelligences, other criteria for other intelligences, but how would one even show that "bodily-kinesthetic" skills constitute any kind of unified intelligence, or an intelligence at all? As Michael Jordan discovered when he tried to play professional baseball, athletic abilities, as they are commonly called, can be very specific. Other modern theories of intelligence also have been proposed (e.g., Baron, 1985; Ceci, 1990, 1996; Perkins, 1995), but these theories, like Gardner's, have yet to yield programs of research that either test the theories globally or even test predictions about specific aspects of the theories against predictions from other theories. Hence at this point one might simply wish to suspend judgement on them. What then, is intelligence? I argue next that it comprises three things, each of which is a different aspect of intelligence.

Three aspects of intelligence

The intelligence one needs to attain success in life and success in learning a foreign language as well comprises analytical, creative, and. practical aspects. According to the proposed theory of human intelligence and its development (Sternberg, 1984, 1985a, 1990, 1997), a common set of processes underlies these three aspects of intelligence. Metacomponents, or executive processes, plan what to do, monitor things as they are being done, and evaluate things after they are done. Examples of metacomponents are recognizing the existence of a problem, defining the nature of the problem, deciding on a strategy for solving the problem, monitoring the solution of the problem, and evaluating the solution after the problem is solved. For example, a foreign-language learner in an introductory course must decide what to study, how to study it, how to test his or her knowledge, and so forth.

Performance components execute the instructions of the metacomponents. For example, inference is used to decide how two stimuli are related and application is used to apply what one has inferred (Sternberg, 1977). For example, in translating a document in a foreign language, there often is no word in the mother tongue that quite matches the meaning of the word to be translated. There may be a number of words that are close in meaning, however. The individual must infer which word comes closest in meaning to the foreign word. It may not be the word whose denotation is the closest match. Knowledge-acquisition components are used to learn how to solve problems or simply to acquire declarative knowledge in the first place. For example, selective encoding is used to decide what information is relevant in the context of one's learning. In making sense of a passage in a foreign language, the individual often has to make use of extensive selective encoding in locating clues to figure out the meanings of unknown words. Selective comparison is used to bring old information to bear on new problems. For example, the individual will have extensive knowledge, from his or her first language that will help him or her make sense of a passage written in a foreign language. Although the same processes are used for all three aspects of intelligence, these processes are applied to different kinds of tasks and situations, depending on whether a given problem requires analytical thinking, creative thinking, practical thinking, or a combination of these kinds of thinking.

Analytical intelligence

Analytical intelligence is involved when the components of intelligence are applied to analyze, evaluate, judge, or compare and contrast. It typically is involved when components are applied to relatively familiar kinds of problems where the judgments to be made are of an abstract nature.

In some of my early work, I showed how analytical kinds of problems, such as analogies or syllogisms, can be analyzed componentially (Sternberg, 1977, 1983; Sternberg & Gardner, 1983), with response times or error rates decomposed to yield their underlying information-processing components. The goal of this research was to understand the information-processing origins of individual differences in (the analytical aspect of) human intelligence. With componential analysis, one could specify sources of individual differences underlying a factor score such as that for "inductive reasoning." For example, response times on analogies (Sternberg, 1977) and linear syllogisms (Sternberg, 1980) were decomposed into their elementary performance components so that it was possible to specify, in the solving of analogies or other kinds of problems, several sources of important individual or developmental differences:

1. What performance components are used?
2. How long does it take to execute each component?
3. How susceptible is each component to error?
4. How are the components combined into strategies?
5. What are the mental representations upon which the components act?

Studies of reasoning need not use artificial formats. In a more recent study, we looked at predictions for everyday kinds of situations, such as when milk will spoil (Sternberg & Kalmar, 1997). In this study, we looked at both predictions and postdictions (hypotheses about the past where information about the past is unknown) and found that postdictions took longer to make than did predictions.

Research on the components of human intelligence yielded some interesting results. For example, in a study of the development of figural analogical reasoning, we found that although children generally became quicker in information processing with age, not all components were executed more rapidly with age (Sternberg & Rifkin, 1979). The encoding component first showed a decrease in component time with age and then an increase. Apparently, older children realized that their best strategy was to spend more time in encoding the terms of a problem so that they would later be able to spend less time in operating on these encodings. A related finding was that better reasoners tend to spend relatively more time than do poorer reasoners in global, up-front metacomponential planning, when they solve difficult reasoning problems. Poorer reasoners, on the other hand, tend to spend relatively more time in local planning (Sternberg, 1981). Presumably, the better reasoners recognize that it is better to invest more time up front so as to be able to process a problem more efficiently later on. In learning a new language, investing more time up front in deciding on a learning strategy can also pay off better than plunging in but then using an ineffective strategy, such as rote memorization of paired associates. We also found in a study of the development of verbal analogical reasoning that, as children grew older, their strategies shifted so that they relied on word association less and abstract relations more (Sternberg & Nigro, 1980). Although older foreign-language learners are at a disadvantage in terms of acquiring a native accent, they typically are at an advantage in being able to turn their superior abstract-thinking abilities to their advantage in understanding the structure of the new language.

Some of our studies concentrated on knowledge-acquisition components rather than performance components or metacomponents. For example, in one set of studies, we were interested in sources of individual differences in vocabulary (Sternberg & Powell, 1983; Sternberg, Powell, & Kaye, 1983; see also Sternberg, 1987b). We were not content just to write these off as individual differences in declarative knowledge, because we wanted to understand why it was that some people acquired this declarative knowledge and others did not. Rather, we studied learning from context, which is the way most words in both a native language and a foreign language ultimately are learned. What we found is that there were multiple sources of individual and developmental differences. The three main sources were in knowledge-acquisition components, use of context clues, and use of mediating variables. For example, in the sentence, "The blen rises in the east and sets in the west," the knowledge-acquisition component of selective comparison is used to relate prior knowledge about a known concept, the sun, to the unknown word (neologism) in the sentence, "blen." Several context cues appear in the sentence, such as the fact that a blen rises, the fact that it sets, and the information about where it rises and sets. A mediating variable is that the information can occur after the presentation of the unknown word.

We did research such as that described above because we believed that conventional psychometric research sometimes incorrectly attributed individual and developmental differences. For example, a verbal analogies test that might appear on its surface to measure verbal reasoning might in fact primarily measure vocabulary and general information (Sternberg, 1977). Thus, someone might be a very able thinker, but look relatively stupid on a verbal-analogies test, especially if it involves very low-frequency words in a second or third language. In fact, in some populations, reasoning might hardly be a source of individual or developmental differences at all. And if we then look at the sources of the individual differences in vocabulary, we would need to understand that the differences in knowledge did not come from nowhere:

Some individuals had much more frequent and better opportunities to learn word meanings than did others.

The kinds of analytical skills we studied in this research can be taught (see Ross, Yoshinaga and Sasaki, this volume, for evidence that the language analytic skills measured by more traditional aptitude tests can also be learned). For example, in one study, we tested whether it is possible to teach people better to decontextualize meanings of unknown words presented in context (Sternberg, 1987a). In one study, we gave participants in five conditions a pretest on their ability to decontextualize meanings of unknown words. Then the participants were divided into five conditions, two of which were control conditions that lacked formal instruction. In one condition, participants were not given any instructional treatment. They were merely asked later to take a post-test. In a second condition, they were given practice as an instructional condition, but there was no formal instruction, per se. In a third condition, they were taught knowledge-acquisition component processes that could be used to decontextualize word meanings. In a fourth condition, they were taught to use context cues. In a fifth condition, they were taught to use mediating variables. Participants in all three of the theory-based formal-instructional conditions outperformed participants in the two control conditions, whose performance did not differ. In other words, theory-based instruction was better than no instruction at all or just practice without formal instruction.

Research on the componential bases of intelligence was useful in understanding individual differences in performance on conventional tests of intelligence. But it became increasingly clear to me that this research basically served to partition the variation on conventional tests in a different way, rather than serving to uncover previously untapped sources of variation. Children develop intellectually in ways beyond just what conventional psychometric intelligence tests or even Piagetian tests based on the theory of Piaget (1972) measure. So what might be some of these other sources of variation? Creative intelligence seemed to be one such source of variation, a source that is almost wholly untapped by conventional tests.

Creative intelligence
Intelligence tests contain a range of problems, some of them more novel than others. In some of our work we have shown that when one goes beyond the range of unconventionality of the tests, one starts to tap sources of individual differences measured little or not at all by the tests. According to the theory of successful intelligence, (creative) intelligence is particularly well measured by

problems assessing how well an individual can cope with relative novelty. Thus it is important to include in a battery of tests problems that are relatively novel in nature. These problems can be either convergent or divergent in nature. Learning a new language, of course, always involves coping with relative novelty. One has some knowledge available from the first language, but any new language will present novelties and, at times, knowledge from the first language actually may interfere with the learning of the second or subsequent language. As one approaches learning of subsequent languages, however, it seems likely that one forms some level of linguistic meta-knowledge that is more easily transferred from the learning of one language to the learning of others.

In work with convergent problems, we presented individuals with novel kinds of reasoning problems that had a single best answer. In this research, individuals had to learn meanings of new concepts that not only were different from concepts they were familiar with, but were different in kind. This is an experience that all foreign-language learners confront. For example, even as simple a concept as "to be" has one representation in English but two in Spanish. In our study, for example, individuals might be told that some objects are green and others blue; but still other objects might be grue, meaning green until the year 3000 and blue thereafter, or bleen, meaning blue until the year 3000 and green thereafter. Or they might be told of four kinds of people on the planet Kyron, blens, who are born young and die young; kwefs, who are born old and die old; balts, who are born young and die old; and prosses, who are born old and die young (Sternberg, 1982; Tetewsky & Sternberg, 1986). Their task was to predict future states from past states, given incomplete information. In another set of studies, people were given more conventional kinds of inductive reasoning problems, such as analogies, series completions, and classifications, but were told to solve them. But the problems had premises preceding them that were either conventional (dancers wear shoes) or novel (dancers eat shoes). The participants had to solve the problems as though the counterfactuals were true (Sternberg & Gastel, 1989). Much of living in a foreign culture — not just the speaking of the language — involves dealing with counterfactuals, or states of the world that are viewed in one way at home and in another way in the new culture. For example, a cultural assumption as simple as how one should greet a superior may differ radically from one culture to the next.

In these studies, we found that correlations with conventional kinds of tests depended on how novel or nonentrenched the conventional tests were. The more novel the items, the higher the correlations of our tests with scores on the conventional tests. We also found that when response times on the relatively novel problems were componentially analyzed, some components better measured the creative aspect of intelligence than did others. For example, in the "grue-bleen" task mentioned above, the information-processing component requiring people to switch from conventional green-blue thinking to grue-bleen thinking and then back to green-blue thinking again was a particularly good measure of the ability to cope with novelty.

In work with divergent reasoning problems having no one best answer, we asked people to create various kinds of products (Lubart & Sternberg, 1995; Sternberg & Lubart, 1991, 1995, 1996) where an infinite variety of responses were possible. Individuals were asked to create products in the realms of writing, art, advertising, and science. In writing, they would be asked to write very short stories for which we would give them a choice of titles, such as "Beyond the Edge" or "The Octopus's Sneakers." In art, they were asked to produce art compositions with titles such as "The Beginning of Time" or "Earth from an Insect's Point of View" In advertising, they were asked to produce advertisements for products such as a brand of bow tie or a brand of doorknob. In science, they were asked to solve problems such as one asking them how people might detect extraterrestrial aliens among us who are seeking to escape detection. Participants created two products in each domain. We found that creativity is relatively although not wholly domain-specific. Correlations of ratings of the creative quality of the products across domains were lower than correlations of ratings and generally were at about the $r=.4$ level. Thus, there was some degree of relation across domains, at the same time that there was plenty of room for someone to be strong in one or more domains but not in others. More importantly, perhaps, we found, as we had for the convergent problems, a range of correlations with conventional tests of abilities. As was the case for the correlations obtained with convergent problems, correlations were higher to the extent that problems on the conventional tests were nonentrenched. For example, correlations were higher with fluid than with crystallized ability tests, and correlations were higher, the more novel the fluid test was. Even the highest correlations, however, were only at the $r=.5$ level, suggesting that tests of creative intelligence tap skills beyond those measured even by relatively novel kinds of items on conventional tests of intelligence. Thus, the creativity one exhibits in learning a foreign language or adjusting to a foreign culture is not likely to be highly predictable from the creativity one exhibits in a wholly different domain. It is for this reason that one needs a language-aptitude test that measures creative coping-with-novelty skills in the specific domain of learning a foreign language, whether that language is real or artificial.

The work we did on creativity revealed a number of sources of individual and developmental differences.

1. To what extent was the thinking of the individual novel or nonentrenched?
2. What was the quality of the individual's thinking?
3. To what extent did the thinking of the individual meet the demands of the task?

We also found though that creativity, broadly defined, extends beyond the intellectual domain. Sources of individual and developmental differences in creative performance include not only process aspects, but aspects of knowledge, thinking styles, personality, motivation, and the environmental context in which the individual operates (see Sternberg & Lubart, 1995, for details).

Creative-thinking skills can be taught and we have devised a program for teaching them (Sternberg & Williams, 1996). In some of our work, we divided gifted and nongifted fourth-grade children into experimental and control groups. All children took pretests on insightful thinking. Then some of the children received their regular school instruction whereas others received instruction on insight skills. After the instruction of whichever kind, all children took a post-test on insight skills. We found that children taught how to solve the *insight* problems using knowledge-acquisition components gained more from pretest to posttest than did students who were not so taught (Davidson & Sternberg, 1984).

Tests of creative intelligence go beyond tests of analytical intelligence in measuring performance on tasks that require individuals to deal with relatively novel situations. But how about situations that are relatively familiar, but in a practical rather than an academic domain? Can one measure intelligence in the practical domain, and if so, what is its relation to intelligence in more academic kinds of domains?

Practical intelligence
Practical intelligence involves individuals applying their abilities to the kinds of problems that confront them in daily life, such as on the job or in the home. Practical intelligence involves applying the components of intelligence to experience so as to (a) adapt to, (b) shape, and (c) select environments. Adaptation is involved when one changes oneself to suit the environment.

Shaping is involved when one changes the environment to suit oneself. And selection is involved when one decides to seek out another environment that is a better match to one's needs, abilities, and desires. People differ in their balance of adaptation, shaping, and selection, and in the competence with which they balance among the three possible courses of action. In adjusting to a new culture, for example, one primarily needs to adapt to the mores of that culture. But one is unlikely to give up all of the native culture one brings to the new culture, so that one is likely also to want to shape the environment so as to allow one to retain some or even many aspects of one's original cultural heritage. Of course, one may decide that the new culture is a bad match, and therefore leave it if one has the luxury of being able to leave.

Much of our work on practical intelligence has centered on the concept of tacit knowledge. We define this construct, for our purposes, as what one needs to know in order to work effectively in an environment that one is not explicitly taught and that often is not even verbalized (Sternberg & Wagner, 1986; Sternberg, Wagner, & Okagaki, 1993; Sternberg, Wagner, Williams, & Horvath, 1995; Wagner & Sternberg, 1985; and see the review of implicit L2 learning studies in Robinson, this volume). Most cultural knowledge is tacit. And when we move to a new culture, we find that we have to pick up a tremendous amount of this tacit knowledge that native residents have and have had for a long time. Often, they cannot help in teaching it, because they are not even aware they have it. We represent tacit knowledge in the form of production systems, or sequences of "if-then" statements that describe procedures, which one follows in various kinds of everyday situations.

We typically have measured tacit knowledge using work-related problems that present problems one might encounter on the job. We have measured tacit knowledge for both children and adults, and among adults, for people in various occupations such as management, sales, academia, and the military. In a typical tacit-knowledge problem, people are asked to read a story about a problem someone faces and to rate, for each statement in a set of statements, how adequate a solution the statement represents. For example, in a paper-and-pencil measure of tacit knowledge for sales, one of the problems deals with sales of photocopy machines. A relatively inexpensive machine is not moving out of the show room and has become overstocked. The examinee is asked to rate the quality of various solutions for moving the particular model out of the show room. In a performance-based measure for sales people, the test-taker makes a phone call to a supposed customer, who is actually the examiner. The test-taker tries to sell advertising space over the phone. The examiner raises various objections to buying the advertising space. The test-taker is evaluated for the quality, rapidity, and fluency of the responses on the telephone.

In our studies, we found that practical intelligence as embodied in tacit knowledge increases with experience, but it is profiting from experience, rather than experience per se, that results in increases in scores. Some people can have been in a job for years and still have acquired relatively little tacit knowledge. We also have found that subscores on tests of tacit knowledge — such as for managing oneself, managing others, and managing tasks — correlate significantly with each other. Moreover, scores on various tests of tacit knowledge, such as for academics and managers, are also correlated fairly substantially (at about the $r=.5$ level). However, scores on tacit-knowledge tests do not correlate with scores on conventional tests of intelligence, whether the measures used are single-score measures or multiple-ability batteries (cf. similar findings for the relationship between a traditional measure of intelligence [Wechsler, 1939, 1997], implicit learning and incidental SLA, reported in Robinson, Chapter 10, this volume). Despite their lack of correlation with conventional measures, the scores on tacit-knowledge tests predict performance on the job as well as or better than do conventional psychometric intelligence tests. In one study done at the Center for Creative Leadership, we further found that scores on our tests of tacit knowledge for management were the best single predictor of performance on a managerial simulation. In a hierarchical regression, scores on conventional tests of intelligence, personality, styles, and interpersonal orientation were entered first and scores on the test of tacit knowledge were entered last. Scores on the test of tacit knowledge were the single best predictor of managerial simulation score. Moreover, they also contributed significantly to the prediction even after everything else was entered first into the equation. In recent work on military leadership (Hedlund, Horvath, Forsythe, Snook, Williams, Bullis, Dennis, & Sternberg, 1998), we found that scores on a test of tacit knowledge for military leadership predicted ratings of leadership effectiveness, whereas scores on a conventional test of intelligence and on our tacit-knowledge test for managers did not significantly predict the ratings of effectiveness. Perhaps most interestingly, we have found that, at least in entry-level office-type occupations (e.g., clerk), the tacit knowledge used in the U.S. and in Spain are very similar. The correlation between response patterns on a test of tacit knowledge for U.S. participants and Spanish ones (taking a Spanish version of the inventory) was over $r=.91$ (Grigorenko, Sternberg, & Gil, 1999).

We also have done studies of social intelligence, which is viewed in the theory of successful intelligence as a part of practical intelligence. In these studies, individuals were presented with photos and were asked to make judgments about them. In one kind of photo, they were asked to evaluate whether a male-female couple was a genuine couple (i.e., really involved in a romantic relationship) or a phony couple posed by the experimenters. In another kind of photo, they were asked to indicate which of two individuals was the other's supervisor (Barnes & Sternberg, 1989; Sternberg & Smith, 1985). We found females to be superior to males on these tasks. Scores on the two tasks did not correlate with scores on conventional ability tests, nor did they correlate with *each other,* suggesting a substantial degree of domain specificity in the task. It is quite possible and indeed likely that the nonverbal cues used to decode social situations vary from one culture to the next.

Practical-intelligence skills can be taught. We have developed a program for teaching practical intellectual skills, aimed at middle-school students, that explicitly teaches students "practical intelligence for school" in the contexts of doing homework, taking tests, reading, and writing (Williams, Blythe, White, Li, Sternberg, & Gardner, 1996). We have evaluated the program in a variety of settings (Gardner, Krechevsky, Sternberg, & Okagaki, 1994; Sternberg, Okagaki, & Jackson, 1990) and found that students taught via the program outperform students in control groups that did not receive the instruction.

Combining analytical, creative, and practical intelligence

The studies described above looked at analytical, creative, and practical intelligence separately. But a full validation of the theory of successful intelligence would require research that looks at all three aspects of intelligence in conjunction. To date, we have done two such sets of studies.

In one set of studies, we explored the question of whether conventional education in school systematically discriminates against children with creative and practical strengths (Sternberg & Clinkenbeard, 1995; Sternberg, Ferrari, Clinkenbeard, & Grigorenko, 1996; Sternberg, Grigorenko, Ferrari, & Clinkenbeard, 1999). Motivating this work was the belief that the systems in schools strongly tend to favor children with strengths in memory and analytical abilities. In particular, students might have substantial foreign-language learning abilities, but not for the method of instruction by which they are taught.

We devised a test for high-school students of analytical, creative, and practical abilities that consisted of both multiple-choice and essay items. The multiple-choice items required the three kinds of thinking in three content domains: verbal, quantitative, and figural. Thus there were 9 multiple-choice and 3 essay subtests. The test was administered to 326 children around the United States and in some other countries who were identified by their schools as gifted by any standard whatsoever. Children were selected for a summer program in (college-level) psychology if they fell into one of five ability groupings: high analytical, high creative, high practical, high balanced (high in all three abilities), or low balanced (low in all three abilities). Students who came to Yale were then divided into four instructional groups. Students in all four instructional groups used the same introductory-psychology textbook (a preliminary version of Sternberg, 1995) and listened to the same psychology lectures. What differed among them was the type of afternoon discussion section to which they were assigned. They were assigned to an instructional condition that emphasized either memory, analytical, creative, or practical instruction. For example, in the memory condition, they might be asked to describe the main tenets of a theory of depression. In the analytical condition, they might be asked to compare and contrast two theories of depression. In the creative condition, they might be asked to formulate their own theory of depression. In the practical condition, they might be asked how they could use what they had learned about depression to help a friend who was depressed.

Students in all four instructional conditions were evaluated in terms of their performance on homework, a midterm exam, a final exam, and an independent project. Each type of work was evaluated for memory, analytical, creative, and practical quality. Thus, all students were evaluated in exactly the same way.

Our results suggested the utility of the theory of successful intelligence. First, we observed when the students arrived at Yale that the students in the high creative and high practical groups were much more diverse in terms of racial, ethnic, socioeconomic, and educational backgrounds than were the students in the high-analytical group. In other words, just by expanding the range of abilities we measured, we discovered more intellectual strengths than would have been apparent through a conventional test. Moreover, the kinds of students identified as strong differed in terms of populations from which they were drawn in comparison with students identified as strong solely by analytical measures.

When one does principal-component or principal-factor analysis, one always obtains a general factor if one leaves the solution unrotated. Such a factor is a mathematical property of the algorithm used. But we found the general factor to be very weak, suggesting that the general factor of intelligence is probably relevant only when a fairly narrow range of abilities is measured, as is typically the case with conventional tests. A similar result has been obtained with a Spanish translation of the test administered to Spanish high school students (Sternberg, Castejón, Prieto & Grigorenko, 2001). We found that testing format had a large effect on results: Multiple-choice tests tend to correlate with other multiple-choice tests, almost without regard to what they measure. Essay tests show only weak correlations with multiple choice, however. We further found that after we controlled for modality of testing (multiple choice versus essay), the correlations between the analytical, creative, and practical sections were very weak and generally nonsignificant, supporting the relative independence of the various abilities. We found that all three ability tests — analytical, creative, and practical — significantly predicted course performance. When multiple-regression analysis was used, at least two of these ability measures contributed significantly to the prediction of each of the measures of achievement. Perhaps as a reflection of the difficulty of de-emphasizing the analytical way of teaching, one of the significant predictors was always the analytical score. (However, in a replication of our study with low-income African-American students from New York, Deborah Coates of the City University of New York found a different pattern of results. Her data indicated that the practical tests were better predictors of course performance than were the analytical measures, suggesting that what ability test predicts what criterion depends on population as well as mode of teaching.) Most importantly, there was an aptitude-treatment interaction whereby students who were placed in instructional conditions that better matched their pattern of abilities outperformed students who were mismatched. In other words, when students are taught in a way that fits how they think, they do better in school. Children with creative and practical abilities, who are almost never taught or assessed in a way that matches their pattern of abilities, may be at a disadvantage in course after course, year after year.

In a follow-up study (Sternberg, Torff, & Grigorenko, 1998), we looked at learning of social studies and science by third-graders and eighth-graders. The third-graders were students in a very low-income neighborhood in Raleigh, North Carolina. The eighth-graders were students who were largely middle to upper-middle class studying in Baltimore, Maryland, and Fresno, California. In this study, students were assigned to one of three instructional conditions. In the first condition, they were taught the course that basically they would have learned had we not intervened. The emphasis in the course was on memory. In a second condition they were taught in a way that emphasized critical (analytical) thinking. In the third condition, they were taught in a way that emphasized analytical, creative, and practical thinking. All students' performance was assessed for memory learning (through multiple-choice assessments) as well as for analytical, creative, and practical learning (through performance assessments)

As expected, we found that students in the successful-intelligence (analytical, creative, practical) condition outperformed the other students in terms of the performance assessments. One could argue that this result merely reflected the way they were taught. Nevertheless, the result suggested that teaching for these kinds of thinking succeeded. More important, however, was the result that children in the successful-intelligence condition outperformed the other children even on the multiple-choice memory tests. In other words, to the extent that one's goal is just to maximize children's memory for information, teaching for successful intelligence is still superior. It enables children to capitalize on their strengths and to correct or to compensate for their weaknesses, and it allows children to encode material in a variety of interesting ways. Thus the results of two sets of studies suggest that the theory of successful intelligence is valid not just in its parts but as a whole. Moreover, the results suggest that the theory can make a difference not only in laboratory tests, but in school classrooms as well.

How we got to where we are

Academic factors

Large numbers of psychologists, cited in books on the g factor, accept the conventional model and tests of intelligence (see Brand, 1996; Jensen, 1998). Why do they support the theory and tests if the data do not support them?

The answer, I believe, is that it depends on which data one chooses to discuss. The fact is that there is an overwhelming amount of evidence that (a) conventional tests of intelligence yield a general factor and (b) these tests predict a large variety of outcomes in school, in the work place, and in other aspects of people's lives in school, in the work place, and in other aspects of people's lives (Herrnstein & Murray, 1994). But the argument of this article is that the general factor is general only with respect to the academic or analytical aspect of intelligence. Once one includes in an assessment creative and practical abilities, the general factor is greatly diminished or disappears. Moreover, although the conventional tests do have predictive validity for a variety of types of situations, as almost all psychometricians have agreed, so do other types of measures (see Anastasi & Urbina, 1997; Cronbach, 1990). The argument of this article is not that conventional tests are wrong or somehow inadequate but rather that they are incomplete. As Cronbach (1975) and Messick (1998) have pointed out, any problems with tests would have to be in the interpretation rather than in the tests themselves. In particular, it is the overinterpretation and overgeneralization of test-score results that is most problematical.

I have argued elsewhere that in the field of intelligence, it is possible to do more and more research and, in a sense, know less and less, or at least to become more and more confident about incorrect generalizations (Sternberg, 2002). If we continue to limit the subject populations, material, and empirical methods we use in research on intelligence, we can continue to get support for conventional theories and measures of intelligence. As the literature review above should make clear, pointing out the limitations of traditional theories requires the use of broader subject populations, broader types of materials, and new types of measurement techniques.

Societal factors

If conventional (and even some modern) theories of intelligence are inadequate, how have we gotten to where we are? The U.S. has developed a multimillion dollar testing industry whose tests are based on conventional notions of intelligence. Other countries may not use U.S. tests, but may have comparable tests of their own. Whether of abilities or achievement, often the tests measure largely the same thing (Sternberg, 1998). The testing industry is a curious industry, in many ways. Whereas the ideas in most technologies have moved forward by leaps and bounds over the last few decades, the testing industry has remained largely (although not entirely) stagnant. For example, the modern version of the Stanford-Binet Intelligence Tests (Thorndike, Hagen, & Sattler, 1986) or the Wechsler Adult Intelligence Scales Revised (WAIS-R) (Wechsler, 1997) look amazingly like the original tests, whether of Binet and Simon (1905) or of Wechsler (1939). Thus, whereas old computers and old VCRs and old telephones rapidly go out of date, old tests never seem to die, except for updating of norms and cosmetic changes.

Why have conventional tests held on so long? I believe there are several reasons, which I discuss in this section. These reasons are so powerful that they probably will lead to conventional tests holding onto their power into the indefinite future, no matter how inadequate they are.

First, the tests are there — their use is entrenched in the entire country, in testing for (a) mental retardation, (b) learning disabilities, (c) private-school admissions, (d) college admissions, (e) graduate school and professional school admissions, and other uses. Any change in the paradigm underlying testing would require a massive reeducation effort. It is not clear who would undertake such an effort or how it would be accomplished.

Second, training in the use of traditional tests is not going away. School psychologists still learn how to use many of the same tests school psychologists have learned to use for several decades, with only the editions changing. They may also learn how to use more modern tests, but the testing industry has been rather reluctant to introduce highly innovative changes, so the number of newer options is strictly limited. Third, in the United States, not only students, but teachers, principals, superintendents, and entire school districts are being judged on the basis of scores on conventional tests. The news magazine U. S. News and World Report did more for traditional tests than perhaps any other single source in the past several decades when it started publishing rankings of undergraduate and graduate institutions based in large part, although certainly not exclusively, on test scores. Other countries may have similar publication of test scores, for example, by university. In consulting with admissions offices at the undergraduate and graduate levels, I have found that these best-selling issues of the magazine have resulted in schools placing even more emphasis on test scores in order to improve their rankings. Administrators may hate the ranking system but they are subject to it nevertheless. The problem is not limited to the college and university level. Many states give conventional statewide mastery tests of achievement and publish the results district by district. This publication practice puts pressure on administrators, teachers, and parents to teach in ways that produce higher scores for their children, whether or not these ways of teaching are what the adults perceive as best educationally for the children.

Fourth, the kinds of skills measured by conventional tests do matter for school achievement. Conventional tests predict roughly 25% of the individual-differences variation in school performance (Anastasi & Urbina, 1997). Although that percentage leaves a lot of variation unaccounted for, it is nevertheless impressive. As shown above, however, the percentage would probably be substantially lower if instruction and assessment took into account a broader range of skills (Sternberg, Ferrari, Clinkenbeard, & Grigorenko, 1996;

Sternberg, Torff, & Grigorenko, 1998). Moreover, if we only consider straight-forward memory skills, we need to recognize that these skills are essential antecedents of analytical, creative, and practical abilities. One cannot analyze information if one has no information to analyze. One cannot go beyond the given if one does not know what the given is. One cannot apply what is known if one does not know anything. At the same time, one might be concerned that the use of tests has become blind. Studies of the validity of these tests for pre-diction to particular situations are conducted only fairly rarely. It is not enough just to go by studies conducted in another time or another place. For example, we conducted a study of the predictive validity of the Graduate Record Examination, a test widely used for graduate admissions in the United States, for predicting graduate success at Yale. All matriculants into the grad-uate program over a 12-year period served as participants. As predictors, we used the verbal, quantitative, analytical, and subject-matter (psychology) tests. As criteria, we used first-year and second-year grades; advisors' ratings of students' analytical, creative, and practical abilities; the same advisors' rat-ings of the students' research and teaching abilities.; and the dissertation com-mittee's averaged evaluation of the doctoral dissertation. We found that the GRE was a fairly good predictor of first-year grades, in line with what other studies have found. However, we found that for women, the GRE significant-ly predicted nothing else. For men, only the analytical section significantly predicted other criteria, and this prediction was relatively weak, at about the $r=.3$ level of correlation. Various corrections for restriction of range improved prediction of first-year grades but little else. The predictive validity obtained scarcely seems to justify the costs to students both in time and in money or the weight that universities often put on this test. Of course, results might be dif-ferent elsewhere. But regardless of where the tests are used, closed systems, described below, make the tests look better than they are.

Closed systems

According to Herrnstein and Murray (1994), conventional tests of intelligence account for about 10% of the variation, on average, in various kinds of real-world outcomes. Although this percentage is not trivial, it is not particularly large either, and one might wonder what all the fuss is about in the use of the tests. Of course, one might argue that their estimation of the percentage is an underestimate, but given their very enthusiastic support for conventional tests, it seems unlikely they would underestimate the value of the tests.

In fact, I would argue, they rather substantially overestimate the value of the tests for predictive purposes. In their book, they refer to an "invisible hand of nature" guiding events so that people with high IQs tend to rise toward the top socioeconomic strata of a society and people with low IQs tend to fall toward the bottom strata. They present data to support their argument, and indeed, it seems likely that although many aspects of their data may be arguable, this one is not in U. S. society. Lawyers and doctors probably have higher IQs, on average, than do street cleaners, for example.

The problem is that although the data are probably correct, the story about the data probably is not. The United States and other societies have created societies in which test scores matter profoundly. High test scores are needed for placement in higher tracks in elementary and secondary school. They are needed for admission to selective undergraduate programs. They are needed again for admission to selective graduate and professional programs. It is really quite difficult to imagine how one could gain the access routes to many of the highest-paying and most prestigious jobs if one did not test well. Low GRE scores, for example, will tend to exclude one not only from one selective graduate school, but from all the others as well. To the extent that there is error of measurement, it will have comparable effects in many schools. Of course, test scores are not the only criteria used for admission to graduate and professional schools. But they count enough so that if one "bombs" one of the admissions tests, one can kiss admissions to many selective schools good-bye.

The 10% figure of Herrnstein and Murray implies that there are many able people who are disenfranchised because the kinds of abilities they have, although important for job performance, are not important for test performance. For example, the kinds of creative and practical skills that matter to success on the job typically are not measured on the tests used for admissions. At the same time, society may be overvaluing those who have a fairly narrow range of skills, and a range of skills that may not serve these individuals particularly well on the job, even if they do lead to success in school and on the tests.

It is scarcely surprising that ability tests predict school grades, because the tests originally were explicitly designed for this purpose (Binet & Simon, 1905). In effect, U. S. and other societies have created closed systems: Certain abilities are valued in instruction, for example, memory and analytical abilities. Ability tests are then created that measure these abilities and thus predict school performance. Then assessments of achievement are designed that also assess for these abilities. Little wonder that ability tests are more predictive in school than in the work place: Within the closed system of the school, a narrow range of abilities leads to success on ability tests, in instruction, and on achievement tests. This applies as well in the foreign-language classroom as in any other. But these same abilities are less important later on in life, including the actual use of a foreign language in real-world communication.

Closed systems can be and have been constructed to value almost any set of attributes at all. In some societies, caste is used. Members of certain castes are allowed to rise to the top; members of other castes have no chance. Of course, the members of the successful castes believe they are getting their due, much as did the nobility in the Middle Ages when they rose to the top and subjugated their serfs. Even in the U.S., if one were born a slave in the early 1800s, one's IQ would make little difference: One would die a slave. Slave owners and others rationalized the system, as social Darwinists always have, by believing that the fittest were in the roles they rightfully belonged in. Closed systems also can be created on the basis of language facility. For example, at the time this chapter is being written, individuals in Estonia (usually Russian) who do not speak Estonian are losing jobs. This situation, in one form or another, is common. In the U.S., lack of facility in English is a pathway to economic destitution.

The mechanism of a closed system can be illustrated by the fact that any attribute at all can be selected for. Suppose we wished to select for nose length. Only those with the longest noses would be admitted to the most prestigious undergraduate programs. People with shorter noses would have enroll in less prestigious places. Nose jobs, of course, would be forbidden, in the same way that cheating on tests is forbidden. Nose-length standards for graduate admissions would be even more rigorous. Eventually we would find people in the top socioeconomic strata tended to have very long noses. In general, closed systems seal off individual options and distort society, depriving many individuals of opportunities they arguably should have. Society is also deprived of their talents.

Lest this all sound hypothetical, when I was in Jamaica, I attended classes in a number of one-room elementary schools. In a typical school, there was no barrier separating the many classes in the single room so that the noise level was constantly high. I found myself asking what Binet might have put on his intelligence test if he had formulated his tests for these schools in Jamaica. I concluded that he might have decided to include in his test battery tests of hearing and auditory selective attention, the two skills that seemed most important for hearing both the instruction and the test items, which typically were orally administered. People who heard better fared better, especially if they had the bad fortune to be anywhere but the front center of the classroom. Indeed, when I mentioned this observation in a colloquium, an individual from Guyana commented that she had grown up in similar schools and always wondered why the smartest children sat in the front of the class. In this case, sitting in the front of the class may well have made them appear smart.

The experience in Jamaica also pointed out one other important fact, namely, that the assumption in much research on intelligence is that every child has an equal chance to succeed on ability tests and in school. In fact, they do not. In a study we did in Jamaica (Sternberg, Powell, McGrane, & McGregor, 1997), we studied the effects of intestinal parasitic infections (most often, whipworm) on children's cognitive functioning. We knew that children with moderate to high loads of intestinal parasites tended to perform more poorly in school, and we were interested in why. Our study revealed that infected children tended to do more poorly on tests of higher order cognitive abilities, even after controlling for possible confounding variables such as socioeconomic class. The data also revealed that although antiparasitic medication (albendazole) improved physical health, it had no effect on cognitive-ability test scores. Presumably, the deficits that were occurring had built up over many years and were not alleviated by a quick-fix pill. Children who are parasitically infected find it hard to concentrate on their schoolwork because they just do not feel well. Our data showed that the cumulative effect of missing much of what happens in school probably cannot be reversed quickly.

Conclusion

The time has come to move beyond conventional theories of intelligence. In this article I have provided data suggesting that conventional theories and tests of intelligence are incomplete. The general factor is largely an artifact of limitations in populations of individuals tested, types of materials with which they are tested, and types of methods used in testing. Indeed, our studies show that even when one wants to predict school performance, the conventional tests are fairly limited in their predictive validity (Sternberg & Williams, 1997). 1 have proposed a theory of successful intelligence and its development that fares well in construct validations, whether one tests in the laboratory, in schools, or in the work place. The greatest obstacle to our moving on is in vested interests, both in academia and in the world of tests, where testing companies are doing well financially with existing tests. We now have ways to move beyond conventional notions of intelligence; we need only the will.

We also need to move beyond conventional notions of testing for language aptitude. I have suggested several ways in which this can be done (see also Grigorenko, Sternberg, & Ehrman, 2000). First, we need to test for creative and practical language-acquisition abilities, not just for memory and analytical ones. Second, we should recognize the need for a more refined analysis that does not just give a general language-aptitude score, but subscores that suggest appropriate forms of instruction (see Skehan, this volume for detailed discussion of this issue). Finally, we should consider the use of dynamic testing, whereby testing and instruction occur at the same time so that the examiner can assess the ability to learn in real time.

Lay conceptions of intelligence are quite a bit broader than psychologists' professional ones. For example, in a study of people's conceptions of intelligence (Sternberg, Conway, Ketron, & Bernstein, 1981; see also Sternberg, 1985b), we found that lay persons had a three-factor view of intelligence as comprising practical problem solving, verbal, and social-competence abilities. Only the first of these abilities is measured by conventional tests. In a study of Taiwanese Chinese conceptions of intelligence (Yang & Sternberg, 1997), we found that although Taiwanese conceptions of intelligence included a cognitive factor, they also included factors of interpersonal competence, intrapersonal competence, intellectual self-assertion, and intellectual self-effacement. Even more importantly, perhaps, we discovered in a study among different ethnic groups in San Jose, California, that although parents in different ethnic groups have different conceptions of intelligence, the more closely their conception matches that of their children's teachers, the better the children do in school. In other words, teachers value students who do well on the kinds of attributes that the teachers associate with intelligence. The attributes they associate with intelligence are too limited. The time has come to expand our notion of what it means to be intelligent. It also has come to expand our notion of language aptitude.

Note

* Preparation of this article was supported under the Javits Act Program (Grant No. R206R950001 and R206R00001) as administered by the Office of Educational Research and Improvement, U. S. Department of Education. Grantees undertaking such projects are encouraged to express freely their professional judgment. This article, therefore, does not necessarily represent the position or policies of the Office of Educational Research and Improvement or the U. S. Department of Education, and no official endorsement should be inferred.

CHAPTER 3

Motivation, anxiety and emotion in second language acquisition[*]

Peter D. MacIntyre
University College of Cape Breton

Introduction

When we think of individual differences among language learners, motivation springs quickly to mind as one of the most important of these variables. In this chapter, language learning motivation theory will be examined from three approaches. First, Gardner's (1985) socio-educational model, whose tenets have been studied for over 40 years, will be examined. This model has been widely accepted in the language learning area, but some recent critics argue that its popularity has led to its unhealthy dominance among language researchers and educators, preventing the exploration of other motivational frameworks. The model and its critique will be summarized. This leads to a second focus of this chapter, representing a sort of criticism of the Gardner critics. Those critics proposed a long list of motivational variables for inclusion in models of language learning motivation. The interrelations of such variables are likely to be more complex than has been suggested, possibly paradoxical. Some examples from the literature on motivation within psychology will be offered to illustrate some of the unexpected effects of the motivational processes proposed for study. Finally, the third major section of the chapter will deal with the concept of emotion, one that has been closely linked to motivation in the literature of psychology over the years. Emotion has not been given sufficient attention in the language learning literature, with the exception of studies of language anxiety. It will be argued that emotion just might be the fundamental basis of motivation, one deserving far greater attention in the language learning domain.

What is motivation?

As a starting point, this is probably not a good question. The question seems to imply that motivation is a "thing" or a "condition." In spoken English, we use phrases like "she is motivated" or "I can't motivate my students." As a working hypothesis, let us assume that most human behavior is motivated. This helps put motivation for language learning into context, as one of the many motives a person might possess. People are motivated to eat, play games, work, socialize, on so on, with potentially hundreds or thousands of more specific motives that could be cited. The number is not as important as the observation that all of these motives occur, to some smaller or larger degree, at the same time. There are a multitude of motives present in every person and these motives wax and wane as time moves along.

Given that individual motives rise and fall over time, we can conceptualize motivation theory in general as an attempt to explain that which "…gives behavior its energy and direction" (Reeve, 1992, p. 3). In other words, questions about motivation tend to address two issues: (1) why is behavior directed toward a specific goal, and (2) what determines the intensity or effort invested in pursuing the goal. A third key question, embedded in the first two, involves a search for explanations for individual differences in motivation: why do different people in the same situation differ in the direction and strength of motivated behavior? Against this larger theoretical backdrop, we can examine the leading theory of motivation in the area of language learning, Gardner's (1985) socio-educational model. It is possible that the success of this model over the years has been due to its ability to answer all three questions.

Motivation in the socio-educational model: Gardner and his critics

A schematic representation of the socio-educational model, taken from Gardner and MacIntyre (1992), is presented in Figure 1. Gardner (1985), in defining motivation, argues that four elements must be present for a student to be considered motivated: a goal, desire to achieve the goal, positive attitudes, and effort. This is an expansion upon the definition offered above, to include attitudes and desires. Gardner has referred to these as "affective variables," clearly differentiating them from the more purely cognitive factors associated with language learning such as intelligence, aptitude and related variables (see Gardner & MacIntyre, 1992, 1993a). This definition of motivation is consistent with definitions in the general literature on motivation, but allows Gardner's model to address a wide

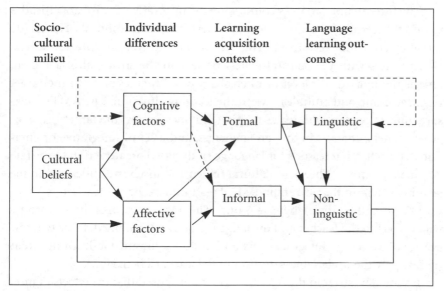

Figure 1. The socio-educational model (Gardner & MacIntyre, 1992)

range of issues under the motivation rubric. It also allows for tapping of the link between motivation and emotion, an essential link that is often missing from motivational concepts emerging from cognitively-oriented psychology.

Four major parts of the model are shown: the socio-cultural milieu, individual differences, language acquisition contexts, and language learning outcomes. According to Gardner and MacIntyre (1992), the socio-cultural milieu plays a role in influencing both cognitive and affective individual differences among language learners. Affective variables include attitudes and motivation, language anxiety, and self-confidence. Cognitive factors include variables such as intelligence, language aptitude, and language learning strategies. These individual differences, especially the affective variables, have been the focus of most of the studies done by Gardner and his colleagues (see Gardner, 1985). Gardner and MacIntyre (1992) state that "there are probably as many factors that might account for individual differences in achievement in a second language as there are individuals" (p. 212). Given this proviso, it is well known that Gardner's primary research interest is directed toward the integrative motive, its key concepts measured by the Attitudes/Motivation Test Battery (AMTB, Gardner, 1985)[1]. The focus on the integrative motive allowed the socio-educational model to concentrate on a specific subset of variables in a veritable conceptual jungle, and this, coupled with the AMTB, allowed research to proceed in an orderly, programmatic fashion.

The three major variables comprising the integrative motive are attitudes toward the learning situation, integrativeness, and motivation. We can divide the integrative motive into integrativeness and motivation. Integrativeness, which begins with the cultural beliefs present in the socio-cultural milieu, reflects the individual's level of interest in social interaction with the target language group and attitudes toward the learning situation. The AMTB measures integrativeness with scales tapping attitudes toward the target language group, general interest in foreign languages, and a set of integrative orientation items reflecting reasons for language study based on attraction to the target language group. The socio-cultural milieu also fosters attitudes within the learning situation that are embodied, at least in part, by the teacher as a representative of the target language group. The AMTB captures these attitudes with respect to the teacher and the language course. Combined, these two categories of attitudes (integrativeness and attitudes toward the learning situation) supply the underlying direction in the learner's behavior.[2]

It should be stressed that Gardner (1996) proposed that the effects of integrative motivation on language learning are largely the result of the motivation component. This component is defined by Gardner as a combination of motivational intensity, desire to learn the language, and attitudes toward learning the language. Gardner emphasizes that it is the active learner, the student who engages with the language, who can be considered motivated. The student who endorses the integrative attitudes, or more simply an integrative orientation or goal, but who does not show effort and engagement with the language, is simply not a motivated learner. This satisfies Gardner's (1985) four-part definition of motivation, having a goal, desire to achieve the goal, positive attitudes, and exerting effort. Gardner and MacIntyre (1993a) argue that this helps to explain why studies of orientations alone produce inconsistent correlations with various specific measures of language achievement (such as cloze tests and course grades).

To complete the socio-educational model, Gardner and MacIntyre (1992) propose that individual differences act in both formal and informal language learning situations, generating linguistic and non-linguistic outcomes. Formal situations refer primarily to classroom settings where direct language instruction is provided. Both cognitive and affective variables operate directly in formal contexts where the focus is on teaching language skills. Informal situations refer to language acquisition contexts where learning is incidental to some other activity, as when one "picks up" another language from friends or co-workers during interactions with them. In informal contexts, the exposure to the language can be considered voluntary; one might encourage or discourage friends or co-workers from using the L2. Gardner and MacIntyre (1992) suggest that, because entry into these situations is voluntary, motivation will play a substantial role in an individual's exposure to situations that provide such opportunities for language learning. Once an individual has decided to enter informal situations, both cognitive and affective variables will operate.

The outcomes of language learning may be either linguistic or non-linguistic. Linguistic outcomes describe the skill, knowledge, and competence in the language itself. A variety of non-linguistic outcomes also are possible, with some of these outcomes being the very same individual difference variables described earlier in the model. That is, as a student progresses through the language learning process, changes in attitudes and motivation are to be expected. In this way the socio-educational model is dynamic, describing how changes in individual difference variables occur over time. For example, one would expect that positive experiences in learning a language will tend to improve objective language proficiency, but also increase motivation and positive attitudes, among other things.

Over the years, the socio-educational model has been widely studied with two purposes, often within the same study: to establish that motivation is related to language achievement and to investigate the structure of the integrative motive. There has been variation in the social and learning contexts and in the focus of research from study to study, as well as some variation in the resulting empirical model. For example, Lalonde and Gardner (1984) found that attitudes toward the learning situation and integrativeness formed two separate factors, but Gardner and Lysynchuk (1990) found that they could be combined into a single factor. Further, Gardner, Lalonde and Pierson (1983) report a model in which attitudes toward the learning situation influence integrativeness but MacIntyre and Charos (1996), in a different social context, report that the influence runs in the opposite direction. Given that these variables are hypothesized to be related, and even derived from the same socio-cultural factors, it should not be surprising that they are highly correlated. In some studies, the variables are so highly correlated that it is empirically justified to consider them part of one construct. Indeed, the major theoretical propositions remain unchanged even if the structure of the model representing them changes slightly in form and empirical results (see Gardner & MacIntyre, 1993a). Thus some variability in the model is to be expected from one study to the next as one reviews the literature on the socio-educational model. However, results consistently support the general hypothesis that elements of the integrative motive are significantly correlated with indices of language achievement (Gardner, 1985; Gardner & MacIntyre, 1993b; Clément & Gardner, 2001).

The early critics of Gardner, such as Au (1988) and Oller (1981), when discussing the impact of attitudes/motivation on language achievement, spent a great deal of time criticizing Gardner's conceptual and operational definitions on the basis of inconsistencies such as the ones just described. The same authors were far less concerned with the arguably more difficult task of defining language achievement. Various studies from various authors have employed various definitions of language achievement. As Gardner and MacIntyre (1993b) show, even within a single sample, attitudes and motivation will display a wide range of correlations with different measures of language achievement. The effect of using a variety of indices of language achievement, such as course grades, standardized achievement tests, or specific language performance tasks (such as the cloze test), on theorizing in the language area should not be underestimated. It would be difficult to justify an expectation that all indices of L2 proficiency correlate uniformly with the variety of attitude and motivation variables under consideration here. Similarly, as noted by Au (1988), theoretical difficulties can be created when variables with names similar to those included in the socio-educational model are used but measured differently from those in the AMTB (Gardner, 1980, 1996). The AMTB has been widely tested showing satisfactory reliability and validity; measures adapted or written for use within a specific study must be assessed for reliability and their validity established empirically, over several samples. Adaptations of the AMTB itself suffer from a similar problem. To the extent that items are omitted, altered, or replaced, and to the extent that contrasting cultural beliefs create different connotations for the items, the theory underlying the AMTB should be examined closely for its applicability.

In the early 1990s, three papers were published that were critical of Gardner's socio-educational model. The critics sought to expand on the socio-educational model to include a host of additional motivational variables. Given their potential impact on the study of motivation for language learning, and their particular relevance to language pedagogy, let us consider each of the studies in depth.

Crookes and Schmidt (1991)
The first of the "critique" papers was by Crookes and Schmidt (1991), who took issue with the social-psychological approach adopted by Gardner, Lambert and

their associates. They argue that the socio-educational model has been so dominant in the language learning field, that other approaches to the study of motivation have "not seriously been considered" (p. 501). This resulted in an unbalanced picture, involving a conception that was, as Skehan (1989) put it, "limited compared to the range of possible influences that exists"(p. 280). However, the socio-educational model covers some of these variables to a greater extent than first meets the eye (see MacIntyre, MacMaster, & Baker, 2001).

Crookes and Schmidt (1991) discussed three other approaches to motivation: Giles and Byrne's (1982) speech accommodation theory, Schumann's (1978) acculturation model, and Krashen's (1985) monitor model. Crookes and Schmidt (1991) strongly support both Gardner's and Schumann's emphasis on the active learner, stating "...it seems reasonable that motivation, as it controls engagement in and persistence with the learning task, should also be considered worthy of renewed scrutiny" (p. 480). This point is well taken.

Crookes and Schmidt (1991) spend the majority of the article discussing practitioners' usage of the term motivation. They argue the

> "... invalidity of SL treatments of motivation in terms of their distance from everyday, nontechnical concepts of what it means to be motivated. When teachers say that a student is motivated, they are not usually concerning themselves with the student's reason for studying ... Teachers would describe a student as motivated if he or she becomes productively engaged in learning tasks, and sustains that engagement, without the need for continual encouragement or direction. They are more concerned with motivation than affect" (p. 480).

This is an error in focus. A consideration of affect is valuable, if not essential, to any discussion of the source of the engagement that many authors see as the key to motivation.

Crookes and Schmidt used Keller's (1983) education-oriented theory to define motivation as the choices people make about the experiences and goals they approach or avoid, and the degree of effort they exert. According to Keller four major determinants of motivation are interest, relevance, expectancy, and outcomes. Crookes and Schmidt apply these four determinants at the micro-level, the classroom level, the syllabus level, and to informal experiences outside the class. Clearly their emphasis is on classroom-based approaches to understanding motivation, though they indicate that motivation extends beyond the classroom into naturalistic settings. Much as Gardner does, they assert that motivation will operate in both settings in similar ways because essentially "...no different processes of learning are involved" (p. 494).

The discussion by Crookes and Schmidt is both interesting and valuable.

They offered the harshest of the three critical evaluations of the socio-educational model under discussion here, and helped to inspire the other two. Unfortunately, they exhibit a tendency to speculate on what empirical research might demonstrate, without explicitly considering the intricate relations among motivation-related variables that necessarily would be involved. For example, at the classroom level, Crookes and Schmidt suggest that students who experience failure and blame themselves for it "…are likely to have a low estimate of their future success in SL learning, which may in turn lead to low risk-taking, low acceptance of ambiguity, and other behaviors that are probably negatively correlated with success in SL learning" (p. 490). They propose cooperative learning as a way to prevent or modify this undesirable sequence of events because such techniques allow the underachiever to feel that success is possible.

The proposed effects of failure seem reasonable and the advocacy for cooperative learning comes across as plausible. But we should not assume that these are the necessary, common, or only psychological and behavioral consequences of failure experiences. Nor should we assume that underachievers would react as proposed. Further, it is possible that high achievers, introverts, and anxious students might be frustrated by group-work, and these potential effects are not mentioned. This highlights the need for empirical work, for which there is no substitute.

Dörnyei (1994a)

To a much greater extent than Crookes and Schmidt, Dörnyei (1994a) acknowledges the important role that the social dimension of second language (L2) motivation plays. Dörnyei also outlines the distinction between integrativeness and instrumentality, as discussed by Gardner. Dörnyei seems to imply that the distinction between integrativeness and instrumentality emanates largely from the Canadian context, although he does indicate that "…broadly defined 'cultural-affective' and 'pragmatic-instrumental' dimensions do usually emerge in empirical studies of motivation" (p. 275). Dörnyei goes on to refer to these as "…broad tendencies — or subsystems — comprising context-specific clusters of loosely related components."

Dörnyei (1994a) then elaborates on what he calls "further" components of L2 motivation. After listing and describing several concepts related to motivation in the broader psychological and educational literatures, Dörnyei integrates these concepts into a three-level framework of motivation. The broadest level is termed the "language level" and is primarily defined by the concepts of integrative and instrumental motivation. Secondly, the "learner level" describes individual differences among learners using familiar motivational concepts such as need for achievement and self-confidence. The "learning situation level," to which Dörnyei devotes considerable attention, is the one over which educators have the most control. The learning situation level can be divided into course-specific, teacher-specific, and group-specific motivational components. Dörnyei argues that this level is especially pertinent to classroom teachers and is not sufficiently considered in the socio-educational model. Particularly relevant to this last point are 30 strategies that teachers might use to motivate learners. Given Dörnyei's emphasis on the language classroom, 20 of these 30 strategies are presented at the learning situation level.

Dörnyei (1994a) examines a wider variety of motivation variables than do Crookes and Schmidt (1991) and the various concepts are grouped into a three-level taxonomy that includes the language level, the learner level, and the learning situation level. It is the learning situation level that most clearly distinguishes Dörnyei's (1994a) approach from Gardner's. Yet Dörnyei is the most accommodating of Gardner's theory. There is a tremendous amount of theoretical work required to integrate the concepts proposed by Dörnyei (1994a) and demonstrate how their interactions affect L2 learning. As well, much empirical research is required to test the ideas. One cannot fault Dörnyei for taking this as the first step. Indeed, to his credit, he has been the most active of the critics in developing and testing an expanded motivational framework (Dörnyei, 2001; Dörnyei & Kormos, 2000).

Oxford and Shearin (1994)

Oxford and Shearin also propose expanding the theoretical framework for language learning motivation. Like Dörnyei (1994a), they argue that the socio-educational model proposed by Gardner is limited in scope and must be expanded "outward" to include a number of other motivational variables. According to Oxford and Shearin (1994), four conditions impede our full understanding of students' motivation: lack of consensus on a definition of motivation, the difference between second and foreign language situations, key motivational variables are missing from the models, and teachers do not understand their students' real motivation for learning. Each of these assertions should be examined in detail before being accepted at face value.

As noted earlier in this chapter, the issue of definition is complex and pervades the study of motivation in general. In discussing this issue, Oxford and Shearin state that "the goal thus helps define the motivational orientation of the student, which in the best-known version of [the socio-educational] model must be either instrumental or integrative..." (p. 13). The statement likely reflects an overly rigid interpretation of Gardner's work. Gardner has not stated that motivational orientations must be one of these two types (see Gardner & Tremblay, 1994). Dörnyei (1994a, 1994b) is quite correct in noting that Gardner's point has been that the student who values the L2 community will tend to show higher levels of achievement than a student who does not, an idea whose impact has been substantial.

The issue of second vs. foreign language situations will vary in importance depending on the perspective one takes on the definition of motivation. To use Dörnyei's (1994a) terminology, if one focuses on the learner level, this issue is less relevant than if one is concerned with the language level. The focus on the learner level, or on individual differences, will tend to emphasize internal representations of external phenomena. Such an emphasis will attempt to explain why some students develop certain orientations, and other students do not, given similar external environments (e.g., the same teacher and course materials). The focus on the teacher or the language level will tend to emphasize similarities among the students in this same context, glossing over the individual differences. It is quite likely that if one looks for individual differences, they will be found; if one looks for broader commonalities, they also will be found.

The omission of key motivational variables might be interpreted as emphasis on understanding what makes language learning motivation unique, as compared to motivation to learn other subjects. Variables such as intrinsic motivation, goal-setting, need for achievement, expectancy-value, and others will be relevant to motivation theories in general, educational motivation theories in general, and theories of language learning motivation in particular. It is the emphasis on culture, psychological identification with a specific cultural group, and changes in identity that most clearly distinguish language learning from other subjects studied in school. Given this emphasis, Gardner's focus on integrative motivation seems appropriate. None of Gardner's critics have argued that this focus is incorrect, rather they argue that other variables should be considered in addition to those involving integrative motivation. Thus, the question appears to be one of emphasis.

Finally, the lack of teachers' knowledge about the motivation of their students, suggested by Oxford and Shearin, is likely to vary substantially from one teacher to another. However, given the experience brought to the issue by Oxford and Shearin, I cannot dispute the point. Indeed, it will be argued later in this chapter that an empirical measurement of motivation and its relation to achievement is a desirable goal. Language teachers are capable of asking students about the motives for taking a given course, using any one of several instruments available (for example, see Chapter 12 in Dörnyei, 2001 and the appendix to Oxford's 1996 book). To the extent that teachers employ well known, standardized instruments, their results can be compared to prior research.

The rest of the Oxford and Shearin paper is devoted to summarizing a number of motivational variables that likely relate to language learning. They examine need theories, expectancy-value theories, equity theories, and reinforcement theories. They also add social-cognitive concepts, emphasizing self-efficacy and reward satisfaction. They round out their inventory with a description of the mastery model and the work of Piaget and Vygotsky. The paper concludes with five practical implications for L2 teachers, including identifying students' reasons for learning, shaping learner beliefs about success and failure, emphasizing that the benefits of L2 learning are worth the cost, enhancing the L2 classroom, and facilitating the transition from extrinsic to intrinsic rewards.

A comment on the critics

An interesting series of responses to these articles appeared in the *Modern Language Journal* in 1994. Oxford (1994), Dörnyei (1994b), and Gardner and Tremblay (1994) each attempted to elaborate on their prior contributions and clear up misconceptions. The critics indicate that they value Gardner's socio-educational model but wish to explore other areas of motivation. In the original critical articles (Crookes & Schmidt, 1991; Dörnyei, 1994a; Oxford & Shearin, 1994), a long list of potential constructs was proposed and grouped into a taxonomy but these constructs were not integrated with each other to show their interrelationships (see Table 1). It might be noted that examination of the literature on motivation would show that a long list of additional concepts could be offered as well (the subject index to Reeve's (1997) motivation text is 14 pages). Indeed, listing potential additions to the literature is not at all difficult compared to the heavy theoretical and empirical work required to specify how these concepts interact. Studying just the variables in Table 1 would keep the field busy for a very long time.

It must be acknowledged that given its considerable breadth, studying motivation necessarily means slicing off a small piece of the theoretical pie. It would be impossible to include all potentially relevant variables in a single model. The socio-educational model mapped out a specific domain within the field of language learning motivation, and research proceeded in a programmatic fashion. Gardner should not be faulted simply for omitting variables; such an approach is absolutely necessary if knowledge is to be advanced in an area. Testable hypotheses can be generated from the list of variables in Table 1, but there is a lot of work in understanding the influence of any one of them. A point on which Dörnyei (1994b) agrees with Gardner and Tremblay (1994) is the need for empirical research to test the hypotheses, intuitions, and potential applications of any expanded model of language learning motivation. It is a point that cannot be reinforced strongly enough.

A study by MacIntyre et al. (2001) has employed factor analysis to examine the degree of overlap among a long list of motivational constructs. The variables studied were drawn from Gardner's model, as discussed above. Scales from Pintrich, Smith, Garcia, and McKeachie's (1991) classroom-oriented Motivated Strategies for Learning Questionnaire, including self-efficacy, task value, and beliefs about the degree of student control over learning were used. Tendencies toward preoccupation, hesitation, and rumination (see Dörnyei & Otto, 1998), three variables drawn from Kuhl's (1994a) Action Control Model, a general model of motivation, were measured. Also measured were the three communication-related variables willingness to communicate, perceived competence, and communication apprehension, that have been investigated by McCroskey and associates over the years (McCroskey & Richmond, 1991). These scales, 23 in all, represented a wide variety of concepts emerging from theoretical models that have been developed independently. However, all can be applied to language learning research and would be suggested by the Gardner critics as expansions of the motivational research base.

Results showed that the 23 scales could be summarized by three underlying factors. The first factor, by far the largest, was labeled *attitudinal motivation*. It was defined primarily by the Gardner and Pintrich concepts. Included on this factor were several AMTB scales: attitudes toward learning French, integrative orientation, instrumental orientation, motivational intensity (effort), interest in foreign languages, attitudes toward French Canadians, French use anxiety, desire to learn French, and self-confidence (from Gardner, Tremblay, & Masgoret, 1997). The other measures on this factor, from Pintrich et al. (1991), were task value, self-efficacy, extrinsic orientation, intrinsic orientation, and control over learning beliefs.

The second factor in that study was labeled *self-confidence* and was defined by measures of anxiety and perceived competence in L2 communication. Such a factor has often emerged in studies by Gardner and associates

Table 1. Motivational concepts offered for application to language learning research

	Dörnyei	Oxford/Shearin	Crookes/Schmidt
Interest	☞	Based on previous experience	☞
Relevance	☞	☞	☞
Outcome	Satisfaction: Grades and rewards	Reinforcement	Reward and punishment
Need for achievement	☞	☞	X
Personality traits	X	☞	X
Expectancy	☞	☞	Success or failure
Experience	X	☞	X
Expectancy-value	X	☞	X
Goal-setting	☞	☞	X
Self-efficacy	☞	☞	X
Self-confidence	☞	X	X
Direction	X	X	☞
Persistence	X	X	☞
Continuing motivation	X	X	☞
Classroom motivation	☞	X	X
Intellectual curiosity	☞	X	X
Teacher feedback	☞	X	X
Anxiety	☞	X	X
Perceived competence	☞	X	X
Activity level	X	X	☞
Security needs	X	☞	X
Equity	X	☞	X
Growth needs	X	☞	X
Age of acquisition	X	☞	X
Fear of failure	X	☞	X
Fear of success	X	☞	X
Environmental stimulation	X	☞	X
Mastery vs. relative performance	X	☞	X

Note: ☞=included x=excluded

(Gardner, Smythe, & Lalonde, 1984; Clément, Gardner, & Smythe, 1977, 1980) leading Clément (1980) to propose self-confidence as a secondary motivational process. The third factor was called *action motivation* and was largely defined by the Kuhl (1994b) action control scales. Dörnyei and Otto (1998) have argued that understanding the initiation of behavior, or "crossing the rubicon of action," is a area of emerging importance in L2 motivation research. It is interesting that willingness to communicate, defined as the intention to initiate communication if given the choice, was found to be related to all three factors (see MacIntyre, Clément, Dörnyei, & Noels, 1998). As a whole, the results of this investigation, particularly the *attitudinal motivation* factor, indicate a great deal of overlap among seemingly disparate motivational variables...

> It might be surprising that there is such a high degree of overlap, but it should be noted that the Gardner model has always covered a great deal of conceptual ground. Perhaps it is not surprising that the value students place on a language course and their expectancies for success in that course would be reflected in the same factor. Whereas the concepts clearly can be distinguished theoretically, the degree of empirical similarity is quite high in this sample (MacIntyre et al., 2001).

Clearly it is possible to define a wide variety of motivational influences in theory, but the empirical results must support such distinctions if they are to be useful both in theory and in practice. In this study, the greater empirical distinction appears to be between *attitudinal motivation* and *action motivation*. This presents an exciting challenge for the field, to examine the transition from attitudes to action (see Ajzen, 1988; Dörnyei, 2001; Dörnyei & Otto, 1998) and the way in which willingness to communicate in the L2 seems to connect them (MacIntyre et al., 1998).

The need for empirical research

There is no shortage of empirical research in the study of motivation, broadly defined. Sustaining this effort over the years have been interesting, at times paradoxical, results. Studies address what might seem to be simple questions, but generate complex answers. It is vital that those conducting theoretical work on motivation for language learning, as well as those reading it, be prepared for contradictory, paradoxical, and unexpected empirical results. To introduce this issue, let us consider one of the most fundamental laws of motivation, homeostasis. Homeostasis is a term coined by Walter Cannon (1932) to describe the regulation of levels of vital substances in the bloodstream. It has been expanded to connote the body's tendency to maintain a steady state. Motivational processes almost always display a tendency toward homeostasis, the key implication being that the regulation of motivation must include both arousing and calming processes, approach and avoidance tendencies. Therefore, when one describes the motives in favor of a particular action, such as integrativeness or additive bilingualism, one must immediately be aware that there will be motives that counteract action, such as fear of assimilation (Clément, 1986) or subtractive bilingualism (Gardner & Lambert, 1959).

Some examples from the general motivation literature will help to illustrate this point. They are being presented in this chapter because they represent the sort of variables proposed by the critics for addition to the literature on language learning motivation, there has been empirical research on each of them, and the results were more complex than expected. Three research areas will be described: the hidden cost of reward, opponent process theory, and psychological reactance.

The hidden cost of reward

Also called the "overjustification effect," the hidden cost of reward refers to the paradoxical tendency for external rewards to damage pre-existing intrinsic motivation. It might seem obvious that to increase motivation one can offer a reward; by conventional wisdom, the larger the reward the greater the motivation. However this is certainly not always advisable, and in some cases the strategy should be avoided. The classic study in the field by Lepper, Green, and Nisbett (1973) showed that children who enjoyed drawing before the research began actually drew less after having been rewarded for their drawing. A great deal of research demonstrated the generality and limitations of this finding and it seems clear that offering a reward that is tangible, expected, and highly salient (emphasized) has the potential to create a decrease in intrinsic motivation (Reeve, 1992). For example, a language teacher who accentuates only instrumental goals, such as getting high grades on a test, might actually discourage some students, specifically those who are interested in the language for its own sake. The effect occurs because the reward itself is made the prominent motive for action. Most teachers likely dread the perennial question from students, "Will this be on the test?" because the teacher's emphasis is on the students' mastery of the material, but the students' emphasis is on getting the highest possible grade (reward) on the test. It should be noted that the overjustification effect can be observed with a task that was intrinsically motivating *before* the reward was offered. If intrinsic motivation is low to begin with, adding an extrinsic reward, such as grades, money, or even gold stars, can produce the desired behavior because of an absence of other motivational support.

Opponent process theory

According to opponent process theory (Solomon, 1980; Solomon & Corbit, 1973, 1974), feelings of pleasure and aversion can be acquired in situations that initially produce the opposite feelings. To take a simple example, consider stepping into a hot bath. Initially the hot water produces feelings of pain and tendency to pull one's foot out of the water. This initial reaction, however, soon gives way to feelings of relief and pleasure that slowly dissipate over time. Unknown to the individual, the initial experience of pain automatically triggers the opposite, or opponent, feeling of pleasure. This helps to maintain the tendency toward homeostasis. Over time, emotional reactions change, and we come to associate the experience of stepping into a hot bath with pleasure rather than pain. Opponent process theory helps to explain apparently contradictory tendencies such as why people long to go home during their vacation and enjoy feeling terrified while watching a scary movie. Of course, there are limits to the situations in which opponent process theory applies (see Mauro, 1988; Sandvik, Diener, & Larsen, 1987). Nevertheless, the counterintuitive nature of the process is noteworthy.

Reactance theory
Reactance theory attempts to explain behaviors normally thought of as demonstrating stubbornness. The theory suggests that when a person's ability to control important outcomes is threatened, he or she will act to re-establish control. This theory can help explain why forbidden fruit is the most attractive, why some people don't like to receive a favor, and why making a course mandatory creates ill-will. According to Brehm and Brehm (1981), human beings want to have the freedom to decide which behavior they will pursue at any particular time. Something that interferes with a person's freedom to choose will meet with attempts to re-establish control. These attempts become more vigorous to the extent that the outcomes are of higher importance and people expect to have some control over events. Perhaps paradoxically, however, after several attempts to exert control in the face of a truly uncontrollable event, a person's behavior may show signs of "learned helplessness" where responding stops altogether. The effects that learned helplessness, which are similar to depression (Rosenhan & Seligman, 1984; Seligman, 1975), are likely to be more severe when the outcomes were initially considered more important.

The three examples briefly described here show the complexity of our motivational experiences and the operation of automatic processes that maintain homeostasis. They demonstrate how difficult it is, in the absence of empirical research, to speculate on the effects of attempts to alter motivation. Strongly implicated in these, and indeed most other, motivational processes is emotion. Indeed, the link between motivation and emotion is strong, intricate, and fascinating.

Emotion as motivation

The motivational properties of emotion have been severely underestimated in the language learning literature. A detailed description of the neurobiology of emotion, applied to L2 experience, is provided by Schumann (1998). In general, there exists a close relationship between motivation and emotion; indeed, there is a scholarly journal of that very title. Silvan Tomkins (1970) notes that throughout the history of psychology, drives have been considered the most basic motives. Tomkins has argued quite convincingly that it is preferable to conceptualize affect as the primary human motive. Emotion functions as an amplifier, providing the intensity, urgency, and energy to propel behavior. In contrasting the primacy of affect with the primacy of "drives," Tomkins outlines three lines of evidence in favor of the primacy of emotion. First, "drives require amplification from the affects, whereas the affects are sufficient motivators in the absence of drives" (p. 104). Take oxygen deprivation as an analogy. Humans require oxygen and are therefore driven to breathe, but it is not oxygen deprivation per se that is motivating — it is the emotions related to fear and panic. Consider the affective difference between holding one's breath for 30 seconds while swimming versus choking for 30 seconds. The level of oxygen deprivation is similar between the examples, but the panic that sets in when one is choking creates extremely intense behavior, and does so immediately, before any effects of oxygen deprivation could possibly be felt. It is the emotion that is motivating.

The second argument in favor of the primacy of affect is the generality of the affective system, which is not limited to time-specific or rhythmic activation. Hunger, thirst, and other drives have particular rhythms; for example, one is not hungry immediately after eating. Affect is not constrained in this way. One may feel anxious for just a moment, for an hour, or consistently for a week. Personality temperament, which is regarded as primarily inherited, describes typical emotional reactions and is responsible for a great deal of the individual differences in personality profiles (Kagan, 1989).

Tomkins' final point is that emotion is continually present, varying in type and intensity. We are always experiencing some sort of emotion. Emotion therefore pervades all of our activities. Given its function as an amplifier, emotion has some impact on everything we do; the stronger the emotion, the greater the impact. Strong emotion can disrupt cognitive and physiological processes, as when high anxiety initiates the powerful "fight or flight response" of the autonomic nervous system. Its effects include halting digestion, increasing muscle tension and blood pressure, pupil dilation, and directing cognition toward battle or escape plans. The onset of these effects can be very rapid, even in the absence of any physical threat, and take a long time to wear off. Emotions are highly sensitive to the immediate environment, or more specifically, changes in the environment (see Buck, 1984). With emotional experience so pervasive, sensitive, and potentially powerful, emotion can be seen as a fundamental motivator of behavior.

Motivated action is particularly relevant to the present discussion. As Parkinson (1995) notes, emotions often carry with them impulses to act in a particular way appropriate to the emotion. It can be added that these impulses to act might be highly appropriate or inappropriate for smooth social functioning, including L2 interaction. For example, feeling embarrassed usually produces the urge to withdraw and hide oneself, regardless of the source of the embarrassment. It is virtually impossible to imagine a L2 learner who does not embarrass himself or herself from time to time. How an individual reacts will be governed in large measure by the intensity of the emotional reaction. It might be in the learner's best academic, financial, cultural, and social interest to keep talking, but if the emotion is too strong, the person will try to withdraw. It stands to reason that L2 students should talk in order to learn, but reason and emotion are separate issues.

There exists a complex link between reason and emotion. Seymour Epstein (1994) has written a number of descriptions of Cognitive-Experiential Self Theory in which a basic distinction is made between an "experiential" system and a "rational" system. The rational system is seen as being logical, analytic, and based on conscious appraisals of events. The experiential system often operates based on subtle feeling states that occur instantly, automatically, and often below the level of conscious awareness as pervasive, subtle, and influential emotions. These feeling states, which Epstein (1993) calls "vibes," operate to shape both cognition and behavior. "A typical sequence of behavior is that an event occurs; the experiential system scans its memory banks for related events; and vibes from the past events are produced that influence conscious thoughts and behavior" (Epstein, 1993, p. 323). Buck (1984) proposes that emotion is a more basic system than cognition (p. 58), because in both human evolution and personal development, emotional systems are fully developed very early on, and rational systems much later. Buck further discusses a two-system view of emotion itself. One system is primitive, subcortical, and visceral, the other a more modern evolutionary development, seated in the cerebral cortex of the brain, and consciously evaluative based on the social and cultural learning history of the individual. Thus, the cognitive system itself can stimulate emotion without an external prompt, as when we reminisce about fond memories, recall an embarrassing incident, or nervously contemplate an upcoming examination. These two routes to emotion, reactions to the situation and reactions to our ongoing thoughts, are separate but coordinated and synchronized (see also Panskepp, 1994).

Given the pervasiveness of emotions, their role in energizing behavior, and their flexibility over time, it is clear that emotion forms a key part of the motivational system. Using Buck's two-system view, it can be seen that the attitudes toward language learning tapped by Gardner's AMTB and represented in the socio-educational model have strong reciprocal links to emotion. Indeed, items such as "I love learning French," "I find the study of French very boring," "I really like learning French," and others tap directly into emotional reactions. The role that emotion, to the extent that it can be split off from attitudes and motivation, plays in the language learning process has yet to be widely studied. Researchers in the field of language learning have not paid sufficient attention to emotional phenomena. Even Krashen's (1981, 1985) well-known concept of "affective filter" seems too passive to fully capture the role of emotion as studied elsewhere by Epstein, Buck, Panskepp, and others.

It is proposed here that the difference between the engaged and unengaged learner, discussed by Gardner (1985), Crookes and Schmidt (1991), Oxford and Shearin (1994), and Dörnyei (1994a), lies in the emotions experienced during language learning. Attitudes alone are not likely to be sufficient to support motivation. This helps to account for the finding, often lamented by Gardner and others (see Gardner & Tremblay, 1994), that integrative or instrumental orientations, which are the goals endorsed for language learning (purely attitudinal in nature) and a subcomponent of integrative motivation, often do not correlate with language proficiency. A better understanding of emotion has the capacity to explain cases where students endorse orientations but might not be energized to take action, and also cases where action is prevented by emotional arousal, either present or anticipated. MacIntyre and Noels (1996) have applied this idea to language learning strategy use, arguing that reasons to approach a language learning task must be juxtaposed with reasons to avoid it, and that the two processes seem to occur simultaneously.

The implications of a more explicit focus on emotion must be worked out. However, we already have a pretty good start. The Gardner model refers to its key components as "affective variables," implying an emotional component. Similarly, the test items used by Gardner and associates in the AMTB

over the years clearly have drawn on emotional phenomena, but have organized the results around attitude clusters, rather than emotions. The link
between emotions and attitudes is one of Buck's (1984) two systems, meaning
that more attention to emotional explanations can be added to the prior
research by Gardner and associates. In future research, we can look for a close,
reciprocal, mutually enhancing relationship between emotion and attitude, as
applied to language learning.

The other of Buck's two systems is a more visceral, low-level, uncontrollable emotional response. These emotions tend to be more intense, at times
overpowering cognitive processes, as when an upset person is asked to "stop
and think." These emotions are strongly rooted in physiological processes, are
relatively universal and independent of culture, are displayed uniquely and
can be clearly differentiated, and are automatic reactions to external events
(Ekman & Davidson, 1994). Some theorists call these "primary" emotions
and the list is typically a short one. Approximately a half-dozen primary emotions are usually proposed, including joy, interest, sadness, disgust, anger, and
fear (Reeve, 1997). The only emotion of this sort to be studied in detail in the
language learning area is anxiety, a variant of fear. For this reason, we now
turn to a detailed discussion of language anxiety.

Language anxiety

Language anxiety has long been included as a variable in Gardner's socio-educational model, but within the model it has not received the attention
assigned motivation nor has it been assigned a consistent place (MacIntyre &
Gardner, 1991). In some formulations, anxiety is an antecedent to motivation
(see Tremblay & Gardner, 1995) and in others a product of proficiency
(Gardner, Tremblay, & Masgoret, 1997). Gardner and MacIntyre (1993a) suggest that the two variables have a reciprocal relationship, that anxiety affects
motivation and motivation affects anxiety. Richard Clément (1980, 1986) has
proposed a model in which anxiety combines with self-perceptions of language proficiency to create self-confidence which is viewed as a second motivational process (see also MacIntyre et al., 2001). The relationship between
anxiety and L2 proficiency is a larger issue and raises an important question
about causal direction.

Does anxiety cause poor performance or does poor performance cause
anxiety? (see Young, 1986). This is the prototypical question asked about the

interpretation of correlations. Take, for example, a study by MacIntyre and Gardner (1994b) where language anxiety was shown to correlate with a number of specific L2 performance measures. Is this evidence that difficulties in language learning create anxiety or that anxiety reduces the quality of performance on these tasks? It is possible that a third variable, such as motivation or aptitude, might be influencing both test scores and anxiety levels. Along these lines, Sparks and Ganschow (1991, 1993a, 1993b) have declared that anxiety is epiphenomenal, proposing that differences in native language linguistic coding create different levels of achievement, and that anxiety is an unfortunate byproduct of poor performance.

A study by MacIntyre and Gardner (1994a) essentially puts the key part of this question to rest, demonstrating that anxiety-arousal can lead to poor L2 performance. Drawing on a model proposed by Tobias (1979, 1980, 1986), MacIntyre and Gardner (1994a) attempted to create anxiety at each of three stages of cognitive processing in order to observe its effects. A video camera was used in order to arouse anxiety during a computer-mediated vocabulary learning session that had been split into the input stage (where material is encountered for the first time), the processing stage (where connections between new material and existing knowledge are made), and the output stage (where knowledge is demonstrated). Experimental groups were created by randomly assigning learners to a control group or one of three anxiety-arousing conditions. During the study, an anxiety-provoking video camera was introduced immediately prior to the input stage, the processing stage, or the output stage. The control group never saw the video camera. Results showed that anxiety increased most, and performance suffered most, immediately after the camera was introduced. As learners adapted to the camera and their anxiety dissipated, some recovery from the effects of anxiety was evident, as expected. This provides support for the idea that anxiety creates disruption in cognitive activity at each of the stages. Further, the study showed that as anxiety dissipated, learners were able to partially compensate for difficulties at previous stages by increased effort, showing the link between emotion and motivation. To be sure, these results do not rule out the possibility that anxiety might result from poor performance, or that both anxiety and poor performance could result from other factors, such as linguistic coding deficits (see Grigorenko, and Skehan, this volume, for further discussion of both of these possibilities). However, these results do clearly indicate that anxiety can play a causal role in creating individual differences in language achievement.

Most of the research into language anxiety has been correlational or qualitative in nature. MacIntyre (1999) summarizes research on the effects of language anxiety in four areas: academic, cognitive, social and personal.

Academic

In the academic area, several studies have demonstrated that language anxiety is negatively correlated with language course grades (Aida, 1994; Horwitz, 1986; Young, 1986). MacIntyre and Gardner (1994b) report a correlation of $r=.65$ between language anxiety and grades in a French course. Ironically, language learners complain of "overstudying" as a result of anxiety arousal (Horwitz, Horwitz, & Cope, 1986). Gardner, Smythe, Clément, and Gliksman (1976) investigated attitudes, motivation, and anxiety in several locations across Canada and found that anxiety was consistently among the strongest predictors of language course grades, particularly as students got older. Language teachers have indicated concern for the reduction of language anxiety and have proposed instructional methods, such as "the natural way," that address the issue (see Koch & Terrell, 1991).

Cognitive

The source of these academic effects can be explained by looking at the disruption in thinking and reasoning caused by anxiety. Eysenck (1979) has proposed that anxiety arousal is accompanied by distracting, self-related cognition — the higher the anxiety levels, the greater the disruption. Eysenck further noted that a frequent response to anxiety, especially at milder levels, is an increase in effort. This explains the inverted "u" function of anxiety arousal (see MacIntyre, 1999), and leads to a distinction between the effects of facilitating and debilitating anxiety (Leibert & Morris, 1967). Facilitating anxiety can lead to better performance as a result of increased effort. The more common use of the term "anxiety," however, is in the debilitating sense where the negative effects of anxiety are harmful to performance (see MacIntyre & Gardner, 1989).

Social

Perhaps the most dramatic social effect of anxiety is a reluctance to communicate. MacIntyre and Gardner (1991) have found that the most anxiety provoking aspect of language learning is the thought of future communication. Communication research (see Daly & McCroskey, 1984) has shown that avoiding communication produces a number of negative social perceptions. Clément (1986) has argued that the social experience of language anxiety is different for members of majority vs. minority groups. We can extend that to suggest that the experience of language anxiety might be different for learners of second vs. foreign languages. One issue that has not been addressed in the literature, but can be observed informally among students, is the extent to which language anxiety provides a common experience and an opportunity for social exchange. After all, if anxiety leads to misery and misery loves company, then it follows that commiserating about anxiety can be a positive experience, even if the anxiety itself is not. This would make for an interesting study.

Personal

The personal effects of anxiety should not be underestimated. Some interesting qualitative research has demonstrated the intense anxiety felt by some students. Students have reported feeling like an idiot, a babbling baby, and a total dingbat. A student in the study by Cohen and Norst (1989) was particularly strong in stating that language learning was "pure trauma" and represented the "smashing of a well-developed self concept" (pp. 68–69). Horwitz et al. (1986) argue that language learning is so anxiety provoking, in part, because learners may have the sophisticated thoughts and emotions of an adult, but the language of a child in which to express them. To some extent language learning itself is prone to creating intense emotion because of the close connection between language, culture, and identity (Noels, Pon, & Clément, 1996).

In reading the reactions of anxious language students provided by Cohen and Norst (1989) and Price (1991) with a critical eye, it seems reasonable to ask whether these students have exaggerated their emotional reactions or overstated the case. However, even if overstated, such a pattern of thought might itself exert an impact on language learning. MacIntyre, Noels, and Clément (1997) demonstrated that anxious language learners tend to underestimate their level of proficiency, and relaxed students overestimate it. If this represents a prevalent tendency, then anxious language learners will tend to remain anxious because they tend to withdraw from situations that might increase their proficiency, creating a self-fulfilling prophecy.

Conclusion

This chapter began by suggesting that language learning is motivated behavior, but that among learners, motives will rise and fall in influence, and several will operate at any given time. Clearly, one of the most important developments in the field has been Gardner and associates' work on the integrative motive as part of the socio-educational model. The insights gained from this body of work should not be lost in the pursuit of concepts novel to the language learning area. We also owe a debt of gratitude to the authors collectively labeled here as "the critics" (Crookes, Schmidt, Dörnyei, Oxford, and Shearin) for so strongly restating the case in favor of studying motivation as an individual difference variable in language learning. We are now in a position to suggest the consideration of a multiplicity of competing motives, some leading to approach and others leading to avoidance of the L2. If we adopt the assumption that even language learning will tend toward a form of homeostasis, interesting research scenarios begin to suggest themselves. For example, (1) does rewarding successful classroom task performance bring a cost to intrinsic, maybe even integrative, motivation that can be examined, (2) can opponent emotional processes be studied for their motivational or restraining properties, and (3) how do we investigate the effects of choice over learning from a variety of perspectives, at the learning situation level (as in choice of tasks) and at the language level (as in the choice of language to be studied or abandoned). Perhaps the strongest message to be offered in the present chapter is to encourage a detailed study of the motivational properties of the emotions experienced during language learning. Regardless of the avenues chosen for future research, the possibilities are exhilarating.

Notes

* This research was facilitated by a grant from the Social Sciences and Humanities Research Council of Canada. Thanks are extended to Zoltán Dörnyei and Leslie Donovan for comments on an earlier draft. Correspondence may be addressed to Peter MacIntyre, Department of Psychology, University College of Cape Breton, Sydney, Nova Scotia, Canada, B1P 6L2 or by e-mail peter_macintyre@uccb.ns.ca

1 For a recent revision to the AMTB see Gardner, Tremblay and Masgoret (1997).

2 It should be noted that some authors, including Dörnyei (1994b), have indicated that various uses of the term "integrative" have created confusion in the literature over the years. To clarify, integrative orientation refers only to a set of specific reasons for language learning. Integrativeness refers to a broader concept representing an interest in the target language group, which subsumes the orientation and supports it with positive attitudes and interest. The integrative motive represents self-reported energized behavior specifically combined with integrativeness as the affective support for the effort. Integrative motivation requires all three elements to meet Gardner's definition of the motivated language learner.

CHAPTER 4

Theorising and updating aptitude

Peter Skehan
King's College, London

Introduction

Research and theorising on foreign language aptitude has languished over the last thirty years, with relatively little empirical work (compared to other aspects of applied linguistics), and remarkably little theorising. It is the purpose of the present paper to contribute to a change in this situation. Early aptitude research is briefly reviewed, as are reasons for the relative unpopularity of aptitude research, and then a survey is presented of what empirical work has been carried out in recent years. It is argued that the contribution of this work, although not widely cited, is far from negligible. Given that one reason for a lack of interest in aptitude is its perceived irrelevance to language acquisition within communicative contexts, the remainder of the paper explores potential connections between what we understand of stages of second language acquisition (SLA), and putative aptitude constructs. It is argued that, taking a componential approach to aptitude, successive stages that are proposed for development are frequently the basis for a number of aptitudinal components, and that these are relevant not simply for formal classroom learning, but for any SLA. It is argued that if we explore the relationship between existing aptitude sub-tests and the possible components, a research agenda emerges regarding the areas where new aptitude sub-tests could beneficially be developed.

Earlier investigations of foreign language aptitude have had a very practical orientation. They have mainly focussed on the scope for predicting how well foreign languages can be learned. The essence of this work has therefore been pragmatic, and while there have been notable theoretical formulations of aptitude (as we will see below) the "payoff" has generally been to assess how effectively prediction of speed of learning can be achieved.[1]

One consequence of this approach has been that as instructional method-ologies have changed, foreign language aptitude tests have been perceived as irrelevant. As a result, they have fallen into disfavor. This too is regrettable, since, as this chapter will argue, the construct of foreign language aptitude has a great deal to offer. This chapter will review research into foreign language aptitude, and then, more significantly, explore aptitudinal constructs theoret-ically, so that they can be related to contemporary accounts of SLA. It will be seen that aptitude, far from being outmoded, could be central for future progress in the second language (L2) learning domain. In part, this is because a componential model of foreign language aptitude fits in well with the stages involved in SLA processing. But there is also the added theoretical dimension that aptitude is illuminating regarding the nature of a talent for learning, and for nature of cognitive abilities more generally. It is also central to any evalu-ation of the relevance of Universal Grammar (UG) for L2 learning.

Traditional investigations of aptitude

Aptitude research

A "modern" approach to foreign language aptitude emerged with the work, in the 1950s, of the American psychologist J. B. Carroll, who established the methodology for studying aptitude as well as its nature (Carroll, 1962). He devised a large number of tests which were hypothesized to implicate funda-mental capacities involved in foreign language learning. He then administered these tests to learners about to embark upon a course of foreign language learn-ing. The different potential aptitude tests were correlated with one another, and also with tests of end-of-course performance. In this way Carroll was able to eliminate candidate aptitude tests which did not correlate with end-or-course performance, as well as candidate aptitude tests which merely duplicated one another, i.e., intercorrelated highly. He retained those candidate tests which suc-cessfully predicted foreign language learning, and which made independent contributions to such prediction. As a result of this work, he published (with Stanley Sapon) the *Modern Language Aptitude Test* (MLAT). (Carroll & Sapon, 1959), a measure which generated reasonably high correlations with language course performance (correlations of $r = .4$ to $.6$ being typical), and a measure which has been the cornerstone of aptitude research ever since.

Aptitude structure

The MLAT generated a total score, and this total score was the basis for predictions of language learning success. This might be taken to mean that aptitude is a monolithic construct. But Carroll also made suggestions regarding the sub-components which make up the broader construct of aptitude, and this more detailed view has proved to be more enduring and interesting than the MLAT test battery itself[2]. The four components are:

Phonemic coding ability	Capacity to code unfamiliar sound so that it can be retained
Grammatical sensitivity	Capacity to identify the functions that words fulfil in sentences
Inductive language learning ability	Capacity to extrapolate from given corpus to create new sentences
Associative memory	Capacity to form links in memory

The table makes it clear that aptitude contains sub-components. One of these is concerned with the auditory aspects of language learning, two with the processing of linguistic material, and one with memory. Each of these areas has its interest. The auditory component is not simply a capacity to discriminate sounds. Rather, it draws upon analysis of sound for the purpose of retention. In other words, this is a "depth-of-processing" interpretation of the capacity to deal with unfamiliar sound: imposing structure on unfamiliar sounds makes them more memorable and less transitory. The two language material factors also concern analysis, but of different material. The first is concerned with analyzing given material to extract function. The second focuses on a capacity to make generalizations and extrapolate. Grammatical sensitivity, in other words, is more passive, while inductive language learning is more active. Finally, the memory component concerns the capacity to make associations between L1 lexis and target language items. In this respect, the analysis reflects the views which prevailed in psychology at the time. Memory was simply conceived by psychologists in associational terms, a viewpoint which also reflected a simplistic equivalence view of word meaning. As we will see below, this is the aspect of the MLAT which has least stood the test of time.

Critiques of aptitude

The study of aptitude, and the impact of aptitude research, diminished considerably by the 1970s. There were several reasons for this. First of all, foreign language aptitude was perceived as anti-egalitarian. To test someone's aptitude and to assign them a score does have a forbidding quality. It implies that a fixed endowment of language learning capacity has been measured, and, to the extent that such an endowment shapes the level of achievement which is possible, the consequence of aptitude was taken to be that the value of individual effort was diminished. Many were disinclined to take this perspective, and, rather than wrestle with the nature of aptitude and its measurement, preferred to explore other options in researching the effectiveness of instruction.

Equally damaging, aptitude came to be associated with particular, and outmoded methodologies. The bulk of aptitude research had been done with learners instructed through audiolingual methodologies. As a result, aptitude itself was associated with these methodologies, and thought to be uniquely adapted to prediction in such circumstances. Two developments marginalised such methodologies. First, as the communicative approach became more influential, the relevance of aptitude was questioned. It was seen as predictive for the context of structured input and practice oriented activities, but not for the sort of information gap, meaningful language use that characterized CLT. Second, the impact of SLA research also grew after 1970. This research highlighted the naturalistic engagement of acquisitional processes, as well as the capacity of the learner to deal with whatever input was received in communicative contexts. Once again, aptitude was seen to be irrelevant, and more appropriate to old-fashioned class learning. Most forcefully, this was argued by Krashen (1981), who conceded that aptitude might have importance, but only for *learning*, not *acquisition*. Since Krashen was arguing for the marginality of learning (as opposed to the centrality of acquisition), this was a very damaging assessment of the role of aptitude. Gardner (1985), Spolsky (1989, and Cook (1996) also relegated aptitude to effects only on classroom learning.

A third reaction to aptitude work is just as important as these, more scholarly critiques. It is that the profession of English Language Teaching has been remarkably uninterested in the differences that exist between learners. This may partly be connected, over the last thirty years especially, with the enormous growth in importance of language teaching materials. Despite a flirtation with the teaching of English for Specific Purposes, the thrust of such materials has necessarily been generalist, as publishers have sought to identify the largest markets for main coursebook series. Such coursebook series, as they have sold in increasingly large numbers, reflecting the growth in importance of English as a world language, have become more international and generalist in scope. Each coursebook series is well-researched, piloted, and represents a significant commitment of resources. There is not scope, therefore, to do other than to try to make such publications appeal to the largest possible number of potential buyers. In other words, catering for individual learning preferences, styles, or aptitudes is not an attractive commercial option. It is a more convenient fiction to believe that all learners are the same, and the excellence of the materials is the over-riding issue. The existence of learner differences based on a generalized aptitude score, or, worse, different aptitude profiles, is not attractive, and the thrust within English language teaching therefore, is to regard mixed-ability classes as the responsibility of the teacher, not the coursebook writer. So once again, the learner fades from focus.

Post-MLAT research into language aptitude

Subsequent to the publication of the MLAT in 1959, there has been some research into foreign language aptitude. Broadly speaking, this research has not reconceptualised aptitude in any significant manner, and most of the research has operated fairly clearly within the aptitude agenda set by Carroll. The research can be portrayed as falling within four broad headings: practical measurement oriented research; research into the components of aptitude; research into contexts in which aptitude results may be used; and broader theory. We will examine each of these in turn.

Measurement oriented research

The MLAT is still, more than forty years after its publication, the most influential current aptitude measurement battery. Nonetheless, there have been several subsequent initiatives to produce alternative or complementary batteries. The most widely-used of these, mentioned above, was Pimsleur's *Language Aptitude Battery* (PLAB)(Pimsleur, 1966b). The motive to produce this commercially-available battery was to have a measuring instrument appropriate to high-school students. Further, Pimsleur (1966a, 1968; Pimsleur et al., 1966) was concerned about the under-achievement of school-children in the foreign language domain, and hypothesized that much of this under-achievement was the result of deficient auditory skills. For this reason the PLAB, compared to the MLAT, emphasizes auditory factors, somewhat at the expense of memory. In addition, it contains a sub-test of inductive language learning ability, whereas the MLAT, despite Carroll's theorising on the four-component structure of aptitude, only contained a measure of grammatical sensitivity. The PLAB, like the MLAT, was a commercially-available and carefully normed test battery, with accompanying manual and support material. In passing, one can also mention the York Language Aptitude Test (Green, 1975), devised to provide a measure of inductive language learning and memory for school-age children in the UK. This less comprehensive aptitude test, loosely modeled on Part 5 of the PLAB, has also been used in a number of research studies.

Interestingly, other initiatives to produce aptitude batteries have been associated with military or government contexts, with the result that the batteries which have been produced have been restricted in availability. Petersen and Al-Haik (1976) produced the Defense Language Aptitude Battery (DLAB), intending it to discriminate at the top end of the ability range, where the MLAT was not so effective. The battery emphasized auditory and inductive language learning factors, and incorporated quite a lot of visual material as prompts for the inductive language learning sub-tests. In practice, the validation studies comparing the DLAB with the MLAT indicated no clear superiority regarding validation coefficients amongst high-aptitude subjects. A later initiative produced VORD (Parry & Child, 1990). This battery used an artificial language (resembling Turkish) to generate sub-tests focussing on noun and verb morphology, sentence syntax, and a cloze format to measuring principally grammatical sensitivity (although with memory influence also operative). Once again, the predictive validity correlations which are quoted do not indicate any advance on the MLAT. Most recently of all, Grigorenko, Sternberg and Ehrman (2000; Sternberg & Grigorenko, 1998; Sternberg, this volume) have developed a new aptitude test, CANAL-F, for use in government contexts.

Research into aptitude components
A different perspective on aptitude research is to avoid the need to construct an entire aptitude battery, but instead to explore one of the components proposed by Carroll (1962), and to try to understand it better, and/or produce more refined measurement. For example, Sparks and his collaborators, in a series of studies (Sparks & Ganschow, 1991; Sparks et al., 1992; Ganschow et al., 1998) have explored the relationship between Carroll's phonemic coding

ability and measures of mild dyslexia (for review, see Grigorenko, this volume). It will be recalled that while early investigations of aptitude tended to assume that sound discrimination was the component of auditory processing that defined an "ear for languages", empirical studies of relevant auditory processing abilities initially were more consistent with the label "sound-symbol association ability", bringing out the capacity to make links between sound and symbol. Later Carroll renamed this component *phonemic coding ability*, capturing the way that linking sound and symbol enables auditory material to be coded in such a way that retention of unfamiliar sound over more than a few seconds was more likely. In effect, Sparks et al.(1992) have generalized this idea of the coding of sound, mediated by symbol, and proposed the *linguistic coding deficit hypothesis*, which suggests that an impaired ability in this domain not only compromises foreign language learning, but is the same deficit implicated in mild dyslexia. They draw attention to the similarity of sub-tests which measure phonemic coding ability in aptitude batteries and the sub-tests that are used in assessing dyslexia. In other words, we seem to have one underlying ability here, the capacity to process sound in a particular way, and this manifests itself in different ways in different contexts.

The component of aptitude that has received far and away the most research attention over the last thirty years is that of memory. Recall here that Carroll, reflecting the prevailing views in psychology contemporary with his investigations, emphasized simple associations between verbal elements. Since then, views of memory within psychology have changed considerably, and some of the aptitude research has reflected these developments. Skehan (1982), for example, showed that association memory is not the most predictive component of memory for language learning. He showed that memory for unfamiliar material, as well as the capacity to impose organizational structure on the material to be learned were better predictors of language learning. In addition, the capacity to memorize and apply rules was also strongly predictive of language learning success. Interestingly, using a simple digit span test, Skehan did not find any relationship between short-term or working memory and language learning success. In contrast, Harrington and Sawyer (1992) and Robinson (Chapter 10, this volume) have reported correlations between working memory, as measured by a version of Daneman and Carpenter's Reading Span test, and foreign language learning performance. Skehan (1982) only used a simple span test, which did not require strong executive involvement of working memory, but only rehearsal. The reading span test is designed to provoke significant computation within working memory, and so it appears that it is the need to operate upon the material that is held in immediate memory that is the key issue. This fits in nicely with contemporary views of working memory. Gathercole and Baddeley's formulation (1993) has a clear distinction between buffer components (phonological loop, visuo-spatial sketch pad) and more active, transformative components (the central executive). Other models of working memory differ in terms of details, but all propose that it is the operations carried out within working memory that are crucial (see reviews in Miyake & Shah, 1999).

There has been little research into the language analytic components of aptitude, but three studies bear upon the operation of these components. Harley and Hart (1997; this volume) have explored the way that language analytic components and memory components of aptitude change in their relevance as a function of age of onset of L2 learning. In studies focussing on children in Grade 11 of an immersion program, they have shown that there are higher correlations between the memory component of aptitude and foreign language achievement amongst children with an early age of L2 learning onset, while the correlations between language analytic components of aptitude and achievement are greater for children with a later age of onset. It appears, in other words, that children whose exposure to the L2 takes place at a later age more likely to capitalize upon the systematic aspects of language than those who get early exposure. Skehan (1986a), researching with adult learners of colloquial Arabic in the British military, also examined the relationship between language and memory components of aptitude. He used cluster analysis to explore patterns in aptitude score profiles associated with success in the Arabic course. He was able to show that proposing general flat profiles consistent with different degrees of (monolithic) aptitude did not correspond to the data. Instead there seemed to be uneven profiles such that successful learners either achieved their success through strong involvement of language analytic abilities *or* through high memory, but surprisingly few students appeared to have high scores in each of these. In other words, there may be different routes to success, with some learners capitalizing on memory abilities and others on linguistic abilities. Finally, and slightly differently in understanding language analytic components of aptitude, we have research by Sasaki (1991, 1996) exploring the relationship between aptitude and intelligence. She administered a range of aptitude tests (Japanese versions of MLAT sub-tests) and intelligence tests. She was able to show that with a first order factor analysis of the resulting data matrix, the aptitude and intelligence scores showed some separation, consistent with earlier research (e.g., Skehan, 1982;

Gardner, 1985) indicating separation between the two areas. But a second order factor analysis suggested that one factor could account for variance in the intelligence measures and some of the aptitude variables. Most interestingly of all, it was the language analytic aspects of aptitude which were closest in their relationship to intelligence, while the phonemic coding ability and memory components still showed separation. This suggests that in older learners (Sasaki's subjects were Japanese university students) general learning ability (as indexed by intelligence) and language analytic ability are closely related. In contrast the other components of aptitude are still separate.

Contexts of language learning
There have been two studies of how aptitude functions in relation to different circumstances. First of all, Wesche (1981) explored the connections between aptitude profiles and instructional treatments. Using a language analytic vs. memory contrast (as in Skehan, 1986a), based on aptitude score profiles, she also explored the consequences of matching and mismatching students with methods. When analytic learners were taught by analytic methodology, the learners did particularly well, and reported greater satisfaction with the instruction. In contrast, when such learners were paired with a memory-oriented methodology, they did more poorly than would have been expected from their aptitudinal abilities *and* they were not happy with the methodology they were being exposed to. Learners strong in memory abilities also did well in a memory-oriented methodology. This study (and see others in this volume) provides clear evidence that a componential approach to aptitude is desirable, and that by exploring aptitude-treatment interactions, one can see how aptitude information can be used to adapt instruction so that it is more appropriate for the individual learner. Reves (1982) also researched the relationship between aptitude and context but in her case the comparison was between formal and informal environments for learning language. She researched L1 Arabic learners in Israel, of English (in a classroom environment) and Hebrew (in an informal environment). She administered aptitude tests to all these learners, and in this within-subjects design, was able to show that the aptitude tests predicted learning in the acquisition-rich informal environment as well as the conventional classroom environment. These results bear upon the claim that aptitude is only relevant for classrooms and has little to say about acquisition, since they show that aptitude is relevant for non-instructed learning contexts also. Skehan (1989) suggests that one can argue that aptitude may be *more* important for informal environments, in that

classrooms will be based on controlled and structured input, to some degree, with the result that learners are not set the same unstructured problems that they are in informal environments. The result is that their capacity to process input (phonemic coding ability), their capacity to analyze that input and make generalizations (grammatical sensitivity, inductive language learning ability), and their capacity to assimilate new material (memory) may all be put under *greater* pressure, with the result that aptitude based differences between learners will assume even greater significance. In any case, these two studies, by Wesche and Reves, indicate clearly the relevance of aptitude for a range of contexts, and its potential for instructional design.

Aptitude and second language acquisition processes

When the MLAT and PLAB were developed, the prevailing instructional methodologies were grammar translation and audiolingualism. Hence the dismissal of aptitude when communicative approaches grew in importance and when SLA research blossomed. Given this marginalisation, it is not surprising that there was little attempt to relate the emerging field of SLA to aptitudinal concepts. But this has changed in recent years, and there is now the beginning of a research tradition which tries to link these two areas. For example, de Graaff (1997b) reports a study into the effects of explanation (and non-explanation) on the performance of learners of eXperanto (an artificial language) and Spanish, with each of these languages represented by simple and complex versions of morphological and syntactic rules. In this regard, the study resembles many SLA studies where the focus is on the contrast between implicit and explicit learning. In addition, however, de Graaff (1997b) gave subjects in his study an aptitude test. This test correlated significantly with performance in both eXperanto and Spanish, and for the explicit *and* implicit conditions. Indeed, there was no difference in strength of relationship with aptitude between these two conditions. Consistent with this, Robinson (1995c) examined the level of correlation between aptitude measures (grammatical sensitivity and memory) and performance in the learning of English, for both an easy and a hard rule, for four conditions: instructed (where learners were given explicit instruction); rule-search (where they were provided with material and told to search for a rule); implicit (where learners were simply provided with material which was consistent with the rule in question, but where their attention was not drawn to this); and incidental (where learners were given a meaning-related task, but with the same rules built in to the material). There were significant correlations with the aptitude measures for all conditions except the incidental one, with correlations in all the significant conditions being above $r = .5$ ($p < .05$) , for both easy and hard rules.

These two sets of results are intriguing. They suggest that aptitude is relevant not simply for conventional, explicit, rule-focussed teaching contexts but also when the learning is implicit. In fact, the one non-significant correlation in Robinson's (1995c) study (for the incidental condition) is equally intriguing. This suggests that aptitude may not be so relevant when the focus is on meaning. As de Graaff (1997b, pp. 158–9) puts it, this suggests that "the evidence cannot be generalized to non-instructed learning without any focus on form." Aptitude, it would seem, presupposes a requirement that there is a focus on-form, precisely the same claim made currently by a range of SLA researchers (Doughty & Williams, 1998) (though cf. Robinson, Chapter 10, who argues learning under *any* condition, whether it involves focus on form or not, is potentially sensitive to individual differences in measures of aptitude).

The origin of aptitude, modularity, and the existence of a critical period for second language learning

Carroll (1973) addressed the issue of the origin of foreign language aptitude. First of all, he proposed that aptitude has to be regarded as fairly stable. This is necessary, in a sense, for us to take aptitude seriously: if a capacity to learn languages is malleable, easily influenced by the environment, e.g., through the learning of other areas, through training, or through the learning of other languages, then the concept of aptitude loses its contribution: it would have to regarded simply as a disguising label for relevant experience. But Carroll (1973) also drew this conclusion based on the research results which are available, particularly that of Politzer and Weiss (1969) who attempted, unsuccessfully, to train aptitude. The truth of this matter is that there is simply not enough evidence to argue for the stability of aptitude with any certainty, but for now, following Carroll, we will assume that aptitude does not change with the seasons! This allows us to explore a number of interesting questions. The first concerns where aptitude comes from. Carroll (1973) was neutral as to whether aptitude is largely fixed at birth, or is the result of early experience. In this latter case he argued that if early experience is important, the evidence is consistent with aptitude achieving some sort of stability early in life, so that it does not matter much whether it is genetically determined or shaped by early experience: its malleability is constrained by age (say) four.

Carroll (1973) went on to argue that, given the differences that exist in speed of first language (L1) learning, foreign language aptitude might be the residue of a first language learning ability. Virtually all first language learners achieve success, (despite differences in rate), and Carroll speculated that while such a pre-wired capacity to learn one's L1 is universal, there may be differential fading of such abilities, so that in the L2 case, some learners would have more complete access to these earlier abilities[3]. If one accepts this interpretation of the origin of aptitude, one would predict some sort of relationship between (variation in speed of) L1 learning ability and foreign language aptitude. Skehan (1986a, 1986b, 1989) reports precisely such a relationship. Researching children studied as part of the Bristol Language Project (Wells, 1981, 1986), he was able to administer aptitude tests to these children some ten to twelve years after they had been studied in relation to their L1 development. Skehan (1986a) reports correlations between first language rate indices and subsequent aptitude scores of above $r = .4$, remarkable values given the ten year span when the two sets of measures were taken. These findings argue that foreign language aptitude is connected to L1 learning, implying a generalized capacity to process language data. This manifests itself in differences of rate in the L1 context which do not prevent all children acquiring "native like" competence, while the differences in rate in the foreign language case are associated with the majority of learners, at least in school situations, not achieving anything like a comparable competence in the L2 they are studying.

But there is also evidence pointing to a discontinuity between first and foreign language learning ability. Indirect, but very telling, evidence is provided through work on a critical period for language learning. If there is a critical period for language learning, such that L1 learning is qualitatively different from L2 learning, the consequences for foreign language aptitude are clear. This would imply that the obligatory involvement of some sort of language acquisition device is consistent with a modular organization for language such that language learning is different from learning in other domains. In this case, exposure to input would be sufficient to trigger the operation (and inevitable success) of this language learning device. If, in contrast, there is no critical period, this would suggest that general purpose learning mechanisms can account for first *and* foreign language learning. In the former case, foreign language learning aptitude would be the abilities relevant for the different sort of learning that foreign language learning is. In the second, such an aptitude would consist of the general learning abilities most relevant to the case of language development.

The arguments rage either way. Bialystok and Hakuta (1994) and Kellerman (1996) argue that the evidence for a discontinuity between first and foreign language learning is not convincing. In contrast, a number of other authors argue that the evidence is sufficiently clear to enable us to conclude that learning one's first language is qualitatively different from learning L2s. Until recently, the seminal study has been Johnson and Newport's (1989) exploration of the effects of age of learning on ultimate attainment, where they report a gradual decline in language learning abilities from around age three to age seventeen. Bialystok and Hakuta (1994) argue that the interpretations made of the data in Johnson and Newport (1989) are invalid; that the measures used to assess language development are suspect; and that affective influences on language learning were not sufficiently taken into account.

In an attempt to address these criticisms, DeKeyser (2000) has replicated Johnson and Newport's (1989) study, while attempting to overcome many of the methodological shortcomings alleged by Bialystok and Hakuta (1994). (Note that Bialystok and Hakuta did not establish, through independent evidence, that there is not a critical period, merely that Johnson and Newport's conclusions were open to critique.) The details of this debate do not concern us here. But two things are highly relevant from the DeKeyser study. First, with methodological improvements, he reports essentially the same results as Johnson and Newport (1989). In other words, we can more surely conclude that the Johnson and Newport results were not due to defective research techniques or subjective interpretations. DeKeyser reports very similar results, consistent with a gradual decline by age 17 in language learning abilities. Second, DeKeyser (2000) used aptitude tests with the subjects in his study. Very interestingly, he was able to show that for learners who had immigrated to the US before the onset of the critical period, there was no correlation between the aptitude scores and proficiency in English. In contrast, for learners who had immigrated after the proposed end of the critical period, there was a clear and significant correlation between aptitude and attained proficiency in English. Further, the post-critical period learners who attained high proficiency in English were all high aptitude scorers. It appears, therefore, that having high foreign language aptitude confers no advantage in the proficiency level that is attained prior to the end of the operation of a qualitatively different talent for language learning, but aptitude is related to level of achieved success once this milestone is passed.

One final aspect of this debate concerns the nature of modularity in language learning. The existence of a critical period is consistent with different mechanisms for language learning before and after the end of this period. Given that it has been proposed that modularity effects are strong in relation to language learning, it might therefore be the case that the nature of modularity changes as the critical period ends. Skehan (1998a) argues precisely this. He suggests that the L1 evidence is consistent with the existence of separate syntax vs. semantics modules. In contrast, he proposes that modularity in the L2 case is based on three modules, each of them connected to an aptitude component:

– auditory processing
– language processing
– memory

The first module here is connected to the operation of phonemic coding ability; the second to grammatical sensitivity and inductive language learning ability; and the third to the extended conceptualization of the functioning of memory. Further, Sasaki's research (1991, 1996), as indicated above, is strongly consistent with the first and third of these modules being only weakly connected to measures of general intelligence, but with the second much more related to such measures.

We can sum up these claims as in Table One. What this table shows is that in the first language case, defined as it is by the availability of qualitatively different learning mechanisms for language, the contrast is between a pre-wired module uniquely adapted for the learning of syntax, compared to a semantics module, not subject to the end of a critical period, and which continues to operate throughout life. In contrast, the L2 learning phase does not have access to the pre-wired system, to enable primary linguistic data to be processed obligatorily and automatically, and so instead has to resort to more general learning mechanisms. As it happens the second of these relates strongly to general intellectual function. In other words, it appears that the abilities implicated in searching for, and internalizing patterns in language are strongly connected with general cognitive abilities. In slight contrast, the capacity to handle what might be termed more peripheral areas, particularly input processing, assimilation of new material, and retrieval for fluent performance, as less related to general cognitive abilities. In other words, there is partial evidence of separation between general abilities and specifically linguistic abilities, but only in these two more peripheral domains.

To conclude this section, it has to be recognized that the evidence on the connections between first and foreign language learning abilities is mixed. There is evidence of continuity, as reflected in the correlations between speed of L1 development and foreign language aptitude scores (Skehan, 1986a, 1989).

Table 1. Modularity in first and foreign language learning

	Modularity influences
First language learning	Syntax vs. Semantics
Second language learning	Input processing vs. Central processing vs. Memory and Retrieval

But the critical period evidence, especially that associated with the DeKeyser (2000) study, together with Sasaki's factor analytic work, suggest that foreign language learning abilities, while modular, are different in kind from the modules which exist in the first language case. In fact, the foreign language case is more consistent with modules being appropriate for different stages of information processing: input, central processing and output.

Second language acquisition and foreign language aptitude

Earlier in this chapter it was mentioned that aptitude's marginalisation was partly the result of its perceived irrelevance to emerging views of communicative language teaching, as well as the significance of SLA research. But it was also pointed out that there is no "in principle" reason to justify such a perceived irrelevance. In fact, the available evidence (the impressive correlations between aptitude scores and naturalistic learning (Reves) as well as the connections between aptitude scores and acquisitional measures (de Graaff, 1997a, 1997b; Robinson, 1995c) points more towards the centrality of aptitude in relation to L2 acquisition processes. For that reason, this section will attempt to relate insights from SLA and emerging understandings of foreign language aptitude at a fairly general level. The section is organized under the four headings of a capacity to process input; central representation; output; and then the importance of a Focus on Form.

Capacity to process input
Earlier approaches to SLA emphasized input, and some even went so far as to claim that requiring learners to process comprehensible input for meaning would automatically engage language acquisition mechanisms (Krashen, 1985). Subsequent developments have indicated limitations with this approach (see, e.g., Swain, 1985, 1995). A key research tradition in this respect is that associated with Bill VanPatten (1990, 1996), who has explored how input can

be processed most effectively. In a seminal study, Van Patten (1990) showed how, if learners are put under any degree of information processing pressure, they use their limited processing resources to attend to meaning. Learners only attended to form in input if they had have spare processing capacity available. In other words, if meaning-processing predominates (as it naturally will), then form becomes an optional and resource-requiring "extra" which often loses out to meaning. In a related series of papers, Schmidt (1990, 1993, 1994, 1995b, 2001) has argued cogently for the importance of *noticing*, i.e., that learners need to direct attention to some aspects of the input. Krashen, it will be recalled, advocates the processing of comprehensible input, and claims that such processing will lead to development in the nature of an underlying implicit system *without learner awareness*. Schmidt, in contrast, is arguing that noticing is a precondition for development: aspects of form which need to be developed *must first be noticed, consciously, in the input*. This does not mean that the learner has to understand the complexity and ramifications of the aspect of form involved, merely that it will be in focal attention. Then, additional processes, implicit or explicit, can be brought to bear. So noticing becomes a pre-requisite condition, rather than a complete explanation.

Central representation
The main problem facing the foreign language learner is how to move from an initial state, where the target language is not known, to an end-state, where the learner has some command over the system of the target language and some capacity to use that system for communication. The learner, in other words, has to gain control over a progressively complexifying system, in such a way that continued development is possible. A first aspect of this development is that some degree of *structure* is going to be involved. There is now widespread evidence of systematicity in foreign language development (Larsen-Freeman & Long, 1991; R.Ellis, 1994a). In other words, it appears that while some degree of flexibility in the order with which elements are learned is possible, there are also strong constraints such that in some areas, natural orders for development are attested. It appears, that is, that learners are interacting with data in ways that consistently lead to similar paths of development (Pienemann, 1998). Any account of L2 development has to take account of this.

A second aspect of foreign language learning is that whatever structural developments take place, there is also the issue of the *processes which drive forward that development*. Connected with this is the nature of the system which is being developed. A lively debate in this respect is whether the processes which drive forward the interlanguage system are implicit, (and not amenable to conscious introspection) or explicit (where some degree of awareness is involved). In the former case, learners would process linguistic data, and without conscious application and organization on their part, change would occur. In the latter, it is assumed that the involvement of the learner, and their focussed attention would facilitate speed and perhaps nature of learning. Linked with this is the possibility that sustained development is itself problematic. It is clear that a reality in foreign language learning is the process of *fossilization*: learning may be continuous and ultimately successful, or it may be the case that some learners reach a plateau of development and find it difficult to move beyond particular areas of interlanguage. Some areas, that is to say, even though they have not become target-like may ossify, and be resistant to further change. They may then co-exist with other areas which *do* change. This too is an aspect of foreign language development which requires explanation.

Finally, in this necessarily brief overview of SLA , there is the issue of the *external influences* which impact upon the nature and speed of foreign language development. Earlier proposals that it was simply comprehensible input which would suffice have been abandoned. Now, even within the constraints that individual factors have great importance, it is nonetheless accepted that modifications of input, as well as types of feedback on learner production, can have some impact. Regarding input, proposals have been made that input enhancement and input flooding can be beneficial. Regarding feedback, and moving beyond proposals on negotiation for meaning, a number of research have advocated the central role of recasts in language development. There is also the issue of differential capacities on the part of learners to derive "uptake" from given quantities and types of feedback. In other words, if there is a predisposition to process language for meaning, but that interlocutors may be providing useful feedback if it is only attended to, there are questions to be asked about the capacities that learners have to benefit from such feedback and to notice what use it may be (see Mackey et al., this volume; Robinson, Chapter 6, this volume).

Output
The study of output has not been central within SLA. The focus of most activity has been on competence-oriented analyses of structural change. As a result, output has been viewed either as the immediate and pervasive consequence of underlying structural change (in which case it has little significance for theory), or the result of a process of automatisation (in which case it is also

theoretically uninteresting). In the last decade or so, new analyses of output have given it a more central role. There are three major aspects to this. First, there are strong arguments that the use of communication strategies can have an impact on language development. It may be that the use of such strategies enables the effective communication of meanings, but at the expense of pressure for structural change. In other words, resorting to a communication strategy which circumvents interlanguage limitations may be effective in the short term, but runs the risk of being proceduralised, in such a way that underlying change is thereby made less likely. The need to communicate in the here and now, that is, may make more fundamental change more difficult (Schmidt, 1983; Skehan, 1992, 1998a).

Second, the nature of fluency has become better understood, and seen as an interesting acquisitional problem in its own right. In particular, it is now clear that learners (as well as native-speakers), make considerable reliance on time-creating devices to ease the pressure of real-time processing (Bygate, 1988). In addition, they rely on lexicalised chunks of language which function as "wholes" and thereby ease processing demands since they are retrieved without internal analysis or construction (Foster, 2001). Third, this view of language as reliant on lexicalised chunks requires a different analysis of the role of memory within language processing. Rather than imagining a parsimonious slot-and-filler approach, which could operate upon syntactic rules and individually-stored lexical elements, the view of language-as-memory-reliant requires a capacious, redundantly-stored memory system from which large numbers of pre-formed lexical units may be retrieved as independent units. Only this enables speakers to keep up with the pressures of real-time processing.

The result of these three factors and of this reanalysis of output itself has two consequences for present purposes. First, the puzzle of fluency (Pawley & Syder, 1983) becomes much more interesting. Second, the analysis changes, in a significant way, the functioning of memory within the study of aptitude. In this regard, the "model" of memory underlying earlier aptitude work emphasized encoding, and the way material enters the memory system. Clearly, and following consensus views of memory theorising, we have to now distinguish between encoding, storage, and retrieval. If we do this, it is clear that classical views of aptitude do not take sufficient account of the storage and retrieval phases. Storage, clearly, needs to be redundantly structured, with often multiple entries for a particular lexical item, as it is linked in different prefabricated chunks. Retrieval, then, becomes a key issue, since if speakers follow

Sinclair's (1991) "idiom principle", they will first attempt to retrieve memorized chunks, since these confer such processing advantages. Only if such lexicalised retrieval fails or is inappropriate will speakers resort to rule-constructed language. Aptitude tests therefore need to take this changed perspective into account.

The role of a focus on form (FonF)

An over-riding generalization which goes beyond the separate analyses of input, central representation, and output is that language learning, in the post-critical period case, requires some degree of Focus on Form (Long, 1991; Long & Robinson, 1998). In the pre-critical period phase, there is inexorable involvement of a language learning system on exposure to primary linguistic data, whereas this no longer occurs in such an obligatory way in post-critical period phase. In other words, it is of central importance that there should be some device which brings about a Focus-on-Form to overcome the predisposition of L2 learners to focus on meaning, partly because of their limited information processing capacities, partly because a Universal Grammar is no longer available, and partly because older learners take meaning and communication as more important than form. Drawing on this insight we can return to the three information processing phases we have already covered to reinterpret the role of a Focus on Form. Clearly, the noticing hypothesis presupposes that the learner is able to, or inclined to notice formal aspects of language. It centrally claims that exposure to input, and subconscious processing are not enough for language development to take place — there has to be awareness of some aspect of form. Regarding central representation the details of the functioning of a Focus on Form are different but the central principles are the same: structural change does not take place in a vacuum — it has to be stimulated by a concern, on the learner's part, for the formal elements of language. Hence the need for not simply initial pattern recognition in language, but also the capacity to extend such pattern and to try to combat fossilization in language. This also means a greater capacity to notice relevant material in feedback on one's own performance, and to assume its helpfulness for continued change. Finally, at the level of output, Focus on Form concerns ways the learner may not exclusively try to communicate meanings, possibly relying on lexicalised language, but may also be concerned with the underlying form of the language which is used. There is also the issue that learners do not simply recycle limited repertoires of language elements, but may also try to use and incorporate newly learned or emerging forms. In all these case, it is clear that the L2 learner is advantaged if there is awareness of the importance of form, and some degree of prioritization of it against the pressure to communicate meanings.

Relating second language acquisition to foreign language aptitude

The discussion in the last section has represented current SLA research in a manner suitable for connections to be made to aptitude. Essentially, the three phases of language use, which all embrace the need for a Focus-on-Form, show that the 'language learning challenge', so to speak, is differently understood now to the way it was in the past. We can draw upon the successive sections to propose that language learning needs to be concerned with the following stages:

SLA Processing Stage	Nature of Stage
noticing	learner directs attention to some aspects of the language system, or is led to direct attention in this way
pattern identification	on the basis of the focal attention, the learner makes a hypothesis or generalization, implicitly or explicitly, about the target language, based on a perceived pattern or regularity
extending	the learner extends the domain of the hypothesis, without changing it fundamentally in kind
complexifying	the learner apprehends the limitations of the identified pattern, and restructures it, as new aspects of the target language are noticed
integrating	the learner takes the output of this process of complexification and integrates the new sub-area of interlanguage into a larger structure
becoming accurate, avoiding error	the learner becomes able to use the interlanguage area without making errors, although this use may be slow and effortful
creating a repertoire, achieving salience	not only can error be avoided, but the interlanguage form can be accessed at appropriate

	places — it becomes part of a *salient* (not latent) language repertoire
automatising rule-based language, achieving fluency	the domain is now used not simply without error, but with reasonable speed, and the role has become, to some degree, proceduralised
lexicalising	the learner, at this stage, is also able to produce the interlanguage form in question as a lexicalised element. In other words, language which may be analyzable, (and has been produced on the basis of analysis) is now also available as a lexical element. In addition, the learner is able to choose freely, and as appropriate, between lexicalised representation of an interlanguage form, and its rule-based creative version

Clearly different parts of the interlanguage system will be at different points on this sequence: some areas, for example, will already have reached the dual-coding stage, while others may not yet have been noticed, or may be at some intermediate point in the sequence.

It should be said, at the outset, that this is hardly a universally-accepted sequence of development in SLA. It draws upon contemporary accounts which emphasize an information-processing perspective, and a Focus-on-Form. But the details, in this respect, are not important. What is important is only that the different stages are seen as plausible, even if they will be replaced by others in fuller, later analyses. The real purpose of outlining such stages is to enable us to relate SLA processes to foreign language aptitude. In Table 2, the same stages are reproduced, but now each of them is related to a putative aptitude component.

If the stages on the left-hand side are accepted provisionally, then the aptitude question which needs to be asked, at each of these stages, is:

–   is there variation in speed of learning in this area?

If the answer to this question is positive, then we have to consider that these differences constitute some component of aptitude.

It is important to note here that we are not taking existing aptitude tests and then seeing if SLA relevance can be perceived for each of them. Rather, we are taking SLA stages, and exploring whether aptitude would be relevant for

Table 2. SLA processing stages and potential aptitude components

SLA Processing Stage	Aptitude Component
1. noticing	auditory segmentation attention management working memory phonemic coding
2. pattern identification	fast analysis/ working memory grammatical sensitivity
3. extending	inductive language learning ability
4. complexifying	grammatical sensitivity inductive language learning ability
5. integrating	restructuring capacity
6. becoming accurate, avoiding error	automatisation proceduralisation
7. creating a repertoire, achieving salience	retrieval processes
8. automatising rule-based language, achieving fluency	automatising, proceduralisation
9. lexicalising, dual-coding	memory, chunking, retrieval processes

each of these stages. In this respect, it can be seen that some of the time, existing aptitude components can indeed be related to SLA stages. In other cases, though, it is clear that there are no relevant existing aptitude sub-tests. In these cases, Table Two constitutes a research agenda — it reveals where it would be useful to produce aptitude tests if we are to be able to predict effectively in acquisition-rich contexts.

We can explore this research agenda by reworking Table 2 slightly, in that one can portray the stages in more macro terms, as follows:

Stage 1	Noticing
Stages 2–5	Patterning
Stages 6–8	Controlling
Stages 8,9	Lexicalising

This re-presentation of the stages allows us to see more clearly where there are strengths with existing aptitude components and where there are weaknesses, omissions, and limitations.

The first stage in this sequence, noticing, is concerned with the initial inroad, the first insight (within any particular domain) that some aspect of form is worth attention. For there to be relevant aptitudinal individual differences, we have to assume that some people are better able to notice form in this way, other things being equal. The aptitudinal component of phonemic coding ability is obviously relevant to this, but is not enough. It needs to be supplemented by some form of attentional management and working memory operation. In other words, simply being able to process sound is not enough. It is also vital here to assign significance to some aspects of sound, relative to others, in order that form which may be relevant to future change can be made salient. The findings reported by Harrington and Sawyer (1992) fit in with this interpretation, since they report correlations between reading span based measures of working memory (as an aptitudinal component) and language learning success. It is clear that there is scope for additional work in this regard.

Stages 2 to 5 from Table Two reflect the capacity to detect and manipulate pattern in the target language. They require (noticed) input to be analyzed, processed, generalizations made, and then extensions achieved. It is assumed that in order to be successful in these areas, learners will not only have to perceive patterns, but they will also have to realize that the first pattern they perceive may be overly limited in scope and require modification. Learners may also need to be sensitive to feedback which will help them to continue to make progress (Mackey et al., this volume). To address these areas the two components from Carroll's model, grammatical sensitivity and inductive language learning each appear to be able to make contributions. The first of these is more relevant to initial pattern detection, as learners process material and extract generalizations. The second is more concerned with learners' capacities to go beyond the data given and extrapolate. Even so, these components of aptitude do not quite capture the problems associated with modifying a pattern (a) to extend it, and/or (b) to modify it. In other words, the two components do not quite deal with the problems associated with restructuring of language, even though that language may appear serviceable as far as communicating meanings is concerned. There is scope to add to aptitude measures to deal with this issue.

Stages 6–8 from Table Two concern the development of control, in a process where a rule-based generalization, initially handled with difficulty, becomes proceduralised. Existing aptitude sub-tests do not ignore this potential component of aptitude, but they do not emphasize it either. There is an element of cumulative learning which impacts upon some of the MLAT subtests, and it is clearly an advantage with the York test if candidates internalize the rules which emerge so that they do not have to return to earlier sections of the test to check whether a generalization was as they remember it. But these sub-tests do not really address what it means to proceduralise. It is interesting that Grigorenko et al.'s CANAL-F (2000) does incorporate cumulative learning into the aptitude materials. Even so, there is clear scope to develop new aptitude sub-tests which do address this issue, and which provide more basic measures of the capacity to proceduralise with linguistic material.

Finally, we come to the area of lexicalisation, represented by Stages 8 and 9. Here the issue is how the learner is able to go beyond rule-based processing, however fast, and build a lexical system which can be used to underlie real-time performance. In other words, to become native-like, the learner needs to put in place a repertoire of linguistic expressions which can be accessed very quickly, and without need for extensive internal computation. Clearly, what aptitude tests have to offer in this area is not adequate. The MLAT only contains an associative memory test, principally concerned with the level of memory encoding. What are needed are tests which are more concerned with storage, and especially retrieval. The other work on memory within aptitude (e.g., Harrington & Sawyer, 1992; Skehan 1986a) indicates promise but does not address the area of retrieval memory, or memory organization in an effective manner. This too is an area where future research would be desirable.

Conclusions

The earlier sections of this chapter were concerned with a general updating of research into foreign language aptitude. The area may not have been one of the most productive in the study of L2 learning, but the surveys which were provided have indicated two things:

- traditional views of aptitude are still relevant to applied linguistics and SLA
- post-MLAT research into aptitude, while not comprehensive or co-ordinated, has not been negligible, and has added to our understanding in significant ways.

This earlier discussion also showed that the concept of aptitude could have centrality in relation to some of the loftier questions in applied linguistics, especially in relation to the existence of a critical period for L2 learning, and also to the nature of modularity in the case of first and second language learning.

The final section of the chapter has taken a different approach, and attempted a reconceptualisation of aptitude consistent with SLA research. Previous characterizations of aptitude have tended to bring together, without much over-arching theory, a range of possible contributing skills for language learning. What the second half of the chapter has shown is that an information processing perspective, as well as an analysis of stages of L2 processing, can generate a principled component structure for aptitude. In other words, we now have the beginnings of foreign language aptitude theory which provides a basis for a more comprehensive understanding of aptitude, as well as a research program to generate new aptitude sub-test components. It is to be hoped that research in this vein would finally enable the study of foreign language aptitude to come in from the rather isolated position it has occupied in applied linguistics for the last half-century.

Notes

1. One aspect of this pragmatic orientation to researching aptitude is worth particular comment. Researchers, e.g., J. B. Carroll, have been at pains to point out that what is being predicted by aptitude tests is *speed* of learning. Discussions of aptitude by such researchers typical assert that everyone can learn a foreign language. What aptitude tests predict therefore is whether a particular level of proficiency can be achieved in the time available. Unfortunately, one of the common popular interpretations of aptitude is that it claims that some learners simply cannot learn languages. Following from this, aptitude test results are seen as devices which cause some learners to be de-selected from courses of language study. This interpretation is to be regretted, not least because aptitude researchers are careful to avoid such claims.

2. The only other commercially available battery, Pimsleur's *Language Aptitude Battery*, was produced in the 1960's (Pimsleur, 1966b). It is very similar in its components to the MLAT, although it somewhat de-emphasises memory, putting more store by the auditory component of aptitude.

3. It is worth noting, in passing, that if this speculation is correct, it has great significance for research into the impact of Universal Grammar on second language acquisition. One of the debates in this literature concerns the relative likelihood that UG is still available to second language learners compared to a situation where it is not, but that its effects, e.g.,parameter settings, from L1 learning, are still operative. If there is differential fading of UG, then very mixed results are likely to be found, depending on the chance aptitude distribution of the subjects who have been researched, (see Chapters 10 and 11, by Robinson, and Ross et al., this volume for empirical studies relevant to this issue).

CHAPTER 5

Foreign language acquisition and language-based learning disabilities

Elena L. Grigorenko
Yale University / Moscow State University

Introduction

Although most newborns acquire as one developmental milestone their native language (NL), first orally and then in its written form, there are some for whom this developmental landmark remains too difficult to master completely. When such difficulties unfold in the absence of general developmental and acquired challenges and in the context of normal intelligence and adequate education, they are referred to as specific language impairment (when the most pronounced deficit is that expressed in the oral language domain) and specific reading disabilities (when the most pronounced deficit is that expressed in the domain of written language).

Dissimilarly, only a relatively small portion of newborns master one or more foreign languages. The main reason for this situation is lack of environmental challenge — the majority of people are never required to develop communication skills in addition to those in their NL. A relatively small number of people ever have the opportunity to try to master a foreign language (FL); of those, only a few reach some proficiency level, whereas the majority remain barely familiar with a FL (just enough to earn an academic credit), and some find it extremely difficult to master even the very beginnings of a tongue different from their native one. Of course, there is a continuum of mastery levels among those who have ever attempted to study a FL.

The simplest intuitive model of individual differences in FL learning predicts success on the basis of skills that have already been acquired and demonstrated in native language (NL) acquisition. According to this model, a learner with high linguistic abilities in her NL (e.g., extensive vocabulary, efficient word processing, high automaticity of lower-level processes, solid ortho-graphical, morphological, and syntactic skills, good comprehension) should also demonstrate high abilities in FL. However, there is a significant amount of evidence that challenges this simple intuitive model.

This evidence is clustered around the following four statements. First, there are different levels of FL mastery among people with similar NL skills. Moreover, the acquisitions of NL and FL are noticeably different, with extremely different timelines and amount of teaching required to achieve mastery. Third, the acquisition and maintenance of a FL requires different amounts of motivation and scaffolding as compared to NL acquisition. Finally, in most cases, by the time a FL is approached, NL skills have been solidified and automatized, which results in a suppressed variation among NL skills of those students who attempt to learn a FL.

Nevertheless, although the predictive power of NL skills across a complete distribution of levels of FL mastery is rather low, this power is strong at the lower tails of the distribution, linking the failure to master a FL and challenged NL oral and written skills.

The purpose of this chapter is twofold. First, I shall briefly review the literature reporting the evidence in support of the link between the lower tail of the NL and FL skills' distributions. Second, I focus on findings that have been accumulated in the framework of studies of challenged NL oral and written skills and their potential relevance for understanding causes of FL learning failures.

A capsule review of the evidence linking difficulties in NL and FL learning

Different sources of information have brought together the evidence stressing that difficulties in NL and FL learning cluster. The first, and most long-last-ing, source of information originates from accounts of educators and researchers interested in the "mechanics" of FL acquisition. These accounts are of two types. The first group is research-based, where, having adminis-tered tests of FL aptitude to many students, researchers always found a few who scored very low on these tests (e.g., Carroll, 1962; Pimsleur, 1961).

This evidence has accumulated in the context of utilizing a number of so-called FL aptitude tests. These tests were based on certain models of FL acqui-sition and generated scores for a variety of processes that, as the authors of the tests claimed, are involved in FL mastery. For example, one such test, the

Modern Language Aptitude Test (MLAT, Carroll & Sapon, 1959), includes the following dimensions: (1) phonetic coding (the ability to learn, recognize, and remember correspondences between particular sounds of a language and the printed representation of those sounds; (2) grammatical sensitivity (the ability to distinguish the grammatical rules of a linguistic system); (3) inductive language learning ability (the ability to infer linguistic rules, forms, and patterns while being exposed to a new linguistic context); and (4) rote learning ability (the ability to learn quickly a large number of new linguistic associations). According to Carroll and Sapon, all four factors are predictive of FL learning in traditional classrooms.

In developing his test of FL aptitude — the Pimsleur Language Aptitude Battery (PLAB), Pimsleur (1966b) added new dimensions: (1) verbal intelligence (the breadth and depth of the NL vocabulary); (2) motivation (the extent to which a person studying a foreign language was interested in learning it); and (3) auditory ability (the ease of establishing sound-symbol associations). According to Pimsleur, the auditory ability is the primary source of variation between successful and unsuccessful FL learners when the variation in intelligence and motivation has been accounted for.

The second group contributing to this informational source is experience-based. Having taught many students foreign languages, teachers sometimes tell anecdotes about students who appeared to be unable to master a foreign language in spite of their motivation and efforts (e.g., Gass & Selinker, 2001). FL mastery usually assumes the formation and development of five basic skills — pronunciation, listening, speaking, reading, and writing. The literature contains sporadic reports pointing to individuals who (1) fail FL learning in all five domains and (2) demonstrate uneven profiles of FL acquisition, with relative success in some areas and rather dramatic failures in others (Ohta, 2001).

The second source of information originated in the literature on dyslexia and specific language impairment. One of the first links connecting the two fields of research, dyslexia and FL studies, was established by Dinklage (1971), who claimed that the students observed by him who were unable to master a foreign language often had learning difficulties in their native language. Specifically, Dinklage described three types of students who experienced difficulties with FL learning: (1) students who exhibited poor reading and spelling skills, reversals, and left-right confusions; (2) students who had poor auditory discrimination skills; and (3) students who had poor memory for auditory symbolic materials (often in addition to poor auditory discrimination).

In the mid-1980s it was accepted that students with dyslexia have particular difficulties when faced with the task of acquiring a FL. This acceptance was based on anecdotal evidence linking both inability to master a foreign language to dyslexia (e.g., Cohen, 1983; Demuth & Smith, 1987; Fisher, 1986; Ganschow & Sparks, 1986, 1987; Ganschow, Myer, & Roeger, 1989; Ganschow & Sparks, 1986; 1987; Geschwind, 1986; Sparks, Javorsky, & Ganschow, 1990; Vogel, 1988) and referrals for dyslexia evaluations as a result of inability to master the foreign language (Lefebre, 1984; Pompian, 1986; Sparks, Ganschow, & Pohlman, 1989).

The first study of success in acquiring a FL in students diagnosed with learning disabilities was conducted by Gajar (1987). In this study, the MLAT performance was compared in groups of students diagnosed and not diagnosed with learning disabilities (LD). The results indicated that the performance of students diagnosed with LD was significantly lower as compared to those not diagnosed with LD. An interesting detail of this study is Gajar's indication that two particular subtests of MLAT (IV-sensitivity to grammar and V-listening rote memory) were the most informative predictors of foreign language aptitude. This finding was supported in a more recent investigation done by Ganschow and colleagues (1991), in which successful and unsuccessful foreign-language learners were compared on a number of indicators, including intelligence, MLAT scores, and native oral and written language skills. One of the major results of this study was one indicating an absence of intelligence-, vocabulary-, and comprehension-based differences in foreign-language learning, but the presence of an MLAT-based difference and a difference in native language word identification, phonology, spelling, and grammar. A similar pattern of findings was obtained for three groups of high-school students: high- and low-risk students for learning a foreign language and students receiving LD services (Ganschow & Sparks, 1991). Results indicated significant differences among all three groups on native language measures of reading, spelling, and written grammar and on all MLAT subtests, but there were no differences on measures of picture vocabulary, antonyms-synonyms, and reading comprehension. Moreover, the only differences between the high-risk and the LD students were on measures of word recognition and spelling, but there were no differences on phonological, syntactic, semantic, rote-memory tasks, and any MLAT subtests. So, it appears that students who have difficulties in mastering their native language also have difficulty mastering a foreign tongue (Morris & Leuenberger, 1990).

A number of researchers have attempted to describe, label, and quantify this difficulty. Sparks and colleagues (Sparks & Ganschow, 1991; Sparks,

Ganschow, & Pohlman, 1989) referred to this difficulty by the term "linguistic coding deficit," introduced in the context of studying individuals with dyslexia by Vellutino and Scanlon (1986). It is assumed that foreign language learning is a generic linguistic process that can be either enhanced or limited by the degree to which students have control over the phonological, syntactic, and semantic components of their native language. Whereas, due to multiple remediation efforts and the pressure of their native linguistic environment, children with language difficulties learn to compensate for their weaknesses in their native language, the encounter of a new, unfamiliar linguistic system challenges and often makes inadequate these compensatory strategies. The more deficits students exhibit in their native language, the more difficult it is for them to master a foreign language. In this view, motivation, language-learning attitudes, and affective reactions (e.g., anxiety) are not causal but rather outcome indicators of the mastery of a FL.

To stress the salient nature of severe difficulties experienced by some students with FL acquisition, Ganschow and Sparks (1993) introduced the term "foreign language learning disability" (FLLD). Diagnostic issues related to the FLLD are blurred by the fact that students referred for evaluations are highly compensated because they are exhibiting relevant success in mastering post-secondary education. Sparks and colleagues (Ganschow & Sparks, 1993) proposed the following system for diagnosis of FLLD: (1) an inquiry into the student's developmental and family learning history; (2) an inquiry into the student's elementary and secondary educational history; (3) an inquiry into all previous experiences with foreign languages; (4) assessment of intelligence, language functioning, and academic achievement; and (5) administration of linguistic process-based assessment instruments.

Correspondingly, the authors have revealed the following links in their research. Students with FLLD are often reported to have: (1) histories of delayed development of speech and subtle or overt language problems; (2) low grades in elementary and secondary school language arts subjects and subjects involving a substantial amount of reading and writing (e.g., social studies); (3) difficulties and frustration with their previous encounters with foreign languages (both at school and while traveling abroad or interacting with foreigners).

The work of Sparks and colleagues showed that the most immediate and severe impact on FL learning was caused by phonological problems (Sparks et al., 1989), with syntactical (grammatical) difficulties in native language being of major importance as well (Ganschow, Sparks, Javorsky, Pohlman, & Bishop-Marbury, 1991). Moreover, students whose educational careers were marked by difficulties in FL learning had weaker oral reading (Ganschow et al., 1994), skills in single-word silent reading, and spelling (Ganschow et al., 1991; Ganschow & Sparks, 1995; Sparks et al., 1992) than successful FL learners.

Summarizing their evidence, Sparks and Ganschow (1993) suggested the importance of considering a unified phonological module that malfunctions both in NL and FL acquisitions, questioning the validity of the assumption of the specificity and unique nature of cognitive processes involved in FL. To enhance this hypothesis, Ganschow and Sparks (1995) investigated an impact of phonology-based FL intervention on students identified at risk for FL failure. The effect of the intervention was positive and manifested itself, not only in improvement in FL aptitude, but in improvement in NL phonological/orthographical measures. However, despite these improvements, at-risk students, even two years later, did not achieve the level of performance comparable to non-at-risk students (Sparks, Ganschow, Artzer, & Patton, 1997).

Thus, the field converges around the statement that there is a nonrandom association between failure to master FL and difficulties in acquiring NL in both its oral and its written formats. Can we pinpoint specific cognitive processes that are challenged in students with specific language impairment and specific reading disability, and therefore might impede the acquisition of foreign languages?

Selected findings from the literature on specific language impairment and developmental dyslexia (specific reading disability)

The concept of interest in the context of this discussion is that of the *FL aptitude complex* (Robinson, 2001c; Chapter 6, this volume; based on Snow, 1994). This concept refers to a cluster of cognitive functions recruited for input processing during foreign-language learning and is defined as a combination of aptitude variables that jointly influence learning in specific situations. According to Robinson, this complex involves cognitive resources (e.g., attention, working, short-, and long-term memory, basic processing speed) as they manifest themselves in primary linguistic abilities (e.g., linguistic pattern recognition, phonological memory, grammatical sensitivity); these primary abilities, in turn, cluster into sets of higher-order abilities engaged in language learning (e.g., noticing the gap, memory for contingent speech, deep semantic processing, memory for contingent text, metalinguistic rule rehearsal); higher-order abilities form aptitude complexes.

The concept of FL aptitude complex appears to be of significance for the present discussion in light of two lines of evidence: (1) FL failure is not a homogeneous phenomenon — there are many diverse reasons that may lead to FL failure, linguistic difficulties in the FL learner's NL being only one possible cluster of these reasons, and (2) there is a diverse variety of linguistic difficulties in NL acquisition, and each of them, or any combination of them, may result in difficulties and/or failure in FL acquisition.

The purpose of this part of the chapter is to investigate those components of the FL aptitude complex that appear to be weakened in students with specific language and reading impairments, and that might result in a failure to master a FL. The point of view advanced here is that FL failure, at least to a significant degree, is a manifestation of NL linguistic difficulties as expressed in specific language disorder and specific reading disability. To enhance this point, consider the following: only 5–10% of children who read satisfactorily in the primary grades ever stumble later, but 65–70% of children referred to as having reading difficulties early continue to read poorly throughout their school careers and beyond (Scarborough, 2001). FL failure is often only one example of these children's stumbling.

FL dimensions and corresponding acquisition challenges

Languages differ on a number of dimensions. In this chapter I will by no means attempt to summarize all of them, but rather briefly point out only those dimensions which are central to our discussion of the difficulties faced by students with disabilities (primarily, specific reading disabilities) when attempting to master a FL.

Languages differ in the regularity of phoneme-grapheme correspondence (Vanezky, 1970). A number of languages (e.g., Polish, Hungarian, Spanish, Kiswahili) are delightfully consistent in their phoneme — grapheme correspondence systems. Such consistency is based on the single letter — single phoneme link and guarantees consistent mapping from phonemes to graphemes as well as from graphemes to phonemes. In such languages, almost any word can be spelled correctly when it is presented orally and pronounced correctly when it is presented visually. Another group of languages (e.g., German, Dutch, Russian) loosens the consistency rule on one side of the system. Namely, these languages preserve the consistency in the mapping of clusters of graphemes to phonemes, but introduce a fair amount of indeterminacy in the phoneme — grapheme mapping. In these languages, one knows how to pronounce a new word if it is presented visually, but is not sure how to spell a new word if the word is presented auditorily. Yet one more group of languages (e.g., English, French) is mysteriously inconsistent. These languages tolerate remarkable amounts of irregularity; in them, one can almost never be sure how a word is spelled when it is presented orally or how it is pronounced when it is presented visually.

Moreover, languages differ by grapheme — phoneme-correspondence systems (i.e., by their orthographies). The majority of linguistic systems employ phonemic scripts with an analytic basis for phoneme — grapheme mapping. There are, however, two major challenges. The first is associated with the system of correspondence between the learner's native characters and the characters of the language she/he aimed to master. If the correspondence is easy (e.g., that between Roman characters in different languages), learning is facilitated. On the contrary, learning is challenged when the correspondence is difficult (e.g., that between Roman and Cyrillic characters). Second, a challenge of a different magnitude is imposed on a learner who tries to master a script of a type different from that of his or her native language. For example, a Russian-speaking learner faces a very difficult task in mastering the linguistic system of Chinese, which is based on characters that have no match to individual sounds. Obviously, both of the challenges mentioned here "map" themselves onto the issue of individual differences in FL acquisition.

Furthermore, languages differ in terms of their morphological complexity. To illustrate, Russian and German, being relatively transparent and therefore not extremely phonologically challenging, are viewed as hard in terms of their morphology. In general, typological categories of languages are based on the average number of morphemes per word and the amount of information contained in each morpheme. Specifically, languages vary remarkably in the degree to which they utilize nominal declension, verbal conjugation, and other morphosyntactic systems (Bloomfield, 1961; Greenberg, 1978). There is an implicit continuum on which, simplifying the dimensionality of the morphosyntactic systems, languages can be placed. One extreme of this continuum, then, is marked by languages such as Navajo, which employs a complex system of aspects, person, case, number, location, and voice. At the other extreme, are languages such as English, Afrikaans, or Kiswahili: these languages have only a few affixes, and their morphosyntactic systems are comparably easy.

Among other dimensions of similarities and dissimilarities between languages, of special interest for this discussion is the dimension of grammatical differences. Grammar is concerned with the syntactical relations of sentence components (e.g., word order, word agreement, clausal links). Some languages, such as Kiswahili, are considered easier grammatically when compared to more difficult languages, such as German.

Thus, even when only these dimensions of linguistic variability are considered, it appears that there is no "simplest" FL: any language can be characterized by a number of dimensions, each of which might create obstacles on the way to its acquisition. In other words, each particular "dimension" of a FL might introduce specific difficulties to students attempting to acquire it.

Specifically, four hypotheses of why phonological acquisition of a new language can be impeded can be generated. The first hypothesis links the FL deficit to ossification of the perceptual system, i.e., the speech perception system addressed initially in the early work with children with specific language impairment of Tallal and colleagues (e.g., Tallal & Piercy, 1973, 1975). The second hypothesis links the FL deficit to difficulties in establishing new procedures for controlling motor output (e.g., phoneme and single-word production in FL — Liljencrants & Lindblom, 1972; MacNeilage, 1970; McNeil & Kent, 1990; Odell et al., 1991). The third hypothesis suggests that, at least partially, FL acquisition troubles in students with specific learning disabilities are related to memory (Gathercole & Baddeley, 1989b, 1990b). Finally, the fourth hypothesis assumes that FL difficulties are intimately related to phonological difficulties experienced in the NL (e.g., Sparks & Ganschow, 1991).

Morphology also appears to be a source of individual variation in the degree of FL mastery. Specifically, individuals differ in their skills of dividing words into morphemes and of modifying morphemes (Feldman, 1995). Moreover, there is a significant developmental variation in these skills, with younger children having difficulty manipulating morphemes (e.g., Gerken & Ohala, 2000). Jointly, such morphology-related skills are referred to as morphological awareness. Thus, the hypothesis links FL failure to lack of morphological awareness.

People also differ in the degree of the mastery of grammatical structures of languages. This is true for students of both NL and FL. To acknowledge this variability, researchers refer to grammatical ability (e.g., Leonard, 1998). Here this ability is referred to as "syntactic awareness."

Below I will, in turn, consider evidence from the literature on specific learning disabilities that might help us understand the nature and types of difficulties experienced by FL learners whose linguistic abilities are challenged.

Speech perception

The research on deficiencies of speech perception in groups of individuals with dyslexia as compared to groups of individuals without dyslexia has resulted in controversial findings: there is some evidence for and against group differences, with the deficit present in children with dyslexia both at the levels of separate sounds and single words (for review, see Snowling, 2000). Of special relevance to this discussion is the hypothesis forwarded by McBride-Chang (1995), which points to the possibility of difficulty in speech perception being one of the early precursors of subsequent phonological difficulties — although speech perception difficulties are easily remediable, in the case of lack of remediation they may lead to phonological difficulties. Transferred to the domain of FL learning, it might be that, although the initial stage of FL acquisition (which is stringing and dissecting foreign sounds into meaningful chains — words and phrases) is a challenge to everyone, it is a particular challenge to students with specific language and reading impairments.

Speech production

Children with reading problems are often reported as having difficulty saying certain words, especially polysyllabic words (e.g., Snowling, 1981). Poor readers have been shown to speak at a slower rate than good readers (McDougall, Hulme, Ellis, & Monk, 1994; Stone & Brady, 1995). Moreover, individuals with dyslexia are more prone than those without dyslexia to make errors when articulating words speedily (Stone & Brady, 1995). Obviously, these deficits might impede the capacities of readers with dyslexia to master FL pronunciation and listening comprehension.

Memory

One of the early hypotheses explaining FL failure linked difficulties in FL acquisition to memory weaknesses. Different forms of memory have been subjected to different explorations in the context of understanding both dyslexia and FL learning failures.

Visual memory
Vellutino, Pruzek, Steger, and Meshoulam (1973) asked 10–13-year-old readers with and without dyslexia to copy printed words of three, four, or five let-

ters from memory, following short exposure. Readers with dyslexia did worse than readers without dyslexia. However, when the same groups of children were asked to copy from memory words printed in Hebrew orthography (neither of the groups had special exposure to the Hebrew language), children with and without dyslexia performed at comparable levels. Thus, it is possible to infer that, when exposed to a FL, students with dyslexia can rely on their visual memory at least as much as students without dyslexia.

Verbal memory

It has long been noticed that readers with dyslexia can remember fewer verbal items than is expected for their age (Hulme, 1981; Shankweiler, Liberman, Mark, Fowler, & Fischer, 1979). Since FL learning requires memorization of large amounts of verbal material, the weakness of verbal memory, which was consistently shown to be one of the major weaknesses in dyslexia, is certainly a component of the FL aptitude complex that, while challenged, can trigger FL learning difficulties.

Short-term memory

Gathercole and Baddeley (1993) have thoroughly reviewed the neuropsychological and developmental evidence causally linking phonological short-term memory and word learning in one's first language. There is strong and extensive evidence linking the capacity of the verbal component of working memory (so-called phonological loop, for review see Baddeley, Gathercole, & Papagno, 1998) and language acquisition of both native and foreign languages (e.g., Masoura & Gathercole, 1999). Specifically, the phonological loop capacity, often measured by nonword repetition tasks, (see Mackey et al., this volume, who use such a measure) has been shown to be predictive of vocabulary development in native (e.g., Gathercole & Baddeley, 1989a, 1990a; Service, 1992) as well as foreign-languages (e.g., Service & Kohonen, 1995). In fact, short-term memory capacity is an especially good predictor of success in foreign-language learners at the initial stages of foreign language exposure, when the acquired vocabulary is relatively poor; this predictive power diminishes significantly in learners who have already acquired an extensive vocabulary in their foreign language (Chen & Leung, 1989). Children with specific language impairment (SLI) have also been shown to have deficient phonological loop capacity (Gathercole & Baddeley, 1989b, 1990b). Children with dyslexia, as well, have been shown to demonstrate this deficit.

Long-term memory

Researchers have shown that success in acquiring new foreign-language vocabulary is linked with the amount of vocabulary already mastered in this language (Cheung, 1996). This finding matches well with the earlier finding indicating that vocabulary itself becomes the best predictor of further vocabulary development at the age of five and, later on, remains so and, moreover, determines the performance of phonological memory (Gathercole, Willis, Emslie, & Baddeley, 1992) and other phonological processes (Perfetti, 1987). These and other findings led to the acceptance of the reciprocal model of the short-term/long-term memory relationship in the context of language acquisition (both native and foreign): phonological loop capacity promotes learning of phonological patterns of new words, and the building long-term word knowledge capacity enhances the limits of short-term memory. Moreover, it has been shown that vocabulary acquisition at early stages of FL learning is mediated through native language concepts (Kroll, 1990; Kroll & Sholl, 1992). This strategy adopted by the majority of FL learners, can be both beneficial (if the FL is close to the native language of the learner) or detrimental (if the FL is very different from the learner's first language). Readers with dyslexia have been shown to have deficient long-term memory (for review, see Snowling, 2000). Moreover, early research on dyslexia has shown that it is more difficult for poor readers, compared to their age-matched control, to learn the first ten words above their own ceiling on a picture vocabulary test (Nelson & Warrington, 1980). Aguiar and Brady (1991) showed that, although poor readers were as successful as normal readers in terms of learning the meanings of new concepts, they were far behind the normal readers in their ability to retrieve quickly the name of the word whose meaning they had just learned. Finally, it has been shown (Wimmer, 1996; Windfuhr, 1998) that children with dyslexia have a harder time learning associations between new words (which sound like nonwords to them) and objects, although their general associative abilities might not suffer.

Phonological deficits

Phonological processing deficits have been recognized as one major, if not the most important, source of developmental dyslexia. The cognitive sequels of this deficit are variable, and not necessarily related to dyslexia (Fowler, 1991; Snowling & Hulme, 1994). However, it is important to keep in mind that the literacy problem, which is central to dyslexia, is one of many cognitive sequels of phonological deficits. In turn, the term "phonological deficits" refers to a number of deficits including (but not limited to) naming difficulties, poor repetition ability, and phonological awareness. Here I shall briefly discuss a set of findings linking phonological deficits and FL failure.

Verbal naming deficits

Long-term memory retrieval difficulties lead readers with dyslexia to have word-finding problems. In the context of their NL, poor readers often give up the effort to retrieve a specific word and resort to long, windy descriptions to express their ideas. In experimental conditions (e.g., Katz, 1986; Snowling, Wagtendonk, & Stafford, 1988), poor readers have difficulty retrieving the names of objects with which they are familiar (both when they are asked to attach a word label to a picture or to a verbal and written description). Anecdotally, many FL learners experience a so-called 'tip-of-the-tongue' state, when the learner has a semantic representation of a word, can provide its description, but cannot retrieve the word itself. The difference between good and poor readers is that good readers experience these phenomena much more seldom, and that they recover and do recall the word much quicker. The frequency and lack of recovery of the 'tip-of-the-tongue' state experienced by FL learners with challenged phonological skills can be accounted for by the lack of phonological specification. Moreover, when a phonological cue (a similar sounding word or the beginning of the word) is provided to such a learner, often the cue is ineffective — such learners appear to be clustering the information lexically, not phonologically.

Another challenge imposed by deficits in naming on FL learners with dyslexia is that this deficit might be an outcome of the impairment of a general timing mechanism linked to skill automatization (Wolf & Bowers, 1999). Viewed in this way, naming deficits might impede such an important in FL acquisition process as establishing a sight vocabulary (Bowers, 1993; Wimmer, Mayringer, & Landeri, 1998).

Repetition

Subsequent to difficulties experienced by children with dyslexia and specific language impairment during speech production, word repetition is difficult for them as well. Researchers (e.g., Bishop et al., 1999; Snowling, Goulandris, Bowlby, & Howell, 1986) have shown that a special challenge to students with specific learning disabilities is repetition of nonwords (i.e., combinations of sounds that do not have any semantic meaning). Of course, most words encountered in the process of FL learning are perceived, at least initially, as nonwords. Thus, it is plausible that the repetition of unknown FL words is of significant difficulty to individuals with reading and language impairments. It has been suggested that nonword repetition is critical for vocabulary acquisition (Gathercole & Baddeley, 1989a; Gathercole, Hitch, Service, & Martin, 1997). Therefore, the impediment to repeating new FL words becomes a major obstacle in building FL vocabulary.

Phonological awareness

The current leading idea in the field of dyslexia and specific language disorder capitalizes on the importance of so-called metaphonological skills. The idea is as follows. There is a significant phonological component in all processes in which students with specific language and reading problems exhibit substantial deficits. Thus, it is fair to assume that one source of these deficit manifestations can be referred to as a deficit in the awareness of phonological units of language, or metaphonological deficit. Having defined this awareness as a metacognitive ability that tops the organization of the phonological system and requires conscious reflection (Gombert, 1992), researchers have described its hypothetical hierarchical structure. It appears that phonological awareness includes: i) rhyming awareness, i.e., the ability to become aware of certain words rhyming with each other or of these words' shared phonetic similarity of the end sounds; ii) syllable and sub-syllable (or word chunks) awareness, i.e., the ability to become aware of large chunks of words — syllables, rimes (a sub-syllabic unit, containing a vowel and the succeeding consonant or consonants), and onsets (a sub-syllabic unit containing the first phoneme or cluster of phonemes); iii) morphological awareness, i.e., the ability to become aware of word morphemes; iv) and phonemic awareness. These "awarenesses" do not appear simultaneously in development (e.g., Liberman, Shankweiler, Liberman, Fowler, & Fischer, 1977), and contribute differentially to spoken and written word acquisition (e.g., Swan & Goswami, 1997) with phonemic awareness being the latest to occur and the most powerful predictor of written NL acquisition.

It is important to note that phonological processing and NL acquisition are reciprocal processes. Phonological processing predicts linguistic performance and, in turn, linguistic performance predicts phonological processing at subsequent stages (e.g., Lundberg, 1994; Morais, Cary, Alegria, & Bertelson, 1979; Perfetti, Beck, Bell, & Hughes, 1987). This holds true for FL acquisition as well. For example, Grubb, Bush, and Geist (1998) investigated the effects of the acquisition of a FL on discrimination of the FL phonemes. The researchers have found that the more prior experience with FL phonemes the participants had, the more accurate was their FL phoneme discrimination.

Where does this take us? Although this hypothesis has not been verified, it is plausible to suppose that FL acquisition unfolds in a fashion similar to the one described above: a student starts by mastering large chunks of phonological information and then turns to fine-tuning this information down to the level of phonemes. If this is the case, then a student whose phonological awareness is challenged in his or her NL will be expected to have difficulties in mastering a new phonological system. And, as in the remedial training developed for the purpose of strengthening phonological skills in their NL, a deepened phonological training should be offered to such students in a FL they are trying to master. It is desirable that such remediation covers a spectrum of phonological skills in the FL — from rhyming to fine phoneme manipulations.

Morphological awareness

Recently, there have been a number of studies addressing the existence and role of individual differences in ability to master morphosyntactic systems (e.g., Gopnik, 1990; Gopnik & Crago, 1990; Pinker, 1991; van der Lely, 1992; van der Lely & Howard, 1993). Among other findings, this research has featured the observation that children with language disorders may have specific difficulties in mastering morphosyntactic paradigms in their native language.

Specifically, students with developmental dyslexia have been shown to have a lack of understanding of the morphological relations among forms derived from a common root (Carlisle, 1988; Elbro, 1990; Vogel, 1975). Researchers have proposed two possible explanations for these findings. Some investigators have proposed that these difficulties reflect a deficit in morphosyntactic development, over and above the phonological deficit (Stein, Cairns, & Zurif, 1984; Vogel, 1975). Other researchers, however, claim that these morphological difficulties and deficiencies in phonological processing are guided by common underlying processes (Feldman, Fowler, Andjelkovic, & Oney, in press; Fowler & Liberman, 1995; Shankweiler & Grain, 1986; Shankweiler et al., 1995).

Similarly, researchers have shown that students with specific language impairment demonstrate morphological awareness deficits. Specifically, children with specific language impairment are late in acquiring grammatical morphemes (Bishop, 1997; Leonard, 1998). For example, inflectional morphemes such as tense markings have been found to be a major source of difficulty for children diagnosed with this condition (e.g., Rice, & Wexler, 1996).

Syntactic awareness

Students with learning disabilities find it difficult to process specific syntactic structures in their NL, specifically passives, relative clauses, and sentences containing adjectives with exceptional control properties. These observations have been initially explained by references to a deficiency in somewhat independent "syntactic ability." However, a number of researchers have shown that children with developmental dyslexia can process such syntactic structures nearly as well as normal readers when comprehension is assessed by a task that minimizes demands on working memory (Bar-Shalom, Crain, & Shankweiler, 1993; Fowler, 1988; Macaruso, Shankweiler, Byrne, & Crain, 1993; Smith, Macaruso, Shankweiler, & Grain, 1989). This second hypothesis assumes that the deficit in syntactic awareness is secondary to the deficit in working memory, and therefore does not have an independent origin.

The story is quite different for students with specific language disorder, for which lack of grammatical development is viewed as the behavior marker of the condition (e.g., Rice, 2000). Specifically, individuals with this condition demonstrate syntactic difficulties with lower-level grammar such as case-marking (e.g., Loeb & Leonard, 1991). Higher-level grammar (e.g., sentence clauses) is an especially weak area for student with specific language disorders (e.g., Cleave & Rice, 1997; Oetting & Horov, 1997). It is interesting to note that children with specific language impairment who are acquiring a language with a rich inflectional morphology (e.g., Italian, Hebrew) seem less impaired in the use of grammatical inflections than their counterparts who are acquiring a language with a sparse inflectional morphology (e.g., English) (Leonard, 2000).

Comprehension

Up to now I have concentrated mostly on components of the FL aptitude complex, which, presumably, might be challenged in students with various forms of language-based learning disabilities and, therefore, might constitute stumbling blocks for these students in FL acquisition. Each of the components reviewed above can contribute to a difficulty in any number of domains of FL learning (e.g., pronunciation, listening, speaking, reading, and writing). However, it is important to remember that our very attempt to master a FL is driven by the hope to eventually fully comprehend this language. It appears that, once again, a parallel can be drawn between NL and FL comprehension. Specifically, although there are strong relationships between the processes discussed above and comprehension, these relationships are not really clear, I will briefly list these findings (for review, see Cain & Oakhill, in press).

First, it appears that individuals with comprehension difficulties do not necessarily have any deficiency in the skills described above (i.e., memory, phonemic, morphological, or syntactic awareness). Second, although phonological processing difficulties are likely to be experienced by poor comprehenders, there is no direct causal link between phonological processing skills and comprehension skills. Third, there is evidence of reciprocity between semantic representation and comprehension; it is unclear whether good semantic knowledge is a by-product of experience with both NL and FL speech and text, or whether it is (at least in part) contributive to success in text comprehension. Fourth, there are also correlations between comprehension and syntactic knowledge; less skilled comprehenders are less likely to draw upon sentence context to guide their comprehension of unknown words and expressions. Fifth, less skilled comprehenders experience difficulties with a wide range of comprehension-related skills: making inferences, decoding continuity, metacognition, and use of context. Finally, it has been established that poor comprehension is related to limitations in the ability simultaneously to store and process information.

Conclusion

Given the number of cognitive skills contributing to the FL aptitude complex and therefore associated with FL mastery, it would be surprising (and totally unrealistic) if *all* the skills and abilities discussed above were deficient in *all* individuals with learning disabilities attempting to study a FL. Although the evidence is very sparse, what is available in the literature suggests that the population of students with learning disabilities who experience difficulties with FL learning is very heterogeneous. It may be that, although diagnosed with a specific learning disability or an FLLD, the population of students with FL difficulties will include individuals with different profiles of deficiency: some may have a fundamental weakness in working memory that restricts their ability to build a vocabulary and make inferences while storing, others might have metaphonological difficulties that will impede their ability to combine or divide strings of verbal and written communication into meaningful units. Thus, different students diagnosed with the same or different learning disabilities may experience FL learning failure because of different underlying impairments.

This very circumstance, according to which the FL failure manifested by students with learning disabilities is, most likely, marked by extreme etiological heterogeneity, brings up the question of adequate teaching techniques. Although researchers, practitioners, and policy makers all acknowledge the difficulties in FL acquisition that are experienced by students with learning disabilities, nobody says that mastering a FL is an impossible task for these students. Just as there are many successful techniques to ensure remediation of difficulties in NL acquisition, so there can be successful techniques ensuring mastery of a FL. The challenge is to identify and describe the particular variety of difficulties being experienced by a group of children with language-based learning disabilities in FL acquisition and then to develop matching teaching techniques.

CHAPTER 6

Learning conditions, aptitude complexes, and SLA*

A framework for research and pedagogy

Peter Robinson
Aoyama Gakuin University

Introduction: individual difference/learning condition interactions

Profiling individual differences in cognitive abilities, and matching these pro-files to effective instructional options, such as types of pedagogic tasks, inter-ventionist 'focus on form' techniques, and more broadly defined learning con-ditions, is a major aim of pedagogically oriented language aptitude research (see the chapters by Sternberg, and Skehan, this volume). Research into the effects of individual differences (IDs) in cognitive abilities on learning under different conditions of exposure is well established outside the field of SLA, for example in the fields of instructional psychology (Corno, Cronbach, Kupermintz, Lohman, Mandinach, Porteus & Talbert, 2002; Cronbach & Snow, 1977), and psychotherapy (Dance & Neufeld, 1988; Snow, 1991). As Corno et al. (2002, p.110) point out, the classic design for such studies involves:

- Alternative methods of teaching the same content
- Random assignment of students to treatments
- Initial testing to measure propensities hypothesized to be more relevant to one treatment than another

In this chapter I argue that such 'aptitude-treatment' interaction research — and in particular Snow's notion of 'aptitude complexes' (Snow, 1987) — also has much to contribute to our understanding of SLA; in particular such cen-tral issues in SLA theory as explaining variation in language learning success under particular instructional conditions; explaining differences between implicit, incidental, and explicit learning processes; and explaining child adult differences in language learning abilities. Aptitude, awareness, and age are important learner variables, and any general theory of SLA will be incomplete without an explanation of how, and under what conditions, IDs in each impact upon learning.

Instructional contexts

Consequently I propose a framework for such research which suggests that sets of cognitive abilities, or 'aptitude complexes' are differentially related to language learning under different psycholinguistic processing conditions. Such conditions can be described at the situational level of classroom instructional treatments; at the more constrained situational level of the specific pedagogic tasks that learners perform in classrooms; and at the cognitive level of implicit, explicit, and incidental learning processes. Matching learner's strengths in particular aptitude complexes to options in the delivery of learning conditions and instructional techniques at each of these levels, then, is therefore an important element in the delivery of optimally effective classroom exposure and practice for second language (L2) learners.

Snow argued (see Corno et al., 2002; Snow, 1994) that a theory of the cognitive abilities contributing to IDs in aptitudes for learning (person variables) also needed to be accompanied by a theory of contextual constraints on these (situational variables). To take one example of how a theory of situational constraints might be developed, elsewhere I have argued that in 'task-based' approaches to syllabus design and pedagogy (see Long & Crookes, 1992; Skehan, 1998a; Skehan & Foster, 2001; Robinson, 1994a, 1996c, 1998, 2001b) situational constraints can be broadly divided into two categories; i) the cognitive demands of the task contributing to its relative *complexity* which can be determined along a number of information processing dimensions, e.g., whether the task requires reference to the 'here and now', or more complex reference to the 'there and then' (Rahimpour, 1997; Robinson, 1995a); and ii) the interactive *conditions* under which the task is performed, e.g., whether the participants are familiar, or previously unfamiliar with each other (Plough & Gass, 1993), or whether the solution to the task is 'open' and negotiable, or fixed and 'closed' (Long, 1989). Effects of manipulating task factors, such as cognitive complexity, and condition factors, such as the familiarity of participants, are also likely to be influenced by person variables, such as differences in anxiety, motivation, and aptitude, which contribute to individual learners' perceptions of task *difficulty* (see Robinson, 2001a, 2001b). One aim of this chapter, then, is to propose a methodological and conceptual framework for examining these *situation* (task complexity, and conditions) and *person* (task difficulty) interactions in the domain of adult L2 learning, and to summarize findings from some recent research (particularly studies described in detail in the following section of this volume) which cast light on their nature.

SLA processes

Research into aptitude-treatment interactions also has theoretical relevance, and potential explanatory value, in addition to pedagogic utility. It has been argued that an explanation of SLA requires both a transition theory, which specifies relationships between cognitive abilities, acquisition processes and the mechanisms which implement them in moving knowledge from point A to point B, and also a property theory which characterizes the properties of knowledge at points A and B (see N.Ellis, 1998, 1999; Gregg, 2001, for discussion). Accounting for the findings from research into the effects (or not) of IDs in cognitive abilities on acquisition processes should therefore form an important part of any *transition theory* and the causal relationships it proposes between cognitive resource allocation and learning mechanisms — illuminating 'how' these mechanisms are integrated in cognitive architecture. However, while working memory capacity effects on parsing mechanisms have been studied in L1 and more recently L2 sentence processing (see Harrington, 2001), IDs in other cognitive abilities, such as the intensity and extensiveness of focal attention allocation (see Santostefano, 1978) have not to date been the subject of SLA research, despite their likely relevance to recent claims about the important role of detection, and 'noticing' in SLA (Robinson, 1995b, in press; Schmidt, 1990, 2001; Tomlin & Villa, 1994). I address this issue later in this chapter.

An interactionist perspective

Individual differences research into cognitive resources and abilities is therefore relevant not only to decisions about matching learners' aptitude profiles to appropriate instructional conditions, but also to a transition theory of SLA. Though I briefly mention options in *property theories*, in this chapter I only address in any detail one candidate, which Gregg (2001) has claimed meets the 'theoretical framework' condition — Bley-Vroman's Fundamental Difference Hypothesis (1990). The Fundamental Difference Hypothesis (FDH) argues general cognitive abilities are drawn on in adult SLA, in contrast to L1 acquisition, which develops under the constraints of Universal Grammar (UG) (see also the chapter by Ross, Sasaki and Yoshinaga, this volume, for discussion). I argue that explaining how, when and why these abilities are drawn on during adult SLA will require linking 'patterns' of abilities to acquisition processes, *and* the information processing demands of learning contexts, which *together* cause their effects on SLA. In doing this I adopt the interactionist perspective on ID research which Snow (1994) has described 'in which the relevant aspects of person and situation are specified, their interaction is demonstrated empirically, and some process explanation of how and why this occurs is offered' (Snow, 1994, p.4). In this approach correlations between cognitive variables and outcome measures of learning (such as the acquisition of a particular structure, or stage of development) are examined in relation to the information processing demands of different conditions of exposure. I argue that where interactions between cognitive variables (e.g., phonological working memory capacity) and learning conditions occur these are attributed to acquisition processes, which draw on the cognitive variable of interest, but which are argued to be facilitated or inhibited by the information processing demands of one of the conditions.

In this chapter I describe some ways in which the issues I have referred to above might, and are beginning to be, conceptualized and empirically investigated by SLA research into the effects of IDs in cognitive variables on L2 learning. The chapter proceeds by describing four interlocking hypotheses, and where possible, evidence to support them: i) the Aptitude Complex Hypothesis; ii) the Ability Differentiation Hypothesis; iii) the Fundamental Difference Hypothesis; and iv) the Fundamental Similarity Hypothesis. These hypotheses, and the relationships between them, lead me to propose an Aptitude Complex/Ability Differentiation framework for researching the effects of IDs in cognitive abilities on L2 learning, and for developing theoretically motivated measures of language learning aptitudes.

Abilities, aptitudes, and instructed learning

Snow (1994) and others (e.g., Carroll, 1993) assume cognitive abilities can usefully be viewed hierarchically and based on extensive factor analyses of performance on psychological tests, have identified hierarchical models of the structure of cognitive abilities. These models distinguish between first order abilities (e.g., working memory capacity, and analogical reasoning) which are directly measured by performance on a psychological test, and second order abilities which are argued to result from specific combinations of first order abilities (e.g., fluid intelligence, Gf; broad speediness, Gs; and crystallized intelligence, Gc). These second order abilities in turn are proposed to contribute to a unitary, third order 'g' (or general intelligence), and to academic success in a variety of educational contexts (see e.g., Hakstian & Cattell, 1976; Jensen, 1998). Early developed measures of language learning aptitude, based in part on these hierarchies, placed a high priority on predictive validity and ease of administration, and didn't have the benefit of recent SLA research into cognitive processes and abilities in motivating its constructs. As Grigorenko, Sternberg and Ehrman (2000), and Skehan (this volume) make clear, in the case of Carroll and Sapon's (1959) Modern Language Aptitude Test (MLAT) this involved wide scale piloting of a great number of subtests of primary abilities which were 'statistically winnowed' by selecting those with the lowest intercorrelations, and the greatest predictive validity. Predictive validity was determined by correlating performance on these tests with measures of school age achievement in predominantly Audiolingual courses of instruction. Given the changing nature of classroom instruction since the 1950s and 1960s, however, it is questionable whether these tests are optimally predictive of development taking place during some current approaches to instruction where oral interaction and communicative activities predominate. This issue of 'treatment' validity — whether an aptitude test is equally predictive of language learning under different instructional treatments — is an empirical one. Results of recent studies do show significant positive correlations of some of the subtests and achievement in communicative classrooms, particularly measures of grammatical sensitivity (e.g., the Words in Sentences, WS, subtest of the MLAT) (see, e.g., chapters by Harley and Hart, and Ranta, this volume). But there is likely margin for improvement, as Sternberg, and Skehan, this volume, also note. So how, therefore, to proceed?

The aptitude complex hypothesis (the ACH)

With these issues in mind, Figure 1 (based on Snow, 1994, p.10) illustrates a *hypothetical* subset of the hierarchical structure of abilities for language learning during instructed SLA. Some of these may be suited to measuring aptitude for learning from some techniques for 'focus on form' delivered in communicative classrooms (see Doughty, 2001), as well as aptitudes for learning during immersion/content-based and more traditional grammar based forms of instruction. Cognitive *resources* (e.g., attention, working, short and long term memory, basic processing speed) implement cognitive *processes* drawn on by primary *abilities* involved in language learning task/test performance (e.g., pattern recognition, speed of processing in phonological working memory (WM), grammatical sensitivity). Primary abilities combine to define sets of higher *second order abilities* hypothesized to support language learning (e.g., noticing the gap, memory for contingent speech, deep semantic processing, memory for contingent text, and metalinguistic rule rehearsal). These abilities themselves can be grouped into aptitude *complexes* (Snow, 1987) which 'represent hypothesized combinations of aptitude variables that jointly influence learning in some particular situation'(Snow, 1994, p. 9).

An example given in Figure 1 is a complex of memory for contingent speech and noticing the gap (possibly related to the factor 'general speediness', Gs), representing the possibility that learners may be classified as high in both of these abilities (HH), high only in one (HL, or LH), or low in both (LL). Such a complex may be particularly relevant, for example, to distinguishing between learners who benefit from implicit negative feedback provided by targeted recasts during oral interaction (see Doughty, 2001; and Mackey, Philp, Egi, Fujii & Tatsumi, this volume) versus those who do not, helping, in part, explain conflicting findings for short term uptake, and the long term developmental change hypothesized to result from it, in this area of research. Learners with relatively low phonological WM capacity and speed, that is, may be less able to accurately and actively rehearse targeted recasts in WM, despite the fact they may have noticed them in the input. They may thus may fail to learn from (via a process of cognitive comparison), and use the information in recasts in a subsequent turn. Alternatively, phonological WM capacity may be high, and memory for contingent speech consequently high, but the ability to notice the gap (Schmidt & Frota, 1986) between their own production and the recast may be low, because of poor pattern identification/ discrimination ability (see Grigorenko, this volume), again leading to missed learning opportunities and lack of uptake (see Mackey et al., this volume, for an empirical study of this issue). Other potential, and researchable, aptitude complexes are suggested in Figure 1. These are made up of combinations of the abilities I have termed memory for contingent speech, deep semantic processing, and memory for contingent text (possibly related to fluid intelligence, Gf), and metalinguistic rule rehearsal (possibly related to crystallized intelligence, Gc). Figure 1 also speculatively relates these complexes to some options in instructed language learning.

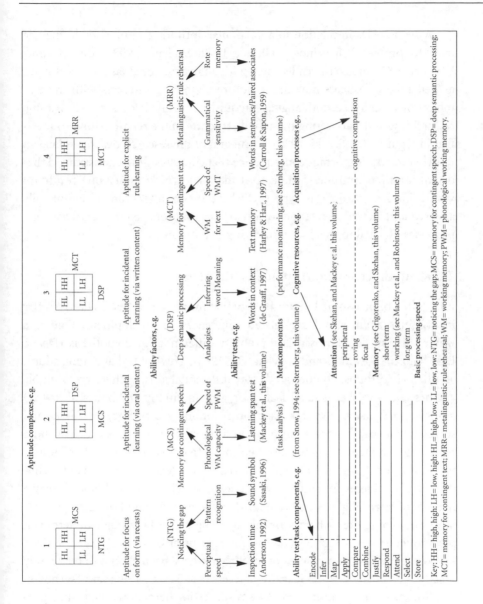

Figure 1. Hierarchical model of cognitive abilities showing two levels of ability factors (primary abilities, and second order ability factors for language learning aptitude), ability tests used as markers for the central ability, and component processes involved in these tests. Aptitude complexes at the top are intended to suggest combinations of abilities drawn on under particular learning conditions(based on Snow, 1994, Figure 1.1, p.10).

Assessing IDs in relation to a particular aptitude complex, then, may be used to profile (Pellegrino & Glaser, 1979; Skehan, 1998a, this volume; Wesche, 1981) and so match learners with an instructional task, or treatment, as well as to investigate how the structure of abilities interacts with these to inhibit or facilitate second language acquisition (SLA) processes. Motivating, researching, and elaborating the actual structure of the relationships exemplified in Figure 1 (cf. Sasaki, 1996) is one aim of the research described later in this chapter. An important consequence that could result is a constrained theory of multiple aptitudes, where aptitude for learning under one condition versus another, or on one type of task versus another, can be empirically assessed and viewed in relation to constraints on proposed universal learning processes. Related to this is the following hypothesis.

The ability differentiation hypothesis (the ADH)

It has often been assumed in psychology that there are similarities between IDs in cognitive abilities and age-related differences in development. One area where this link is addressed is the ability differentiation hypothesis (Deary, Egan, Gibson, Austin, Brand & Kellaghan, 1996). This holds that among adults, and high-IQ groups, abilities are better differentiated (i.e., there are multiple abilities and a weaker general factor, or g) than among children and low-IQ groups (see Stankov, 1999, for discussion). Similarly, therefore, for adults, and successful language learners this hypothesis predicts that abilities such as those represented in Figure 1 should also be more differentiated (there will be multiple abilities, or aptitudes for learning, and a weaker general factor) than for children and less successful adult language learners. The former should display a number of High-High, as well as High-Low/Low-High, and Low-Low patterns in aptitude complexes, whereas for the latter High-Low, Low-High, patterns will predominate (I return to this point in my conclusions).

While traditional measures of intelligence have been shown to relate only weakly — if at all — to L2 learning success (see Sasaki, 1996; and Sternberg, and Robinson, this volume), what I am suggesting here, however, is that aptitude, and the proposed abilities (such as noticing the gap, deep semantic processing, etc.) which contribute to it, *may* show a similar pattern of ability differentiation to the one observed in intelligence research (see also Grigorenko's summary of Native Language ability differentiation research, this volume). Although it will not be unproblematic to operationally distinguish between high and low measures of the abilities contributing to SLA, this has not inhibited Deary et al., 1996, and others concerned with general intelligence from pursuing this issue, and I would argue it is similarly susceptible to empirical investigation in the domain of SLA.

Levels of learning conditions

Clearly, SLA takes place under a great variety of conditions of exposure, which help determine how information available to the learner is processed and which may be specified and delivered at a variety of levels. Classroom ethnographies, and learner protocol analyses (see Jourdenais, 2001) provide important windows on the contexts in which learning takes place, yet from an information processing perspective it is largely in the specifics of a particular ID-outcome relationship that claims about IDs are interpretable. Without knowing what the processing demands of a learning task are, it is difficult to know why IDs in resources and abilities lead to learning differences. As Snow notes, 'both persons and situations ... need description at several "grain-size" levels. Different levels involve different kinds of aggregation across persons, tasks, and time. Interactions at one level may thus appear to be quite different from those at another' (1994, p.8). IDs/learning condition interaction research therefore should ideally be multilevel, while looking for patterns of systematicity and consistency across them. Areas of relevant current ID research include the following;

–   conditions specified in terms of SLA theory and delivered experimentally during laboratory studies (e.g., implicit, explicit, incidental, and intentional learning conditions, see N.Ellis, 1993, 1994; de Graaff, 1997a; DeKeyser, 1995, in press; Hulstijn, 1997, 2001; Robinson, 1996a, 1997a, this volume);

–   conditions specified according to principles of L2 learning task design and delivered experimentally contrasting the effects of performance on e.g., simple v. complex tasks (Niwa, 2000; Robinson, 1995a, 2000, 2001a, 2001b, 2002; Robinson, Ting & Urwin, 1995); open v. closed tasks (Long, 1989; Rahimpour, 1997, 1999); or planned v. unplanned tasks (Foster & Skehan, 1996; Ortega, 1999; Ting, 1995);

–   and conditions specified pedagogically and delivered methodologically in classroom settings (e.g, via grammar-based, content-based, task-based (see Dörnyei, this volume) or communicative approaches (see Ranta, this volume), and sometimes contrasted with the effects of 'naturalistic' exposure, (see DeKeyser, 2000; Harley & Hart, 1997, this volume; Ross, Yoshinaga & Sasaki, this volume).

I briefly summarize research findings at two of these levels later in this chapter. Of essential theoretical interest, then, in this research is a characterization of how these variously specified *learning conditions* constrain information processing, and how the information processing *resource demands* of these conditions are affected by IDs in the extent of *resource availability* and the structure of abilities. (For a stimulating account of how such research can be carried out in child developmental psychology, where learning conditions are operationalized as tasks at different levels of complexity, and where the cognitive resource of interest is changes in working memory capacity throughout childhood, see Halford, 1993, and for an attempt to apply this easy-hard task paradigm to SLA research see Robinson, 2001a, 2001b, 2002.)

Correlates, components and explanation

Most summaries of the influence of IDs in abilities, dispositions and states on SLA point to the clear contrast between L1 and L2 acquisition in terms of outcomes (e.g., as assessed by measures of lexical and/or structural development) — L2 acquisition is characterized by considerable variation in rates and levels of attainment, whereas L1 acquisition leads to native speaker ability, with some, though much less variation in rate of progress. IDs in aptitude and motivation have been shown to correlate highly with variation in SLA outcomes, (multiple r = between .4 and .6), and to be the most robust predictors of instructed language learning success (as measured, predominantly, by measures of achievement and proficiency). Skehan and Dörnyei (in press) refer to this as the 'correlational challenge' posed by IDs research to SLA theory. But as Skehan and Dörnyei (in press), Sawyer and Ranta (2001), and others have also noted, for these correlational findings to contribute to a cognitive 'explanation' of SLA (its representation and process) they must be related to one or more theoretical models of acquisition processes and mechanisms. As Segalowitz has noted, while SLA research into IDs has produced a substantial body of correlational findings, it has been 'relatively silent about... mechanisms' (1997, p. 87).

A major challenge for ID/ condition interaction research, then, is to try and explain *why* patterns of abilities lead to learning outcomes in any one context in terms of proposed SLA processes and mechanisms. These include, for example;

– 'triggering' in UG (Gibson & Wexler, 1994; Robinson, and Ross et al., this volume);

– 'competition' and 'cue salience', or 'chunking' in emergentist theories of SLA such as the Competition Model or connectionist approaches (N.Ellis, 1998, 2001; MacWhinney, 2001);

– rule 'compilation' and 'automatization' in skill theory (DeKeyser, 1997, 2001; Skehan, this volume);

– and use of 'operating principles' and 'cognitive comparison' of input models or recasts and learner utterances in interactionist theories (Doughty, 2001; R.Ellis, 1995; Mackey et al., this volume; Nelson, 1987).

This means that proposals for the second order abilities suggested in Figure 1 should, where possible, be motivated by these theoretical constructs, and related to acquisition processes and the cognitive resources that implement them. Crucial to this is the notion of 'components' of the information processing demands of *tests* which mediate this relationship. Sternberg (1977, and this volume) and Pellegrino and Glaser (1979) identified a series of these, holding the view that;

> 'the significant use of measures of intelligence and aptitude is not primarily for the purposes of prediction, but for indicating how intellectual performance can be improved. This desired goal might be achieved if individual differences could be interpreted in terms of processes that enhance or retard cognitive performance. Conditions of education might then be implemented that adapt to these individual characteristics…'(Pellegrino & Glaser, 1979, p.61).

From this 'componential' perspective, Figure 1 attempts to describe how 'cognitive comparison' as Doughty (2001) has described it, might be related to a relevant measure or test of one of the primary abilities (pattern recognition) contributing to the hypothesized second order ability of noticing the gap (NTG). This is done by identifying 'compare' as a theoretically relevant component process of the test of the primary ability, pattern recognition (as operationalized, for example, in Sasaki's (1996) sound symbol test of pattern recognition) which underlies the second order noticing the gap ability.

Clearly, each of the above mentioned, theoretical proposals for relationships between input, output and SLA processes (triggering, chunking, competition etc) has different consequences for how a relevant measure of IDs in cognitive capacities can be identified. In some cases, such as Anderson's theory of skill learning, the theory is explicit about the relationship between mechanisms and cognitive resources, and areas of potentially important IDs in abilities. However, in other cases, such as triggering in UG, or mechanisms for 'implicit' learning in Reber's (1989) theory, IDs in cognitive resources and abilities are proposed to be irrelevant. I deal with this issue in the following section.

The fundamental difference hypothesis and the fundamental similarity hypothesis

Two, complementary, hypotheses in the SLA literature both argue that IDs in cognitive resources and abilities are fundamental to understanding SLA processes and the causes of variation in levels of adult language learning attainment. Bley-Vroman's (1990) Fundamental Difference Hypothesis (FDH) contrasts L1 and adult L2 acquisition, proposing that L1 acquisition and adult SLA are fundamentally different since post critical period adults have no access to the domain specific 'innate' learning mechanisms that guide L1 development. Adult language learners must rely on L1 knowledge, plus domain general problem solving procedures in L2 learning, and IDs in the resources and abilities these problem solving procedures draw on contribute to differentials in levels of L2 attainment. The Fundamental Similarity Hypothesis (FSH) (Robinson, 1996b, 1997a) describes only adult L2 learning, but complements Bley-Vroman's FDH, arguing that in adulthood there is no evidence for a dissociation between dual systems of 'unconscious' implicit learning (Reber, 1989), or L2 acquisition (Krashen, 1981), and conscious explicit 'learning'. The general cognitive abilities contributing to focal attention allocation, 'noticing' (Schmidt & Frota, 1986), and rehearsal in memory (Robinson, 1995b, in press; Williams, 1999) are argued to be implicated in the learning that results from exposure to L2 input in any condition. However, experimental task, and classroom learning conditions differ in the extent to which they predispose the input to be processed, and it is these differences, interacting with the structure of information processing abilities, that contribute largely to differences in learning outcomes. Implicit and explicit learning, and separate learning systems, may be ways of distinguishing child and adult learning, as Bley-Vroman (1990) claims, but no longer dissociable processes once maturational constraints make access to ontogenetically earlier evolved implicit learning mechanisms problematic, and once domain independent problem solving procedures become established in the adult. Recent findings from two areas of IDs research relevant to these issues are described below.

UG, access, age and IDs

Given the proposed modularity of input-systems to central processes (which IDs clearly *do* affect), and informational 'encapsulation' of fast obligatory processing in the language module in some accounts of UG (see e.g., Fodor, 1983), and assuming, contrary to the FDH, that modular representations remain fully accessible in adult SLA (Schwartz, 1986), there would seem to be little way in which IDs in the cognitive processes and abilities described in Figure 1 could contribute to differentials in the ability to successfully detect 'triggers'. Recent IDs research has addressed this issue. Ross, Sasaki and Yoshinaga (this volume), working in the Principles and Parameters UG framework — and targeting an aspect of core grammar where triggering would be expected to have an effect — examined the influence of aptitude (Sasaki's, 1996, Language Aptitude Battery for the Japanese, LABJ) on intuitions of the grammaticality of subjacency violations by Japanese learners of English, who differed in their critical-period language learning profiles. Results showed, that for the three groups (those who had naturalistic exposure in childhood; teenage L2 learners; and foreign language learners) IDs in grammatical analytic abilities systematically emerged to positively influence post critical period learners grammaticality judgements, but showed little relationship to the accuracy of judgements of those with childhood L2 exposure. Related to this DeKeyser (2000), in a partial replication of an earlier study by Johnson and Newport, found that of 57 adult Hungarian-speaking immigrants to the US, very few adult immigrants scored within the range of child arrivals on a grammaticality judgement test, and that for all adults there were strong significant positive correlations of verbal analytic ability and performance (using a modified version of the WS subtest of the MLAT, aptitude complex 4 in Figure 1). The grammatical sensitivity, analytic component of aptitude was not a significant predictor for child arrivals. These findings suggest that post critical period learning mechanisms, as Bley-Vroman has claimed, are influenced by IDs in relevant 'problem solving' capacities, in particular, metalinguistic ability, in contrast to pre-critical period learning.

Harley and Hart (1997, this volume) went beyond these findings by examining the interaction of IDs in aptitude and age with learning outcome, *and* learning condition (exposure during immersion education, versus exposure during a 3 month bilingual home stay in Quebec by English native speaking children). Harley and Hart (1997) found that aptitude as measured by measures of memory for text predicted successful learning for pre-critical period, early immersion students, whereas post-critical period, late immersion students' learning was significantly and positively related to measures of language analytic ability (using a measure based on Pimsleur's Language Aptitude Battery). Suspecting that the correlation between language analytic ability and achievement for the older learners may have been found because the mode of instruction in the late immersion classes was of a more 'analytic' orientation than in the early immersion classrooms Harley and Hart (this volume) conducted their follow up study. The same relationship, though weaker, between gain during naturalistic exposure in the three-month home stay and language analytic abilities was found, though no relationship was found there between gain and memory ability.

The findings of DeKeyser, and Harley and Hart, of course, can't be taken as clear evidence for or against access to UG for post critical period learners, since in these studies the outcome measure was not acquisition of a specific feature of grammar hypothesized by the property theory to be triggered by exposure to a certain class of input (however, it *was* in the Ross et al. study). Rather, in DeKeyser's case, it was grammaticality judgements of a wide range of structures, and in Harley and Hart's case it was changes in proficiency, assessed by a number of tests of listening/reading comprehension, and oral/written production. Nevertheless, taken together the studies suggest that age and aptitude(s) interact in predicting language learning, with precritical period learning related to a different pattern of abilities than post critical period learning (as Bley Vroman's FDH predicts).

A way to interpret within the framework proposed here is suggested in Figure 1. The abilities contributing to aptitude complexes 2 and 3 in Figure 1 are largely drawn on during pre critical period learning, whereas the abilities comprising aptitude complex 4 are also drawn on in post critical period learning (cf. Karmiloff Smith, 1992). It seems possible, and researchable, that metalinguistic abilities, as represented by aptitude complex 4 in Figure 1, are also related to the abilities described in aptitude complex 1, which lead learners to 'notice the gap'.

Incidental learning and aptitude

The studies reviewed above also suggest that learning context (instructed immersion, versus home stay exposure) exhibits an influence on the abilities-outcome relationship, with naturalistic 'incidental' adult learning during the home stay exposure being relatively less sensitive to aptitude differences than instructed classroom learning — which as Harley and Hart, this volume, note, was analytic in orientation, therefore favoring those learners with the abilities measured by aptitude complex 4 in Figure 1. The issue of the sensitivity of aptitude measures to incidental, naturalistic learning during adulthood is taken up and considered in relation to the FSH, and findings from recent laboratory studies of SLA in the chapter by Robinson, in the following section of this volume.

Robinson takes as his starting point claims by Reber (1989, 1993) and Krashen (1981, 1982) that implicit (unaware) and incidental (non intentional) learning are insensitive to individual differences in cognitive abilities measured by intelligence, or language aptitude tests, in contrast to explicit, and intentional instructed learning. Reber has argued that there are two distinct *modes* of adult learning — implicit (unintentional, inaccessible to awareness) as revealed in transfer test evidence of above chance accurate induction of the rules of the letter display in the memorize only condition — and explicit (intentional, and accessible to awareness), as revealed by the, often poorer, performance of subjects asked to find the rules. Implicit learning (and memory) processes, Reber argues, are phylogenetically and ontogenetically earlier evolved than their explicit counterparts. IDs are claimed not to affect implicit processes, which show very little population variance, in contrast to explicit processes which are sensitive to IDs, and which exhibit large variance in the population (Reber, Walkenfield & Hernstadt, 1991; cf. Feldman, Kerr & Streissguth, 1995). Implicit processes are also argued to be robust in the face of aging and neurological insult, whereas explicit processes are much more affected by them (Reber & Allen, 2000).

Similarly, Krashen (1981, 1982, 1985) has proposed a dual-system theory of SLA, and claims aptitude tests measure the abilities drawn on in conscious 'learning', but not in unconscious 'acquisition', or incidental learning during processing for meaning. Supporting this Zobl (1992, 1995) has claimed that within group variance in L2 learning during meaning focused instructional treatments is much lower than when learning in formS focused instructional treatments.

In a previous study, Robinson (1996b, 1997a) found significantly less variance in transfer test evidence of grammar learning (English) for adult Japanese learners who were instructed in easy and hard pedagogic rules then asked to apply them to examples during training, than for implicit learners (who as in the implicit 'unaware' conditions of Reber's experiments were instructed only to memorize co-occurring stimuli in sentences viewed during training), or for incidental learners (instructed only to process sentences viewed during training for meaning), or for learners instructed to search for rules. However, that study also showed aptitude, as measured by the WS, and PA subtests of the MLAT, positively affected learning in all conditions *except* the incidental, meaning focussed condition (see Robinson, 1997a, p. 67). In other words, in contrast to learners in the other conditions, those learners who had incidentally gained grammatical knowledge of the easy and hard rules while processing for meaning did so *without* drawing on the abilities measured by the aptitude tests. This finding, while contrary to the predictions of Reber for implicit L2 learning,apparently *does* support the claims for the aptitude independence of incidental l2 learning made by Krashen. However, in line with the FSH I reasoned that the apparent aptitude insensitivity of learning in the incidental condition of Robinson (1997a) was probably because the measure of aptitude used in that study didn't measure the abilities needed to meet the conscious processing demands of the training task. That is, the measures of aptitude used draw only on the abilities contributing to aptitude complex 4 in Figure 1, not to aptitude complex 2 and 3.

In the follow up study (Robinson, this volume) a replication and extension of Reber et al. (1991), I further addressed the issue of the aptitude sensitivity of incidental learning. Three measures of IDs were used; a reading span measure of WM capacity (Osaka & Osaka, 1992), a measure of language learning aptitude (Sasaki's, 1996, LABJ), and a short form of the Wechsler Adult Intelligence Scale (as in Reber et al.). In the incidental learning condition participants first rote learned translation equivalents of words in an unknown language (Samoan) then viewed 450 sentences in two training sessions (lasting approximately three and a half hours, spaced from three to five days apart) in order to answer comprehension questions. Comprehension was high, at over 95% correct, for all subjects on the last trial of training. Results of immediate, one week, and six month delayed posttests comprising, a computer delivered grammaticality judgement test, an aural grammaticality judgement test; and a guided sentence production test, showed positive correlations of incidental Samoan grammar learning with aptitude and WM scores, though not with intelligence. The strongest pattern of significant positive correlations with incidental Samoan grammar learning was for the reading span measure of WM (with aural grammaticality judgements, and guided production, on immediate, one week and six month delayed posttests). This most clearly, of the three ID measures used, *matches the processing demands* of the training task, i.e., reading sentences for meaning, while incidentally attending to, and in many cases learning, aspects of the grammar.

While this finding for a strong relationship between WM for text and incidental learning from written input is therefore support for the FSH, interestingly, once again, aptitude, as measured by Sasaki's LABJ (which consists of tests of grammatical sensitivity, paired associate learning, and phonemic sensitivity, and is similar in design to the MLAT used in the earlier study), was only very weakly related to incidental learning on one, six month delayed, measure of guided sentence production. This, I would argue, confirms the position taken at the beginning of this chapter, and illustrated in Figure 1, that sets of abilities, or aptitude complexes, may be differentially related to learning outcomes that result from learning under different processing conditions. In summary, the reported results demonstrate, contrary to the claims of Krashen, that adult incidental learning of natural L2 grammar during processing for meaning is sensitive to measures of IDs in cognitive capacities, but only where these are relevant to the *consciously regulated processing demands* of the learning task (the FSH).

Summary of the aptitude complex/ability differentiation framework

Let me now bring together the hypotheses I have described, and show how I think they are related, defining the Aptitude Complex/Ability Differentiation framework I have outlined in this chapter;

1. There are child-adult differences in language learning; adults rely heavily on general problem solving abilities and exhibit much greater variation in levels of attainment (the FDH). But the Fundamental Difference Hypothesis alone does not explain *why* variation in levels of attainment should be so great.

2. The information processing demands of tasks draw differentially on cognitive abilities, or aptitude complexes (the ACH).

3. Therefore, adult learning under any condition is fundamentally similar, since it is a result of the interaction between a pattern of cognitive abilities and the consciously mediated processing demands of the task (the FSH).

4. Points 2 and 3 together help explain variation in adult L2 learning outcomes;
(i) patterns of abilities need to be matched to learning tasks and conditions to be effective, and they often aren't; and (ii) some learners may have differentiated abilities (a number of High-High's, as well as High-Low's, and Low-Low's

in aptitude complexes) (i.e., exhibit multiple aptitudes), whereas others have less differentiated abilities (High-Low's, and Low-High's) (i.e., exhibit a stronger general aptitude factor) (the ADH). (iii) It follows that for groups of learners with more differentiated abilities, there will be more variation in learning in any one environment, or on any one task (i.e., less matching of abilities and processing demands) than for groups of learners with less differentiated abilities.

Conclusion: research issues for SLA theory and pedagogy

Four issues future research in this framework could address are raised briefly here, in conclusion.

Aptitude treatment/pedagogic technique interactions

Firstly, in the framework I have proposed here it will be important to study the effects of individual differences in the cluster of abilities (aptitude complexes) that are hypothesized in Figure 1 to support language learning under particular conditions of exposure. Such aptitude-treatment interaction studies are theoretically important, since they can help to cast light on the cognitive correlates and components of implicit, incidental, and explicit L2 acquisition processes, as I have argued above (see also DeKeyser, in press, for review, and Robinson, Chapter 10, this volume).

Aptitude-treatment interaction studies are also particularly important in the light of recent developments in L2 pedagogy, such as the use of various interventionist techniques to deliver focus on form (see Doughty & Williams, 1998; Long & Robinson, 1998; Doughty, 2001) in communicative classrooms. For example, do those learners scoring high on measures of perceptual speed and pattern recognition, which I have argued may contribute to the ability to notice the gap (NTG), outperform learners scoring lower on these measures when instruction involves learning from the implicit negative feedback available in recasts? One study (Robinson, 1999; Robinson & Yamaguchi, 1999) has suggested this is so, since learners high in phonological sensitivity (measured using Sasaki's sound symbol correspondence test of pattern recognition) were also those who showed most evidence of pre to posttest gain in percentage correct relative clause use (the form targeted by recasts in the study) as assessed by an elicited imitation measure.

Figure 1 also proposes that memory for contingent speech (MCS) will contribute to the ability to notice the gap and learn from the information available in recasts. This has also found to be so in the study of the effect of IDs in phonological working memory on noticing and uptake from recasts reported by Mackey, et al. (this volume) with the caveat that learners at lower developmental levels showed stronger positive correlations of working memory capacity, noticing and uptake than learners at higher developmental levels.

Uptake of learning from other techniques for focus on form, other than the use of recasting, are also likely to be affected by IDs in the abilities drawn on by the aptitude complexes described in Figure 1. One example is the use of visual input enhancement techniques to provide a flood of instances of a particular form (see e.g., White, 1998). This is likely to be related to the third aptitude complex for incidental learning from written text, drawing on working memory capacity, and speed of working memory for contingent text (MCT), as well as deep semantic processing (DSP). In contrast, input processing instruction, as described by Van Patten (1996) may be a technique for inducing focus on form that is differentially affected by the fourth aptitude complex illustrated in Figure 1 — particularly the grammatical sensitivity component of what I have termed metalinguistic rule rehearsal (MRR). No studies of processing instruction or input enhancement, to date, have used such ID measures to examine the extent to which effects of instruction are sensitive to IDs in these aptitude complexes, but it will be important to do so if a clearer understanding of what 'causes' the effects of these different forms of intervention is to be achieved.

In summary, matching instructional *treatments*, and also different *techniques* for focus on form that those treatments may make use of, to aptitude complexes will be an important element of optimally effective classroom L2 instruction and is an area of needed research. The full range of focus on form techniques described by Doughty and Williams (1998), from the least communicatively intrusive 'input flood', to the most intrusive, 'input processing' or 'metalinguistic instruction', can be expected to be differentially related to clusters of cognitive processing and learning abilities, i.e., aptitude complexes. Using such measures of IDs in aptitude complexes as covariates in studies aiming to assess the global effects of focus on form, versus focus on formS, and focus on meaning (see Long, 1991) on instructed SLA will therefore be important to further clarifying overall differences in effect size attributable to these global treatments (see Norris & Ortega, 2000).

Ability differentiation

A second area for research in the proposed framework concerns the issue of whether abilities contributing to aptitude complexes can be clearly differentiated, such that learners high in, for example noticing the gap and memory for contingent speech (High-High) can be clearly distinguished from learners high in only one (High-Low), or low in both of these (Low-Low). If so, then the important further claim of the ability differentiation hypothesis (the ADH) could then be addressed, i.e., that for those learners with more differentiated abilities, there will be more variation between them in learning in any one environment, or on any one task, or from any one focus on form technique, than for those learners with less differentiated abilities.

Age related changes in abilities

The proposed framework also offers potential explanations for age-related changes and differentials in learning processes and capacities (as described by Harley & Hart, and Ross et al., this volume). For example, Salthouse (1996) has proposed that declines in processing speed across the lifespan can explain the apparent age-related declines on a variety of memory, problem-solving, reasoning and other cognitive tasks. If noticing the gap is an important aspect of learning in naturalistic environments, during oral interaction, as suggested in Figure 1, and if processing speed contributes to this ability, this could explain, in part, child-adult differences in learning in such environments — children of course being much better — and additionally support arguments for the need to adopt more explicit techniques for focus on form, in addition to recasts, thereby facilitating such noticing for older adults during oral interaction in classrooms.

Operationalizing ability tests

Finally, developing appropriate measures and tests of the hypothesized abilities themselves (such as noticing the gap, NTG) will be an important agenda item for SLA oriented individual differences research. For example, is the ability to notice the gap best measured by the inspection time (for perceptual speed, see Anderson, 1992, and also Salthouse, 1996), and sound symbol tests (for pattern recognition, see Sasaki, 1996; Robinson, and Ross et al., this volume) I have nominated in Figure 1, or by other tests?

These are issues, and challenges, and a *program* for future research, with potentially important theoretical, and practical pedagogic consequences.

Note

* I thank Martin Bygate, Robert DeKeyser, Jan Hulstijn, Alison Mackey, Jonathan Newton, Miyuki Sasaki, Mark Sawyer, Richard Schmidt and Larry Selinker for comments on an earlier version of this paper, which appeared in *Second Language Research, 17*, 368–392. I also thank the Aoyama Gakuin Soken Research Institute for supporting the Language and Comprehension Research Project, and the writing of this paper.

Empirical Studies

CHAPTER 7

The motivational basis of language learning tasks*

Zoltán Dörnyei
University of Nottingham

Introduction

The study of *language learning tasks* offers a particularly fruitful research direction towards the understanding of how instructed second language acquisition (SLA) actually takes place. By focusing on tasks, researchers are able to break down the complex, prolonged learning process into discrete segments with well-defined boundaries, thereby creating researchable behavioural units that have a well-definable profile in terms of the L2 input/output and the language processing operations involved. Thus, tasks can be seen as primary instructional variables or building blocks of classroom learning, and for research purposes they can be used as "logical models that describe what students are doing in classrooms and the context of their actions" (Winne & Marx, 1989, p. 224). For this reason, during the past decade SLA research has paid increasing attention to the analysis of tasks, looking at them both from a theoretical (language processing) and a methodological (instructional design) perspective (e.g. Bygate, 1999; Bygate, Skehan & Swain, 2001, Crookes & Gass, 1993a, 1993b; Dörnyei & Kormos, 2000; R.Ellis, 2000; Foster, 1998; Foster & Skehan, 1996; Long & Crookes, 1992; Robinson, 1995a, 2001a, 2001b; Skehan, 1998a, 1998b; Skehan & Foster, 1997, 1999; Swain & Lapkin, 2000; Willis, 1996; Yule & Powers, 1994).

Taking tasks as the basic level of analysis is also a logical step in the study of motivation to learn a foreign/second language (L2). Traditionally, L2 motivation was examined in a broad sense, by focusing on the learners' overall and generalised disposition towards learning the L2, but the 1990's shifted the emphasis towards a more situated approach, with more and more studies investigating how student motivation is reflected in concrete classroom events and processes (for a recent review, see Dörnyei, 2001). While the former macro perspective is more relevant from a social psychological perspective as it allows researchers to characterise and compare the motivational pattern of whole learning communities and then to draw inferences about intercultural communication and affiliation, the latter micro perspective is more in line with an educational approach whereby the significance of motivation is seen in its explanatory power of why learners behave as they do in specific learning situations. This emerging new perspective of motivation has often been referred to as the 'situation-specific' approach (cf. Dörnyei, 1996; Julkunen, 1989, 2001), and the study of *task motivation* can be seen in many ways as the culmination of this approach: motivation can hardly be examined in a more situated manner than within a task-based framework.

In the light of these considerations, the purpose of this paper is to examine the main characteristics of task motivation. As a preliminary, we should note that although the understanding of the motivational processes fuelling the quantity and quality of learners' on-task behaviour is highly relevant both from a theoretical and a practical point of view, motivational psychology in the past has not generated substantial research on the subject (for a valuable exception, see Winne & Marx, 1989). This paper will address one key aspect of task motivation, its *dynamic nature*, examining how motivation is shaped by various internal and external forces/conditions in an interactive and ongoing manner. I will argue that the actual degree of motivational force associated with an individual's specific on-task behaviour is the composite outcome of a number of distinct motivational influences, many of which are related to the various broader 'contexts' each task is surrounded with, such as:

- the language class the task takes place in;
- the language course the class is part of;
- the school that offers the language course; and
- the particular language that the course is targeting.

I believe that all these 'contexts' function as '*motivational contingencies*' in that they have some bearing on the final task motivation. I will propose a process-oriented approach that is suited for an analysis of such dynamic relationships, and I will also present empirical data from a task-based classroom study that examined the motivational basis of L2 learners' task engagement.

Main aspects of task motivation

In order to study the motivational characteristics of instructional tasks, we first need a definition of what a 'task' is. In view of the conception proposed above whereby instructional tasks are discrete units of situated learning behaviours, the most important specification for a 'task' is the identification of its boundaries, that is, determining when a particular task starts and ends. For the purpose of this study I will conceive a learning task as a complex of various goal-oriented mental and behavioural operations that students perform during the period between the teacher's initial task instructions and the completion of the final task outcome[1]. Accordingly, learning tasks constitute the interface between educational goals, teacher and students.

Let us start the examination of task motivation by considering a basic distinction proposed by Tremblay, Goldberg and Gardner (1995), who distinguished *trait* and *state motivation*, the former involving stable and enduring dispositions, the latter transitory and temporary responses or conditions. The trait/state distinction has been applied in psychology with regard to a number of different individual difference variables (e.g. anxiety; cf. MacIntyre, 1999, this volume) and from the point of view of motivation this dichotomy makes good sense: It is highly likely that, when confronted with a particular task, a learner will be motivated both by generalised, task-independent factors (e.g. overall interest in the subject matter) and situation-specific, task-dependent factors (e.g. the challenging nature of the task). Task motivation would then be the composite of these two motivational sources (cf. Julkunen, 2001).

Although the trait/state approach is a possible way of conceptualising task motivation, its weakness is that it suggests a rather static conception. Instructional tasks involve a series of learner behaviours that can last for a considerable period (e.g. up to several hours) and it is unlikely that the learner's motivation during this period will remain constant. Thus, instead of assuming a simple and stable 'state motivation' component to account for the situation-specific aspect of task motivation, a more accurate characterisation may be provided by taking a *process-oriented approach* that, as the term suggests, looks at the dynamic motivational processes that take place during task completion. The validity of such a conception has received empirical confirmation in a recent study by MacIntyre, MacMaster and Baker (2001), who found a clear factor analytic distinction between what they termed "attitudinal motivation" (associated with Gardner's approach) and "action motivation" (associated with Kuhl's process-oriented '*action control*' approach — see below).

Motivation from a process-oriented perspective

A *process-oriented approach* attempts to account for the ongoing changes of motivation over time. Looking at it from this perspective, motivation is not seen as a static attribute but rather as a dynamic factor that displays continuous fluctuation, going through certain ebbs and flows. In 1998, István Ottó and I attempted to draw up a process model that would describe this evolution (Dörnyei & Ottó, 1998), outlining how initial wishes and desires are first transformed into goals and then into operationalized intentions, and how these intentions are enacted, leading (hopefully) to the accomplishment of the goal and concluded by the final evaluation of the process. Drawing on the work of German psychologists Heinz Heckhausen and Julius Kuhl (e.g. Heckhausen, 1991; Heckhausen & Kuhl, 1985; Kuhl & Beckmann, 1994), we suggested that from a temporal perspective at least three distinct phases of the motivational process should be separated (see Figure 1, for a schematic representation):

– *Preactional stage:* First, motivation needs to be *generated* — the motivational dimension related to this initial phase can be referred to as *choice motivation,* because the generated motivation leads to the selection of the goal or task that the individual will pursue.

– *Actional stage:* Second, the generated motivation needs to be actively *maintained* and *protected* while the particular action lasts. This motivational dimension has been referred to as *executive motivation,* and it is particularly relevant to learning in classroom settings, where students are exposed to a great number of distracting influences, such as off-task thoughts, irrelevant distractions from others, anxiety about the tasks, or physical conditions that make it difficult to complete the task.

– *Postactional stage:* Finally, there is a third phase following the completion of the action — termed *motivational retrospection* — which concerns the learners' *retrospective evaluation* of how things went. The way students process their past experiences in this retrospective phase will determine the kind of activities they will be motivated to pursue in the future.

Because students are rarely in the position of choosing the tasks they would like to engage in, with regard to the understanding of task motivation it is the second, actional, stage that is of the greatest importance for us. According to a process-oriented conception, the learner enters this actional stage with a certain level of motivation (which can be called the 'instigation force'), but very soon a new set of motivational influences — associated with the immediate learning

Preactional stage	Actional stage	Postactional stage
Choice motivation	**Executive motivation**	**Executive motivation**
Motivational functions: – Setting goals – Forming intentions – Launching action	*Motivational functions:* – Generating and carrying out subtasks – Ongoing appraisal (of one's performancel) – Action control (self-regulation)	*Motivational functions:* – Forming causal attributions – Elaborating standards and strategies – Dismissing intention & further planning
Main motivational influences: – Various goal properties (e.g. goal relevance, specificity and proximity) – Values associated with the learning process itself, as well with its outcomes and consequences – Attitudes towards the L2 and its speakers – Expectancy of success and perceived coping potential – Learner beliefs and strategies – Environmental support or hindrance	*Main motivational influences:* – Quality of the learning experience (pleasantness, need significance, coping potential, self and social image) – Teachers' and parents' influence – Classroom reward- and goal structure (e.g. competitive or cooperative) – Influence of the learner group – Knowledge and use of self-regulatory strategies (e.g. goal setting, learning and self-motivating strategies)	*Main motivational influences:* – Attributional factors (e.g. attributional styles and biases) – Self-concept beliefs (e.g. self-confidence and self-worth) – Received feedback, praise, grades

Figure 1. A process model of learning motivation in the L2 classroom

situation — come into force, and a complex process of 'motivational processing' commences (Winne & Marx, 1989). This involves two interrelated submechanisms: *ongoing appraisal* and *action control*. While learners are engaged in a task, they continuously *appraise* the multitude of stimuli coming from the environment and the progress they have made towards the action outcome, comparing actual performances with predicted ones or with ones that alternative action sequences would offer. This appraisal process is closely linked with a second mechanism, *action control*, which refers to "knowledge and strategies used to manage cognitive and noncognitive resources for goal attainment" (Corno & Kanfer, 1993, p. 304). That is, action control processes denote self-regulatory processes that are called into force in order to enhance, scaffold or protect learning-specific action; active use of such mechanisms may 'save' the action when ongoing monitoring reveals that progress is slowing, halting or backsliding.

'Motivational processing', then, is seen as the interplay of the appraisal and the action control systems. Following Winne and Marx's (1989) reasoning, negative signals from the appraisal system may trigger the need to activate action control strategies, and if appropriate schemata are available, certain mental or behavioural adjustments are made and the motivational level necessary for sustaining action is restored. The effective operation of executive motivational processing is, therefore, the function of the learner's willingness to activate action control mechanisms and the availability of these (cf. Dörnyei, 2001, for more detail).

In a recent paper (Dörnyei, 2000), I have concluded that the main strength of a process-oriented approach with regard to the understanding of student motivation is that it makes it possible to interpret and integrate the manifold motivational factors that affect the student's learning behaviour in classroom settings. Using *time* as an organising principle provides a natural way of ordering the relevant motivational influences into various distinct stages of the motivational sequence along a temporal axis. However, one problematic aspect of such an approach is that it implies that the actional process in question is well-definable and occurs in relative isolation, without any interference from other ongoing activities the learner is engaged in. Regrettably, this is rarely true in the strict sense. Where exactly does 'action' start in an educational context? Consider, for example first-year college students: Where would be the borderline between pre-action and action in their case? At the point when they decides to study in higher education? Or enrol in a particular university? Or select the specific courses they will take? Or attend a particular class? Or engage in a particular activity within this class?

It seems logical to assume that taking all these steps will result in somewhat different, increasingly action-oriented contingencies or 'mind sets' in the students. This, however, means that the 'choice' phase of one actional step might happen simultaneously with the executive phase of another, resulting in complex interferences: For example, a British secondary school pupil is in the actional/executive stage of learning in the sense that he/she is actively attending school and trying to meet various curricular requirements, but at the same time he/she may still be in the preactional/choice phase in the sense that he/she may still be contemplating which 'A' level courses to take for specialisation.

Although I believe that the conception of task motivation as a complex of motivational influences associated with various levels of action-oriented contingencies or mind sets provides a more elaborate description than that offered by the trait/state approach, this conception is still incomplete if it does not take into account the *dynamic nature* of motivational processing. It is very likely that the various motivational influences *interact* with each other; for example, certain general orientations (such as an instrumental orientation) may cause the learner to perceive or responded to certain situation-specific motivational features differently from the perceptions/reactions associated with other orientations. In other words, an IF-THEN contingency can occur whereby motives of different levels of generalisation activate each other. Indeed, it is not difficult to find evidence for such IF-THEN contingencies in the L2 motivation literature. For example, in a study conducted by Noels, Clément and Pelletier (1999) focusing on the motivational impact of the language teacher's communicative/instructional style, the researchers have found that — quite logically — the degree of the teachers' support of student autonomy and the amount of informative feedback they provided were in a direct positive relationship with the students' sense of self-determination (autonomy) and enjoyment. However, this directive influence did not reach significance with students who pursued learning primarily for extrinsic (instrumental) reasons, which indicated that those learners who studied a language primarily because they had to were less sensitive to this aspect of teacher influence than those who did it of their own free will.

In my own research, in a study conducted together with Judit Kormos (Dörnyei & Kormos, 2000) we found that students with a more positive versus a more negative attitude towards a particular task displayed significant differences from each other in a number of respects. Their linguistic self-confidence only affected their task engagement among students with a positive attitude towards the task, and social factors such as the learners' social status (i.e. social standing/position in class) affected task engagement positively amongst students with positive and negatively amongst students with negative task attitudes. In addition, when we changed the language of the tasks from English as a second language to the students' mother tongue (L1), we obtained a strikingly different motivational pattern, with several significant *negative* correlations emerging between motivational variables and task engagement factors: in the L1 version learners who did not particularly like the English classes and did not see much point in learning English in general appeared to be more active than their motivated peers. These findings suggested to us that the predictor variables of task performance constituted a complex, multi-level and hierarchical construct.

Research question and design

The study reported in this paper is a follow-up to the Dörnyei and Kormos (2000) investigation and uses data from the same large-scale British-Hungarian research project conducted together with Martin Bygate (University of Leeds) and Anita Csölle, Dorottya Holló, Krisztina Károly and Nóra Németh (all from Eötvös University Budapest). The research objective was to examine a yet uncharted aspect of motivational processing, the motivational impact of the fellow-participant in a task. It has been suggested by several scholars in the past that peer influences constitute an important motivational factor (for a review, see Dörnyei, 2001), but I am not aware of any concrete research that would have examined this relationship in actual terms. Thus, the main research question of this study is to examine the extent to which task motivation is *co-constructed*, that is, shaped by the dynamic interplay of the task participants' motivation.

The design of this study was relatively straightforward: Following a correlational research design, a number of individual difference (mainly motivational) and language variables were identified and assessed, and then correlations were computed between them. The language variables were objective measures of the participants' actual language output in a communicative language task (performed in dyads): the *size of speech* produced (measured by the number of words) and the *number of turns* the participants' exchange comprised. These were taken as an index of the learners' *task engagement*, which is a central issue in instructed SLA because it is a prerequisite to any language processing to take place; to put it broadly, if students are not actively involved in the instructional tasks and do not produce a certain amount of language output, L2 learning is unlikely to be effective in developing communicative skills. Therefore, all the cognitive and linguistic processes discussed in the L2 task literature depend, to some extent, on this initial condition. This importance attached to task engagement is consistent with findings in educational psychology; as Winne and Marx (1989, p. 225) summarise:

> In order to promote, facilitate, or develop students' knowledge and skills in any subject, contemporary research about learning converges on at least one clear prescription: Teachers must arrange for students to engage in cognitive activities in which they manipulate and transform information.

The individual difference variables included various attitudinal/motivational measures related to learning English in general and to the language course the students were attending in particular. Because the language measures concerned the quantity of the speech produced by the participants, one further individual difference variable was added to the research paradigm, the learners 'willingness to communicate' (WTC) in the L1, which refers to the person's general readiness to enter into discourse. According to McCroskey and Richmond (1987), WTC is a personality trait that is responsible for the "regularity in the amount of communication behaviour of an individual across situations" (p. 138) and it is related to a number of enduring personality variables such as introversion/extroversion, self-esteem and communication apprehension (for more details, see MacIntyre, Clément, Dörnyei & Noels, 1998, who conceptualised WTC in the L2 to be an important language learning variable).

In order to assess participant effects, I correlated the interlocutor's predictor and the speaker's criterion variables, that is, looked at the association between an individual's language output and his/her interlocutor's motivational disposition. Finally, correlations were also computed between the motivational and language measures with the dyads as the basic units of analysis, that is, with the communication partners' scores pooled.

Method

Participants

The participants of the investigation were 44 Hungarian students (aged 16–17) studying English at an intermediate level in 5 classes in 2 Budapest secondary schools. The two schools were of the same type, "gimnázium" (similar to the former British grammar schools), providing general instruction and preparing students for further studies in higher education. The English curriculum involved teaching integrated skills with an emphasis on developing communicative competence and students in all five groups used coursebooks published in Great Britain. The group sizes ranged from 12–16 (but not every student participating in the large-scale longitudinal project was present when the data reported here were gathered).

Task

The task used is the study was an *oral argumentative task*. This task was designed as an interactive problem-solving activity, aimed at eliciting arguments concerning everyday school matters (see Appendix). Students (working in pairs) were given a list of items and they were asked to select and rank-order some of these individually, based on an imaginary situation. Following this, they were to compare with their partners their preferences and come to a compromise by means of a negotiation process.

Data collection and processing

All the data collection for the study was carried out during the students' regular English classes. The students' performance on the research task was recorded and then transcribed. As mentioned above, we used two measures to describe the quantity of learner engagement, the *speech size* measured by the number of words produced and the *number of turns* generated by the participants. This second measure was included because it was assumed that the successful completion of a problem-solving, negotiation-based task such as the one we had used would require a considerable amount of turn-taking to take place. In contrast, a hasty and unmotivated solution in which no real arguments or attempts at persuading the interlocutor are involved can be achieved by using very few turns. Therefore, the number of turns used by a speaker can be seen as an indicator of the level of student involvement. We must note that there is a difference between the two language measures in that the number of turns depends more directly on the quality of the joint interaction than the number of words does. For example, if the interaction itself is not very productive but one person offers lengthy monologues, this will result in a high word count but a low turn number on his/her part. Indeed, turn number is a function of the interlocutor's active contribution, since in turn-taking the number of turns produced by the two speakers is by definition roughly equal.

Students also filled in a *self-report questionnaire,* which focused on various attitudinal/motivational issues, based on Clément, Dörnyei & Noels's (1994) instrument specifically developed for Hungarian learners. The data from the questionnaire were computer coded and the number of variables was reduced by computing six multi-item scales (summarised below) by summing the thematically corresponding items. As mentioned before, a seventh background variable was added to these six scales, the learners' *willingness to communicate* (WTC) in their L1, in order to account for their general communication orientation. This scale was obtained by another self-report questionnaire and the actual items used in our study were adapted from an instrument developed by the originators of the construct, McCroskey and Richmond (1991).

Because there was considerable between-group variation in the learners' language output (recall that the learners came from five class groups in two schools), we computed standard scores within each class for both the motivational and language variables and used these rather than the raw scores for the computations. This involved mathematically converting the distribution of the scores within each class sample in a way that the mean was 0 and the standard deviation 1, which is an established statistical method for compensating for within-sample differences before pooling the data from various subgroups (see Dörnyei, 2001; Gardner, 1985).

Variables in the study

The following list summarises the seven individual difference variables used in the study, with their description, the number of items they were made up of and the Cronbach Alpha internal consistency reliability coefficient for each scale. The mean Cronbach Alpha coefficient across the six attitudinal/motivational scales is .76, which is adequate for such scales. The coefficient for WTC is lower because the scale deliberately sampled responses concerning different social situations[2].

– *Integrativeness*	A broad positive disposition towards the L2 speaker community, including an interest in their life and culture and a desire for contact with them (7 items, Cronbach α = .80)
– *Incentive values of English proficiency*	A broad factor associated with the various benefits — pragmatic and L2 use-related — of L2 proficiency; e.g. "Learning English is important for me because I may need English in the future (work, further education)" (8 items, Cronbach α = .80)
– *Attitudes towards the English course*	E.g. "I like the English classes"; "I wish we had more English classes at school" and "The things we learn in the English classes will be useful in the future" (3, .83)
– *Linguistic self-confidence*	Factor associated with a favourable self-conception of language aptitude, a satisfaction with progress and a belief in one's ability to succeed in L2 learning; e.g. "I am sure I'll be able to learn English" (6 items, Cronbach α = .76)
– *Language use anxiety*	Anxiety experienced while using the L2; e.g. "I usually feel ill at ease when I have to speak English" and "I often become uncertain when I have to speak in the English classes" (2 items, Cronbach α = .73)
– *Task attitudes*	E.g. "I have found the tasks used in the project useful

for L2 learning" and "I liked the tasks used in the project" (2 items, Cronbach α = .61)

– *Willingness to*   *(WTC)*The learners' readiness to enter into discourse
  communicate   with people in different social situations; e.g. "Standing in the bus stop with friends" (5 items, Cronbach α = .48; see also Note 2)

Results and discussion

Correlations between task attitudes and the other individual difference measures

Let us first look at the correlations between task attitudes and the other individual difference measures (see Table 1). Of the five correlations with motivational variables three are significant, indicating that — in accordance with Tremblay et al.'s (1995) and Julkunen's (2001) claims — the appraisal of the specific task was related to more general motivational variables. The strong correlation with *Course attitudes* was expected because task and course attitudes both concern classroom learning in a situated manner, and the significant correlation with *Integrativeness* is consistent with Gardner's (1985) theory (see MacIntyre, this volume) as well as past findings in Hungarian student samples (e.g. Clément, Dörnyei & Noels, 1994; Dörnyei & Clément, 2001). The positive association with *L2 use anxiety* is somewhat unexpected; it indicates that those learners who take the task more seriously experience more nervousness about speaking in the L2. Recent research by Dewaele (in press; Dewaele & Furnham, 2000) suggests that certain personality variables (e.g. psychoticism, extraversion and neuroticism) are directly related to the

Table 1. Correlations between 'Task attitudes' and the other individual difference variables

	Task attitudes
Integrativeness	.40**
Incentive values	.26
Course attitudes	.58***
Self-confidence	.07
L2 use anxiety	.37*
WTC	.21

$* = p<.05; ** = p<.01; *** = p<.001$

amount of language anxiety one experiences. We can speculate that the same personality variables might also affect one's attitudes towards a communicative task, which then would imply that the association between L2 anxiety and task attitudes is due to mediating personality effects. With regard to WTC, the non-significant correlation indicates that there is no evidence of a relationship between the learners' attitude towards the communicative task used in the study and their WTC orientation.

Correlations between the motivational and language variables

Table 2 presents the correlations between the seven individual difference and two language variables. The table reveals significant positive correlations between the language variables and the two most situation-specific variables, *Course attitudes* and *Task attitudes*, and presents a further significant correlation between *Self-confidence* and speech size. As the multiple correlations show, the motivational variables together explain roughly 35–40 per cent of the variance in the language measures. Although the overall magnitude of the coefficients in Table 2 is similar to correlations reported in the motivation literature, it is lower than what I originally expected. This is because, unlike most studies on L2 motivation in which the criterion measure is some sort of course achievement or standardised language proficiency score, in this investigation the obtained attitudinal/motivational variables were correlated with objective measures directly reflecting the participants' actual language behaviours in a concrete learning task. And since the relationship between motivation and learning behaviours is by definition stronger than that between motivation and learning achievement (because the latter is also influenced by

Table 2. Correlations between the language and the individual difference variables

	Words	Turns
Integrativeness	.17	.07
Incentive values	-.02	.30*
Course attitudes	.41**	.35*
Self-confidence	.35*	.23
L2 use anxiety	-.10	.00
Task attitudes	.35*	.48***
Multiple correlations	*.63*	*.59*
WTC	.25	.38*
Multiple correlations with WTC	*.68*	*.68**

* = *p*<.05; ** = *p*<.01; *** = *p*<.001

other, non-motivational factors such as the learners' ability, learning opportunities and instructional quality), this stronger relationship was expected to show up in the correlations.

With regard to WTC, it shows a significant positive correlation with the number of turns but not with the number of words produced. This is in accordance with the construct of WTC, since it is more a measure of whether someone will initiate talk rather than how much the person actually speaks. Looking at the multiple correlations that include the WTC measure (explaining 46 per cent of the variance), it is clear that WTC explains a considerable amount of unique variance in the language measures.

Separating high-task-attitude and low-task-attitude subsamples

One possible reason why some correlations reported in Table 2 are not as high as expected might be related to the diversity in the learners' task attitudes. Let us, for a moment, look at the task situation from the students' perspective. Although the language tasks were administered during the learners' regular English classes (as mentioned earlier, the study was part of a larger-scale task-based investigation), they were not part of the official syllabus but instead served research purposes. And even though we placed a great emphasis on 'selling' our project to the students, that is, on creating positive task attitudes, it was inevitable that not everybody took the activities equally seriously. We can guess, for example, that some of the students may have looked at our project as a welcome break from the serious, 'real' school activities, whereas others may have found our tasks pointless or a nuisance. This is, in fact, quite understandable and to a certain extent inevitable with a classroom-oriented investigation such as this; however, if this assumption is true, it would mean that the behaviour of some of the students (the ones who did not take the task seriously for some reason) was somewhat disinterested/random and not necessarily reflecting their motivation to learn the L2. Such disinterested task behaviour would, in turn, depress the motivation-behaviour correlation coefficients.

In order to test this hypothesis, I divided the sample into two subgroups based on the *Task attitudes* variable, by assigning learners to the 'high-task-attitude' subsample (LowS) if their score was lower than 4; this resulted in groups of 21 and 23, respectively. Following this, I repeated the correlation analysis reported above in the two subsamples separately (see Table 3)

The results in Table 3 confirm the assumption that the two subsamples

Table 3. Correlations between the language and the individual difference variables in the high- and low-task-attitude subsamples

	High-task-attitude learners		Low-task-attitude learners	
	Words	Turns	Words	Turns
Integrativeness	.44*	.14	-.12	-.08
Incentive values	-.01	.56**	-.11	.07
Course attitudes	.11	.07	.50*	.40
Self-confidence	.53*	.38	.27	.17
L2 use anxiety	-.19	-.22	-.18	.03
Task attitudes	.37	.59**	.19	.38
WTC	.46*	.60**	.07	.18

$* = p<.05; ** = p<.01$

show different characteristics in terms of the relationship between the motivational and language variables. In the HighS, speech size correlates highly significantly with *Integrativeness* and *Self-confidence*, and the number of turns shows a significant positive correlation with *Incentive values*; the same correlations in the LowS are non-significant. This means, firstly, that amongst the learners who had positive task attitudes, the confident ones outperformed the less confident ones, wich makes sense. Secondly, the significant correlations also indicate that learners who had more positive generalised motives to accompany their high situation-specific motives (i.e. task attitudes) also tended to perform better, wich is in accordance with the suggestion presented in the Introduction that task performance is fuelled by a combination of situation-specific and generalised motives.

In the LowS we find only one significant correlation with a language measure, which is consistent with the hypothesis that because these learners failed to take the task sufficiently seriously, their performance would be somewhat disinterested/random. However, the single emerging significant relationship, between *Course attitudes* and speech size, is very important: it shows that among the learners who displayed low task-attitudes, those who had a favourable disposition toward the language course in general participated more actively in the task than those who had unfavourable attitudes toward both the course and the task. In other words, the generalised positive disposition toward the whole course neutralised some of their negative attitudes towards the particular task. This finding indicates that situation-specific motives in educational settings involve at least two distinct levels — task-related and course-related — which provides evidence for the assumption that the complex of task motivation can be better described as a composite of multiple motivational influences related to the various actional/engagement contingencies than as a composite of trait and state motivation.

The most dramatic difference between the HighS and LowS occurs between WTC and the language measures. In the HighS, this relationship is indeed very strong: it explains 36% of the variance in the number of turns (as indicated by the correlation coefficient of .60), and even the somewhat lower (but still significant) correlation with the size of the learner's speech (.46) accounts for 21% of the variance. In contrast, the same correlations in the LowS are non-significant, which again attests to the disinterested/random nature of the performance of low-task-attitude students.

The motivational influence of the interlocutor

The results reported so far have generally supported a process-oriented conception of task motivation, and further support for this perspective would be gained if we could find indications of any impact of the interlocutor's level of motivation on his/her communication partner's task performance. That such an influence exists is a logical assumption because two interacting people affect each other in many ways, and it would also highlight the dynamic, negotiated nature of task motivation. To test this assumption, correlations were computed between the interlocutors' motivational variables and speaker's language output measures (see Table 4); in other words, if Sally and Johnny were paired, Table 4 presents the correlation between Sally's motivation and Johnny's language output.

The results shown in the table are noteworthy. For the whole sample, we find four significant correlations between the individual difference variables and the number of turns and only two with the number of words, wich is in line with the more 'mutual' nature of the former language variable (discussed earlier). The overall pattern provides strong evidence that the interlocutor's motivational disposition is related to the speaker's performance. If we break down the whole sample into HighS and LowS subgroups, we can see that interlocutor effects primarily concern the LowS, where they serve as a 'pulling force': if someone with a low task attitude is matched up with a more motivated peer, the chances are that the person's performance will improve. Although there are only three significant positive correlations in the Lows, we can find here four other correlations of .37, which is significant at the $p<.10$ level, indicating trends. All this points to a very consistent pattern.

Table 4. Correlations between the speakers' language measures and the interlocutors' attitudinal/motivational measures

	Whole sample		High-task-att.		Low-task-att.	
	Words	Turns	Words	Turns	Words	Turns
Integrativeness	.01	.08	-.15	-.20	.09	.21
Incentive values	.31*	.35*	.11	.19	.37	.37
Course attitudes	.25	.41**	.03	.35	.37	.42*
Self-confidence	.04	.20	.16	.26	-.07	.16
L2 use anxiety	.08	.03	-.19	.21	.37	.23
Task attitudes	.42**	.49**	.27	.22	.58**	.69***
WTC	-.01	.35*	.01	.40	.00	.35

$* = p<.05; ** = p<.01; *** = p<.001$

These interlocutor influences can be explained in two ways:

1.   One might argue that the influence is primarily *linguistic* — the partner's motivational disposition affects only the partner's own performance and it is only this increased (or decreased) performance that will indirectly affect the speaker's language output in that if someone's partner initiates more (or less) speech, this will make it easier (or more difficult) for the speaker to produce speech. In other words, if Johnny speaks more, one can argue that his partner, Sally, may also produce more speech simply by reacting to Johnny and completing adjacency pairs.

2.   The alternative explanation centres around *motivation* and states that the actual task motivation of the task participants is not independent from each other. If one is paired up with a highly motivated or unmotivated partner, this will affect the person's own disposition toward the task; that is, task motivation will be *co-constructed* by the task participants, with the interlocutor either pulling 'up' or 'down' the speaker.

I am more inclined towards the second explanation, primarily because I have found in the past that L2 learner interaction can be very uneven, with someone often speaking a great deal more than his/her interlocutor without being much affected by this imbalance. The real impact of the interlocutor on his/her communication partner is, I believe, caused by the 'spirit' he/she brings into the exchange, which functions as a motivational 'turn-on' or 'turn-off'. Looking at Table 4, we can also find some indirect support for this speculation in that the interlocutor's WTC does *not* affect the speaker's speech size. This shows that the fact that one's interlocutor is more talkative does not automatically increase one's language output — which is the basis of the linguistic explanation.

The motivation of the dyads

If it is true that task motivation is (at least partially) co-constructed, this would imply that looking at the communicating dyads — rather than the individual speakers — as the basic level of analysis will produce results of increased explanatory power with regard to the motivation-behaviour relationship. Table 5 presents correlations between the motivational and language variables for the 21 dyads that participated in the study. These correlations were obtained by pooling the data for the two people in each dyad.

Table 5. Correlations between the language and the individual difference variables for the 21 dyads (i.e. with the speaker's and the interlocutor's data pooled)

	Words	Turns
Integrativeness	.13	.09
Incentive values	.22	.43
Course attitudes	.49*	.48*
Self-confidence	.31	.28
L2 use anxiety	-.04	.01
Task attitudes	.72***	.73***
Multiple correlations	*.85** *	*.83** *
WTC	.34	.59**
Multiple correlations with WTC	*.87* *	*.90** *

* = $p<.05$; ** = $p<.01$; *** = $p<.001$

The coefficients in Table 5 are considerably higher than the corresponding correlations for the individual students reported in Table 2. Although some of the correlations do not reach statistical significance, this may in fact be due to the limited sample size caused by halving the number of cases when pooling the communication partners' data. The multiple correlations indicate that the motivational variables together explain 72 per cent of the variance in the total speech size and 69 per cent of the variance in the number of turns generated. These coefficients are over 30 per cent higher than the corresponding figures at the individual level (cf. Table 2), which provides strong support for the thesis of motivational co-construction. Furthermore, if we add the variance explained by WTC to that explained by the six motivational measures, we find that 76 per cent of the variance in speech size and 81 per cent of the variance in the number of turns are explained by the individual difference variables. These unusually high figures mean that at the dyad level the motivational variables accompanied by the WTC personality trait do an excellent job in explaining the bulk of the variance in the language performance measures.

Conclusion

Admittedly, this study has several limitations, the most notable ones being the small sample size and the fact that correlations do not indicate causation (and therefore we cannot take it for granted that the individual difference factors were the independent and the language measures the dependent variables). However, I believe that the results are consistent and powerful enough to suggest some valid patterns and tendencies.

Motivation-behaviour relationship and task based research

The results in this study support the assumption that when the relationship between motivation and concrete learning behavioural measures is assessed we can obtain considerably higher correlations than when motivation is related to global achievement measures. The magnitude of the multiple correlations in Table 5 indicates that if we take into account both communication partners' motivation at the same time, we can achieve highly satisfactory explanatory power, and if we also add an index of the participants' general communicational characteristics (i.e. WTC) to the equation, the individual difference variables account for the bulk of the variance in the language measures. This also confirms, in a more general sense, the suitability of adopting a task-based framework for the purpose of motivation research. Looking at the impact of motivation on concrete learning behaviours in a situated manner will result in a clearer and more elaborate understanding of L2 motivation than the traditional research practice whereby the most common criterion variable was a general achievement of proficiency measure. On the other hand, it must also be pointed out that such a situated approach will make motivation studies more difficult to compare to each other, especially if very different tasks were used.

The relationship between general and situation-specific motives

The findings confirm that both situation-specific and more general motives contribute to task motivation but the overall construct is more complex than the composite of state and trait motivation. It was argued that on-task behaviour is embedded in a series of broader actional contexts (e.g. going to a specific school, attending a particular class, taking up the study of a particular L2) and each of these contexts exert a certain amount of unique motivational influence. That is, it may be insufficient to assume that the learner enters the task situation with some 'trait motivation baggage' and to obtain task motivation this 'baggage' needs to be pooled with the motivational properties of the instructional task. Instead, engaging in a certain task activates a number of different levels of related motivational mindsets and contingencies, resulting in complex interferences.

Motivational processing and the dynamic co-construction of task motivation
The findings also support the conception of 'motivational processing' during task completion. The outcome of this processing is a function of a multitude of perceived information and stimuli, and in communicative L2 tasks that involve several participants, the interlocutors' motivational disposition is a key factor affecting the learner's appraisal and action control processes. In other words, task motivation is *co-constructed* by the task participants.

In sum, the main thesis of this paper is that the full complexity of task motivation becomes apparent only when we consider it within a larger context of dynamically interacting synchronic and diachronic factors and actions. This perspective requires a process-oriented approach which recognises that motivation is never static but is constantly increasing or decreasing depending on the various social influences surrounding action, the learner's appraisal of these influences and the action control operations the learner carries out on such motivational content.

Notes

* I am grateful to Jean-Marc Dewaele, Peter MacIntyre and an anonymous reviewer for their very insightful comments on an earlier draft. The final version of this chapter owes a lot to their suggestions.

1. We must note, however, that the teacher's and the students' views concerning these task boundaries might not coincide (MacIntyre, personal communication, 8 May 2001), which raises the broader question as to whether we can speak about the 'task' in general, without separating different task perceptions according to the teacher, the students and perhaps even the task designer (cf. Winne & Marx, 1989).

2. Students were to indicate on a six-point scale the extent to which they would engage in

an L1 conversation in the following five situations: standing in the bus stop with friends; asking questions in a public "teacher-student forum" at school; at a party where one doesn't know anybody; meeting a (not too close) acquaintance at the post office; and in the lift with a stranger.

Appendix

The task used in the study

You are a member of the school student committee. Your school wants to participate in the district's social life and asks students to offer their help. The following possible options have been suggested:

— Delivering lunch to elderly people in the district
— Publishing a local newsletter
— Helping out in the library
— Providing tourist information
— Performing for children in the kindergarten
— Collecting newspaper/wastepaper
— Feeding birds
— Maintaining the park
— Performing for elderly people
— Organising sports events

First, look at the list alone for three minutes and choose **5 activities** you would find interesting or useful. Put them on these lines *in the order of your preference.*

1. _____
2. _____
3. _____
4. _____
5. _____

Second, compare your list with your partner's. The lists are probably different. Your task is to find the best compromise with your partner and *prepare a final list of 3 activities* you together will recommend to the school management.

1. _____
2. _____
3. _____

You have 10 minutes to convince your partner about your ideas. Make sure you give reasons but remember that you *MUST come to an agreement on the best proposal.*

CHAPTER 8

The role of learners' language analytic ability in the communicative classroom[*]

Leila Ranta
University of Alberta

Introduction

The importance of a learner's language analytic ability in predicting success in second language (L2) learning was well established by research carried out in grammar-translation or audiolingual classrooms (Carroll, 1962). Since the advent of communicative language teaching (CLT), however, educators and scholars alike have cast doubt on the relevance of analytic abilities for L2 acquisition. Although recent studies suggest that language analytic ability continues to be a good predictor of success (Ehrman & Oxford, 1995), relatively little research has been conducted in classrooms that are truly communicative in nature. In this chapter, the findings from a study conducted in a unique language learning environment in Quebec, Canada are presented. The participants were francophone children studying in a five-month intensive ESL program offered at the grade 6 level. The instructional aims of the program focussed on the development of interpersonal communication skills through mainly oral activities rather than on English for academic purposes. A variety of L2 proficiency measures were administered over the course of one academic year; language analytic ability was measured using an error correction task in the L1. Although the L1 task did not have a strong, linear relationship with performance on the L2 proficiency measures, a cluster analysis revealed that language analytic ability was associated with strong performance on the L2 measures for the most successful learners and with weak performance for the least successful students. These results suggest that CLT as instructional treatment cannot wipe out the effect of aptitude differences among learners.

The role of learners' language analytic ability in the communicative classroom

In a recent decision, the Federal Court of Canada ruled that an employee of the federal civil service was discriminated against when she was rejected for language training and thereby lost a job promotion on the basis of poor performance on an aptitude test (Tibbetts, 2000). The test was condemned in the ruling for its emphasis on short-term memory and mimicry which overlooked "broader learning methods". The Public Service Commission used the Modern Language Aptitude Test (MLAT; Carroll, 1958; Carroll & Sapon, 1959) and subtests of the Pimsleur Language Aptitude Battery (PLAB; Pimsleur, 1966b) for the purposes of screening applicants for language training. Apparently, the judges felt that the kind of L2 communication skills required by government bureaucrats could be gained through other abilities than those measured by the aptitude test. Interestingly, this legal opinion is consistent with the views of some applied linguists. For example, Cook (1996, p. 101) discounts the relevance of aptitude, stating that the "MLAT mostly predicts how well a student will do in a course that is predominantly audiolingual in methodology rather than in a course taught by other methods". While Cook is more concerned with the inadequacies of the aptitude test, Krashen (1981) attacks the role of aptitude itself in the L2 acquisition process. He argues that "one characteristic of the ideal second language class is one in which aptitude will *not* predict differences in student achievement [...] because efficient acquisition is taking place for all students" (Krashen, 1981, p. 171). For Krashen (1982), efficient acquisition occurs when learners receive comprehensible input in a positive affective environment.

Krashen's statement echoes the belief of many language educators who see communicative language teaching (CLT) as a way of leveling the playing field for all learners. In technical terms, they see the situation in terms of an aptitude-by-treatment interaction (Cronbach & Snow, 1977; Robinson, Ch. 6, this volume). Readers may be more familiar with the disordinal type of interaction that is depicted graphically by intersecting lines (e.g., McLaughlin, 1980, p. 339). In the case of CLT, we are dealing with an assumed ordinal interaction in which treatment X (i.e., CLT) is superior to treatment Y (i.e., audiolingual) for all students but is vastly superior to treatment Y for lower aptitude students (McCann, Stewin, & Short, 1991). Given the consistency with which the MLAT and the PLAB have been found to predict L2 success in L2 classroom learning (see review in Sawyer & Ranta, 2001), it is important that this belief be put to the empirical test. As the Canadian court case mentioned above illustrates, there are important ramifications of viewing aptitude testing as irrelevant to L2 learning in the classroom. Unfortunately, the empirical evidence available to date does not shed much light on the issue. Little research has been carried out in settings which can unambiguously be described as CLT. In this paper, I report the results of a study which investigated the role of one particular aspect of L2 aptitude, language analytic ability, in relation to L2 learning in a unique CLT environment.

Language analytic ability and metalinguistic skill

The term *foreign language aptitude* is often associated with the work of Carroll (1962, 1981; Carroll & Sapon, 1959) who was responsible for the theoretical model underlying the MLAT. In the model, there are two components which deal with language analysis, namely, grammatical sensitivity and inductive language learning ability (Carroll, 1962)[1]. Grammatical sensitivity is defined as the ability "to recognize the grammatical functions of words in sentences" whereas inductive language learning refers to "the ability to infer or induce the rules governing a set of language materials, given samples of language materials that permit such inferences"(Carroll, 1981, p. 105). Arguing that the two components were really different aspects of the same underlying ability, Skehan (1989, and this volume) later simplified the model of L2 aptitude by collapsing the two components into one called *language analytic ability* and defined it as "the capacity to infer rules of language and make linguistic generalizations or extrapolations" (Skehan, 1998a, p. 207).

The wording of Skehan's definition is sufficiently general to cover both the implicit analysis of naturalistic input by children acquiring their mother tongue and the explicit inference of grammatical rules from a small structured data set on an aptitude test. Given the fact that the distinction between internalized grammar and metalinguistic grammar is a cornerstone of SLA (e.g., Krashen, 1982; Lightbown, 1985), it may seem a surprising claim to make. Indeed, Sharwood Smith (1994) cautions against equating the hypothesis-testing of the child's language acquisition device with the kind of metalinguistic activity of the linguist. There is, however, empirical support for a link between the two types of analysis. In the Bristol Project follow-up study, Skehan (1986b, 1990) administered aptitude measures and L2 proficiency tests to adolescents who had participated in the longitudinal Bristol Language Project when they were young children. He was thus able to examine the relationship between language analytic ability and L1 development, and found significant, moderate strength correlations between scores on the test of grammatical sensitivity and such L1 developmental indices as the mean length of utterance at 42 months, and the range of noun phrase complexity (Skehan, 1990).

A closer scrutiny of the literature reveals that language analytic ability and metalinguistic ability are overlapping concepts. The tasks used to measure language analytic ability (i.e., MLAT's Words in Sentences or PLAB's Language Analysis) are *de facto* metalinguistic tasks[2]. It is hardly surprising then that studies have found correlations between performance on the MLAT and on metalinguistic tasks (Alderson, Clapham, & Steel, 1997; Masny, 1987; Masny & d'Anglejan, 1985). However despite this overlap, aptitude and metalinguistic ability have generally been explored by distinct research paradigms. Aptitude is viewed as a stable *trait* of the individual which predicts how *quickly* he or she will learn a foreign language. Researchers in this paradigm focus on differences among individuals using mainly correlational designs (e.g., Carroll, 1962). Metalinguistic ability, on the other hand, covers a wide range of *skills* which differentially *emerge* over the course of human development, beginning with "the ability to decenter, to shift one's focus from the most salient attribute of a message (its meaning and contextual setting) to structure (the ordinarily transparent vehicle by which meaning is conveyed)" (Ryan & Ledger, 1984, p.157). Here, research focusses on differences between groups on different types of tasks; for example, Bialystok (1987) compared children in junior kindergarten, grade 1 and grade 3 on their ability to judge vs. correct anomalous sentences.[3] Although metalinguistic skill emerges as a function of age, individual differences among children are well attested: in Kessel (1970), for example, some of the seven year olds were better at interpreting ambiguity than some ten year olds. Differences among individuals in metalinguistic ability are not just a matter of rate, but also are a matter of ultimate attainment. Not all adults have the same metalinguistic abilities in their L1; Gleitman and Gleitman (1970) demonstrated that adult speakers of English vary enormously in their ability to think about and comment on syntactic as opposed to semantic novelty.

Van Kleeck (1982) points out that metalinguistic skill is influenced by an interaction between endogenous and exogenous variables. A large body of research by psychologists has investigated two exogenous variables: the onset of literacy (Olson, 1996) and early bilingual exposure (Bialystok, 2001). The findings from the Bristol Project follow-up study suggest that L2 aptitude constitutes an important endogenous variable affecting metalinguistic skill development.

From this perspective, language analytic ability as a trait and metalinguistic skill as a developmental outcome are related to each other in an *epigenetic* way. Epigenesis is the notion that individual development is "a highly variable process resulting from a cascade of immensely complex interactions between genetic information, the developing features of the individual, and the environment in which development is occurring" (Plotkin, 1998, p. 56).[4] While a full exploration of the relationship between language analytic ability and metalinguistic skill is beyond the scope of this paper (see discussion in Ranta, 1998), I wish to highlight here the two main points that have emerged from the literature: (1) language analytic ability and metalinguistic skill are two sides of the same coin, and (2) language analytic ability is likely to be involved in both the implicit analysis of naturalistic input and the explicit analysis required by metalinguistic tests.

Review of relevant research

In a review of the then existing literature on aptitude and L2 learning, Krashen (1981) concluded that ;

a.   aptitude is correlated with success in "learning" contexts, where the emphasis is on formal accuracy and metalinguistic explanation, and on tests of "learned" knowledge under conditions that favour monitoring;

b.   aptitude is not correlated with success in "acquisition" settings, where the emphasis is on the communication of meaning and positive affect, and on tasks that make use of "acquired" knowledge.

Note that, although Krashen uses the term "aptitude" in this review, he concentrates on the relationship between performance on the MLAT Words in Sentences subtest and L2 proficiency measures. One instructional setting which has been characterized as promoting "acquisition" is immersion (Krashen, 1984). Indeed, a relatively recent study by Harley and Hart (1997) conducted in French immersion classes in Canada offers support for Krashen's claims. The study involved a comparison of grade 11 students who had begun French immersion in grade 1 (early immersion) with their peers who had begun French immersion in grade 7 (late immersion). The Language Analysis subtest of the PLAB and a variety of L2 proficiency measures were administered. These included a yes/no vocabulary recognition test, a listening comprehension test, a cloze, and a written response to an open-ended question. In addition, oral production data were collected from a subsample of each group.

The results for the early entry students were as Krashen would have predicted. The Language Analysis subtest was not a strong predictor of L2 performance; it correlated with only one L2 proficiency measure, the listening comprehension test. However, for the late start learners, the PLAB subtest correlated significantly around $r=.4$ with most of the L2 measures (i.e., the cloze, yes/no vocabulary test, accuracy and communicative effectiveness in writing).

In the discussion of their findings, Harley and Hart (1997, and this volume) propose that the different pattern of correlations between analytic ability and L2 outcomes found in the two groups of students may arise in response to differences in the instructional focus of early vs. late immersion programs. The focus of instruction in the early grades is necessarily less concerned with formal accuracy, written language skills, and the development of academic language proficiency. According to the classroom observation study by Dicks (1992) the different instructional approaches associated with early vs. late immersion are maintained in the later grades. He found that teaching in grades 6 and 8 with learners who had started learning French in early immersion incorporated more experiential activities than was the case with late-entry immersion learners.

The study that is most widely cited as demonstrating the role of aptitude in informal as well as formal learning situations is Reves (1983, see also Skehan, this volume, for discussion). The learners were Arabic native speakers in Israel who were acquiring Hebrew "informally" in a bilingual community and studying English "formally" at school. The participants were grade 11 and 12 students who had been exposed to Hebrew since early childhood and had studied English since grade 5. An Arabic version of the MLAT was developed and six criterion measures were collected (ratings of oral fluency and grammatical accuracy for Hebrew and English, and course grades for each language). The multiple regression analysis revealed that aptitude accounted for significant percentages of the variance on all criterion measures for both Hebrew and English. However, it was the Imitation subtest which accounted for most of the explained variance and not the Arabic Words in Sentences. It is important to note that these learners had received massive exposure to Hebrew in the bilingual community they lived in, and that, from grade 5 onwards, they had received formal instruction in Hebrew which focussed on accuracy in the written language. The findings therefore cannot be generalized to the situation of L2 learning in a communicative classroom environment.

Other studies in settings offering a combination of communicative and form-focussed instruction confirm the impact of learners' language analytic ability on learning outcomes. Horwitz (1987) studied American high school students in their second year of French. She selected five classes in which at least a third of observed class time involved communicative activities. Scores on the MLAT's Words and Sentences subtest correlated moderately and significantly with the grammar test and with communicative competence as measured by ratings on oral tasks. Similarly, Ehrman and Oxford (1995) found a relationship between the MLAT and L2 success in their large-scale study of US government employees. The instructional approach in these intensive language courses was largely communicative but also included some features of audiolingual teaching such as drills and dialogues. Ehrman and Oxford found that the Words in Sentences subtest of the MLAT and an "observed aptitude" rating by the instructor correlated moderately with the Foreign Service Institute ratings of speaking and reading.

Unlike earlier studies in audiolingual programs where performance on the MLAT was found to be a good predictor of success in L2 learning (Carroll, 1962, 1981), the studies reviewed here were conducted in instructional environments which were purportedly communication-oriented in nature. Significant, moderate strength correlations between language analytic ability and L2 proficiency measures were found among late French immersion students by Harley and Hart, among high school students of French by Horwitz, and among adult foreign service personnel in Ehrman and Oxford. Surprisingly, the strength of these correlations was not markedly different from those found by Carroll in audiolingual programs. It must be recalled, however, that all of these studies took place in classrooms where learners experienced a mixture of communicative and accuracy oriented activities.

Results from the early-start French immersion learners studied by Harley and Hart provide support for Krashen's claims that the ability to perform metalinguistic tasks is irrelevant when instruction is meaning-oriented (see also Robinson, Ch. 6, this volume). However, in interpreting this finding, it is important to consider the fact that the early immersion learners had been learning and using French for a period of ten years. No data is available about their performance during the early stages of their exposure to the L2. It is quite possible that, as Skehan (1998a, p. 217, and this volume) has suggested, different components of aptitude are important at different *stages* in L2 learning. He argues that analytic ability may have a monotonic relationship with success *throughout* learning; phonemic coding ability is important in the early stages, while memory abilities are most important for attaining native-like proficiency in a L2. However, interestingly, Harley and Hart (1997) found that measures of memory rather than the Language Analysis test correlated with L2 proficiency for the early start learners.

The present study was conducted to examine the role of language analytic ability in the early stages of L2 acquisition in a classroom setting which promoted the development of interpersonal communication skills rather than academic proficiency. The specific research question addressed by the study was:

Is there a relationship between learners' language analytic ability and their performance on measures of L2 learning in an instructional environment that is predominantly communication-oriented?

Method

The research context

The participants in the study were all learning English in an intensive ESL program in the province of Quebec, Canada. This is the Canadian province where the majority is French-speaking and all daily activities are carried out in French. Francophone children attend French schools and receive ESL instruction beginning in grade 4. The ESL curriculum is organized around a set of functions and notions, and emphasizes the development of oral rather than written skills, and fluency rather than accuracy (Gouvernement du Québec, 1981). Most students receive two hours or less of ESL instruction per week. In response to the low levels of English attained in such a drip-feed approach, intensive ESL has emerged as a popular form of instruction (Lightbown & Spada, 1994). Note that subject matter instruction in English is prohibited by law in the French language public school system.

Students in the present study attended a special school where they received five months of intensive ESL instruction in grade 6. In this school, five classes begin the year with an all-day program in ESL while another five classes study the grade 6 French language curriculum. At the end of January, in the middle of the school year, the classes switch. The school provides an English-language environment in that all members of the staff are bilingual to various degrees, and the use of English outside of the ESL classroom is encouraged through a number of different ways (e.g., English tables in the cafeteria, announcements given in English over the public address system). The salient characteristics of this school are summarized as follows:

– every student in the school is in grade 6 (10 classes of 30 students each);
– every student in the school spends one half of the school year in intensive ESL (= 4.5 hours/day);
– prior to the year of intensive study, all students have had a maximum of two years of regular ESL for 2 hours/week;
– English is never used as the medium of instruction for subject matter teaching;
– the ESL program emphasizes oral communication skills over reading and writing skills;
– students are encouraged to use English in the school outside the ESL class;
– students from all levels of academic ability are eligible for this program.

As with most other intensive programs in Quebec, the curriculum used in the Intensive School is based on the regular ESL curriculum mandated for use in primary schools by the Ministry of Education. Learners participate in a variety of oral activities such as games, puzzles, surveys, interviews and discussions which are organized around themes relevant to the interests of students of this age (White, 1996). There are no grammar objectives in the curriculum.

The teachers in the school were well known to have a close working relationship; they planned instructional activities together to ensure that all students received the same instructional input. Three of the five ESL teachers had been observed both informally and formally over a period of ten years (Spada & Lightbown, 1989; Spada, Ranta, & Lightbown, 1996; White, 1996). The formal observations had been carried out using Part A of the Communicative Orientation of Language Teaching (COLT) Observation Scheme (Spada & Fröhlich, 1995). This instrument permits the systematic description in real-time of features characteristic of communicative teaching such as the extent to which classes are teacher- or learner-centred, the amount of instructional time devoted to focus on form or focus on meaning, the amount of time spent on different skills, and the type of interactional organization. For the present study, all five ESL teachers were observed using Part A of the COLT for one full day in May-June 1995. These observational data provided further confirmation of earlier impressions of the teachers' commitment to the communicative approach. The salient features of ESL instruction among the five classes at the Intensive ESL School were:

– English was consistently used for all functions in the classroom (e.g., lesson delivery, classroom management, discipline, etc.);

- pair- and group-work activities predominated over teacher-centered activities;
- student-teacher interaction was characterized by negotiation of meaning;
- when focus on form occurred, it usually took place when homework was corrected.

Additional information concerning the nature of L2 teaching in the school was gathered through a teacher questionnaire. The questionnaire concerning teaching practices had been sent out prior to this study to all the school boards offering intensive ESL programs. Four of the five ESL teachers at the Intensive ESL School responded to the questionnaire. Their responses reflect a commitment to CLT. For example, when their opinion about grammar was elicited, they commented:

> "Learn to speak first, as you learned your mother tongue, then proceed with learning grammar to improve the quality of the language"
> "...Teaching grammar or concentrating on it to learn a language is a false concept"
> "I believe students should learn to communicate before learning grammar structures"
> "They can communicate with kids their age and understand the messages without the grammar"

The findings from the analysis of the COLT and from the questionnaire responses were consistent with the goals of the intensive ESL program and with the principles of CLT as disseminated in teacher training textbooks (e.g., Brown, 1994; Nunan, 1991). On the basis of this information, we may conclude that learners in the school were indeed experiencing a predominantly communication-oriented approach to L2 teaching.

Participants

The participants in this study (N=150) began their ESL instruction in September 1994 and then switched into the French part of their intensive year from February to June 1995. Students in this school represented a range of academic abilities. The only requirement for admission to this special program was that they not be fluent in English. Furthermore, students must show that they have the motivation and parental support to cope with the demands of covering the usual ten-month French language arts, math, and social studies content in a five-month period. Typically, more students apply to attend the program than there are places available, and the final selection is based on a drawing of names. This population of learners was linguistically very homogenous: almost all of the students in the school were francophones from unilingual families whose contact with English prior to participation in the intensive program was limited to English-language media, and the communicative ESL instruction they had received in grades 4 and 5. At the age of 11–13 years, these children were cognitively mature enough to perform the tasks used in this study.

Procedure

The participants were tested on three occasions during their intensive ESL year.[5] The distribution of tests across the school year is presented in Table 1. The selection of tasks was based on the need to be able to assess learners' growing proficiency in the L2. From earlier experience with students in intensive ESL programs, it was known that at the beginning of the school year, learners can only handle simple receptive tasks whereas at the end of the five month period they are capable of performing more complex communication tasks. The French task was administered during the French portion of the academic year for practical reasons: teachers at the school were firmly committed to an *English only* policy in the ESL classroom.

Table 1. Testing schedule

September 1994	January 1995	June 1995
– Aural vocabulary recognition	– MEQ Listening comprehension (32-items)	– Yes/no vocabulary
		– MEQ Listening comprehension (53-items)
– Listening	– L2 Metalinguistic task	
– Cloze-Sept	– Cloze-Jan	– L1 Metalinguistic task

Instruments

The choice of an instrument to measure language analytic ability suitable for use with francophone children posed certain difficulties. Aptitude measures such as the MLAT or the PLAB are intended to be given in the learners' L1. There is a French language version of the MLAT (Wells, Wesche, & Sarrazin,

1982), but it is intended for older learners (grade 9 to adult); the version of the MLAT adapted for elementary school students (the EMLAT; Carroll, 1967) was not available in translation. The issue of ecological validity was also a concern. Given the overall emphasis on communication in the intensive ESL program, it was not considered appropriate to administer an analytic task involving a completely unknown (and irrelevant) language as on the PLAB. Thus, a metalinguistic task administered in the L1 was developed in order to assess learners' language analytic ability.

The L1 Metalinguistic Task was an error detection and correction task (see Appendix A). Unlike the Words in Sentences or Language Analysis subtests from the standardized aptitude batteries, this metalinguistic task was consistent with the type of instructional activities found in the French language arts curriculum in the school. The rationale for using this task was that the correct spelling of many grammatical forms in French requires a grammatical analysis of the sentence and the application of rules of agreement for number and gender. Francophone students in grade 6 do not generally have complete control over the rules of written French which usually requires years of practice and corrective feedback. It was assumed that different levels of success on this task among these learners, who had received the same type of metalinguistic instruction with respect to grammatical spelling in French, would reflect differing abilities to attend to the syntactic and morphological form of sentences. As argued earlier, performance on metalinguistic tasks such as this is influenced by individual differences in language analytic ability.

L2 Proficiency measures

The following L2 measures[6] were administered:

1. Aural Vocabulary Recognition: A list of 64 words was presented to the learners on audiotape. The learner chose the picture that corresponded to the word heard.

2. Listening Comprehension: Learners heard 10 sentences twice and chose the picture that corresponded to the sentence.

3. Cloze: This was a rational deletion cloze consisting of a short passage of 54 words with 10 blanks. Any plausible word was accepted and great leeway was given for spelling (e.g., *skool* and *scool* were accepted for *school*).

4. MEQ Listening Comprehension (32- and 53-items): Learners listened to recorded English statements, questions, or descriptions and selected the

appropriate picture, statement, or response in a multiple-choice format. On the 32-item version, only isolated sentences were targeted. The 53-item version of the test administered in June included additional sections involving more extended discourse, and items targetting pragmatic knowledge.

5. English Metalinguistic Task: Learners read an extended story and identified errors. Of these errors, 21 involved the possessive determiners *his* and *her* and 11 were distractors.[7]

6. Yes/No Vocabulary: Learners were presented with lists of real words and plausible-sounding non-words (e.g., jarvis, savourite) and checked off the words they knew. A score was derived based on signal detection theory in which the number of real words correctly identified was adjusted in relation to the number of non-words accepted as real (Meara & Buxton, 1987; Meara & Jones, 1989).

Analyses

The scores for each student on the various measures were entered onto a spreadsheet and submitted to three types of analyses: Pearson correlations, principal components analysis, and cluster analysis. Correlation is the prototypical analytic procedure for investigating the relationship between two variables. However, when many variables are involved, it is often preferable to use a multivariate analytic technique such as principal components analysis in order to reduce a complex set of correlations into fewer dimensions (Skehan, 1989). The principal components analysis produces a matrix of components and component loadings, which are the correlations between each component and each variable from the data set. By examining these correlations the researcher can name the construct underlying the component. In the present case, a language analysis component could be expected to emerge. The analysis was conducted using the Factor program of SPSS-X 6.1.

Cluster analysis refers to a group of procedures that assembles entities into piles according to their similarities or dissimilarities. Unlike multiple regression or factor analysis, cluster analysis is not limited by the assumption that variables are related to each other in a linear or an additive fashion. The cluster analysis technique has been championed by Skehan (1986a, 1989) for use in the study of individual differences since it allows the researcher to identify subgroups which are maximally similar to each other, and different from other subgroups. Ward's method (Ward, 1963) was chosen to cluster the data using the Cluster program available on SPSS-6.1.

Results

Pearson correlations for all of the variables were computed after an initial inspection of scatterplots led to the identification and elimination of a few outliers. The scores from students who did not complete all of the tests were also removed from the analyses. The correlation matrix is presented in Table 2. Given the relatively large sample size, it is not surprising to find that most of the intercorrelations are significant, although they range from low to moderate in strength. The r correlations between the French Metalinguistic task and the L2 measures range from a non-significant low of $r=.08$ for the September Listening test to a significant high of $r=.42$ for the English Metalinguistic task. This means that the variance in the L1 metalinguistic task accounts for 16% or less of the variance on the L2 measures. The strongest correlations are found between the L1 metalinguistic task and the two English proficiency measures which required a focus on form, that is, the English Metalinguistic task and, to a lesser degree, the cloze.

Table 2. Pearson correlations among test variables ($N=133$)

	AVR	Listen. Sept	Cloze Sept	Cloze Jan	MEQ Jan	MEQ June	L1 Meta	L2 Meta	Yes/ No
AVR									
Listen. Sept	.58								
Cloze- Sept	.55	.33							
Cloze- Jan	.46	.43	.46						
MEQ Jan	.41	.36	.43	.48					
MEQ June	.61	.45	.45	.56	.59				
L1 Meta task	.28	.08#	.39	.40	.26	.32			
L2 Meta. task	.40	.32	.38	.60	.57	.58	.42		
Yes/ No	.46	.26	.36	.51	.47	.60	.34	.53	

Note: All correlations are significant at $p<.01$ except when indicated by #.

Principal components analysis

Table 3 presents the results from the principal components analysis. A three-component solution which accounted for 72.1% of the variance was chosen. The three components were rotated using Varimax rotation in order to arrive at loadings which would be more easily interpretable. The component loadings (i.e., the correlation between each variable and each component) of .40 and stronger are in boldface. Following recommendations by Stevens (1986), these were the loadings used to interpret the component.

Table 3. Principal components of test variables with varimax rotation

Variable	Component 1	Component 2	Component 3
AVR-1 (Sept)	.31	.80	.18
Listening (Sept)	.27	.81	-.15
Cloze-1 (Sept)	.17	.67	.50
Cloze-2 (Jan)	.57	.40	.34
MEQ Listening-32 items (Jan)	.75	.31	.06
MEQ Listening-53 items (June)	.73	.45	.10
L1 Metalinguistic	.25	.02	.89
L2 Metalinguistic (Jan)	.75	.18	.31
Yes/no vocabulary (June)	.80	.13	.17

The first component can be characterized as a Post-Instruction factor since it is the proficiency tests administered after the five months of ESL instruction and not the September tests that contribute to it. In contrast, the three tests administered in September have high loadings on the second component. Since the cloze and the June administration of the MEQ Listening Comprehension test also contribute to this component, it seems likely that it reflects knowledge of L2 vocabulary. Finally, the third component can be labelled as representing L1 Metalinguistic knowledge since the French metalinguistic task was the variable that loaded most strongly on it. The pre-instructional cloze, which was the only L2 measure that involved any writing, also loaded moderately on this component; the second administration of the cloze did not, however, meet the criterion of a .4 loading on this component. It thus appears from this analysis that language analytic ability as measured by the French test is generally unrelated to performance on the L2 measures.

Cluster analysis

The output from the cluster analysis provides solutions for any number of clusters from 1 to *n*. In the present case, this meant that the solutions ranged from having each of the 135 individuals[8] as a unique cluster of one, to having one cluster which includes all 135 individuals. The task of the analyst is to find the best solution somewhere between those two extremes. On the basis of the change in the coefficient and a visual inspection of the clusters on a dendrogram, the four-cluster solution was chosen. This solution provided four groups of sufficient size to make statistical comparisons possible ($N = 53, 41, 28, 13$, respectively). Figure 1 presents the means for each cluster in z-scores so that comparisons can be made across the different tasks[9]. One-way analysis of variance was carried out on the cluster means for each of the nine variables in order to determine where the clusters differed significantly from each other. Based on this display and the ANOVA results, the learner profiles outlined in Table 4 were derived.

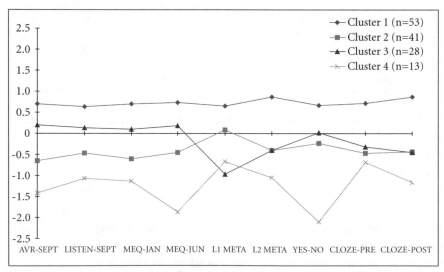

Figure 1. Cluster scores expressed as standardized scores

Figure 1 and Table 4 reveal that a strong performance on the L1 Metalinguistic task is associated with strong performance on all of the L2 measures for the learners in Cluster 1. A similar trend in the opposite direction is evident for the learners in Cluster 4: poor performance on the L1 task is associated with weak performance on the L2 measures. Thus, for the strongest and weakest learners in this population, language analytic ability does predict their degree of success in L2 learning. The learners in Clusters 2 and 3 present a contrary trend. Cluster 2 learners are relatively stronger than the learners in Cluster 3 on the French task, but are significantly weaker on many of the L2 listening tests. Clearly, the interpretation of the results for the two middle clusters requires that factors other than language analytic ability be taken into account.

Table 4. Descriptions of cluster profiles

Cluster	Characteristics
1	– strong on all L2 pre-tests and post-tests – strong on the L1 Metalinguistic task
2	– weak on all L2 pre-tests and post-tests – average on L1 Metalinguistic task
3	– average on measures of L2 vocabulary and listening; below average on cloze, and L2 Metalinguistic task – below average on L1 Metalinguistic task
4	– weak on all L2 pre-tests and post-tests – weak on L1 Metalinguistic task

Discussion

Taken together, the results from the correlations and the principal components analysis suggest that language analytic ability as measured by a L1 metalinguistic task is only weakly associated with L2 learning outcomes in this CLT setting. In line with Krashen's interpretation of earlier aptitude research, the strongest relationships found were between the tasks requiring a focus on form such as the L2 Metalinguistic task and the cloze, but even these were only barely moderate in strength. The cluster analysis, however, sheds further light on the relationship. Recall that there is no assumption of linearity in a cluster analysis; it merely groups individuals based on similarity in the pattern of scores. Performance on the L1 metalinguistic task was associated with the overall superior performance on the L2 measures for Cluster 1 and with the poor performance of the learners in Cluster 4. The non-linearity crops up with Clusters 2 and 3.

On the face of it, Cluster 3 learners appear to be relatively weaker in language analytic ability than their peers in Cluster 2. They may well be the kind of memory-oriented learners described in the learner style literature (Ranta & Derwing, 1999; Skehan, 1986a). The learners in Cluster 2 appear to be stronger in language analysis than they are in the two other components of aptitude, that is, phonemic coding ability and memory (Skehan, 1998a). Support for this lies in their relatively weak performance on the aural vocabulary recognition and listening comprehension tests. It is possible that it is too early in their L2 development for them to benefit from their relatively greater strength in analysis. As Skehan (1998a, this volume) has suggested, different aspects of aptitude may come into play at different stages of language learning. Initially, the more important aspects of learning are auditory processes which are necessary for establishing automatic lexical retrieval; this in turn frees up attention for higher level processes such as grammatical analysis (Hulstijn, 2001; Segalowitz, 1997). It is also possible that the L1 analytic measure did not correlate with L2 measures for Clusters 2 and 3 because it was not sufficiently powerful to discriminate among the learners in the middle range [10].

Let us now consider the consistently strong performance of the learners in Cluster 1. They are clearly "good language learners" like those studied by Naiman, Fröhlich, Stern, and Todesco (1978). The significance of their success must be understood against the backdrop of the type of classroom treatment they experienced. These learners had participated in a variety of communication activities such as games, discussions, stories, creative-projects, etc. which differed greatly from the kinds of things they were asked to do on the proficiency tests. The learners had never practiced identifying errors in a written passage, or filling in a cloze passage, nor had they ever had to distinguish real words from non-real words on a long list. They were not applying "learned" knowledge using their Monitor as suggested by Krashen (1981) but rather performed well on these tasks based on their previous experiences in their French language schooling and on their innate ability to impose structure on linguistic input.

On the one hand, it is clear that these children would have been exposed to considerable metalinguistic information during their French language schooling and that this might be beneficial for performing metalinguistic and other academic tasks. According to Cummins (1987), metalinguistic tasks are particularly good examples of context-reduced, cognitively demanding tasks which involve the type of language skills that transfer across languages. However, such transfer cannot really help when the L2 task requires specific knowledge of the target language. The Cluster 1 learners appear to have "strategic competence" (Bachman, 1990; Canale & Swain, 1980). Bachman defines strategic competence as non-subject specific abilities needed to put language knowledge to use.[11]

The impact of strategic competence on L2 performance measures lies in the fact that language testing almost always involves some degree of decontextualization. Consider, for example, the MEQ Listening Comprehension test used in this study. Like so many others (e.g., TOEFL) it makes use of a multiple-choice format. The test taker is given a number of sentences and short dialogues, each unconnected to the other and listens for one correct response among a number of alternatives, all the while shifting attention from the test booklet to the written response sheet. It is hardly an example of a "natural" listening activity. Furthermore, such tasks place heavy demands on the individual's ability to split attention and thus are affected by individual differences in working memory capacity (Harrington & Sawyer, 1992). It can be argued that the same kind of strategic allocation of attention required by a multiple-choice listening comprehension test is also required to perform metalinguistic tasks where attention must shift from meaning to form. In this study, the similarity in processing demands would account for the fact that the Yes/No Vocabulary test, and the MEQ Listening Comprehension tests loaded together with the English Metalinguistic task onto the same component. Given the decontextualized nature of language testing, then, it is likely that the differences among the learners in the intensive ESL program on the various measures reflects differences in strategic competence as well as in language analytic ability.

The results of this study have implications for ESL instruction in intensive classes in Quebec. It was found that about a third of the learners were able to handle proficiency tests that were more metalinguistic, form-focussed, or decontextualized than the kind of activities they had generally experienced in their ESL classes. On the other hand, this study revealed that many intensive program students appear to have difficulty with vocabulary and that this may be holding back progress in their learning of English. The learners in Clusters 2 and 4 (40% of the learners studied) were significantly weaker in their performance on an aural vocabulary recognition test given at the beginning of the year which measured the knowledge gained from "drip-feed" ESL instruction in grades 4 and 5. Their poor showing on the post-instructional listening comprehension tests suggests continuing problems with lexical retrieval despite greater exposure to the L2. Without automatized access to lexical items, it may be the case that further interlanguage development is hampered since processing the meaning of utterances uses up too many attentional resources (Hulstijn, 2001). It is possible that the Cluster 2 and 4 learners would benefit from a more structured approach to enhance their vocabulary acquisition (see pedagogical suggestions by Gatbonton & Segalowitz, 1988; Hulstijn, 2001; Sparks, Ganschow, Fluharty, & Little, 1997).

To conclude, taken as a whole, the results from this study do not support the claim that a CLT environment can counteract the effects of learner aptitude in an aptitude-by-treatment interaction. It appears that, despite what some Canadian Federal Court judges may believe, the "good language learner" of today has the same characteristics as those successful learners studied in the past (Naiman et al., 1978), at least with respect to language analytic ability.

Notes

* This paper is based on the author's doctoral dissertation completed at Concordia University and funded by doctoral fellowships from Concordia University and the Quebec Ministry of Education (Fonds pour la formation de chercheurs à l'aide à la recherche), and by grants from F. C. A. R. and the Social Sciences and Humanities Research Council of Canada to Patsy M. Lightbown and Nina Spada. Special thanks to John A. Upshur for assistance on the dissertation research, to Randall Halter for the statistical support, to Patsy Lightbown for valuable feedback and guidance throughout, to the principal, teachers, and students for their enthusiastic cooperation, and to an anonymous reviewer. Needless to say, all remaining defficiencies in the text remain my own.

1. The other two components are phonetic coding ability and rote memory. Note that Skehan (1998a) refers to the former component as "phonemic coding ability".

2. The Words in Sentences subtest of the MLAT requires the test-taker to match an underlined word in one sentence with a word or phrase having the same grammatical function in a second sentence. The Language Analysis subtest of the PLAB consists of a series of sentences from an unknown language which are presented along with their English translations; the test-taker must infer the grammatical rules in the language and apply them to novel sentences. See Birdsong (1989, pp. 58–59) for an analysis of different types of metalinguistic tasks, including Words in Sentences, based on Bialystok and Ryan (1985).

3. See Loman (1989) for a discussion of the trait vs. skill paradigms with respect to the study of intelligence.

4. Along similar lines, Chapelle and Green (1992) cite the work of Cattell (1987) and Horn (1989) to argue for a distinction between "general analytic ability" which is fluid (i.e., innate) and language analytic ability which is "crystallized" (i.e., learned). See Sternberg, and Robinson, this volume for discussion.

5. See Lightbown & Spada (1997) for a report of the findings from the larger study in which the present study took place.

6. In addition, oral production samples were elicited from a subsample of 50 students (see Ranta, 1998 for findings).

7. The inclusion of a metalinguistic task which focussed on the possessive determiners *his/her* made it possible to compare metalinguistic performance to oral production on a grammatical feature having a well-established developmental profile (see details in Ranta, 1998).

8. The cluster analysis included all of the individuals who had completed all of the tests, including those who had been eliminated as outliers in the correlational analyses.

9. It should be noted that that the numbering of the clusters is not meaningful in itself but simply reflects the point at which one cluster breaks off from another.

10. The Cronbach alpha for the L1 Metalinguistic task was .62.

11. Note that Chapelle and Green (1992) equate strategic competence with fluid ability which they call "general analytic ability" in their proposed model of aptitude.

Appendix

L1 Metalinguistic task ("Trouve les erreurs")

Instructions: Lis chaque phrase attentivement. Si tu trouves une erreur dans une phrase, encercle l'erreur et corrige-la dans l'espace prévu à cet effet. S'il n'y a pas d'erreur, écris "pas d'erreur". *Chaque phrase incorrecte ne contient qu'une seule erreur alors que quelques phrases n'ont aucune erreur.*

1. Les légumes frais sont plus bons pour la santé que les bonbons.
2. Toutes les enfants prennent l'autobus à 15 heures.
3. Grand-père leurs a raconté une histoire.
4. L'hiver dernier je fais ju ski tous les jours.
5. Nous nous sommes beaucoup amusés à Calgary.
6. Mes parents ont allés à Toronto.
7. Sa mère l'a prêté de l'argent.
8. Nos voisins ont achetaient une nouvelle voiture.
9. Il faut que je vais chez le dentiste.
10. Les joueur de hockey gagnent trop d'argent.
11. Hier soir elles sont sorties pour aller au théâtre.
12. Il a passé les plus beaux vacances de sa vie!
13. Richard sent va à la campagne.
14. Je ne sais pas très bien nagé.
15. Les premières deux personnes ont eu un prix.
16. Ils nous avons offert un repas délicieux.
17. Après nager pendant une heure, on était très fatigué.
18. Lorsque mon oncle a ouvri la porte, il a eu une grande surprise.
19. Nous avons complètement oublié de la téléphoner.
20. J'ai besoin d'une nouvelle bicyclette.

CHAPTER 9

Individual differences in working memory, noticing of interactional feedback and L2 development

Alison Mackey, Jenefer Philp,
Takako Egi, Akiko Fujii and Tomoaki Tatsumi

Georgetown University (Mackey, Egi, Fujii, Tatsumi) /
University of Tasmania, Australia (Philp)

Introduction

Within the interactionist framework of second language acquisition (SLA), recent studies have suggested that individual learners vary in the ways they benefit from interactional feedback (Mackey, 1999; Mackey & Philp, 1998; Polio & Gass, 1998; Swain & Lapkin, 1998). Researchers investigating the relationship between working memory and SLA have suggested that working memory (WM) plays a role in second language (L2) learning (N.Ellis, 1996; N.Ellis & Schmidt, 1997; N.Ellis & Sinclair, 1996; Harrington & Sawyer, 1992; Miyake & Friedman, 1998; Robinson, in press; Valentine & Baddeley, 1991; Service, 1992; Williams, 1999). In this chapter, we explore the relationship between L2 learners' WM capacities, their noticing of interactional feedback, and the ways in which their interlanguage changed after feedback. Psychometric tests of WM capacity were administered to 30 learners in both their L1 (Japanese) and their L2 (English). The learners received feedback in the form of recasts of their non target-like English question forms during three 30 minute sessions of dyadic task-based interaction. Subsequent changes in question formation were tracked through a pretest-posttest design. All learners carried out an immediate posttest. Nineteen learners carried out a delayed posttest, and 11 learners took part in a retrospective interview instead. Results suggest an interesting but complex relationship between WM capacity, noticing of L2 form and interaction-driven second language development.

Interaction, attention and L2 learning

Long's (1996) interaction hypothesis proposes that feedback obtained during conversational interaction promotes interlanguage (IL) development because interaction "connects input, internal learner capacities, particularly selective attention, and output in productive ways" (Long, 1996, pp. 451–452). Research on interaction initially sought to describe interactional modifications (Hatch, 1978, 1983; Long, 1981, 1983a, 1983b; Wagner-Gough & Hatch, 1975). Such work was followed by studies that sought empirical evidence for the impact of interaction on comprehension (Loschky, 1994; Pica, Young, & Doughty, 1987), production (Swain & Lapkin, 1998; Gass & Varonis, 1994) and L2 development (R.Ellis, Tanaka, & Yamazaki, 1994; Mackey, 1999; for review see Gass, Mackey, & Pica, 1998). SLA research on interaction has naturally led to the question of *how* interaction works to bring about L2 development. Most recently, there has been a move in interactional research to explore the specific nature and contribution of different interactional features to L2 learning (Mackey, 2000). A number of researchers have discussed the importance of empirically exploring the role of internal learner capacities (R. Ellis, 1991, 1994a; Faerch & Kasper, 1986; Gass, 1991, 1997; Gass & Varonis, 1994; Long, 1996; Mackey, Gass, & McDonough, 2000; Philp, 1998), and a potential relationship between conversational interaction and L2 learners' internal and attentional processes has been discussed, in particular the link between specific types of interactional feedback, such as recasts, and L2 development. Individual differences in attentional resources may be one factor affecting why interaction 'works' better for some learners than others. Robinson (1995b) has argued that "individual differences in memory and attentional capacity both affect the extent of noticing, thereby directly influencing SLA" (p. 283). The goal of the current study was to investigate the relationship between second language learners' WM capacities, their noticing of L2 form, and their interlanguage development after interactional feedback.

Several recent studies have explored the role of attention in L2 development, although there has been controversy over the definitions and operationalization of attentional constructs such as noticing and awareness, and their roles in L2 development (see for example discussions in Leow, 1999a, 1999b, 2000; Schmidt, 1990, 1993, 1994, 1995; Tomlin & Villa, 1994; Robinson, 1995b; Simard & Wong, 2001; and the critical review by Truscott, 1998). As Leow (1999a, 1999b) points out, until recently, most of these studies utilized the constructs as a post-hoc explanation of learning or as a theoretical premise of research (see also Truscott, 1998) without confirming whether or not learners paid attention to and noticed the input (see for example, studies by Doughty, 1991; Fotos, 1993; Greenslade, Bouden, & Sanz, 1999; Leeman, Arteagoitia, Fridman, & Doughty, 1995; Leow, 1993, 1997a; Shook, 1994; and White, 1998). However, recent adaptations of on-line and off-line measures of attention and noticing have provided empirical evidence for an association between noticing and learning (Alanen, 1995; Leow, 1997b, 2000; Mackey, 2000; Rosa, 1999; Rosa & O'Neill, 1999).

Within SLA, discussions of noticing generally reflect two theoretical positions based on the work of Tomlin and Villa (1994), and of Schmidt (1990, 1993, 1994, 1995; Schmidt & Frota, 1986) and Robinson (1995b, in press). These two theoretical positions center on a distinction between detection of input with and without awareness and are associated with different hypotheses about learning.

Tomlin and Villa (1994; see also Posner & Peterson, 1990) describe noticing very concisely as detection within selective attention, not necessarily involving awareness. They point to a difference between detection with and without awareness, suggesting "registration" rather than "noticing" as a more neutral word "for the cases that do not implicate awareness or for processing of nontargets"[1] (p. 200).

While both Schmidt (1990, 1993, 1994, 1995) and Robinson (1995b, in press) also describe noticing as cognitive registration, in contrast to Tomlin and Villa (1994), they distinguish between detection and noticing on the basis of awareness. Robinson (1995b) defined noticing as "detection with awareness and rehearsal in short-term memory ... necessary to learning and the subsequent encoding in long-term memory" (p. 318). In Robinson's model, activation of information in short-term memory must exceed a certain threshold in order for learners to be consciously aware of it. Robinson (in press) further argues that noticing is "that subset of detected information that receives focal attention, enters short-term, WM, and is rehearsed." (p. 34). Noticing is a consequence of this process of rehearsal, through which information in short-term memory is encoded in long-term memory; thus, noticing is crucial for learning. This follows Schmidt's noticing hypothesis (1990, 1993, 1995), which claims that learning cannot take place without noticing. In Schmidt's model, awareness is crucial and learners must consciously notice linguistic input in order for it to become intake. Noticing that results in intake may lead to restructuring of the learner's IL system. Schmidt has argued against implicit or unconscious learning, claiming that awareness and learning cannot be dissociated. He differentiates two levels of awareness: awareness at the level of noticing, and awareness at the level of understanding. It is awareness at the level of noticing that Schmidt claims is crucial for language learning, adding that awareness at the level of understanding linguistic rules can be facilitative but is not necessary for SLA. In the current study we utilized Robinson and Schmidt's descriptions of noticing, focusing on learners' noticing of feedback in the context of interaction, in the sense of detection with awareness.

While the literature generally suggests that noticing and interlanguage development are likely to be associated, individual differences in various domains may be a mediating factor. Philp (1998; in press) proposed that learners' noticing of L2 form may be modulated by their IL grammars, suggesting that learners' developmental levels may be a factor affecting noticing of interactional feedback (see also Gass, 1991, 1997; Mackey, 1999; White, 1987). The attentional resources of learners may also be constrained by the degree of automaticity or control each learner has over comprehension and production in their L2 (R. Ellis, 1994a; McLaughlin, 1987; VanPatten, 1996). Nick Ellis (2001) argues that language users make use of "ready-made units" or formulae, that is, frequently used analyses already present in long-term memory, for greater efficiency and speed in production and comprehension (see Bresnan, 1999; Nattinger, 1980; Pawley & Syder, 1993 also cited by N. Ellis, 2001). Access to such pre-encoded units may free the L2 user to attend to other demands, including the challenges of producing or comprehending larger complex units, or making comparisons with forms in the input which do not fit with the learner's IL representations.

Robinson (1995b, in press) also suggests that noticing may be constrained by individual differences in WM capacity. Similarly, Schmidt (2001) claims that "At least one aptitude factor, short term or working memory capacity, (Baddeley, 1986; N.Ellis, 1996; Harrington & Sawyer, 1992) is closely related to attention" (p.10). Engle, Kane, and Tuholski (1999) also argue for a model of working memory in which WM capacity refers to the capacity for controlled attention in the face of distraction, and individual differences in WM capacity reflect individual differences in controlled attention.

Working memory in SLA

Within the framework of cognitive or psycholinguistic accounts of SLA (cf. N. Ellis, 1996, 1998, 1999; Healy & Bourne, 1998; Segalowitz & Lightbown, 1999;

Skehan, 1998a), an important role has been ascribed to working memory in relation to verbal input during second language learning (N. Ellis, 1996; N.Ellis & Schmidt, 1997; N.Ellis & Sinclair, 1996; Miyake & Friedman, 1998; Robinson, 1995b, in press; Skehan, 1998a). Research in SLA seems to suggest that individual differences in WM may account for some differences in L2 performance and acquisition.

A range of studies of WM and SLA have been carried out, some focusing on the relationship between individual differences in WM and L2 performance, others investigating the role of various components of WM in second language learning. A number of studies have focused on the role of phonological short-term memory (STM), operationalizing the construct as the ability to repeat phonological input correctly (Daneman & Case, 1981; N.Ellis & Schmidt, 1997; N. Ellis & Sinclair, 1996; Papagno, Valentine, & Baddeley, 1991; Papagno & Vallar, 1992; Service, 1992; Service & Kohonen, 1995; Williams, 1999). Findings generally support an important role for phonological STM in second language learning. For example, earlier experimental studies, such as Daneman and Case (1981), Papagno et al. (1991), and Papagno and Vallar (1992), demonstrated that phonological STM played a role in the learning of novel lexical items. A relationship between phonological STM and second language vocabulary acquisition was also suggested by a longitudinal study by Service (1992) and Service and Kohonen (1995). In their study of Finnish child learners of English as a foreign language, the children's ability to repeat English pseudo words accurately at the outset of their English learning predicted their final grades in the English course and their scores on vocabulary tests after 4 years. More recent studies have suggested that phonological STM may be involved not only in lexical acquisition but also in the acquisition of grammatical rules (N.Ellis & Schmidt, 1997; N.Ellis & Sinclair, 1996; Williams, 1999). Ellis and Sinclair (1996), for example, found from their study comparing the effects of learners' phonological rehearsal of Welsh utterances on elements such as comprehension, metalinguistic knowledge and acquisition, that learners who repeated utterances clearly outperformed those prevented from doing so. They concluded that "individual differences in STM and working memory can have profound effects on language *acquisition*" (p.247) [emphasis in the original].

Other studies (e.g., Ando, Fukunaga, Kurahashi, Suto, Nakano, & Kage, 1992; Harrington & Sawyer, 1992; Miyake & Friedman, 1998) have addressed a more active, simultaneous storage/processing function of WM, referred to as verbal working memory, typically assessed by methods such as Daneman and Carpenter's (1980) sentence span task.[2] For example, Harrington and Sawyer (1992) compared ESL learners' L2 WM capacity and their L2 reading proficiency as measured by the reading/grammar subsections of TOEFL. In their study, learners' performance in the L2 reading span task correlated significantly with their scores on the TOEFL subsections. More recently, Miyake and Friedman (1998) found a similar relationship between ESL learners' performance on an L2 sentence span task and their L2 listening comprehension abilities. Using path analysis, Miyake and Friedman showed that their learners' WM in L1 strongly predicted the learners' WM in L2, which in turn predicted learners' native-like cue assignment during sentence comprehension. In both studies, measures of passive STM (i.e., digit/word span tasks) showed no correlation with the learners' L2 comprehension ability or with measures of verbal working memory (i.e., sentence span tasks). Notably, both studies reported that learners' L1 WM correlated with their L2 WM, moderately in Harrington and Sawyer and more strongly in Miyake and Friedman, suggesting the possibility that performance on WM measures may be language independent, provided that measures are at an appropriate level of difficulty (see Osaka & Osaka, 1992 for supportive evidence). Finally, in a study of interaction between instructional approaches and learners' cognitive differences, Ando et al. (1992) found that Japanese 5th graders' verbal working memory capacity as tested by L1 reading and listening span tests, predicted their relative success in the L2 after 20 hours of explicit form-focused instruction. However, under a more communicatively-oriented condition that included meaning-focused production activities, results were reversed. Learners with low WM span in the L1 benefited more from the implicit communicative approach. Ando et al.'s findings suggest that WM, measured by tasks that require simultaneous input retention and processing, may be a reliable predictor of successful L2 learning for some learning conditions, but not others. The results of these studies suggest that WM is a likely component of language aptitude (see Miyake & Friedman, 1998).

The studies reviewed here provide both indirect and direct empirical support for the involvement of WM in second language learning. As Skehan (1998a, this volume) and Robinson (this volume) point out, more empirical studies are needed in order for researchers to explore the role WM may play in specific linguistic domains and learning conditions. Taken together, the literature suggests an interesting hypothetical link between WM, noticing, and interaction-driven L2 development. The present study aimed to explore the relationship between WM, noticing, and second language development through interaction. To address this issue, the following research questions were posited:

RQ 1. Is there a relationship between WM capacity and noticing of interacional feedback?

RQ 2. If so, is the relationship related to learners' developmental levels?

RQ 3. Is there a relationship between WM capacity and interaction-driven L2 development?

Method

Operationalizations

This study examined the relationship between WM, noticing and second language development.

Working memory
This study focused on two functions of working memory[3]; verbal WM and phonological STM, as both have been linked to different aspects of language learning. As Miyake and Shah point out, several chapters in their volume (1999) propose different explanations of what working memory span tests really measure and why they are often good predictors of complex cognitive tasks. In the current study, verbal WM capacity was operationalized as the ability to recall verbal auditory input while simultaneously processing the input and was measured through a listening span test in L1 (Japanese) and L2 (English) (Daneman & Carpenter, 1980; Miyake & Friedman, 1998). Following Gathercole and her colleagues (Gathercole & Baddeley, 1989; Gathercole, Service, Hitch, Adams, & Martin, 1999), phonological short-term capacity was operationalized as the ability to repeat novel verbal input immediately following its presentation. A non-word recall test was adapted from Gathercole, et al. (1999) and was used to measure this ability. Non-words have been widely used in measures of phonological short-term memory (e.g., Avons, Christopher, Wragg, Cupples, & Lovegrove, 1998; Gathercole & Baddeley, 1989; Gathercole & Martin, 1996; Gathercole, Willis, Emslie, & Baddeley, 1991; and see Grigorenko, this volume, for a review of findings) and have been claimed to be a valid measure of phonological short-term memory, reducing the likelihood of interference from stored knowledge over temporary phonological representation (Gathercole & Martin, 1996).

Noticing

Noticing was defined as "detection with awareness and rehearsal in short term memory" (Robinson, 1995b, p.318), and operationalized as the learner's articulation of response to the input[4], without distinguishing the degree of understanding involved, or the focus of noticing[5]. The following extracts from the data represent instances of what was coded as noticing: "In my head, I was trying so hard to make the question 'What are they doing' and then to say it" "I tend to use a declarative sentence with a raising intonation as a question, but she corrected my questions, so I thought I should say 'do' and 'is' in the beginning of the sentence."

Second language development

Second language development was operationalized as advances through the developmental stages of English question formation identified by Pienemann and Johnston (1987), following studies such as those by Mackey (1999)[6], Mackey and Philp (1998) and Lightbown and Spada (1993, 1998).

Interactional feedback

Interactional feedback encompasses discourse moves such as repetition, prosodic cues, comprehension checks, clarification requests, confirmation checks and recasts (see Long, 1996 for discussion). This study focused on recasts[7] in interaction, defined as utterances which rephrase a learner's production "by changing one or more sentence components (subject, verb, or object) while still referring to its central meanings" (Long 1996, p.434). Example 1 below illustrates a recast; the native speaker (NS) changes the order of the non-native speaker (NNS) utterance, substitutes "other" for "another" and adds a plural to the noun.

Example 1.

NNS   what are there another thing?
NS   ah what other things are there?

ESL learners

Thirty adult ESL participants, whose L1 was Japanese, participated in this study. They were recruited from ESL programs in universities and private institutions in Washington DC on the basis of (a) volunteering for the study, and (b) having lower intermediate proficiency in English as measured by the Test of English as a Foreign Language. The participants' TOEFL scores ranged from 417 to 547, with an average of 491. Participants' ages ranged from 19 to

30 with a mean of 25.7 with the exception of one person whose age was 55. The mean length of stay in the U. S. was 8.6 months, with a range of 3 to 20 months. Of the 30 participants who took part in the study, 11 participated in a stimulated recall session immediately after the treatment period, and the 19 remaining participants took a delayed posttest.

Native speaker interlocutors

A total of 10 native speakers (NS) of U. S. English participated in the experiment as interlocutors for the tasks in the pretest, posttests and treatment sessions. NSs included 9 females and 1 male, and were between the ages of 24 and 38. The NSs were trained to provide recasts of problematic L2 question forms during interaction, while carrying out communicative tasks, in order to control for consistency in the amount and type of interactional feedback provided. Training consisted of reading descriptions of targeted structures and tasks; viewing a video of NS-NNS task-based interaction with recasts; role-playing use of tasks, and discussing strategies for the appropriate delivery of recasts. A written set of instructions was also given to NSs prior to sessions.

Materials

Interaction materials: Communicative tasks

Two types of communicative tasks were used in the pretest and posttests, in order to assess learner's IL production and developmental levels in terms of question forms. Three types of communicative tasks were used in the treatment sessions in order to elicit the greatest variety of forms. These tasks had been used in previous studies (Mackey, 1999; Mackey & Philp, 1998; Philp, in press) to successfully provide contexts for L2 question forms to be used, and therefore to provide opportunities for interactional feedback to be provided. The participants asked questions in order to elicit information from their NS interlocutors. Examples of task types, classification features, and question structures that were targeted are summarized in Figure 1.

Nonword recall test

The phonological STM test consisted of a list of 16 pairs of non-words (32 in total). The non-words were 3–6 moras in length (four sets for each mora length) and consistency with phonotactic rules for Japanese was maintained[8]. Since Gathercole (1995) pointed out that highly word-like nonwords attract

Task	Description	Structures Targeted
Picture drawing	The native speaker has a picture. The participant asks questions to find out about the picture and then draws it.	*Wh*-question, copula inversions, yes/no inversion questions, *Wh/Do*-fronting questions
Picture difference	The native speaker and participant have similar pictures. The participant asks questions to find the differences.	*Wh*-question, copula inversions, yes/no inversion questions, *Wh/Do*-fronting questions, *Neg/Do* second questions
Story completion	Participants are shown pictures one by one. They ask questions to find out the story behind the pictures.	*Wh*-questions, *Do/Aux* questions, SVO questions, *Neg/Do* second questions

Figure 1. Task materials used for test and treatment.

involvement of individuals' long-term lexical knowledge and therefore may reduce the validity of the test, prior to implementation 13 NSs of Japanese rated word-likeness of each non-word on a 5-point Likert scale. Words that were defined as highly word-like (a mean rating of 4 or higher) were excluded from the test in order to minimize the effect of knowledge in long-term memory on participants' performance. During the implementation of the test, the words were first randomized and then presented in a fixed order using an audio cassette player. Prior to taking the test, each participant was presented with pre-recorded instructions, which contained a practice session as well as an explanation of the test procedure. Participants were asked to repeat each set of nonwords after an auditory prompt which was a tone sound.

Listening span tests
Various versions of listening span tests have been used in previous studies as a measure of verbal WM capacity (See for example, Harrington & Sawyer, 1992; Miyake & Friedman, 1998; Niwa, 2000, cited in Robinson, in press; Osaka & Osaka, 1992; Swanson & Berninger, 1996; Turner & Engle, 1989; Waters & Caplan, 1996).

In the current study, the Japanese sentences were taken from advanced level textbooks for Japanese as a foreign language (Miura & Oka, 1998). The sentences were modified to control for some of the factors that may have reduced comparability of sentences. The modified sentences were 8–12 content words in length, contained no embedded clauses, and were affirmative and in active voice (Turner & Engle, 1989). English sentences were taken from English textbooks used in Japanese high schools (Ando & Hale, 1994; Matsumura & Nakatani, 1995; Suenaga & Yamada, 1995) and modified. The modified sentences were 9–13 words in length, contained no embedded clauses, were affirmative, and in active voice. Half of all the Japanese and English sentences were designed as 'nonsense' sentences by rearranging the content words in such a way that sentences were syntactically possible but semantically anomalous (Harrington & Sawyer, 1992; Turner & Engle, 1989; Waters & Caplan, 1996).

During implementation, the participant was presented with pre-recorded sets of sentences. A set consisted of three, four, or five sentences (three sets per each sentence span level; 36 sentences in total). The order of the sets was first randomized and then was presented in a fixed order. As the participant listened to the sentences, he/she was directed to answer "OK" or "nonsense" after presentation of each sentence (during a 2 second interval) and to check the corresponding box on the answer sheet. Approximately half the sentences at each span level of three, four, and five sentences were constructed as semantically anomalous. Similar procedures have been followed by other researchers (Harrington & Sawyer, 1992; Turner & Engle, 1989; Waters & Caplan, 1996) in an attempt to ensure that the participants process the sentences for meaning without focusing only on the retention of recall items.

Finally, to assess the participants' verbal WM capacity, participants were asked to recall all the sentence initial words in the Japanese set and sentence final words in English set, irrespective of the order. Prior to both the L1 and L2 listening span tests, each participant was first presented with pre-recorded instructions which included a practice session. Before the test, participants were told that the end of each set would be signalled by a tone. The words that served as recall items were common nouns and were 3–4 moras in length (Japanese) or 1–3 syllables (English). None of the recalled words in the same set were semantically associated to each other, as subjectively judged by three of the researchers. No set consisted only of words that were highly abstract, another factor that has been found to affect the difficulty of word recall (Turner & Engle, 1989).

Stimulated recall
Stimulated recall protocols (Gass & Mackey, 2000) were elicited to uncover participants' introspective comments about their thoughts during the treatment sessions. Immediately after the final treatment session, videotaped clips

from three treatment sessions (one task from each session) were played for the participant by one of the researchers. The video was paused at any time by participants when they wished to describe their thoughts at any particular point in the interaction. The researcher paused the tape after each recast episode and at other (distractor) exchanges. The researcher provided participants with prompts that oriented them to the time when the original interaction was going on and asked them to recall what they were thinking at that time. The stimulated recall procedure and reports were carried out in the participants' L1 in order to present no barrier to their expressions of their thoughts[9].

Exit questionnaire
A written questionnaire was used to obtain data about noticing and to explore whether participants reported any extra-experimental input. The questionnaire included five questions pertaining to noticing. These focused on: (1) awareness about the goals of the study, (2) perceptions about learning during the treatment, (3) explicit linguistic rules for items they learned, (4) type of linguistic elements attended to, and (5) perceptions about interactional feedback. The questionnaires were given to the participants immediately after they completed their final posttests, or if they were in the stimulated recall group, their stimulated recall interviews[10].

Procedure

The study followed a pretest, treatment, posttest, delayed posttest design, as shown in Figure 2. Each test and treatment session lasted approximately 20–30 minutes. Following the pretest on the first day, three treatment sessions were administered on three consecutive days. After the immediate posttest, the participants were randomly assigned to two groups, a stimulated recall group and a delayed posttest group[11]. The stimulated recall group carried out their stimulated recalls after the immediate posttest on the same day. The delayed posttest group carried out a delayed posttest two weeks after the immediate posttest.

Week/ Day	Immediate Simulated recall group	Delayed posttest group	Activity (number of examples)
1/1	Pretest	Pretest	Picture drawing (2) Story completion (2)
1/2	Treatment 1	Treatment 1	Picture drawing (1) Picture difference (1) Story completion (1)
1/3	Treatment 2	Treatment 2	Picture drawing (1) Picture difference (1) Story completion (1)
1/4	Treatment 3	Treatment 3	Picture drawing (1) Picture difference (1) Story completion (1)
1/4	Posttest immediate SR Exit questionnaire	Posttest	Picture drawing (2) Story completion(2)
3/5		Delayed posttest Exit questionnaire	Picture drawing (2) Story completion (2)

Figure 2. Experimental procedure
Note: Two tasks were used in the pre and post tests for assignment of developmental level. A third task type was included in all treatment sessions to increase variety and ensure maximum opportunities for recasts.

Coding and Scoring

Question production data (pre and posttests)
Each participant's developmental level in terms of question forms was identified, based on their pretest performance, according to the developmental sequence for question forms identified by Pienemann and Johnston (1987; see also Spada & Lightbown, 1993; Mackey, 1999; Mackey & Philp, 1998; Philp, in press). Participants classified as being at Stage 4 produced yes/no questions with an auxiliary or modal in sentence initial position (for example, "Have you got a girl in your picture?" "Can you see 3 aliens?"), and *wh*-questions with inversion of the subject and copula (for example, "Why is she sad?" "Where is the alien?"). Participants classified as being at Stage 5 produced *wh*-questions in which the auxiliary or modal is in second position and is followed by a subject and main verb (for example, "Where are they going?" "What does he do?"). Participants who consistently produced questions in the posttest(s) that were at higher stages than those they produced in the pre-test

were coded as having increased in developmental stage. Evaluation of consistent production of forms at higher stages was based on the production of at least two question forms at higher levels in two different tasks (see Mackey, 1999; Mackey & Philp, 1998).

Noticing data (stimulated recall protocols and questionnaires)

Stimulated recall episodes involving recasts of the target structures were transcribed and coded. A recall episode was coded as a noticing instance when it included either or both of the following points: (1) participants' (metalinguistic) comments regarding English question forms and (2) participants' explicit acknowledgement of interlanguage errors and/or target-like recasts in relation to English question forms, with or without metalinguistic comments. These are seen in Examples 2 and 3, respectively, below.

> Example 2.
>
> "Well, I wanted to say 'doesn't she do other such and such things?' and, I said 'doesn't she such and such' and inserted a verb. Then, she [interlocutor] used a different expression at that time. When we make a negative question, don't we say 'doesn't / don't such and such'? Don't we insert something like 'don't' in the beginning [of a sentence]?" [ ] = transcription note by the researcher

> Example 3.
>
> "Umm, (I was thinking that) I made a mistake. She (the interlocutor) restates (what I said), for example, about 'is', she says 'um, Is?'"[12]

The same coding criteria were used for answers to the five questionnaire questions pertaining to noticing. One point was awarded for a stimulated recall episode or an answer to a question on the exit questionnaire when it satisfied coding criteria described above. The maximum score for the questionnaire answers was five (1 point for each of the five questions pertaining to noticing). The maximum score for the stimulated recall was open-ended, although participants had a similar range of opportunities to report noticing of feedback.

Working memory data (Nonword recall test and listening span tests)

On the nonword recall test, one point was allocated for an exact repetition of an auditory presented nonword and for a repetition which included a maximum of one different phoneme. For example, in response to the stimulus *no-ka-fu*, a repetition including one different phoneme, such as *mo-ka-fu* and *nu-ka-fu*, was counted as a correct response and granted one point. The possible score range was 0 to 32. On the listening span test, one point was awarded for an exact repetition of a word. However, very minor modifications, such as the addition of a Japanese politeness suffix[13] -o to a noun e.g., *furo* and *o-furo* gained the same points as exact repetition. Participants' (judgements regarding) anomaly of the stimuli sentences were analyzed solely to confirm participants' attention to meaning, and did not affect scoring decisions. The possible score range was 0 to 36[14].

Analysis[15]

Participants' WM abilities were assessed through the use of three different tests measuring different, albeit overlapping, memory abilities. As discussed above, these abilities have been associated with L2 learning and production. In addition to the individual tests, composite scores were obtained where the scores for each memory test were converted into z-scores and the sum of z-scores was calculated for each individual. Composite scores for all three tests were obtained, as well as composite scores for verbal working memory. Using a test battery to obtain composite scores as a representative measure of WM was motivated by the multi-component nature of WM suggested by recent research in cognitive psychology, (see for example, Miyake & Shah, 1999). One problem with using composite scores, however, is that two learners may obtain a similar composite result (for example, "high" WM capacity) through different routes, that is they may have completely different strengths/weaknesses in sub-components. However, composite scores may also be more predictive of SLA outcomes. Researchers of foreign language aptitude (for example, Skehan, 1989, 1998a) have argued that tests of language aptitude, such as the Modern Language Aptitude Test (Carroll & Sapon, 1959), can achieve strong predictive ability because of "their hybrid nature" (Skehan, 1989, p.34). That is, while individuals may score differently on subtests of a battery, whether they will be judged as high/low aptitude individuals depends solely on the composite scores. Clearly, by treating a multi-componential construct, such as WM or aptitude, as a monolithic construct, researchers sacrifice the ability to identify precisely the factors among the sub-components that may explain observed trends in dependent variables (i.e., relative success in L2 learning). In the current research both composite scores and subcomponent scores for each test were considered, in order to evaluate the relationship between L2 development, noticing and different aspects of working memory.

Nonword recall and listening span tests

In order to explore the relationship between the three memory tests, scores for each test were converted to z-scores. In a correlation analysis using Pearson's product moment correlation, these data reflect the findings of previous studies (Harrington & Sawyer, 1992; Miyake & Friedman, 1998; Osaka & Osaka, 1992). A low positive correlation was found between the phonological STM measure and the verbal WM tests: a correlation was found for non word recall and L1 listening span ($r=.443^*$, $p=.05$) but not for L2 listening span ($r=.308$). A high correlation was found between the L1 and L2 versions of the listening span tests ($r=.654^{**}$, $p=.01$).

Participants were divided into three groups, high, middle, and low, for each of the three memory tests and on a composite of the three tests, on the basis of their z-scores. Participants with z-scores greater than 0.5 were assigned to the high group and participants with z-scores greater than -0.5 were assigned to the low group. Participants with z-scores between -0.5 and 0.5 were assigned to the middle group. Z-scores were employed so that group assignment was based on the same criteria for all three tests, ensuring comparability of group assignment across tests. The threshold level of +/-0.5 meant that scores of participants in *high* and *low* group were at least one standard deviation apart[16]. The distribution of the groups is shown in Table 1. Since the constructs that the verbal L1 and L2 WM tests measured were closely related, and the test results for these two sub areas correlated highly with each other, composite scores for verbal WM were also calculated for each participant.

Table 1. Memory groups

	High	Middle	Low
Nonword recall test	10	9	11
Listening span test (Japanese)	8	16	6
Listening span test (English)	13	8	9

Measuring noticing

Noticing data from participants who took the delayed posttest came from their answers on the exit questionnaire[17]. Noticing data from 11 participants, who did not take the delayed posttest, came from stimulated recall protocols. In the recall sessions, participants' verbal reports of noticing were elicited as they watched videotapes of their own interactions with the NSs. Participants focused in particular on sequences including recasts provided by the NS. In contrast, the exit questionnaires required participants to answer specific questions about noticing without any visual or aural stimulus. Participants were categorized into two groups according to the amount of noticing registered. Stimulated Recall participants were considered to have reported 'more noticing' if they reported noticing 25% or more[18] of recasts from the three treatment sessions. Of the 11 participants in the SR group, 6 were classified as having reported 'more noticing,'while 5 were classified as having reported 'less noticing'. Delayed posttest participants were classified as having reported 'more noticing' if they provided two or more reports of noticing in answers to five noticing related questions on the exit questionnaires. Of the 16 delayed posttest participants, 5 reports indicated 'more noticing' while 11 reports indicated 'less noticing' on the exit questionnaire.[19]

Results

Research Question 1.: Is there a relationship between WM capacity and noticing of interactional feedback?
As noted above, a composite score was obtained for WM based on a combination of the scores for the three subtests. This exploration focused on data from the twenty participants whose scores were high or low on the composite test for WM. Six of the seven participants whose reports indicated more noticing, had high WM scores and one had a low score. Four of the thirteen participants whose reports indicated less noticing had high WM scores, while nine had low WM scores. These results are shown in Table 2. Statistical analysis indicated that the relationship between learners' reports of noticing and their WM scores was marginally significant[20] (Fishers Exact test, $X^2(1, N=20)=5.49, p=.057$). Figure 3 illustrates this relationship, showing that most learners who reported more noticing also had higher WM scores. Interestingly, the pattern did not approach significance for any of the individual sub-test scores.

Research Question 2.: Is the relationship between WM and noticing related to the learners' developmental level?
No statistically significant patterns were found in the relationship between WM, noticing and developmental level in terms of learners' working memory composite scores. However, when examined in the context of learners' scores on the test for phonological STM, some interesting patterns emerged.

Table 2. Noticing and working memory

| Group | NW/L1/L2 composite ($N = 20$) | |
	High	Low
More noticing	6	1
Less noticing	4	9

Note: NW/L1/L2 = Working memory as a composite of the three tests: nonword recall, L1 and L2 listening span tests.

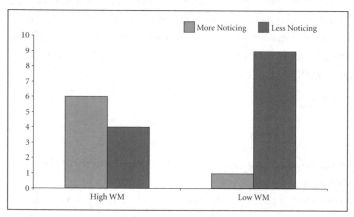

Figure 3. Reported noticing and working memory

Eight learners had high scores on the test for phonological STM capacity, four of these learners were at Stage 4, and four were at Stage 5. All of the Stage 4 learners' reports indicated more noticing. All of the Stage 5 learners' reports indicated less noticing[21]. Nine learners scored low on the test for phonological STM, three of these learners were at Stage 4, and six were at Stage 5. Two of the three Stage 4 learners and five out of six of the Stage 5 learners indicated less noticing, as seen in Table 3. This relationship is illustrated in Figure 4.

Table 3. Phonological short term memory, noticing and level of development

PSTM	Reported noticing	Stage 4	Stage 5
High	More	4	0
High	Less	0	4
Low	More	1	1
Low	Less	2	5

Note: PSTM = Phonological short term memory

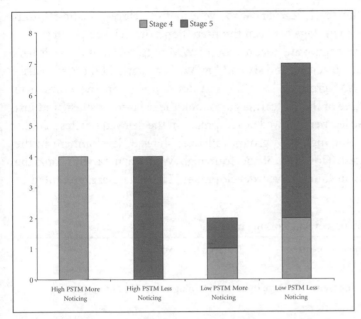

Figure 4. Working memory, noticing and developmental level

These differences were significant for learners with high phonological STM (Fishers exact test, X^2 (1, $N=8$)=8.00, $p=.029$) but not for learners with low phonological STM.

Research Question 3.: Is there a relationship between WM and interactionally driven second language development?

The analysis of working memory and L2 development utilized data from learners[22] who were evaluated as being at Stage 4 or lower at the time of the pretest and whose composite scores on the tests of WM were high or low. Data from 13 learners were examined, since they had potential to develop as a result of the feedback received during interactional treatment. Eleven of these learners were at Stage 4, one was at Stage 3, and one was at Stage 2. Six of the learners were in the stimulated recall group and seven were in the delayed posttest group. The effect of the treatment on the learners' IL grammars was assessed based on an increase in developmental stage between the pretest and the immediate posttest, or between the pretest and the delayed posttest (or the pretest and both posttests). Eleven of the 13 learners demonstrated interlanguage change in their production of question forms in posttests. Seven learners showed a change in the immediate posttest, using structures from higher stages. Five of the seven learners who were in the delayed posttest group showed an increase in stage between the pretest and the delayed posttest.

Based on their composite z-scores on the WM tests, seven of the 13 learners had high WM capacities, and six had low WM capacities. Of the six learners in the low WM group, all six showed development in the immediate posttest. Only three of the six learners also took the delayed posttest, and just one of these three learners showed development in the delayed posttest. Of the seven learners in the high WM group, only one showed development in the immediate posttest. However, of the four high WM learners who took the delayed posttest, all four showed development. These data are presented in Table 4.

Table 4. L2 Development and working memory

	Immediate posttest (N=13)		Delayed posttest (N=7)	
WM[a]	Development	No Development	Development	No Development
High	1	6	4	0
Low	6	0	1	2

Note: Whereas all learners carried out the immediate posttest (N=13), only those not in the SR group performed the delayed posttest (N=7).
[a] Working memory as a composite of the three tests: nonword recall, L1 and L2 listening span tests.

Clearly, the number of learners in this analysis is low and the trends reported here are best seen simply as indicators that this issue may be worthy of future exploration. However, the examination of the IL development of these learners with high and low WM capacities did reveal an interesting pattern. Whereas all six learners with low WM capacity appeared to benefit initially from interactional treatment, this initial benefit did not result in sustained IL development for two of the three learners who also took a delayed posttest. Conversely, all four of the learners with high WM who took the delayed posttest showed development after a two-week interval. Learners with low WM capacities were significantly more likely to develop in the immediate post test than learners with high WM capacities (X^2 (1, N=13)=9.55, p=.005). This pattern of initial change amongst low WM capacity learners and delayed development amongst high WM capacity learners is illustrated in Figure 5. This pattern was significant both for the composite scores, shown in Table 4, and also for the phonological STM scores (X^2 (1, N=21)=5.97, p=.035).

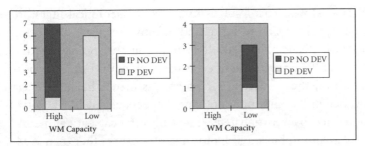

Figure 5. WM Capacity and IL development in the delayed posttest

Summary of results

Research Question 1.: Is there a relationship between WM capacity and noticing of interactional feedback?

Learners whose reports indicated less noticing tended to have low WM capacities. Learners whose reports indicated more noticing tended to have high WM capacities.

Research Question 2.: Is the relationship between WM and noticing related to the learners' developmental level?

Learners who scored high on the test for phonological STM, differed in their reports about noticing according to developmental level. Reports of learners at lower developmental levels indicated more noticing than the reports of learners at higher developmental levels.

Research Question 3.: Is there a relationship between WM and interactionally driven second language development?

Perhaps learners with low WM scores showed most initial interlanguage change. Learners with high WM scores showed more development in delayed post-tests (this finding is based on a very small data set).

Discussion

Working memory and noticing
In this study, the data suggest a relationship between WM composite scores and reports of noticing. When learners with high and low WM capacities were compared, most of the learners whose reports indicated they noticed more

also had higher WM scores. This result is in line with theoretical literature linking WM capacity, processing of input and effective retrieval of existing schematic knowledge (Skehan, 1998a). It is important to point out that whereas all but one of the learners classified as having low WM capacity provided reports indicating they noticed less, learners classified as having average WM capacities varied in the amount of noticing they reported. Clearly, noticing of interactional feedback is not determined by WM capacity alone. As both Skehan (1998a) and Robinson (1996b) suggest, factors other than WM, such as grammatical sensitivity and field independence, as well as socio-psychological factors, may constrain noticing. Our findings concerning the relationship between WM and noticing lend some support to Robinson's claim (1995b, in press) that WM constrains noticing. It is also likely that there is a complex relationship between individual differences in WM capacity, noticing, and the learner's prior knowledge base.

Working memory, noticing and the developmental level of the learner
The developmental level of the learner appeared to be a modulating factor in the relationship between WM capacity and reports about noticing. When the sub-test scores for phonological STM capacity were explored, learners with high scores for phonological STM who were at lower developmental levels reported more noticing than learners at higher developmental levels. Recasts could only be provided in response to learner errors, and thus were relevant to the level of the learners. However, learners who were at Stage 4 apparently noticed the feedback (on both Stage 4 and Stage 5 forms) more than learners who were at Stage 5. A close examination of the data suggests a potential explanation. For the Stage 4 learners, recasts may have been providing crucial input about constituents of question forms and their order, as seen in Example 4 below.

Example 4. Stage 4 learner treatment session
NNS   do do they are they doing are they doing ah on beach?
 NS   what are they doing on the beach (.) one man is resting
        (later turn)
NNS   uh what what do I what do they doing? What?
 NS   what are they doing?

However, for learners classified as being at Stage 5 in terms of question formation, in addition to the sorts of examples found in Example 4 above, there were also many recasts of their non-targetlike forms which corrected what may be viewed as performance lapses, or minor grammatical features such as the inclusion of an article or lexical item. These two trends can be seen in Examples 5 and 6 below.

> Example 5. Stage 5 learner treatment session
>
> NNS   so he what is he getting? Ah in hand?
> NS   what does he have in his hand?
> NNS   uh huh

> Example . Stage 5 learner treatment session
>
> NNS   do you think mm mmm why why did they mistake?
> NS   um (.) why did they make a mistake?
> NNS   yeah

It is possible that the Stage 5 learners reported noticing recasts less because the interactional feedback was less relevant for their emerging grammars. This is in line with previous studies that have suggested there may be a link between noticing and learners' interlanguage grammars. Interestingly, Bloom, Hood and Lightbown (1974) note in a study of FLA, that children responding to recasts were more likely to imitate linguistic items already emerging in their own interlanguage than forms that were completely novel or already acquired. Both in FLA (Gleitman, Newport, & Gleitman, 1984; Newport, Gleitman, & Gleitman, 1977) and SLA (Gass, 1997; Mackey, 1999; Philp, 1998; White, 1987), researchers have argued that the learners' emergent grammars modulate their apperception of the input and therefore the use they might make of interactional feedback. Philp (1998) also provides evidence of less noticing by learners when feedback was beyond their developmental level. However, there were too few learners at lower developmental stages in the current study to further test this claim. Nevertheless, the converse appears to be true: those learners who noticed more may have been those for whom the feedback was most relevant or appropriate. What is of interest here is the connection between WM, noticing and level. It is possible that neither level alone, nor WM capacity alone, nor the combination of these two factors alone accounts for reported noticing. Clearly further investigation with a larger data set is needed.

Working memory and IL development

In terms of how the learners made use of the feedback they received, these results suggest that learners with high WM capacity (based on their composite WM scores) were more likely to benefit from interactional treatment, not immediately after the treatment but after a time interval[23]. Because of the small sample size, we do not make any claims based on these data. However, these findings are considered indicative of a potential relationship between WM and efficiency in use of interactional feedback and seem worthy of testing further with a larger data set. A number of studies, both theoretical and empirical have suggested delayed development may be one effect of interaction (Gass & Varonis, 1994; Mackey, 1999). The results obtained from our limited dataset can be viewed as implicating WM capacity as a factor that constrains IL development through interaction.

Perhaps learners with high WM capacities are more efficient at processing the input they receive. While the current study examined shortterm IL change, other research such as Ando et al.'s (1992) study suggests the need for a comparison of the relationship between WM and long-term IL development. In Ando et al.'s study, learners' WM scores did not correlate with L2 learning under the 'communicative' instructional condition (i.e., the learners engaged in various meaning-oriented, communicative tasks) immediately after the instructional period. The WM scores did correlate, however, with the learners' performance in the delayed posttest, which was administered after a two-month interval. In the present study, a similar disparity was found over time, albeit over a much shorter time frame. Our results point to the complexity of the role of working memory in L2 acquisition. One might expect high WM to be implicated in short term learning or immediate IL change, through use of superior processing capacity and retrieval mechanisms. However, here, as in Ando et al.'s study, it seems that those with high WM took longer to consolidate and make sense of the feedback given them, reflecting change only after an interval. Although speculative, it may be that these learners had gleaned more data to process and consolidated this over time, compared to low WM capacity learners who could not "hold on" to data with great accuracy[24]. It should be emphasized that WM capacity, particularly given the limited nature of the tests and the small data set, is not the only factor in learners' use of interactional feedback, but is more likely to be one of a range of factors.

Limitations and future research

As a small scale exploratory study, the findings presented here have necessarily been modest and suggestive rather than conclusive. However, the study provides some avenues for exploring working memory, noticing and L2 development in the context of interaction.

The use of composite scores for describing working memory is not without its problems, as discussed earlier, however it is reassuring that the WM battery correlated highly with an aptitude test battery[25] and that the correlation produced similar patterns among WM subtests to those found in previous studies concerning L2 learning and use (Harrington & Sawyer, 1992; Miyake & Friedman, 1998; Osaka & Osaka, 1992).

The relationship between WM and noticing found in our study may also be a reflection of the target form employed in the study. Question formation involves word ordering and choice of auxiliary. It is possible that learning how to form questions is largely based on collocation and sequencing, which, as Ellis (N.Ellis, 1996, 2001; N. Ellis & Schmidt, 1997; N. Ellis & Sinclair, 1996) has argued, is constrained by phonological STM. The relative importance of phonological STM, among other functions of WM, in the noticing and developmental level relationship suggested by our results may also be a reflection of the nature of the tasks employed in the study. The tasks used in our study required the participants to engage in meaningful interaction with the native speaker interlocutors. During such task-based oral interaction, which is clearly different from most reading and writing tasks, participants may need to rely strongly on their ability to store phonological sequences, maintaining both the native speakers' and their own utterances in WM. This kind of ability may have been most directly measured by our phonological STM measure [26].

It is also possible that utilizing more refined instrumentation for measuring noticing may have revealed more noticing amongst low WM learners, or may have enabled us to explore the issue at a finer level of granularity. The specific relationship between noticing and interlanguage development is a topic our current research is exploring with a larger data set.

In summary, this study has offered a small window onto the complex relationships between WM capacity, noticing and interactionally driven L2 development. While the majority of studies to date have dealt with WM capacity in carefully controlled laboratory settings, this study has attempted to explore working memory within the dynamic context of oral interaction. While this necessitated the use of a small data set with less control over variables, which led to fewer statistically meaningful results, this type of study also has the advantage of being closer to authentic NS-NNS interactions and resultant learning than a more controlled laboratory study.

Notes

1. Citing various priming studies as providing evidence for implicit learning, Tomlin and Villa argue for the possibility of a dissociation between learning and awareness, as others have done (see Carr & Curran, 1994; Gass, 1997).

2. "Sentence span test" is used as a cover term for both reading and listening versions of the tests, based on Daneman and Carpenter (1980). The terms "reading span test" or "listening span test," are used when referring to the specific type of sentence span test being used. '

3. A discussion of the relationship between STM and WM is beyond the scope of this chapter. We have focused instead on the memory constructs that previous research has linked to aspects of second language learning. Miyake and Shah (1999) and Robinson (in press) provide relevant discussion of models of WM and attention.

4. While watching videotaped clips of their conversations with native speakers, learners were asked about their thoughts during interaction. Questionnaires were also used to elicit data about noticing. Details are provided in the methods section.

5. It should be noted that the construct of noticing has attracted criticism. Carroll (1999) and Truscott (1998) have both criticized Schmidt's noticing hypothesis on the basis of its lack of specificity. In particular, Carroll notes that it does not deal with properties of the input that might trigger noticing, making it pre-theoretical. However Robinson (in press) argues that "these are not valid objections to the noticing hypothesis *per se*, which is not a comprehensive theory, and was not proposed as one," quoting Schmidt's (2001) characterization of what must be noticed as 'elements of the surface structure of utterances in the input, instances of language, rather than any abstract rules or principles of which such instances may be exemplars' and characterizing Carroll's objections as "irrelevant to the noticing hypothesis as stated" (p. 10).

6. Some motivations for using question forms as a measure of development were summarized by Mackey (1999, p. 566), who noted that previous research has shown that the question forms were readily elicited, were present at all stages of learning, fall into the category of complex structures that some researchers have suggested may be affected by interaction (see, e.g., Pica, 1994), and that empirical research for the stages of acquisition of question formation is relatively robust (Mackey & Philp, 1998; Pienemann, Johnston, & Brindley, 1988; Pienemann & Mackey, 1993; Spada & Lightbown, 1993; Philp, in press). Mackey also notes that questions have been fairly well studied in terms of phonology, morphosyntax, and semantics and that the issue of readiness to acquire certain forms can be controlled.

7. Recasts may provide one or more syntactic changes to a learner's original utterance. Research suggests a potential distinction between "simple" and "complex" recasts in terms of provision and learner modification, for both FLA (Bohannon & Stanowicz, 1988; Farrar, 1992) and SLA (Oliver, 1995). The current study did not distinguish between simple and complex recasts, since the focus was WM, noticing and L2 development as opposed to the contribution of different kinds of recasts to L2 learning.

8. It is possible that the ability to perceive and recall nonwords following the phonotactic rules of the L2 might be influenced by familiarity with the L2. Therefore, nonwords fol-

lowing the phonotactic rules of the participants' L1, Japanese, were used in order to minimize effects of L2 proficiency and ensure the validity of the test as a measure of the participants' phonological short-term memory, independent of language proficiency.

9. Eliciting stimulated recall protocols from participants is a labor intensive process, often requiring several researchers to work with individual learners (and data) simultaneously. Data for recalls must be carefully selected in order to maintain comparability and reliability. Although it is very time consuming and often necessitates working with a smaller data set, stimulated recall data can offer an important window into learners' cognitive processes, especially during oral interaction. One hundred and thirty four hours of oral data were analyzed for the current study.

10. For the SR learners the questionnaire data were used simply to rule out extra experimental input..

11. Groups differed in numbers due to constraints of time and equipment.

12. The original SR comments in Japanese were as follows: Example 2: "Eto ne, hokani naninani wa shinai no, tte iu fuu ni hyoogen shitakatta no. De, 'Doesn't she' naninani ga aru no, dooshi o ireta no ne, de, kanojyo ga nanka chigau hyoogen o shita no ne, son toki ni. Hiteikei no gimonbun ni suru toki wa, 'Doesn't, Don't' naninani toka shinai no? 'Don't' toka mae ni irenai no?"; Example 3: "U-n, yappari, jibun no a, machigattyata tte iu no wa. Iinaoshite kureru n desu yo ne, kanojyo ga. Is toka, aa 'Is?' tte."

13. Use of politeness suffixes relates to issues of individually different speech styles and gender.

14. Performance was also scored according to the maximum size of the set of sentences correctly recalled by the participant. The two scoring methods yielded roughly the same rank-order of the participants. However, the total number of recalled words was selected as appropriate scoring criteria for the analysis because of greater variability among scores, which allowed discrimination between high and low WM capacities. This selection procedure was also used by Turner and Engle (1989).

15. The three research questions were addressed by focusing on data from different sets of the 30 participants. Research question 1 was addressed by examining data from learners who scored high and low on the working memory tests; research question 2 was addressed by examining data from learners at Stages 4 and 5 in production of ESL questions; and research question 3 was addressed by examining data from learners who were not at Stage 5. For this reason, the N sizes in tables vary according to the analysis.

16. Data from learners in the middle WM group were not included in the analyses in order to make the group comparison more discriminatory.

17. Questionnaires were obtained from 16 of the 19 delayed posttest participants.

18. The rationale for using a score of 25% or more to indicate "more noticing" was based on L1A research by Bohannon, MacWhinney, and Snow (1990) and SLA research by Oliver (1995, 2000). These researchers argue that corrective feedback need not be provided in response to all error utterances for it to be usable, basing their argument on work by Levine (1963), who demonstrated that concept learning was possible even when corrective feedback was provided on fewer than 25% of trials.

19. Two different measures of noticing were necessary as only 11 of the 30 participants carried out the stimulated recall sessions. Responses to the noticing questionnaire provided a means of examining noticing from those participants in the delayed posttest group. The two datasets, while not viewed as directly equivalent, were carefully scrutinized for obvious disparities, and scores were combined for the purposes of analysis.

20. As small cell sizes precluded the use of chi square tests, Fisher's Exact tests were used for all analyses (Hatch & Lazaraton, 1991).

21. Recasts are contingent upon learner errors. The likelihood of a group of learners producing identical errors is very low. Therefore, the number of recasts, and the types of forms recast in the treatment were obviously not identical for all learners because learners receive recasts in response to their own non-targetlike forms. In this way, recasts have been claimed to provide feedback at the optimal time for learners, both in terms of the immediate discourse, and in terms of their developmental levels. Both in terms of selection of the recall data, and posthoc examination of a sample of the treatment transcripts, learners received roughly similar amounts of recasts, with Stage 5 learners receiving approximately 10% more recasts of Stage 5 forms, and Stage 4 learners receiving approximately 12% more recasts of forms at Stages 3 and 4. Thus, learners had similar opportunities to notice feedback on forms within their levels.

22. Three Stage 4 learners were excluded from the analysis as their WM scores were in the middle range. The other 14 learners in the study were already at Stage 5 at the time of the pretest. As Stage 6 questions were not elicited by the tasks and were rarely produced or recasted, development beyond Stage 5 was not explored in the analysis.

23. We did not consider IL change measured by the immediate posttest as equivalent to evidence of learning, since the change was not sustained after a (two week) interval.

24. We thank an anonymous reviewer for making this suggestion.

25. Language aptitude was measured by Sasaki's Language Aptitude Battery for Japanese (LABJ) described by Sasaki (1996) (see also Ross et al., and Robinson, this volume, who also used the LABJ in their studies). The LABJ consisted of three sub-sections, each measuring associative memory, inductive language learning ability, and phonemic coding ability. The composite z-scores for the LABJ and the composite z-scores for the WM battery positively correlated (Pearson's product moment $N=30$, $r=.762$, $p<.01$), as did the composite scores for verbal WM and the LABJ ($N=30$, $r=.632$, $p<.01$). Correlations among the subtests of WM and the subtests of LABJ were also computed. The results of these are seen in Table 5 below.

26. Clearly, only certain aspects of WM were tapped by the phonological STM measure and the verbal WM tests used. Both the listening span tasks and the nonword repetition tasks measured recall. Hence these verbal WM tests may reflect storage components rather than processing and attention components. Arguably performance on these tests reflects the ability of learners to maintain units in the focus of attention.

Table 5. Correlation between working memory subtests
and aptitude subtests ($N = 30$)

	NW	L1	L2	AptMem	AptLa	AptPhon
NW	1.000	.444*	.308	.582**	.524**	.661**
L1		1.000	.654**	.594**	.452*	.603**
L2			1.000	.482**	.348	.479**
AptMem				1.000	.491**	.753**
AptLa					1.000	.560**
AptPhon						1.000

Note. NW = nonword recall test (a phonological short-term memory measure); L1 = L1 listening span test (the L1 verbal working memory measure); L2 = L2 listening test (an L2 verbal working memory measure); AptMem = LABJ Part 1, associative memory; AptLA = LABJ Part 2, inductive language learning ability; AptPhon = LABJ Part 3, phonological coding ability.
*$p < .05$. **$p < .01$.

CHAPTER 10

Effects of individual differences in intelligence, aptitude and working memory on adult incidental SLA[*]

A replication and extension of Reber, Walkenfield and Hernstadt (1991)

Peter Robinson
Aoyama Gakuin University

Introduction

The extent to which individual differences (IDs) in cognitive abilities differentially affect second language acquisition (SLA) under different conditions of exposure is an issue of theoretical, and practical importance. In recent years a growing number of experimental laboratory studies of SLA have attempted to study the effects of different conditions of exposure on second language (L2) learning, where learning conditions are operationalized as 'instructional set' (Reber, 1976) to the learning task, and where ± *attention* to; ± *awareness* of; and ± *intention* to learn, the structure of the L2 domain are the variables of interest (see N.Ellis, 1993; DeKeyser, 1995, 1997; de Graaff, 1997a; Hulstijn, 1990; Robinson, 1996a, 1997a, 1997b; Robinson & Ha, 1993; Williams, 1999; and see DeKeyser, in press; Hulstijn, 1997, in press, for overviews). The methodology, and explanations of findings in laboratory SLA studies has in large part been stimulated by similar research into the effects of attention and awareness on learning the structure of complex stimulus domains in cognitive psychology (see Cleeremans, Destrebecqz, & Boyer, 1998; O'Brien-Malone & Maybery, 1998 for review). In both lines of research, *implicit* learning conditions (i.e., those that encourage memory based learning, without awareness of the rule governed structure of what has been learned, and without intention to discover it), have often been contrasted with *incidental* learning conditions (in which participants process stimuli for semantic, or other content, and unintentionally learn the rule-governed structure of the domain, though they often become aware of it during processing), and *explicit* learning conditions (in which participants are made aware the domain has a rule-governed structure — by being told there are rules, or by being taught them in advance — and are then instructed to intentionally to search for, or apply, the rules in processing the input they receive during training).

In general the findings from these laboratory studies, supported by results of classroom studies of the effects of instructed SLA (see Norris & Ortega, 2000 for a meta-analysis), have been that; i) attention to input is necessary for SLA; ii) that awareness is facilitative and likely necessary too (though difficult to assess); iii) but that intention to learn — while necessary in many areas of vocabulary acquisition (Hulstijn, 2001, in press) — is not necessary for grammar acquisition, and can sometimes have negative, as well as positive, consequences, especially where the structural domain is complex.

These generalizations are not universally accepted, particularly, i) and ii) above. With regard to the necessity of attention, some have claimed that 'non-attentional' L2 learning is possible (Schacter, Wright, Rounds & Smith, 1996), or that the notion that attention is 'selective' of input is problematic for SLA theory (Carroll, 1999). The necessity of awareness has been more disputed (Truscott, 1998); there have been claims that attention without awareness, i.e., simple 'detection' or preconscious registration of input stimuli, is the level at which L2 learning begins (Tomlin & Villa, 1994); that one can notice L2 data 'subconsciously' (R.Ellis, 1994b, p.95); and that the resulting implicitly acquired L2 knowledge can later 'become' explicit knowledge.

Of less interest, until recently, both in cognitive psychology and SLA research, has been the role of IDs in cognitive abilities in mediating learning under the different conditions of attention to, awareness of, and intention to learn, the structure of the domain. While there are few findings to date in this area, two broad theoretical positions have been put forward in recent years. On the one hand Reber (1993; Reber & Allen, 2000; Reber, Walkenfield & Hernstadt, 1991) has argued that unconscious implicit learning, and in many cases incidental learning (Reber & Allen, p. 238), are unaffected by differences in cognitive capacities measured by currently available intelligence tests, such as the Wechsler Adult Intelligence Scale-Revised (WAIS-R), whereas, the extent of explicit, conscious learning *will* be affected by intelligence measured using this, and similar instruments for assessing intelligence quotient (IQ). One study in particular (Reber et al., 1991) has been claimed to provide direct evidence for this claim, and a few subsequent studies (reviewed below) have been claimed to provide inferential support for the basic finding that IDs in IQ and implicit and incidental learning are unrelated, though Reber admits that this important area is in need of much further research, even commenting that 'the issue of individual differences in implicit learning has gone almost completely unexplored' (Reber & Allen, p. 229). Complementary to this view Stanovich and West (2000) argue there are two coherent and conceptually distinct types of thinking and reasoning, System 1 and System 2. System 2 is later developed, and equated with intelligence whereas System 1 is not. However, others (Newstead, 2000; Oberauer, 2000) see the two types of system as nondistinct, or as lying on a continuum.

Similarly to Reber, Krashen (1982, 1985, 1994, 1999) has argued that unconscious second language 'acquisition' (by which Krashen means both unintentional, incidental, and unaware, implicit L2 acquisition during processing L2 input for meaning) is unaffected by differences in measures of aptitude, whereas the extent of conscious second language 'learning' (the intentional search for rules, or use of pedagogically presented rules) *is* affected by aptitude. Related to these arguments is the claim that access to innate knowledge of constraints on the shape of possible grammars, in the form of Universal Grammar (UG) remains accessible in adulthood (Schwartz, 1986; Schwartz & Sprouse, 1994), and that access to such informationally encapsulated, modularized knowledge is automatic, and unaffected by IDs in measures of general cognitive abilities, which contribute only to distinct, non UG, general learning procedures.

In contrast to these dual system explanations of human learning, following Schmidt (1990, 2001), and transfer appropriate, and episodic-processing explanations of implicit/explicit learning (Blaxton, 1989; Graf & Ryan, 1990; Neal & Hesketh, 1997; Roediger, Challis & Weldon, 1989; Whittlesea & Dorken, 1993; Whittlesea & Wright, 1997) it has been proposed that adult L2 learning under any conditions of exposure is *fundamentally similar* (Robinson, 1996b, 1997a), since it requires conscious processes such as 'noticing' (Schmidt, 1990; Schmidt & Frota, 1986) and rehearsal of noticed input in memory, and that therefore measures of IDs in cognitive abilities relevant to the processing demands of specific learning tasks will be likely to affect the extent of learning. While child L1 and adult L2 learning may be fundamentally different (Bley-Vroman, 1988) — the former drawing heavily on domain specific innate knowledge, and implicit learning mechanisms, and the latter on general problem solving procedures and cognitive resources available during central processing — the Fundamental

Similarity Hypothesis proposes that cognitive maturity, critical period effects, and existing L1 knowledge conspire to prevent adult access back to ontogenetically earlier evolved implicit L1 acquisition mechanisms. Dual systems (acquisition/learning, implicit/explicit, UG/central processing) are not dissociated in the domain of adult SLA, and consequently IDs in cognitive abilities have ubiquitous effects on the effectiveness of the general problem solving procedures, and explicit modes of information processing that adults adopt in learning an L2, accounting in part for the wide variation in levels of attainment, and rate of adult L2 learning progress.

While this issue is therefore of considerable theoretical importance, it is also of immediate practical importance for L2 pedagogy and the use and value of aptitude testing. If the claims of Reber regarding domain general implicit learning, and of Krashen regarding L2 acquisition, are correct then IDs in cognitive abilities, as measured by current intelligence and aptitude tests, are relatively uninfluential on naturalistic, and also classroom learning, especially where the knowledge base is assumed to develop largely incidentally from exposure (Saffran, Newport, Aslin, Tunick, & Barrueco, 1997), e.g., to comprehensible L2 input made available during currently popular approaches to pedagogy such as communicative, immersion, content, or task-based forms of instruction.

Rethinking aptitude: Differentiating cognitive abilities, intelligences, aptitudes, and aptitude complexes

A related claim to that of Reber and Krashen has been made over the last twenty years by educational psychologists concerned with the implications of intelligence theory and research for educational practice. This claim is that traditional measures of IQ, while successfully predicting 'academic' success, do not predict the ability to develop domain specific tacit knowledge, such as that underlying the ability to rapidly calculate and use information about horse 'handicapping' and racing odds to successfully place bets at the race track (Ceci & Liker, 1986), or domain knowledge in other areas of practical life (see Sternberg & Wagner, 1986). Briefly put, one response to such evidence has been to propose constrained theories of 'multiple intelligences' (e.g., Gardner, 1993; Sternberg, 1985a, 1990, this volume), drawing on different constellations of domain appropriate cognitive abilities, each influencing success in different adaptive domains, rather than to limit the scope of a monolithic, 'general' intelligence, or g, to academic contexts and pursuits. Some have argued this response is likely appropriate for models of aptitude for L2 learning too (Grigorenko, Sternberg & Ehrman, 2000; Robinson, 2001c; Robinson & Cornwell, 2000). Rather, that is, than argue aptitude is relevant only to learning under particular 'explicit' conditions of instructional exposure, a range of aptitudes, or aptitude 'complexes' may need to be proposed, and differentially matched to different learning conditions, task types, and instructional interventions (see Robinson, 2001a, 2001b, in press; Snow, 1987, 1994).

For example, Carroll (1993; Carroll & Sapon, 1959) has argued that four factors underlie performance on the Modern Language Aptitude test (MLAT); rote memory for word associations measured by a paired associates (PA) subtest; grammatical sensitivity measured by a words in sentences (WS) subtest; and phonemic sensitivity, and inductive learning ability, measured by other subtests. Predictive validity for the MLAT was initially obtained by correlating performance on the test with success in classrooms operationalizing audiolingual learning conditions (+ attention/ + awareness/ + intention), requiring rote memorization and practice of grammatical patterns, presented aurally, with extensive explicit error correction and little opportunity for group work. However, with the advent of *communicative* approaches to L2 instruction, and in particular recent *task-based* approaches (Long & Crookes, 1992) which advocate meaningful language use on tasks designed to promote interaction, with only occasional 'focus on form' (+ attention/+ or − awareness/ − intention)(Long, 1991; Long & Robinson, 1998) sometimes *reactively* delivered by such techniques as oral recasts, or *proactively* by such techniques as input enhancement, flooding, or processing instruction (see Doughty & Williams, 1998), there is some reason to doubt whether the MLAT has construct validity, and optimal predictive validity, as a measure of the processing demands and learning consequences of these very different learning conditions and pedagogic interventions. But this does not mean aptitude is less influential in these classrooms, but rather that aptitude for learning in these classrooms reflects a reconfiguration of the basic cognitive abilities partially measured by tests such as MLAT. For these classrooms, and learning conditions, a measure of aptitude that reflects the processing demands of simultaneous attention to form and meaning, with its attendant demands on working memory (WM) (Baddeley, 1986; N.Ellis, 1996, 2001; Gathercole & Baddeley, 1993; Mackey et al., this volume; Miyake & Friedman, 1998; Miyake & Shah, 1999) would seem to be necessary. Further, given the on-line, reactive nature of some focus on form techniques, such as recasting, which result in only brief, temporary attention to form, it would also seem plausible that a measure of processing speed (Anderson, 1992; Salthouse, 1996; Stankov, 1999; Willingham, 1998) might also be a valid measure of the necessary cognitive abilities for learning in such classrooms, as might measures of the ability to 'switch' attention between (Segalowitz, in press), and so cognitively compare (Doughty, 2001), learner output and corrective recasts.

If this line of response to critiques that aptitude measures only 'learning', and reflects only academic, crystallized intellingence, is to be seriously pursued, it will involve some reconceptualisation of language learning aptitude, and sustained empirical enquiry into how the structure of mental abilities underlying aptitude interacts with implicit, explicit and incidental learning conditions, and the processing demands of different L2 learning tasks. In summary, the role of IDs in cognitive abilities in learning under different conditions of exposure has important theoretical consequences for our knowledge of the role of attention and awareness in L2 learning, and practical consequences too for the development of new measures of aptitude with 'predictive' validity, in a range of classroom learning environments. These issues are further discussed below, along with others, before the results of a study of the effects of IDs in intelligence, aptitude and working memory on implicit, explicit and incidental L2 learning are described.

Individual differences during implicit, incidental and explicit learning

Many would have argued that processes contributing to implicit learning are variegated, and differentially activated by the processing conditions of different implicit learning tasks, and that it is in investigating the relationship between specific task demands and varieties of implicit learning processes, and their interaction with explicit processes, that future progress in understanding the role of awareness in learning and memory lies (e.g., Butler & Berry, 2001; N.Ellis, 1993; Matthews, Buss, Stanley, Blanchard-Fields, Cho & Druhan, 1989; Perruchet & Amorim, 1992; Rosetti & Revonsuo, 2000; Seger, 1998; Shanks & St. John, 1994; Whittlesea & Dorken, 1993). However, despite this likely multiplicity, DeKeyser (in press) makes an important and useful, *basic* distinction between two broad categories of implicit learning, which helps resolve one ambiguity sometimes present in the SLA literature on implicit L2 learning. This is between implicit inductive learning (resulting from instance-based, data-driven rehearsal of stimuli), and implicit deductive learning (resulting from elaborative rehearsal of stimuli, requiring the activation of preexisting representational schemata)(see also Robinson, 1995b, in press, and Williams, 1999, for discussion).

Individual differences and implicit deductive learning
Concerning implicit deductive learning, Dennet (1988 p. 216) has argued that 'for information to be represented implicitly, we shall mean that it is *implied* logically by something that is stored explicitly (emphasis added)'. Roberts (1998) calls this sense of 'implicit' 'representational implicitness', and it is in this sense that UG can be called a theory of implicit, deductive learning. Positive evidence when attended, is often comprehended and elaboratively rehearsed in memory, but what is *implied* by the triggering feature of the input is a representational specification of the shape of the L2 grammar, as described in UG (Dresher, 1999; Gibson & Wexler, 1994). Given the modular, encapsulated nature of the UG knowledge base, such implicit deduction has been argued to be fast, involuntary and insensitive to IDs in the cognitive abilities drawn on by central processing (Fodor, 1983).

Individual differences and implicit inductive learning
In contrast to this interpretation of implicit learning, Reber has argued against the need to propose any representationally encapsulated, innate mechanisms and knowledge to explain implicit learning, in favor of connectionist, data-driven models of representation (1993), as have many others (e.g., Cleeremans, 1993; Dienes, 1992: Dienes & Perner, 1998; N.Ellis, 2001; N.Ellis & Schmidt, 1997). To this extent, Reber's position is that implicit learning is inductive, and domain general, and results not from automatic, involuntary activation of pre-existing, domain specific, grammatical schemata which guide the analysis of input data (see Carroll, 2001), but simply from 'the absence of conscious, reflective strategies to learn' (Reber, 1989 p. 219) which different experimental conditions aim to induce, or not.

The extent of implicit inductive learning has often been addressed in a research paradigm where participants are exposed to letter strings generated by a miniature artificial Markovian grammar (see Appendix A and the methodology section below) and instructed simply to 'memorize' them (the implicit, unaware condition) or to actively 'search for the rules' governing the sequences of letters (the explicit, aware condition). Reber (1989, 1993) has argued that results of research in this paradigm support the claim that there are two distinct *modes* of adult learning — implicit (unintentional, inaccessible to awareness) as revealed in transfer test evidence of above chance accurate induction of the rules of the letter display in the memorize only condition — and explicit (intentional, and accessible to awareness), as revealed by the performance of participants asked to find the rules. In many cases it has been found that implicit learning is in excess of explicit learning, particularly where the rules governing the display are complex.

Reber has explained the 'primacy of the implicit' in evolutionary terms. Implicit learning (and memory) processes, Reber argues, are phylogenetically earlier evolved than their explicit counterparts. Consequently implicit processes show more cross-species commonality, in contrast to explicit processes which, Reber argues, are phylogenetic latecomers on the evolutionary scene, occurring "in only some (albeit most) of the species tested to date (Wynne, 1998)" (Reber & Allen, 2000, p. 233). Ontogenetically, implicit processes are also argued to be earlier evolved and longer lasting than explicit processes, and to be robust in the face of aging and neurological insult, whereas explicit processes are much more affected by these, being slower to develop in childhood, but also first to decline in late adulthood (Reber, 1993; Reber & Allen, 2000). Complementary to these arguments, IDs in cognitive abilities, such as IQ, are claimed *not to affect* implicit processes during adulthood, which show very little population variance, in contrast to explicit processes which *are sensitive* to IDs in cognitive abilities, and which exhibit large variance in the population (Reber, 1989, 1993; Reber & Allen, 2000).

In support of this latter claim Reber, et al. (1991) reported the results of an experiment which assessed the relationship of IDs in intelligence (measured by a short form of the WAIS-R) with learning under explicit conditions where participants were instructed to try to complete series solution problems (described in detail below) and under implicit conditions, where participants were instructed to memorize examples generated by a finite-state grammar (also described in detail below). Their results showed much greater variance in explicit learning: implicit learning showed a very narrow pattern of variance (see Table 1 below). In addition, explicit learning of the series solution task correlated significantly and positively with IQ, ($r=.69$ $p <.01$) whereas implicit learning of the rules of the finite-state grammar correlated non significantly ($r=.25$ $p >.05$) with WAIS-R scores.

Individual differences and incidental L2 learning
Subsequent to the publication of Reber et al. (1991) a few studies have also been claimed to support the position Reber describes, showing measures of IQ relate to performance on explicit, but not implicit versions of contingency detection tasks by children (Maybery, Taylor & O'Brien-Malone, 1995; McGeorge, Crawford & Kelly, 1987). Reber concedes that "incidental learning is not identical to implicit rule or pattern learning, but is similar in the sense

that it is unintentional and uncontrolled" (Reber & Allen, 2000, p. 238) and reports studies of the incidental acquisition of visuo-spatial, non-complex location information (Ellis, Katz & Williams, 1987), showing that, like the implicit learning studies reviewed, incidental learning also appears to be "unrelated to gross measures of high-level cognitive function" (Reber & Allen, 2000, p. 238). However, reviewing studies of incidental learning that require "processing of verbal or complex material", and so greater depth of processing (Ellis & Allison, 1988; Schultz, 1983), Reber and Allen argue IDs "might" emerge in these domains (p. 238). The issue in question, then, is whether they *do*, since incidental L2 learning is clearly a complex, verbal task domain which would appear to require greater depth of processing than the experiments forming the basis of Reber's claims about implicit processes and IDs.

One categorical answer to this question, however, has been "no", since as briefly described above, Krashen (1982, 1985) also proposed a dual-system theory of instructed L2 development, and claimed aptitude tests measure the abilities drawn on in conscious 'learning', but not in unconscious 'acquisition', or incidental learning during processing for meaning, where IDs in aptitude can be expected to play no role. Supporting this dual-system, noninterface position, Paradis (1994) has argued that neurophysiologically distinct learning and memory systems are responsible for incidental acquisition, versus explicit L2 learning. Similarly supporting this position Zobl (1992, 1995), in reviewing results of previous effect of instruction studies, has claimed that within group variance in L2 learning which takes place during incidental, meaning focused instructional treatments, such as those occurring in Canadian L2 immersion programs (see e.g., Harley, Allen, Cummins & Swain, 1990), is much lower than when learning takes place in formS focussed instructional treatments.

Laboratory studies of IDs, aptitude and incidental SLA
There is some recent counter evidence to these related claims (of Reber, Krashen and Zobl) that IDs in abilities, and aptitude(s), only influence learning in explicit conditions, and where L2s are the learning domain. De Graaff (1997b) found aptitude positively affected learning of both an artificial, and a natural language, in an implicit (exposure and semantic processing without rule explanation) as well as an explicit (exposure and semantic processing with rule explanation) condition. Importantly, in the artificial grammar (experanto) learning experiment de Graaff found two measures of aptitude, a Dutch version of the WS MLAT subtest, and a measure of the ability to infer word

meaning in context, 'tended to be significant' (1997b, p. 261) in predicting learning in both conditions, whereas the rote memory Paired Associates (PA) MLAT subtest did not (although it did not correlate negatively). Collapsed scores from all aptitude subtest showed significant positive correlations with performance on three out of four tests/task types (administered midway through training and on an immediate, and delayed posttest).

Williams (1999) studied the effects of individual differences in memory on implicit L2 learning. Memory was operationalised as the number of correct attempts to recall sentences in a novel language — a corrupted form of Italian — following computer presentation during a training period. Learning was assessed in a transfer translation task requiring participants to demonstrate knowledge of a number of the subrules of the language they had been exposed to. Williams found considerable variance in accuracy of recall at the beginning of training (IDs in memory), for the first 8 Italian sentences viewed and heard (Block 1) but rather less variance at the end of training, on the last 8 sentences viewed and heard (Block 5). Williams also found the translation task revealed accurate learning of *some* of the aspects of grammar, such as verb inflections, but not of others, such as article noun agreement.

Importantly, Williams found that accuracy of recall early during training (on Block 1) correlated significantly, and positively with accuracy during the translation post test. In fact, accuracy of early recall correlated much *more* strongly than accuracy of later, Block 5 recall. Williams concludes, 'It would appear from this result that there is at least some sense in which knowledge of grammatical rules emerges out of memory for input and that individual differences in memory ability that are apparent even in the earliest stages of exposure have consequences for ultimate levels of learning. The results suggest that the learning occurring in this experiment can be characterized as data driven' (p. 22).

Contrary to the claims of Reber, Krashen and Zobl, Robinson (1996b, 1997a) found significantly *less variance* in transfer test evidence of grammar learning (of a natural language, English) for adult Japanese learners *instructed* in easy and hard pedagogic rules of English, then asked to apply them to examples viewed during training, than for *implicit* learners (who as in the implicit 'unaware' conditions of Reber's experiments were instructed only to memorize co-occurring stimuli in sentences viewed during training), or for *incidental* learners (instructed only to process sentences viewed during training for meaning), or for learners instructed to *search for rules*. However, in partial contrast to the findings of de Graaff (1997b), and Williams (1999),

Robinson (1996a, 1997b) also showed aptitude, as measured by the WS, and PA subtests of the MLAT, positively affected learning in all conditions *except* the incidental, meaning focussed condition (see Robinson, 1997a, p. 67). In other words, in contrast to learners in the other conditions, those learners who had incidentally gained grammatical knowledge of the easy and hard rules while processing for meaning did so *without* apparently drawing on the abilities measured by the aptitude subtests. This is as Krashen predicts.

However, there is another possible explanation for the apparent aptitude insensitivity of incidental learning in Robinson's study. In line with the findings of de Graaff and Williams reported above, who used ID measures of inferring word meaning in context, and verbatim recall of sentences previously viewed and comprehended, which *could* therefore be expected to be sensitive to incidental learning during processing for meaning, the finding for the aptitude independence of the incidental learning group in Robinson (1997a) could have been due to the fact that the measure of aptitude used in the study didn't measure the abilities needed to meet the conscious processing demands of the training task. In order to learn incidentally while processing for meaning learners must hold a semantic representation of the input in WM, in order to answer questions about the meaning, while simultaneously imposing a grammatical representation on the input. Attention switching, between the semantic representation and syntactic representation could be expected to occur most often, and most profitably for the learning that results from 'noticing', where the semantic representation does not yield a ready determinate answer to the comprehension question, and some difficulty in answering is experienced. In this view, WM limitations, and IDs in capacity, would play a large role in determining the extent of successful incidental learning, as is suggested by the findings of de Graaff and Williams.

This interpretation of the aptitude independence of incidental learning in the Robinson (1997a) study, differs from that offered by Skehan (this volume) who comments that: 'the one non-significant correlation in Robinson's study (for the incidental condition) is equally intriguing. This suggests that aptitude may not be so relevant when the focus is on meaning. As de Graaff (1997a, pp. 158–9) puts it, this suggests that 'the evidence cannot be generalised to non-instructed learning without any focus on form.' Aptitude, it would seem, presupposes a requirement that there is a focus-on-form'.

In contrast, I have argued that all adult L2 learning is fundamentally similar, drawing on conscious information processes under executive control, and that individual differences in the extent of learning can be predicted by measures of IDs in cognitive resources, but importantly, *only when those cognitive resources are drawn on by the processing demands of specific learning task conditions which implicate them.* In this view, broadly put, aptitude for learning when there *is* a focus on form draws on a different cluster of cognitive resources and abilities — or what I have called 'aptitude complexes' (see Robinson, Chapter 6 this volume; Snow, 1994) — than aptitude for incidental learning without a focus on form. The fact that there is apparently wide variation in the extent of adult naturalistic, incidental learning across individuals implies that this is likely to be so (see e.g., Meisel, Clahsen & Pienemann, 1981; Klein & Purdue, 1992). The issue addressed in the study reported below is what cognitive abilities and resources best characterise the aptitude complex contributing to successful incidental learning.

Implicitly learned representations and awareness

How is the knowledge acquired during implicit learning represented? Reber argues it is rule-based and abstract. Others disagree (e.g., Perruchet & Pacteau, 1990; Servan-Schreiber & Anderson, 1990), arguing the knowledge base that results from exposure in the implicit conditions is the result of fragmentary, instance-based knowledge of cooccurrence restrictions, or bigram and trigram associations between stimuli (usually letters, in letter strings such as XYZYTS generated by a finite-state Markov grammar), further arguing that this knowledge *is* accessible to awareness, but that typical measures of awareness used are insensitive to this content. Such knowledge is only seemingly implicit, and tacit, that is, because participants in Reber's studies are not asked to report awareness of bigrams, trigrams, and associative knowledge, but are instead only asked to verbalize rules, which is an insensitive measure (Brody, 1989; Dulany, Carlson & Dewey, 1984, 1985; Shanks & St. John, 1994; Stadler & Roediger, 1998). Others hold mixed positions (Knowlton & Squire, 1996; Vokey & Brooks, 1992; McAndrews & Moscovitch, 1985; Whittlesea & Dorken, 1993) arguing rules *and* memory for specific instances both contribute to implicit knowledge (see Cleeremans, et al., 1998; and DeKeyser, in press for recent reviews of this debate).

One candidate for an SLA property theory argues (similarly to Reber with regard to the eventual abstractness of the end state of learning, but not with regard to the representational mechanisms implicated in acquiring it), that abstract rules are instantiated by exposure to positive evidence of some aspects of L2 structure, and that this instantiation is automatic (unintentional) and that the rules are inaccessible to awareness (unreportable). Schwartz (1993) proposes this, i.e., that L2 learners have full access to UG. Positive evidence of grammatical examples is all that is needed to initiate access. The claims of UG bear interestingly on the targeted rules for the present study, as explained below.

Incidental learning of Samoan

In the incidental learning component of the study reported below participants were first trained to criterion on translation equivalents (in their L1, Japanese) of words in a previously unknown language (Samoan), then were exposed to grammatical sentences formed from the Samoan words during a task requiring them to demonstrate comprehension of the meaning of the sentences. Training took place in two sessions, consisting of ten trials, during which participants saw 45 sentences, making a total of 450 sentences viewed over the two days (3–4 hours) of training.

Samoan syntax differs from Japanese in a number of ways. Samoan is a verb initial language, in which VSO is the predominant word order, though VOS is possible and common (see Ochs, 1985). This contrasts with the basic SOV and SVO word order of Japanese and English respectively. Like English, heads (e.g., verbs and prepositions) precede their noun complements, in contrast to head direction in Japanese, where heads follow nominal complements. Unlike Japanese or English, Samoan is an ergative language in which the subjects of transitive verbs are marked by an ergative marker. In first language acquisition, formal ergative marking is late developed, though children make ergative distinctions between verbs from an early age, using word order and discourse devices (see Ochs, 1985). Samoan also differs from Japanese and English in allowing noun incorporation, i.e., nouns functioning as direct objects can be incorporated directly into the verb (see Baker, 1988, and Robinson, 1994b).

Based on these areas of difference from Japanese, three types of Samoan sentence, lexicalised in different ways, were presented in equal numbers during training (ia, iia, and iiia below). In the first type, an ergative marker (e) marks, by preceding, the subject (*le tama*/the boy) of the transitive verb (*ave*/drive). In the second type a locative marker (i) precedes a specified location (*le paka*/the park). In the third type the normal VSO structure is changed by noun incorporation of the object noun into the verb (*ave-taavale*/drove-car) and this precedes the subject (*le tama*/the boy) which in this case does not receive ergative marking. During the transfer test of knowledge of grammaticality, ungrammatical versions of these sentence types were also presented (ib, iib, and iiib below). For the ergative sentence, the ergative marker was omitted (e.g., *ave le tama le taavale*), and for the locative sentences the locative marker was omitted (e.g., *taalo le tama le paka*). For the incorporated sentences, a locative complement (e.g., *paka*) was incorporated into the verb. Samoan only allows incorporation of direct object nouns into the verb.

i.   a.   grammatical/ VSO with ergative marking: *ave* (drove) *e* (ergative marker) *le tama* (the boy) *le taavale* (the car)

      b.   ungrammatical/VSO with no ergative marking: * *ave* (drove) *le tama* (the boy) *le taavale* (the car)

ii.   a.   grammatical/ VS loc with locative marking: *taalo* (play) *le tama* (the boy) *i* (locative marker) *le paka* (the park)

      b.   ungrammatical/ VS loc with no locative marking: * *taalo* (play) *le tama* (the boy) *le paka* (the park)

iii.   a.   grammatical (direct object) noun incorporation: *ave-taavale* (drive-car) *le tama* (the boy)

      b.   ungrammatical (locative) noun incorporation: * *taalo-paka* (play-park) *le tama* (the boy)

While OV/VO word order differences, and the pre- versus post-nominal positioning of adjectives in Japanese and Samoan are examples of how languages differentially select from universal, legitimate options in configuring syntax, Universal Grammar makes claims about the reason for the unacceptability, in principle — in *any* language — of example iii b above. Within Principles and Parameters theory (Baker, 1988; Chomsky, 1981; Fodor & Lepore, 1999) the ungrammatical example of noun incorporation in example iii b. is considered an ECP (Empty Category Principle) violation (see Baker, 1988; and Robinson, 1994b for extensive details of this analysis). Within the more recent Minimalist Program (Chomsky, 1995) the movement of the noun complement (paka/ park) over the nearest feature-checking landing site (the prepositional head, *i*) to attach to the verb (*taalo*/play) violates the Minimal Link, or Shortest Move Requirement (SMR). Ferguson (1996) explains the SMR, resulting in the ungrammaticality of *taalo-paka le tama* (play-park the boy), as follows:

> 'In standard accounts, the lexical categories V^o and P^o have the capacity to assign case features to their nominal complements. Since nouns typically incorporate into V and P, and movement is assumed to be motivated only by the need to check features, I argue for the null hypothesis, namely, that incorporation is

motivated by the need for feature-checking, in particular Case-feature checking. Thus the complement N moves to the checking domain of the closest c-commanding head capable of checking case (i.e., it adjoins to V or P).' (p. 106).

Rule complexity, rule difficulty, UG and individual differences

It is important at this point to make a distinction made elsewhere (Robinson, 2001a, 2001b), and to point out its implications for two broad views of the relationship between access to UG (full versus attenuated/no access) and IDs in cognitive abilities. *Complexity* (e.g., of either of tasks, math problems, or grammar rules) is an inherent property of the stimulus display, or problem, or task structure. So simple addition is less complex than calculus: or giving directions from a simplified map, with a route marked on, of a small area, is less complex than giving directions from an authentic map, of a large area, with no route marked on. The differential complexity of these different stimulus displays, problems, or tasks makes differential demands on our cognitive resources and abilities in processing and learning them. In contrast, d*ifficulty* concerns an individual's perceptions, and is dependent on differences in the cognitive resources and abilities learners bring to the stimulus, problem, or task domain. So two learners with *different aptitude* for math will find the same math problem (therefore controlling for complexity) more or less *difficult* than each other as a result of individual differences in the set of cognitive abilities they bring to the problem. Similarly, a single learner will find two stimulus, problem, or task domains, differ in difficulty when the intrinsic structure of the stimulus, problem or task differs in complexity.

This distinction, between complexity and difficulty, does not apply to UG explanations of SLA — assuming full access to the initial state — where the stimulus domain is the syntactic structure of an input L2 sentence, since implicit deduction (described above) is seen to be automatic, encapsulated, and impervious to IDs in cognitive resources and abilities which only affect central processing (Fodor, 1983). So if principles of UG, like the SMR, are fully accessible in adulthood Japanese native speakers exposed to Samoan input sentences like iii b above would unanimously reject them regardless of IDs in cognitive abilities such as those assessed in the present study. However, if access is attenuated, or not possible, and central processing and domain general cognitive abilities play some, or a complete role in learning the structure of the stimulus domain, then rule complexity, perceptions of rule difficulty (and so ID) interactions will play a major role in learning.

Intention, verbalizability, and awareness

The claim that access to UG is automatic and that the knowledge is unreportable, doesn't *necessarily* rule out a role for awareness. Schmidt (1990, 2001) has argued that attention to input accompanied by the subjective experience of 'noticing' positional information regarding its form is necessary for all SLA: 'the objects of attention and noticing are elements of the surface structure of utterances in the input, instances of language, rather than any abstracts rules or principles of which such instances may be exemplars ' (Schmidt, 2001, p.5). In this view positive evidence won't trigger UG representations if you don't attend to, and notice the relevant surface structure correlates of them (though see Tomlin and Villa, 1994, for claims that simple detection, i.e., attention without awareness, is sufficient for learning). What noticing involves, I have suggested, is detection, focal attention allocation, and subsequent rehearsal in short term memory (Robinson, 1995b, in press), and it is differences in the kind of rehearsal processes operating on attended input which give rise to differences in the contents and extent of awareness.

However, Schmidt has also argued that higher levels of awareness than simple 'noticing', such as rule awareness, are strongly facilitative of subsequent learning. Note, what learners *notice*, and may be able to report awareness of, and verbalize, is not abstract structures and principles (Schmidt, 2001) but a much more general testimony to having noticed that something occurs, and possibly, at a higher level of *rule* awareness, some generalization about what the positional restrictions on its occurrence are. Such verbalizations are not veridical, exhaustive or complete accounts of the knowledge domain, or even partial rules, but are evidence, nonetheless, of a level of awareness of it. Consequently, if learners correctly reject ungrammatical type iii b. sentences, and correctly accept type iii a. grammatical sentences, while demonstrating awareness of relevant surface structure characteristics, at either of the levels described above, (e.g., by testifying to having noticed bigram pairs in the input, such as, *ave-taavale went together, but ave-paka didn't* — simple noticing; or producing a generalization such as, *verbs can be followed by nouns unless they are places, like park/paka* — rule awareness) it could then be argued that access to UG is 'gated' by attention to and awareness of the triggering input that constitutes the 'evidence for principles' (cf. Schmidt, 2001, p. 25).

However, if learners do reject those ungrammatical iii b. examples of noun incorporation at high above chance levels of accuracy, *without* any consistently reported awareness of the surface structure constraints on incorporation, it isn't incontrovertible evidence for access to UG without awareness either, since they could reject them for other reasons. That is, they could be mistakenly drawing on awareness of some other surface structure details to make the correct decision (for the wrong reason), e.g., correctly rejecting *taalo-paka le tama*/play-park the boy, but incorrectly rejecting *ave-taavale le tama*/drive-car the boy, and incorrectly accepting *ave le tama le taavale*/ drive the boy the car, because they noticed agent/subjects immediately follow the verb in many sentences and wrongly think word order should always be SVO. Awareness data such as verbalizations and written questionnaire responses to probes about why decisions were made can 'help' clear this up, by revealing when some decisions seem to have been made for the right, and for the wrong reasons. But given the insensitivity of these measures they can never do so incontrovertibly for each participant.

Reber (1989, 1993) has consistently made use of questionnaire data to assess awareness, and since I replicated his methodology in the present study, I also adopted questionnaire measures of awareness. However, it is clearly problematic, using open-ended question formats, to exhaustively elicit first person descriptions of what learners 'noticed' in input, given that noticing itself may be fleeting, and unavailable for off-line recall, and that open-ended questions underdetermine the responses they seek to elicit. Closed-format questions ('did you notice this', or 'what is the rule for using this') also cannot with any certainty be relied on to exhaustively tap the contents of on task awareness since they; i) rely to an extent on the learner's variable abilities to verbalize and describe linguistic content; and ii) may also often draw learners attention to phenomena which they had not been aware of during the task, but when posed with a direct question during the debriefing feel they have to, or want to, describe or explain in some way.

One illustration of the limitations of questionnaire debriefings as a measure of awareness was provided by Matthews et al. (1989) who used an experimental, yoked-control groups design. Participants who had completed an implicit learning artificial grammar learning task were asked to recall their prior training experience, and use this to tell those in a control group how best to perform the same task. Matthews et al. found the information participants gave to the yoked-controls was disjoint with, and often exceeded the information they had given verbally during a preceding questionnaire debriefing.

In summary, questionnaire formats for eliciting awareness cannot be assumed to meet what Reingold and Merickle (1988) called, the 'exhaustiveness assumption', i.e., that a measure of awareness completely measure participants' conscious knowledge. Stadler and Roediger (1998, p. 111) comment that it is 'probably impossible' for any single measure to meet this assumption. The value of such data therefore lies in the preponderant *trend* it indicates, about whether decisions in the overall population seemed to have been based on information that was noticed, or verbalized as a rule, and whether the correct decision seemed to have been made on this basis and not on another.

Research questions and Hypotheses for the present study

The finding that incidental L2 learning in Robinson 1997a (reported above) appeared to be aptitude independent, seemingly supporting Krashen, Zobl and Reber's positions, was the starting point for the present study. While I wanted to further study the apparent insensitivity of incidental L2 learning to IDs in cognitive abilities, as demonstrated in that study, I also wanted to set this study in the context of Reber's work — further examining his claim that implicit learning is insensitive to IDs in cognitive abilities, while at the same time examining the generalizability of his claims for implicit learning to adult incidental L2 learning. No previous studies have directly compared L2 learner performance on an implicit learning task, as used in Reber's studies, with performance on an incidental language learning task. These issues, and the discussion above, motivated the following research questions and hypotheses.

Research Question 1. To what extent can Reber et al.'s (1991) finding that explicit learning is sensitive to individual differences in IQ whereas implicit learning is not, based on evidence of learning rules of an artificial, semantics free finite-state grammar, be generalized to SLA and the incidental acquisition of a previously unknown natural language? To answer this question, in a repeated measures design, I replicated the implicit and explicit learning experiments Reber et al. performed and used the same measure of IQ, a short form of WAIS-R. I also added a third experimental condition, incidental meaning focussed learning of Samoan, a natural language.

Hypothesis 1. Reber et al.'s results will be replicated, but incidental L2 learning will show a different pattern of correlations with individual difference measures than either implicit and explicit learning, suggesting a process sharing some characteristics of each, but identical with neither.

Research Question 2. Will the earlier (Robinson, 1997a) finding for the apparent aptitude independence of incidental learning be replicated in the present study, and will incidental learning, and also implicit learning as operationalized in Reber et al.'s study, be insensitive to a wider range of ID measures? To answer this question I assessed not only individual differences in IQ, but also aptitude (Sasaki's, 1996, Language Aptitude Battery for the Japanese, LABJ), and working memory (Osaka & Osaka's, 1992, reading span test).

Hypothesis 2. Incidental learning will be sensitive to the ID measure *that most closely matches the abilities drawn on during incidental learning task performance.* Research has shown aptitude batteries such as MLAT do measure many of the abilities drawn on in learning from explicit formS focussed instruction. But they lack measures of some of the important abilities drawn on in incidental, experiential or naturalistic learning. One of these is working memory — a fundamental capacity drawn on in 'noticing' grammatical information while primarily oriented to processing for meaning (see Doughty, 2001; N.Ellis, 2001; Mackey et al., this volume). As described above, this was why, I suspect, the aptitude measure in Robinson 1997a did not reflect the learning processes in the incidental condition. Consequently, I predicted that WM differences would most successfully predict incidental learning, compared to intelligence scores (using the WAIS-R), or aptitude scores (using the LABJ).

Research Question 3. Will incidental learning of the targeted rules of Samoan be facilitated by awareness? To examine this learners were asked to complete a debriefing questionnaire following the immediate posttest, and the six month delayed posttest of grammatical knowledge of Samoan.

Hypothesis 3. Higher levels of awareness, as demonstrated by responses to the debriefing questionnaire *will correlate positively and significantly with higher levels of learning,* of all three targeted rules.

Research Question 4. Will incidental learning of Samoan be durable? To examine this question, following the immediate posttest there was a one week delayed posttest, and a further six month delayed posttest.

Hypothesis 4. There will be some deterioration of performance on the delayed posttests, relative to the immediate posttest, but performance will still be above chance. Those demonstrating *higher levels of awareness* will show *greater retention* of incidentally acquired Samoan.

Method

Participants

There were a total of 55 participants. There were 38 participants in the experimental group (12 male, 26 female) who were all undergraduate third and fourth year students at Aoyama Gakuin University in Tokyo, aged between 19 and 24 years. This is a narrow sample, but comparable to Reber et al.'s 20 undergraduate students at Brooklyn College, City University New York (CUNY). A control group of 17 undergraduate third and fourth year students at Aoyama Gakuin University, was also used to calculate effect size for incidental learning. All participants had taken, or were currently taking, English medium university content courses, and had good oral and literacy skills in English. Thus, in contrast to Reber et al.'s sample (psychology majors) the participants for the present study were all experienced L2 learners. All participants were volunteer respondents to a call to participate in a study about computers in education, and were paid 1,000 Yen per hour (for a total of around 8 hours participation in the experimental group, and 2 hours in the control group), in contrast to participants in Reber et al. who participated to complete a course requirement.

Learning tasks : Measures and procedures

All participants in the experimental group completed three experimental tasks (those in the control group only performed the vocabulary learning phase, and the immediate posttests described below). The first two tasks, replicating the tasks presented to participants in Reber et al., were an explicit and an implicit learning task, described below. Order of presentation of these tasks was counterbalanced, as in Reber et al., half performing the implicit task first, and half the explicit task. These tasks were performed on the same day by participants, and together took around forty minutes.

Following these tasks participants completed a third incidental learning task which began on a separate day. This task took considerably longer than the first two tasks, and involved an initial vocabulary learning phase, followed by two separate training sessions, which took place on separate days, followed by a series of three immediate, one week and six month delayed posttests. All of the implicit, explicit and incidental training and transfer tasks were completed on Macintosh computers. All explanation of training and transfer task procedures also took place via Macintosh computers, though in each case the researcher was on hand to clarify any questions participants had about procedures, such as which keys to press, during the explanation and orientation phases.

i. Explicit learning task

This was the forced choice, series-solution problem task used by Reber et al. (1991, p. 891). As in Reber et al., 12 series solution problems were randomly selected from a set of 21 and presented in a fixed random order (see Appendix A). Participants were told that they would see a series of letter strings and that they should try to decide which letter best completed the series. There are two types of problem, randomly interspersed, to make the task more demanding (though participants were not made aware of this during the explanation/orientation phase). Alphabetic problems e.g., ABCBCDCDE_ D* or C, depend on repeating alphabetic sequences, ABC, BCD, CDE, in which the last two letters of one triplet are repeated as the first two letters of the following triplet. Non alphabetic problems e.g., CDEADCA_ E* or D, depend on mirroring, or reversing pairs of letters in the sequence, CD, EA, DC, AE. Six questions of each type were included in the 12 problems making up the test of explicit learning.

The problems were presented on a computer screen (in Times font, size 14), and participants responded by pressing the letter they chose to complete the series from two choices presented on the keyboard. No feedback was given following each answer. Upon selecting the letter of their choice the next problem appeared. As in Reber et al., percentage correct scores for this task were calculated. Reliability using a matched item, split half correlation, corrected with the Spearman Brown prophecy formula was .68. Reber et al. do not report the reliability of this task in their study.

ii. Implicit learning task

Training As in Reber et al. this was described to participants during the initial explanation/ orientation phase as a memory task. During training participants viewed strings of letters generated by a miniature artificial 'Reber' grammar. These were presented for 3s each (in Times font, size 14) on a computer screen. After viewing each string they were instructed to write it down on a piece of paper in response to a prompt on the computer screen 'Now write down the letter sequence you saw'. After they had written down each sequence they then pressed the keyboard in response to the 'Press any key to continue' prompt and a new sequence appeared for 3s. There were two trials of training, as in Reber et al. In each trial of training the participants saw 26 strings, e.g., XXVT, VXJJJJ, XXVJ, XXXVTV, generated by the rules of the artificial grammar. Since Reber et al. do not report their transfer and training set stimuli strings, the artificial grammar chosen for the present study was that used in a number of other reported studies of implicit learning such as Abrams and Reber (1989), and Knowlton and Squire (1996), and the training and transfer sets were those used in Knowlton and Squire (1996) (see Appendix B).

Transfer As in Reber et al. after training the participants were told the strings they had viewed followed a set of rules, and they would now see some more strings. They were asked to decide if they followed the same rules. If they thought they did so they were instructed to press C for correct, whereas if they thought they didn't follow the same rules they were instructed to press M for mistake. This was not a speeded task. There were 32 transfer set items. As in Reber et al., percentage correct scores for this task were calculated. Reliability calculated using the split half, odd/even correlation, corrected by the Spearman Brown prophecy formula was .52. This is low, but almost identical to the reliability of .51 (Cronbach's alpha) reported by Reber et al. for their implicit learning transfer test. The reliability of this measure is discussed further in the following section.

iii Incidental learning task

Training Training for this task was spread over a number of days. The first phase involved learning new vocabulary, followed by two training sessions, spread from two to five days apart, depending on the participant's availability. Immediately following the second training session an immediate posttest took place.

   a. Vocabulary learning Participants were asked to memorize the meanings of 27 new words. One article, 15 nouns, and 11 verbs. These are Samoan words, a language unknown to the participants. English and Japanese translation equivalents, written in English and Japanese, were provided on a study sheet, e.g. *taalo* (play / asobu), *faitau* (read / yomu), *tusi* (book / hon) (see Appendix C). Participants were asked to study them until they could recall all translation equivalents on a test. This generally took around forty five minutes to one hour.

   b. Processing for meaning After completing the word list memorization exercise participants then completed 10 trials of training. During each trial of training participants viewed 45 Samoan sentences of the three types described earlier (ergative, incorporated and locative) making a total of 450 presentations, 150 tokens of each type. Each sentence appeared for 10s on the computer screen, in Times, size 14 font. During the computerized explanation/orientation phase participants were asked to try as hard as they could to understand the meaning of each sentence. No grammar explanation was provided. During training, to test comprehension following the 10s presentation of each stimulus, participants viewed, and were asked to respond to yes/no comprehension questions as illustrated in the following examples:

Screen 1.   taalo le tama i le paka (10 second presentation)
Screen 2.   Does the boy swim in the sea? (no time limit for responding)
Screen 3.   Correct/ incorrect. Press any key to continue. (no time limit for responding)
Screen 4.   inu-pia le tama (10 second presentation)
Screen 5.   Does the boy drink beer? (no time limit for responding)
Screen 6.   Correct/ incorrect. Press any key to continue. (no time limit for responding)

Participants responded by pressing C for yes, or M for no on the keyboard. Feedback was given in the form of correct, or incorrect responses to each answer, before the next stimulus sentence appeared. The mean error rate on the first trial was around 15 %. The mean error rate on the last trial was around 1%. Each trial took around 15 minutes. Total time spent in training, including vocabulary learning, was around 3 hours 15 minutes.

Transfer: Immediate posttest Immediately following the last trial of training participants completed two grammaticality judgement (GJ) tests, presented in the written and aural modalities, a questionnaire assessing participants awareness of the rules of Samoan to which they had been exposed during training, and a word-sort, sentence production measure of ability to form sentences in Samoan. The tasks were presented in this order because it was felt that the guided sentence production task would invite conscious reflection on, and analysis of the grammatical constraints on Samoan sentence construction, and that therefore if it had preceded the questionnaire assessing awareness it could have strongly influenced responses to it.

  a. Computerized GJ test After completing the last trial of training participants were told the sentences they had seen were from a real language, though they were not told which one. They were told they would now see more sentences and they must decide if they follow the same rules as the sentences they had seen during training. They were asked to respond by pressing C for grammatical, and M for ungrammatical. The transfer test was unspeeded. The transfer set consisted of 27 items (comparable to the number of items, 32, on the implicit transfer test, but not the explicit task, 12 items) of the following types; nine *old items* viewed in training (3 for each rule type); nine *new grammatical* items (3 for each type); and nine *new ungrammatical* items (3 for each type). The split half reliability for this test was .72, calculated by correlating scores on odd, and even items from the test, and corrected using the Spearman Brown prophecy formula.

b. Listening GJ test After the immediate computerized GJ test I asked participants to complete a listening GJ test. They heard the same 27 sentences presented during the first GJ test, presented in a different fixed random order, and wrote C or M on a piece of paper after hearing each item. Sentences were taped and spoken at normal speed. Following each spoken sentence there was a 5s pause before the following sentence.

c. Awareness After the two GJ tests participants answered a questionnaire, written in Japanese, which they completed in Japanese. In order to enable comparison of findings between the present study, and the findings for awareness during incidental learning in Robinson 1997a, the questionnaire was close in design and wording to the one used in the earlier study. This asked if participants had: a. noticed any rules during the training session; b. had been searching for rules while they completed the training exercises; c. could say what any of the rules were in the sentences viewed during training; d. could say what " *i* " (the locative marker) meant in the sentences they had seen, and/or state the rule for its use, and give an example; e. could say what " *e* " (the ergative marker) meant in the sentences they had seen, and/or state the rule for its use, and give an example; and f. could say what " — " (the symbol showing noun incorporation) meant in the sentences they had seen, and/or state the rule for its use, and give an example. On the basis of these responses participants were coded from 0 to a maximum of 6 for awareness. Two native Japanese speakers translated the questionnaire responses, and in discussion with the researcher consensus was established for coding decisions. For questions a. and b. participants were given one point for simply saying they had noticed, or searched for rules, and 0 if they said they had not. For question c. statements demonstrating awareness of any rule relating to the sentences viewed during training, such as the typical VOS, and VSO word orders, or that verbs always come first, were accepted. For questions d., e. and f., exhaustive metalinguistic rule statements were not required, simply demonstrating awareness of the different rules, through a partial explanation — often supported by examples — was judged to be enough. For question d. statements to the effect that the locative marker is a preposition; that it is like 'in' in English, or comes before a place or location were acceptable. For question e. statements to the effect that the ergative marker occurs before the subject, or between the verb and the subject, in the order VSO were acceptable. However comments that it was a plural, or tense marker, or that participants had no idea, were common. For question f. statements to the effect that it joins together the verb and the object, supported by an example, were acceptable. In answering questions e. and f. participants often used 'noun' rather than 'subject' or 'object' in the verbalizations. If they did this, while providing an example that illustrated that the nouns were indeed functioning as subjects or objects, this was judged acceptable. However, any answers that consisted only of examples of usage, with no comment on them, were not judged acceptable. Reliability of questionnaire responses was .71, using the split half correlation of odd and even items, corrected using the Spearman Brown Prophecy formula.

d. *Guided Sentence Production* Following the awareness questionnaire participants were given sets of words, with each word written on separate pieces of paper. These sets were stored together in four separate packets. Participants were asked to empty each packet and arrange the words in it to make sentences (see White, 1991, for a similar procedure for eliciting knowledge of adverb placement rules). The packets of words to complete the first three sentences, one of each ergative, locative and incorporated rule type, were presented separately. For example, for the first ergative sentence the words *fau* (build), *fale* (house), *e* (ergative marker), *le* (the), *tama* (boy), *le* (the) were emptied in a jumbled order from a packet. If participants correctly ordered them in the sequence *fau e le tama le fale* they were given one point. Following this they replaced the words in the packet, then emptied and arranged the words in the second packet, illustrating a locative sentence, before replacing them and then doing the same for the third packet, containing words illustrating an incorporated sentence. Following the first three sentences, the words for the second group of three sentences (again illustrating a locative, ergative and incorporated sentence) were emptied simultaneously in jumbled order from one packet, making the second part of the production task much more demanding. On the basis of these responses participants were coded as 0, 1 or 2 for production of each rule, and from 0 to 6 overall for production.

Transfer: One week delayed posttest
Between five to seven days following completion of the first posttest partici-

pants completed an unexpected delayed posttest. Participants were first asked if they correctly remembered the Samoan words they had learned, and given time to look again at the word lists and memorize them. When they demonstrated to a criterion of ten successive correct responses to requests for translation equivalents they proceeded to complete the same computerized, and listening GJ tests used on the immediate pretests, followed by the same measure of ability to produce Samoan sentences by ordering groups of words into six sentences.

Transfer: Six month delayed posttest

Between five to six months following completion of the first delayed posttest participants again completed an unexpected delayed posttest. As previously they were given time to read again the list of Samoan words and their translation equivalents, and proceeded to the second delayed posttest after demonstrating memory for the words by producing ten successive correct responses to requests for translation equivalents. The six month delayed posttest consisted of the computerized GJ test, completion of the last three questions on the awareness questionnaire assessing ability to verbalize rules, and the measure of sentence production ability. Of the original participants, only 26 returned to complete the six month delayed posttest.

Individual difference measures

i. Intelligence test

As in Reber et al. a short form of the Wechsler Adult Intelligence Scale (WAIS-R) was used (Japanese version, Shinagawa, Kobayashi, Fujita, & Mayekawa, 1990). The full form of the WAIS-R has an extremely high reported reliability of $r=.97$ (Kline, 2000, p.451). Reber et al. used a short form which consisted of picture arrangement (PA), block design (BD), vocabulary (V) and arithmetic (A). This short form has been shown to correlate highly with the full test, with a validity and reliability coefficient of $r=.95$ to .96 (see Cyr & Brooker, 1984, p.905; Reber et al., 1991, p.892). Since some participants in the present study had already been exposed to the PA subtest, during participation in an unrelated research project, it was decided to drop scores for this subtest, using a triadic WAIS-R short form (V, A, & BD) which Cyr and Brooker (p.905) also report has a high validity and reliability coefficient of $r=.94$. As in Reber et al. I used the conversion tables in Brooker and Cyr (1986, also reported in Cyr & Brooker, 1984) to convert short form scores to scaled IQ scores. Using the triadic short form (V, A, BD) participants had a mean IQ of 113 which is almost identical to Reber et al.'s participants' mean of 110 using the tetradic short form (V, A, BD, PA) . However, our standard deviation was much narrower (SD 8.2, kurtosis 1.7, skewness, -.8) than Reber et al.'s (SD 21.2), as was our range of scores, from 88–132, compared to 73–151 in Reber et al.'s study. Possibly this difference in range and variance is due to the fact that Brooklyn College, CUNY, has an open admissions policy, whereas entrance to our own university is competitive, and conditional on passing a series of entrance exams.

It is also worth noting here that the unusually wide range of IQ scores, in such a small population, is an aspect of Reber et al.'s study, which has conse-quences for any study attempting to replicate their findings, since if the two participants at either end of this range, with IQ scores of 73, and 151, per-formed poorly, and reasonably well respectively on the explicit learning task, this would contribute substantially to high positive correlations of IQ and explicit learning, as Reber et al. indeed found. Notably, as is reported below, the positive correlation of IQ and explicit learning reported in Reber et al. is much higher, $r = .69$, than the positive correlation found in the present study.

ii. Aptitude test

I used Miyuki Sasaki's (1996) Language Aptitude Battery for the Japanese (LABJ). This consists of three sections based on Carroll and Sapon's MLAT and Pimsleur's PLAB, and took about 30 minutes to administer. The sections are Memory (M) a measure of rote memory for 24 paired associates; gram-matical sensitivity (GS) a measure of the ability to identify grammatical pat-terns in a new language; and phonemic sensitivity (PS) a measure of the abil-ity to match sounds and symbols. Mean scores for the 60 item test were 46.6 (SD 8.2, kurtosis, -.48, skewness -.69). Reliability for this test was .85 (KR21).

iii. Working memory test

I used Osaka and Osaka's (1992) reading span test of WM, which took about 40 minutes to administer. In this test participants are presented with sets of Japanese sentences written on cards and are asked to read them aloud. After reading them aloud they are asked to recall individual words which were underlined in each sentence. The sentence sets increase from 2, 3, 4 to 5 sen-tences throughout the test. I scored this using total number of correctly recalled words. Mean scores on this 70 item test were 44.8 (SD 9.3, kurtosis -.74, skewness -.1). Reliability for this test was .83 (KR21).

Results

The presentation of results for the present study is divided into three main sections. Firstly I discuss issues concerning the variance, and reliability of the implicit, explicit and incidental learning tasks, relating the findings of the present study to those of Reber et al. (1991). I then describe findings for correlations of ID measures and learning under these three conditions, again comparing the present findings to those of Reber et al. Following this I describe in detail the extent of incidental learning of Samoan, focussing first on the results of the three GJ, LGJ and Production measures used, on immediate, one week and six month delayed intervals, and then at learning of the three different ergative, incorporation, and locative sentence types in the incidental transfer set data. Finally, I describe the interactions of individual differences and learning on the three sentence types, over time, and on all measures.

Distributions, variance and reliability

Variance
All data was normally distributed, showing no excessive kurtosis or skewness. Reber et al. (1991) found almost identical means for performance on their implicit and explicit tasks, allowing them to perform direct comparisons of variance. Their F-test showed significantly greater variance on the explicit learning task, as predicted by Reber's evolutionary theory of implicit/explicit learning described previously. As shown in Table 1, the mean difference in accuracy of performance on the implicit and explicit tasks in the present replication is much greater than in Reber et al., while there is somewhat more variance in implicit learning, and less variance in explicit learning than found by Reber et al. Nonetheless, the variance data is in line with the findings of Reber et al., and an F-test also shows this to be a significant difference (F, .502, p <.05). F-tests show no significant differences in variance between incidental, and implicit or explicit learning.

Reliability
Reber et al. report only the reliability of the implicit learning transfer task, which was .51. The reliability of the implicit learning task in the present replication was almost identical, using split-halves, corrected by Spearman Brown Prophecy (.52). Reliability for the incidental learning task was somewhat higher, calculated using the same procedure (.72). Reber et al. argue that "generally

Table 1. Mean percent accuracy, variance and reliability for implicit, explicit
and incidental learning

	M%	(RWH'91)Variance	(RWH'91)Kurtosis	Skewness	Reliability	(RWH'91)
Imp	55.2	60.9	88.3	51.84	-1.19	-.18	.52	.51
Exp	68.5	61	176.1	237.5	-.59	-.17	.68	nr
Inc	63.8	–	102.7	–	.38	-.23	.72	–

Key: M% = Mean percentage correct, Imp = Implicit learning condition, Exp = Explicit
learning condition, Inc = Incidental learning condition, RWH'91 = Reber, Walkenfield
and Hernstadt's 1991 results, nr = Not reported.

speaking, a Cronbach α above .4 or .5 is taken as reasonable support for the
internal reliability of a test" (p.893), and further that, despite the low variance
on the implicit task, and low reliability, in performing correlations of implicit
learning with individual difference measures, such as IQ, "the observed patterns of *r*s are unlikely to be due to attenuated or truncated variance in the
implicit task. That is, our observed variance is not attenuated in the sense that
the real variance is actually large and our procedure somehow squeezed it
down; it is small because the underlying factor being assessed actually shows
little in the way of individual variation" (p.893).

Nonetheless, given the difference in reliability between the dependent
measures of implicit and explicit learning in the present study, and the higher reliabilities for the ID measures reported previously, uncorrected correlations (as reported in Reber et al.), together with correlations corrected for
attenuation, are given below in Table 2.

Individual difference measures

Correlations of IDs and implicit, incidental and explicit learning The findings
for correlations of IQ and implicit and explicit learning in this replication differ from Reber et al.'s (1991) findings (see Table 2). The positive correlation of
explicit learning and IQ only approaches significance (p=. 06), while the negative correlation of implicit learning and IQ is significant (r = .-34, p < .05). The
corrected correlation of explicit learning and IQ is significant (r = .47, p < .01),
but not as large as the correlation observed in Reber et al. (r = .69, p < .01),
while the correlation of implicit learning and IQ is in a reverse, i.e., *negative*,
direction to Reber et al.'s finding (i.e., of r = .25, p > .05), and significant both

Table 2. Intercorrelations of implicit, explicit and incidental learning, awareness and individual differences

	Int	WM	Aw	Imp	Exp	Inc GJ1		LGJ1	P1
Apt	.17	.35 *	.44 **	.03 (.04)	.38 * (.66)***	-.25		.22	.3
Int	–	.13	-.08	-.34* (-.5)**	.3 (.47)**	-.11		.18	-.07
WM	–	–	.03	.09 (.14)	.04 (.07)	.08		.42 **	.05
Aw	–	–	–	.15 (.25)	.22 (.45)**	-.002		.11	.05
Imp	–	–	–	–	-.13 (-.36)*	.06 (.09)		.1	.28
Exp	–	–	–	–	–	-.21 (-.3)		-.02	.09

n.b. (bracketed correlations are corrected for attenuation).

Key: * = $p < .05$, ** = $p < .01$, *** = $p < .001$, Apt = Aptitude, Int = Intelligence, WM = Working memory, Aw = Awareness, Imp = Implicit condition, Exp = Explicit condition, Inc = Incidental condition, GJ1 = Grammaticality judgement, immediate posttest, LGJ1 = Aural grammaticality judgement, immediate posttest, P1 = Guided production, immediate posttest

with and without correction for attenuation.

While the present findings, then, are in line with Reber's claim that IQ positively affects explicit learning, they also show — contrary to Reber et al.'s findings — that individual differences in IQ *do* affect *implicit* learning, i.e., those with lower IQ scores on the WAIS-R outperform those with higher IQ scores on this task. However implicit learning is not related to the two other measures of individual differences — WM or aptitude.

In contrast, in addition to the positive relationship with measures of IQ ($p = .06$), *explicit* learning shows a significant positive relationship to two other measures; a correlation with language learning aptitude ($r = .38$, $p < .05$), and also a corrected correlation with the measure of awareness of grammar during the incidental learning task ($r = .44$, $p < .01$). However, interestingly, as found in Robinson 1997a, once again aptitude is unrelated to any measure of immediate posttest *incidental* learning, as is intelligence, and also awareness. Only WM is positively and significantly related to immediate posttest measures of incidental learning, on one test — the listening GJ task ($r = .42$, $p < .01$). Neither is incidental learning of Samoan related to implicit or explicit learning, using the tasks in Reber et al., and replicated in this study, since there are no significant intercorrelations of implicit/explicit learning with any of the measures of incidental Samoan learning.

These findings raise two paradoxes, in need of explanation. Why should implicit learning be *negatively* correlated with intelligence? And why should

Table 3. Intercorrelations of IDs, awareness and measures of incidental learning over time

	GJ test			LGJ test		Production test		
	T1	T2	T3	T1	T2	T1	T2	T3
Apt	-.25	-.09	.13	.22	.08	.3	.18	.56 **
Int	-.09	-.03	-.07	.18	-.02	-.007	.1	.16
WM	.07	.06	-.12	.42 **	.48**	.06	.33 *	.44 *
Aw	.003	.11	-.02	.11	.12	-.03	.04	.28
Aw2	–	–	.18	–	–	–	–	.45 *

Key: * = $p < .05$, ** = $p < .01$, Apt = Aptitude, Int = Intelligence, WM = Working memory, Aw = Awareness, immediate posttest, Aw2 = Awareness, six month delayed posttest, GJ = Grammaticality judgement, LGJ = Aural grammaticality judgement, T1 = Immediate posttest, T2 = One week delayed posttest, T3 = Six month delayed posttest

incidental Samoan learning be unrelated to measures of language learning aptitude, and attested awareness of grammar during the incidental training task, as well as being related to WM on only *one* of the three immediate posttests?

Correlations of IDs and incidental learning on delayed posttests

As Table 3 shows, GJ measures of incidental learning are not correlated significantly with any measures of IDs, either on the immediate, or one week and six month delayed posttests. WM alone is positively and significantly related to performance on both the immediate ($r = .42$, $p < .01$) and one week delayed ($r = .48$, $p < .01$) listening GJ tests, as well as to performance on the one week ($r = .33$, $p < .05$) and six month delayed ($r = .44$, $p < 01$) production tests. It is clear, then, that of the three measures of IDs in the present study, *working memory* appears to have the strongest influence on incidental Samoan learning. It also appears that of the three tests used, production data on the six month delayed posttest shows the strongest pattern of influence by ID measures, since it is positively related to WM, and to aptitude ($r = .56$, $p < .01$), as well as to awareness ($r = .45$, $p < .05$).

Two further conclusions can be drawn from Table 3, therefore, which also are in need of explanation. Firstly, the influence of IDs on learning appears strongest on the one week, and six month delayed posttests. Immediate posttest performance shows very little relationship to measures of IDs. Secondly, there are no significant correlations of any IDs and performance on the computer presented GJ test, on immediate, one week or six month posttests. One likely explanation for the observed interaction of test time, and IDs lies in the possibility that learning continued as a consequence of the immediate delayed transfer test experiences, and that IDs in relevant abilities contributed to the capacity to build on initial exposure during training, and continue to learn during the posttests. In this view, for example, aptitude would contribute to the capacity to continue to learn from additional exposure to Samoan input during the posttests, culminating in an eventual strong correlation of aptitude, as well as of WM, and production test performance on the six month delayed posttest.

An explanation for the second finding, that GJ measures are insensitive to IDs, whereas the same task in an aural modality shows strong positive correlations with WM, likely lies in the different processing demands of the two transfer tests. Computer presented grammaticality judgements were not speeded, and participants did not need to rehearse the stimuli in memory in order to make a judgement, as they did when stimuli were presented aurally. Working memory was drawn on when meeting processing demands of the latter transfer test, but not the former.

Neither of these explanations, though, suggests that IDs are implicated in the *learning* that results from *initial* exposure to Samoan sentence stimuli during the incidental training task, but rather argue different IDs are important in managing the processing demands of different posttest formats, or in further learning from repeated exposure during the posttests. Tables 2 and Table 3, therefore, seem to strongly suggest that incidental learning during training is uninfluenced by IDs in measures of conscious information processing abilities and capacities, as Krashen claims, and as Reber also claims for implicit learning.

However, one issue not discussed so far is that the aggregate measures of incidental learning presented in Tables 2 and 3 are actually based on transfer test responses to sentences illustrating three very *different rule types,* as described earlier — an ergative type, an incorporated type, and a locative type. It is possible that these rules differ in their complexity, and therefore that learner characteristics (IDs) interact with rule types to determine their relative difficulty, and so learnability (see Robinson 2001a, and the earlier discussion of the complexity/difficulty distinction). Therefore it is to examining differential performance in aggregate incidental learning of these three rule types that I now turn, before looking again at the specific interaction of IDs on learning each rule type in the final section.

Summary of results for individual differences

i. In contrast to Reber et al.'s finding, implicit learning and IQ are significantly (though negatively) correlated.

ii. In line with Reber et al.'s finding, explicit learning and IQ are positively related, (though the correlation is significant only when corrected for attenuation).

iii. IDs in WM have the strongest relationship with incidental learning.

iv. Aptitude and awareness are only weakly related to incidental learning, on one, six month delayed, production test.

v. Grammaticality judgement measures of incidental learning are unrelated to IDs, on immediate and delayed posttests.

Incidental learning of Samoan

Grammaticality Judgement Test

i. Immediate GJ posttest The repeated measure ANOVA shows significant main effects for Type (F, 67.096, $p < .001$), Rule (F, 41.743, $p < .001$) and a significant interaction of Type and Rule (F, 28.332, $p < .001$). Chance performance on items of each type (old, new grammatical and new ungrammatical)

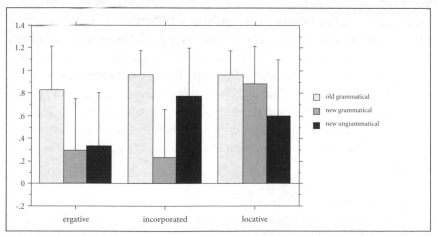

Figure 1. Mean percent accuracy on Samoan sentence types in the immediate GJ posttest

and rule (ergative, incorporated, locative) is between 41.8% and 58. 2 % correct. As Figure 1 shows accuracy is high and above chance on old items for each rule. For new items grammatical locative sentences are correctly accepted (87%) and ungrammatical locative sentences are correctly rejected (59%) at

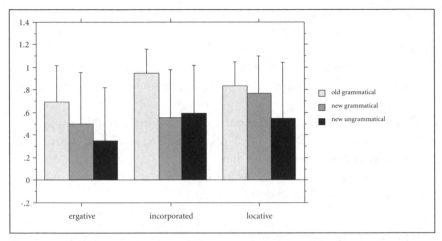

Figure 2. Mean percent accuracy on Samoan sentence types in
the one week GJ posttest

above chance rates. New ungrammatical incorporated sentences are correctly
rejected at above chance rates (76%), but new grammatical sentences are
wrongly rejected and accuracy is at only 22% on these items, suggesting that
participants adopted a strategy of rejecting most new examples of incorporation, whether grammatical or ungrammatical. Performance on new ergative
sentences is above chance, but incorrect and accuracy is low on both grammatical (28%) and ungrammatical (32%) items. Since ungrammatical examples of
ergative sentences are those with VSO word order, but lacking the ergative
marker *e* before the subject, this suggests that learners are actively (and incorrectly) rejecting new grammatical sentences that contain the ergative marker,
and accepting (wrongly) those that do not contain it. Only the locative rule,
therefore, accompanied by memory for old instances of all rule types, seems to
have been learned.

Effect size and Power
A control group of 17 participants completed the incidental vocabulary learning task, and then took part in the transfer GJ task. Mean performance for the
control group is at chance (53% accurate), and performance on sentences of
each rule type is almost identical (ergative, 52.9%; incorporated, 53.6%; locative 53.6%). An ANOVA shows a significant difference between the control
group and the incidental learning group's immediate posttest (F, 12.535, p
<.001/ Power, .953). There is also a significant difference between the control
group and the incidental learning group's one week delayed posttest perfor-

mance (F, 12.523, $p <$.001/Power, .952), though not between the control group and the incidental learning group's six month delayed posttest (F, 3.566, $p =$.06/Power .439).

Effect size (Cohen's d) was calculated (see Norris & Ortega, 2000, p. 424) and was .978 for the immediate posttest/control group comparison, . 956 for the delayed posttest/control group comparison, and .533 for the six month delayed posttest/control group comparison. Effect size was also calculated for performance on each rule by comparing the control group with the immediate, one week and six month delayed posttest performance of the incidental learning group. Effect size for the *ergative* rule on immediate, one week, and six month delayed posttests is .27, .08, and .23 respectively. For the *incorporation* rule it is .77, .97 and .74 respectively, while for the *locative* rule it is 1.3, 1.06 and .58 on the three posttests.

ii. Immediate and delayed GJ posttest An ANOVA of immediate and delayed posttest GJ accuracy shows no significant main effect for Time (F, 0.329, $p =$ .56). The results of the repeated measure ANOVA for the delayed GJ task shows significant main effects for Type (F, 30.444, $p < .001$)and Rule (F, 20.816, $p <$ .001) and an interaction of Type and Rule (F, 2.744, $p < .05$) (see Figure 2). As on the immediate posttest, old items on the one week delayed posttest are correctly accepted at above chance rates for all rules. Performance on new grammatical and ungrammatical locatives is still above chance and accurate (77% and 65% accurate respectively). Performance on new grammatical incorporated sentences is at chance (55%) and on ungrammatical incorporated sentences is still, but only just, above chance (59%) and accurate. New grammatical ergatives are at chance (48%) and ungrammatical ergatives are below chance but inaccurate (41%). Overall the results of the immediate posttest are maintained on the delayed posttest — only the locative rule appears to be known, as evidenced by accurate above chance responses to grammatical and ungrammatical items. However, participants have made small, though non significant, gains in mean accuracy on all ergative and incorporated sentences, and declined slightly in accuracy on locative sentences.

iii. Six month delayed GJ test The repeated measure ANOVA for the six month delayed GJ test shows significant main effects for Type (F, 32.478, $p <$ .001), Rule (F, 7.422, $p < .01$) and a significant interaction of Type and Rule (F, 2.489, $p < .05$). As Figure 3 shows accuracy is above chance on old items for each rule, but only marginally so for ergatives (59%), higher for locatives

(78%), and very high for incorporated sentences (91%). For new items performance on grammatical ergative sentences are at chance, locative sentences are correctly accepted at above chance levels (66%), and new grammatical incorporated sentences are accepted at the highest level of accuracy (73%). New ungrammatical locative sentences are accepted at chance levels, while new ungrammatical ergatives, and incorporated sentences are accepted inaccurately, at above chance levels (30% and 29% respectively). As with the earlier GJ results, performance on ergative sentences is poorest, demonstrating no generalizable knowledge of this rule, while grammatical examples of both locatives and incorporated sentences are correctly accepted at above chance rates. This contrasts strikingly with the initial reluctance to accept any new examples of incorporated sentences on the immediate pretest. However, the results suggest that learners are still unaware of the restriction on incorporation, since ungrammatical examples are wrongly accepted at above chance rates. Once again, therefore, the strongest evidence is for learning of the locative rule, accompanied by memory for old instances.

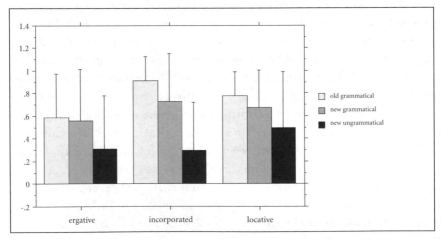

Figure 3. Mean percent accuracy on Samoan sentence types
in the six month GJ posttest

Listening grammaticality judgement test
i. Immediate listening GJ posttest The repeated measure ANOVA for the listening GJ posttest shows evidence of cross modal transfer of learning (see Figure 4). There are significant main effects for Type (F, 34.888, $p < .0001$), Rule (F, 13.261, $p < .0001$) and a significant interaction of Type and Rule (F, 10.997, $p < .0001$). As on the computerized reading GJ posttest, performance

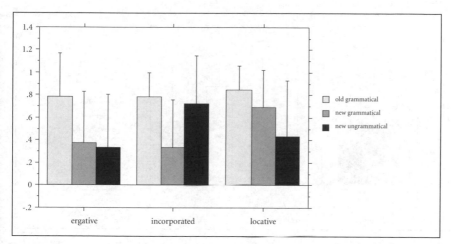

Figure 4. Mean percent accuracy on Samoan sentence types in the immediate
　　　LGJ posttest

on old items is above chance and accurate for all rules. As with the reading GJ
test, for new items, performance on ungrammatical incorporated sentences
(73%), and grammatical locative sentences is above chance (69%). However
performance on ungrammatical locative sentences, in contrast to the reading
GJ test, is at chance. As with the reading GJ test, performance on both grammatical (38%) and ungrammatical (34%) new ergative sentences is above
chance, but inaccurate.

ii. Immediate and delayed listening GJ posttest A repeated measure ANOVA
for immediate and delayed posttest performance on the listening GJ test shows
an effect for Time which approaches significance (F, 3.816, p=059). Accuracy
on all rules is higher on the delayed than on the immediate posttest. This is possibly a result of learning occurring *during* performance on the immediate and
delayed posttests rather than maturation of learning occurring during training
task exposure. As with the delayed reading GJ test, the repeated measure
ANOVA for the delayed listening GJ test (see Figure 5) also shows that performance on old items remains accurate and above chance. As with the reading GJ
test, accurate rejection of ungrammatical incorporated sentences is maintained (69%) as is accurate acceptance of grammatical locatives (68%).
Performance on new ergatives has improved from below chance and inaccurate, but is still at chance (55%), while performance on ungrammatical ergatives remains below chance and inaccurate (39%).

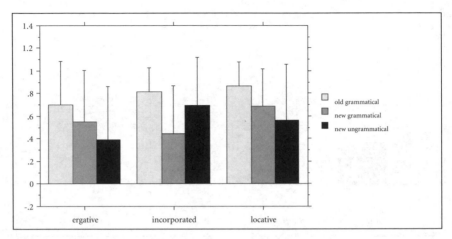

Figure 5. Mean percent accuracy on Samoan sentence types in the one week LGJ posttest

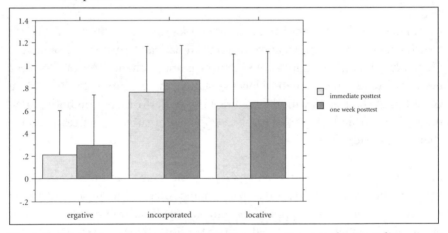

Figure 6. Mean percent accuracy on Samoan sentence types in the immediate and one week delayed production posttests

iii. Written versus aural GJ modalities While both the written and aural GJ tests show participants have learned to recognize old sentences presented during training, and to generalize knowledge gained during training to above chance, correct judgements of locative sentences, there are differences in performance on tests in these modalities. A repeated measure ANOVA of immediate written and aural GJ responses shows a significant main effect for modality (F, 8.819, $p < .01$), and a significant interaction of Modality and Rule (F, 7.415, $p < .001$), but no interaction of Modality and Type (F, 2.730, $p = .07$). Accuracy on locative sentences is significantly higher on the written GJ test (88%) than on the aural GJ test (66%). However, performance on the delayed listening GJ test improves considerably, with the result that a repeated measure ANOVA of delayed written and aural GJ responses shows no significant main effect for Modality, or interaction of Modality and Rule, or Type. On the delayed aural and written GJ tests accurate judgements of the ergative (55% and 51%), incorporated (65% and 70%) and locative sentences (65% and 71%) is very similar.

Summary of Grammaticality Judgement Test results over time

In summary the results of immediate and delayed posttests on reading and listening GJ tests show:

i.   clear evidence of generalizable knowledge of the locative rule;
ii.   evidence of the increasing acceptability of new grammatical examples of incorporated sentences, without knowledge of the scope of restrictions on this rule;
iii. and no evidence, beyond memory for old instances, of learning the ergative rule.
iv.   The six month delayed GJ test suggests that accurate rule knowledge may have been maintained most clearly in the case of the locative sentences.
v.   There is evidence of cross modal transfer of incidental learning, with information presented during exposure to written input available to guide grammaticality judgements presented aurally.

Sentence Production Tests

i. Immediate and one week delayed production test

The repeated measure ANOVA for the immediate posttest of production shows a significant main effect for Rule (F, 28.674, $p < .001$), with percent accurate production of incorporated (77%) and locative sentences (65%) being significantly better than production of ergatives (20%) (see Figure 6). The repeated measure ANOVA for delayed production also shows a significant main effect for Rule (F, 29.514, $p < .001$), and an improvement in accuracy for production of all sentence types. Mean accuracy of production on the ergative is still significantly poorer than production of the other two sentence types. Production of incorporated sentences is highly accurate (90%) and is significantly better than production of locatives (70%). Production of all sentence types improves from immediate to one week delayed posttest, but this improvement is significant only in the case of ergatives ($p < .03$), and a repeated measure ANOVA shows no main effect for Time (F, 2.301, $p = .14$) on production on the two tests.

ii. Six month delayed posttest

The six month delayed production test shows a similar pattern to the two ear-lier tests. There is a significant effect for Rule (F, 19.338, $p < .001$), with accu-rate production of ergatives (20%), much lower than of incorporated (77%), or locatives (65%). There is a decline in overall ability on each of the rules in the production test, compared to one week delayed performance, but perfor-mance on the six month delayed and immediate posttests is almost identical

Summary of results on the sentence production test over time

In summary, the production tests show:

i.   as with the GJ tests, learners have little knowledge of the ergative rule.
ii.   In contrast to the GJ tests, productive ability is higher on the incorporat-ed than locative sentences.
iii. Performance on both incorporated and locative sentences is high, above chance, and accurate on immediate, delayed and six month delayed tests;
iv.   this suggests stronger retention over time of accurate production ability than of knowledge guiding accurate grammaticality judgements.

Awareness questionnaire data

Following the coding criteria described earlier, all participants demonstrated high levels of awareness on the immediate posttest debriefing questionnaire, with the exception of verbalizable knowledge of the ergative rule, as shown in Table 4 . Following the six month delayed GJ test the last three questions on the original questionnaire, asking participants of they could verbalize the three rules, were readministered. As can be seen from the bracketed percent-ages, there is some decline in overall ability to verbalize the locative and incor-porated rules, but still substantial awareness of them, in contrast to verbaliza-tions and awareness of the ergative rule.

Table 4. Questionnaire awareness data on the immediate and six month posttests

Noticed	Searched	Verbalized	Locative	Ergative	Incorporated
89%	70%	81%	81%(73%)	02%(07%)	81% (73%)

Note: Bracketed percentages are for performance on the three questions administered on the six month posttest

Interactions of rule type, test format,time, and individual differences

Individual differences, rules, and GJ and LGJ tests over time
The results reported in Table 3 above showed no correlations of individual differences and incidental learning of Samoan on any of the three GJ posttests. Table 5 shows that in general this finding is not affected by the type of rule to be learned. There are no significant correlations of ID measures and ergative learning on any of the posttests, and only one significant correlation of incorporated rule learning and IDs (with awareness, $r = .35$, $p < .05$) on the delayed posttest, and one significant correlation of locative rule learning and IDs (with aptitude, $r = . 47$, $p < .05$) on the six month delayed posttest.

Table 3 also showed that working memory alone predicted successful performance on the Listening Gramaticality Judgement test, on both immediate and one week delayed posttests. Table 6 shows this is in large part the result of significant correlations of WM and incorporated rule learning (immediate posttest, $r = . 41$, $p < .05$; delayed posttest, $r = . 52$, $p < .01$), and with ergative rule learning on the delayed posttest ($r = . 49$, $p < .01$). Of the three rules, incorporation is most clearly affected by IDs, particularly on the immediate posttest, where accuracy correlates significantly with aptitude ($r = . 54$, $p < .01$), intelligence, ($r = .46$, $p < .05$), as well as WM. Locative rule learning is unrelated to any measure of IDs on the Listening GJ posttests.

Table 5. Intercorrelations of IDs, awareness and incidental learning of three rules, as measured by performance on the GJ test over time

% Correct	Apt	Int	WM	Aw
Ergative T1	-.26	-.11	-.04	-.22
Ergative T2	-.27	-.03	.002	-.25
Ergative T3	-.13	-.15	-.06	-.16
Incorporated T1	-.02	-.03	-.06	.17
Incorporated T2	.11	-.003	.24	.35*
Incorporated T3	-.22	.2	-.13	.15
Locative T1	-.13	-.03	.27	.19
Locative T2	.05	-.08	-.06	.28
Locative T3	.47*	-.19	.16	.36

Key: * = $p < .05$, T1 = immediate posttest ,T2 = one week delayed posttest, T3 = six month delayed posttest, Apt = Aptitude, Int = Intelligence, WM = Working memory, Aw = Awareness

Table 6. Intercorrelations of IDs, awareness and incidental learning of three rules, as measured by performance on the listening GJ test over time.

% Correct	Apt	Int	WM	Aw
Ergative T1	-.22	-.08	.18	-.08
Ergative T2	-.1	-.08	.49 **	.03
Incorporated T1	.54**	.46*	.41*	.23
Incorporated T2	.14	.24	.52**	.02
Locative T1	.02	-.06	.16	.04
Locative T2	.08	-.15	-.04	.07

Key: * = $p < .05$ ** = $p < .01$, T1 = immediate posttest, T2 = one week delayed posttest, Apt = Aptitude, Int = Intelligence, WM = Working memory, Aw = Awareness

Table 7. Intercorrelations of IDs, awareness and incidental learning of three rules, as measured by performance on the production test over time

% Correct	Apt	Int	WM	Aw
Ergative T1	.11	.55 **	-.006	.03
Ergative T2	.1	.2	.42*	.14
Ergative T3	.44*	.18	.2	.43*
Incorporated T1	-.04	-.27	-.13	.03
Incorporated T2	.02	-.22	-.1	-.04
Incorporated T3	.35	.26	.36	.25
Locative T1	.47*	-.17	-.01	.03
Locative T2	.08	.05	.21	-.11
Locative T3	.5 **	.07	.19	.35

Key: * = $p < .05$ ** = $p < .01$, T1 = immediate posttest, T2 = one week delayed posttest, T3 = six month delayed posttest, Apt = Aptitude, Int = Intelligence, WM = Working memory, Aw = Awareness

Individual differences, rules, and the sentence production data over time
In contrast to the findings reported above in Tables 5 and 6, on the Sentence Production test it is accuracy in forming ergative sentences that is most strongly, and positively influenced by all measures of IDs, though this influence changes over time (see Table 7). Intelligence ($r = .55, p < .01$) and working memory ($r = .42, p < .05$) are related to accurate immediate and delayed posttests peroduction respectively. Six month delayed production is positively related to both aptitude ($r = .44, p < .05$), and awareness ($r = .43, p < .05$).

In contrast to the findings reported for the Listening grammaticality tests in Table 6, there are no significant correlations of IDs and incorporated rule learning. Of the measures of IDs, aptitude is most related to learning on this tests, with ergative learning on the six month posttest ($r = .44$, $p < .05$), and particularly with locative learning on the immediate ($r = .47$, $p < .05$) and six month delayed posttests ($r = .5$, $p < .01$).

Summary of interactions of IDs, rule types, test formats, and time
Correlations of IDs and performance on rule types, on test formats over time show:

i.   Accuracy on the Grammaticality Judgement test is the least sensitive to IDs.
ii. Accuracy on the Listening Grammaticality Judgement test is most strongly influenced by WM (three out of five positive correlations), and accuracy on the Production tests is most strongly influenced by aptitude (three out of six positive correlations).
iii. IDs most strongly influence ergative rule production on the Sentence Production test, and IDs most strongly influence accuracy of judgements of incorporated sentences on the Listening Grammaticality Judgement tests.
iv. Overall, IDs are not more influential on immediate, delayed or six month delayed posttests.
v.   The strongest, ID by rule and time relationship, is for *aptitude* and *locative* performance on the six month delayed Grammaticality Judgement ($r = .47$, $p < .05$), and Sentence Production tests ($r = .5$, $p < .01$).

Discussion

Summary of findings for the Main Hypotheses

The generalizability of Reber et al.'s (1991) findings for implicit learning
Implicit learning, as studied by Reber and replicated in the present study, shows a different pattern of correlations with ID measures than incidental learning. Incidental learning is not related to intelligence, whereas implicit learning is significantly, albeit negatively, related to intelligence (see Table 2). Possibly this is due to the fact that the participants in the present study were experienced language learners and adopted an explicit code-breaking set

towards the implicit learning task, and since the rules governing the implicit learning task display are extremely complex, this had negative effects — particularly for those who with higher IQ scores were most disposed to adopt an explicit code-breaking set to the task. Further, the present study found that incidental learning and implicit learning are unrelated on any of the immediate posttest measures of incidental learning (see Table 2). Neither is incidental learning related to explicit learning, suggesting a process which is different from both implicit learning of the artificial grammar, and explicit learning of the series solution tasks replicated in this study.

These results, then, demonstrate that the claims about implicit learning and IDs made by Reber et al. are not generalizable to incidental SLA. While this may be expected, since the stimulus display in the artificial grammar learning experiment requires non semantic processing, in contrast to the stimulus display in the incidental learning condition, Reber and Allen (2000) do argue that incidental learning *in general* shares many characteristics of implicit learning, and that robustness in the face of IDs in cognitive abilities may be one of them. This was not found to be so in the particular case of incidental L2 learning operationalized in the present study, and this finding is in line with Reber and Allen's (2000, p.238) speculation that "individual differences might emerge in processing of verbal or complex material" under incidental, unintentional learning conditions.

While this study is the first attempt to directly compare, in an experimental, repeated measure design, implicit learning as operationalized by Reber, and adult incidental SLA, the present finding for the nongeneralizability of Reber et al.'s findings to SLA also confirms other research findings which have attempted to investigate the relevance of Reber's research to SLA. It confirms, for example the findings of Robinson (1996a, 1996b) where it was shown that implicit learning of an L2 (operationalized as instructions to memorize examples as in Reber's studies) was not superior to explicit learning of complex rules, as claimed by Reber, and also by Krashen, who argues unconscious acquisition is most effective in the case of complex L2 rules, though simple L2 rules can be learned explicitly. Robinson showed that on both simple and complex rules, structured explicit learning was superior to implicit SLA, as did Ellis (1993).

In another sense there is also doubt about the generalizability of Reber et al.'s (1991) basic findings to a different population, since with the present population of participants — who were all experienced and proficient language learners — significant *negative* correlations of IQ and implicit learning were obtained, and the correlation of IQ and explicit learning only approaches significance. To this extent, IDs in IQ *do* affect implicit learning, albeit negatively, in the present study (perhaps for the reasons given above), contra the claims of Reber et al. The results therefore only partially support hypothesis 1 of the present study, that; i) Reber et al.'s results will be replicated, but that ii) incidental L2 learning will show a different pattern of correlations with ID measures than either implicit and explicit learning, suggesting a process sharing some characteristics of each, but identical with neither. The first claim was not supported though the second was.

It must be noted however, that the findings reported above are not in themselves reason for dismissing, or even for doubting the fundamental validity of, Reber's claims for implicit learning outside the domain of adult incidental SLA. As argued above, the finding for a significant negative correlation of IQ and implicit learning in the present study may be attributable to the narrow sample of subjects — university students who, importantly, had some level of *expertise* in foreign language (FL) learning, and considerable FL classroom learning *experience*, and who may have therefore have adopted *conscious strategies*, drawing on the abilities measured by the IQ test, to solve the implicit learning task. More research is needed, replicating basic findings from cognitive psychology (such as Reber's) with different pools of experienced L2 learner participants, with different levels of L2 expertise, resulting from naturalistic, as well as instructed exposure, and of different ages.

Neither do the findings of the present study negatively imply that *any* attempts to relate research in cognitive psychology to SLA are likely to produce results which are discontinuous with the original findings. Despite the special nature of the SL learner population, in terms of their expertise and experience in FL learning settings, most SLA processes, I would argue, are not categorically different from the learning processes studied in general cognitive psychology (see e.g., the positive results from DeKeyser's (1997) application of Anderson's ACT* theory to SL automatization). However, they are unlikely in all cases to be identical, and it is the *precise nature of the overlap* from findings in cognitive psychology, with the particular processes involved in SLA that needs to be explored. Positive, as well as negative findings can be expected to result from such research. The latter point is fundamentally important to any sustained research program into the cognitive basis of SLA, and to identifying its areas of similarity, and difference, from general learning processes.

Aptitude, intelligence, working memory and incidental learning
The second hypothesis for the present study, based on the transfer-appropriate processing explanations of learning offered by Roediger et al. (1989), was largely confirmed. Incidental learning was found to be most sensitive to the ID measures that most closely matched the abilities hypothesized to be drawn on during incidental learning task performance, i.e., aptitude and working memory. Intelligence assessed by the WAIS-R measure of IQ was not strongly related to incidental L2 learning. However, I also predicted that WM differences would most successfully predict incidental L2 learning, compared to intelligence scores (using the WAIS-R), or aptitude scores (using the LABJ). There was evidence for this, but only in overall performance on the immediate and one week Listening GJ test, which WM strongly predicted, and for performance on the one week and six month delayed Production tests (see Table 3), though rule type interacted with ID measure and test type as Tables 5 and 6 show. Working memory, however, was unrelated to immediate GJ tests of overall incidental learning.

Clearly then, while WM does predict successful incidental learning, it does not do so ubiquitously, on all tests. It does so most successfully on tests which themselves tap WM capacity — in the same way it was hypothesized the incidental L2 learning process would — such as the listening GJ test versus the unspeeded computerized GJ test. This confirms points made elsewhere in the SLA literature about the need to develop process continuous, and therefore acquisitionally sensitive measures of varieties of L2 learning, resulting from exposure under different instructional conditions (see e.g., Robinson, 1995b, p.311; Long & Robinson, 1998, p. 40), in line with similar arguments for transfer appropriate tests of learning in general cognitive psychology (e.g., Graf & Ryan, 1990; Jacoby, 1983; Roediger, et al., 1989) Further, the effects of WM on incidental learning are most clearly apparent (not surprisingly) on the rules which *can* be learned (i.e., locatives versus ergatives, which are difficult to learn) and has clearer effects when learning is assessed over time.

Awareness, retention, and incidental learning
The third hypothesis for the present study was not confirmed. Higher levels of awareness, as demonstrated by responses to the debriefing questionnaire did not correlate positively and significantly with higher levels of learning, of any targeted rules. Awareness, though significantly and positively related to WM and aptitude (see Table 2), was only related to six month delayed Sentence Production posttest performance on the ergative rule (see Table 7), and one

week delayed posttest accuracy of performance on the GJ delayed posttest for incorporated rule sentences (see Table 5). In my introduction to this paper I acknowledged the problems inherent in questionnaire measures of awareness, such as their potential lack of sensitivity and exhaustiveness as elicitation measures, but adopted them in this study because they are consistent with measures of operationalizing awareness in Reber's studies, and it was those findings I principally wanted to compare my own with (see e.g., Reber 1989, 1993). However, the preponderant trend in the questionnaire awareness data was to awareness of the two rules, locatives and incorporation, which also were clearly most learnable. The rule for forming ergative sentences was poorly learned, as evidenced by performance on GJ, and production tests, over time, and it was this rule in particular participants demonstrated least awareness of in their questionnaire responses, suggesting that awareness is necessary for learning, but not coextensive with it — as Schmidt (2001) has claimed.

The greater awareness of the structural correlates of the locative and incorporation rules, versus the ergative rule, is also no doubt a consequence of the semantic processing induced by the incidental learning task. To answer questions about the meaning of sentences containing locative phrases requires that the semantic information conveyed by the prepositional marker i has to be attended to. Similarly, in processing sentences which contained examples of incorporated nouns, the argument structure of the verb, and so the proximal relationship of the verb to the noun, had to be attended to and semantically processed. In contrast, sentences containing ergative markers can be successfully processed without attending to the ergative marker e , which is semantically opaque and communicatively redundant. As Ochs (1985) notes, for this reason ergative marking is late acquired during Samoan L1 development, since ergative distinctions between verbs can be, and are, made from an early age using discourse, word order, and other devices. As many have argued, it is therefore in precisely cases such as the ergative marker that additional intervention may be needed in instructed settings to focus learner attention on form that otherwise may go shallowly processed, unnoticed, and so unlearned (Doughty & Williams, 1998; Long & Robinson, 1998).

In the present study I also examined a purely formalist explanation (as opposed to the functional rationale offered above) for why constraints on noun incorporation might be learned quickly, and independently of the influence of individual differences, i.e., the Minimalist UG proposal that incorporation of a noun into a verb from a locative phrase violates the Shortest Move Requirement, or Minimal Link Condition (Chomsky, 1995; Ferguson, 1996), or in Government and Binding theory, the Empty Category Principle (Baker, 1989; Robinson, 1994b). If the present study had shown accurate rejection of such ungrammatical sentences, independently of the influence of IDs in cognitive abilities deployed during central processing, there would have been strong evidence for this. However, as illustrated in Figure 1, in the present study there is evidence that participants adopted a strategy of rejecting most new examples of incorporation, whether grammatical or ungrammatical, and this must be taken as counterevidence to the proposal adult L2 learners have full and automatic access to UG, in this case. Further, as shown in Tables 4, 5 and 6, while production of incorporated sentences, and accuracy in GJ responses to them is independent of IDs in the cognitive abilities measured in this study, accuracy of listening GJ judgements of incorporated sentences is strongly influenced by IDs in aptitude, intelligence *and* WM on the immediate posttest.

Finally the fourth hypothesis was only partly confirmed. There was evidence of *long term retention* of incidental learning, but only for locative rule learning on all posttests (see Figures 3, 5 and 7). There was evidence that learning of the locative rule that occurred during incidental exposure was maintained on the one week and six month delayed posttests of Grammaticality Judgement and Sentence Production. Sentence Production tests revealed maintenance of learning of the incorporated rule on posttests, though the ergative rule did not appear to be learned. However the further claim of hypothesis four, that those *demonstrating higher levels of awareness will show greater retention of* incidentally acquired Samoan, was also not found to be true. As implied in the comments immediately above, awareness may be necessary to initiate learning, but maintenance of learning draws on a different cluster of cognitive abilities and capacities, one of which may be WM capacity, and related processes for elaboratively rehearsing the learned material in WM (see Robinson, 1995b, p. 297; Williams, 1999).

Further discussion and conclusions

As might be expected in replicating a study from general cognitive psychology (Reber et al., 1991), and additionally examining its relevance to a specific learning domain — adult incidental learning of a natural L2 — the present study has identified some areas of similarity with findings from the replicated study, as well as important areas of difference. A further motivation for the present study was the finding in an earlier study (Robinson, 1996b, 1997a) that incidental learning, in contrast to rule-search, and rule instructed learning, was unrelated to two measures of language learning aptitude, the MLAT WS and PA subtests. The present study adopted a different measure of aptitude, Sasaki's LABJ, as well as WAIS-R measures of IQ, and a reading span measure of WM. The findings of the present study *do* show some of these measures of IDs to be influential on incidental learning. Brief further discussion of these main findings is given below.

Individual differences and variance

As in Reber et al. the present study shows significantly *greater variance in explicit learning* than in implicit artificial grammar learning (Table 1). Incidental natural L2 learning displays more variance than implicit learning, but the difference is non significant. The results contradict claims by Zobl (1992) that incidental SLA occurring during communicative courses of instruction exhibits less variance than SLA occurring during traditional grammar focussed instruction. There was no significant difference between variance in the incidental and explicit conditions of the present study; and in an earlier study, where a direct comparison of incidental learning and rule-instructed SLA was made (Robinson, 1996b) it was shown that incidental learning exhibited *greater* variance than instructed learning.

Also, as in Reber et al. explicit learning shows positive correlations with intelligence, though the correlation is not as strong in the present study. However, in contrast to the findings of Reber et al., implicit learning is negatively, and significantly, related to intelligence. Overall, on the immediate posttest (see Table 2) *incidental learning appears unaffected by individual differences,* even in aptitude and awareness.

However, while seemingly supporting the claims of Krashen (1982) and Zobl (1992) this latter basic finding masks the contribution of rule complexity to incidental L2 learning. On GJ and Listening GJ immediate posttests, as well as on Sentence Production immediate posttests there is clear evidence that learners are above chance and accurate in performance on *locative* sentences, and this is maintained, with some decline, over time. Sentence Production tests show ability to accurately produce *incorporated* sentences, and this is also maintained over time, though this is not reflected in accuracy on GJ tests at any time. In contrast, there is *no* evidence that *ergative* sentences have been learned, at any time, on any test. However, although the awareness data in Table 4 shows much greater awareness of the rules which *are* learned, locative and incorporated, and little awareness of the rule that wasn't, ergatives, there are few correlations of awareness and actual measures of learning.

Individual differences also interacted with the type of rule learned. Performance on *locative sentences* which learners were most successful on and could verbalize positively *related to aptitude,* on two six month delayed posttests, though *not as strongly related to working memory or* awareness (see Tables 5 and 7). Performance on ergative rules, which learners were least aware of and could not verbalize is consistently negatively related to aptitude and other ID measures on the immediate GJ test (Table 5), but is positively related to a number of measures of IDs in the Sentence Production test (Table 7). Clearly then, adult incidental L2 learning is variably affected by the complexity, and nature, of the rule to be learned, and IDs in cognitive abilities interact with rule complexity and rule type during incidental learning. The true nature of the influence of IDs on incidental learning is therefore to be found in the specific details of such interactions (see Whittlesea & Dorken, 1993), and this is not, ultimately, reducible to general statements that IDs do, or do not, affect global incidental, explicit, or implicit learning.

Incidental learning of Samoan
There was maintenance of incidental Samoan learning, and interesting evidence of gain over time on the delayed GJ tests. Notably, learners learned more of, and gained most over time on the two rules they demonstrated the greatest ability to verbalize, i.e., rules for locative and incorporated sentences — evidence perhaps that greater awareness can lead to more successful learning, and maintenance rehearsal of verbalizable rules, leading to subsequent gain.

Strangely, for incorporated sentences, there was a mismatch between the high level of ability demonstrated in production of these sentences (the most accurately produced on the posttest and the delayed posttest) and poor performance on accepting new grammatical examples of them during the GJ tests. Learners produced sentences they rejected during the GJ test. *Declarative knowledge,* perhaps, accessed during the GJ test, *is disjoint with the procedural knowledge* drawn on in the production test. This could be interpreted as consistent with the claims that Universal Grammar (which prohibits the ungrammatical examples of word formation in the form of noun incorporation presented in the GJ test) is not accessible explicitly, in the form of conscious judgements of grammaticality, but can be accessed without reflection in the sentence production test. However, there was widescale testimony to having noticed, and ability to verbalize some of the constraints on noun incorporation evident in the responses to the questionnaire, suggesting, as Schmidt argues, that even access to UG may be gated by attention and awareness. But this interpretation begs the question of whether the incorporated rule was actually learned, and there is no conclusive evidence (accurate above chance rejection of ungrammatical examples of noun incorporation in the GJ tests) that this was so (see Figure 1). Rather the production tests show only that learners are able to produce well formed grammatical examples, and this is in itself not evidence that they have learned restrictions on the scope of the rule.

In the present study there is also evidence of *crossmodal transfer of learning*, from learning via reading and comprehending computerized stimuli to correct acceptance of sentences presented in the aural modality. This also suggests, in addition to the findings for individual differences described above, that incidental learning of Samoan in the present study differs from implicit learning as described in the studies of Reber, since widescale evidence has been reported that implicit learning in those studies is extremely sensitive to modality matches between learning and testing (see e.g., Cleeremans, et al. 1998), and that where the modality for learning and testing is not matched, there is lack of transfer of implicit (though not explicit) learning.

Incidental learning, aptitude, and working memory

Incidental learning in Robinson 1997a, though it did occur, was not significantly related to aptitude. In contrast, in the present study aptitude was shown to influence incidental learning, particularly of the locative rule on the six month delayed posttests, and is most strongly related to overall Sentence Production ability on the six month delayed posttest. The influence of aptitude, as measured by the LABJ, therefore, appears to be most effective over time, and on rules which are easier and more learnable. However, overall, the LABJ measure of aptitude is a weak predictor of successful incidental learning, and this may be for the reasons that I gave in my introduction, that aptitude tests such as the LABJ, and MLAT, need to be revised if they are to capture the cognitive abilities drawn on in learning under incidental (as opposed to audiolingual, or grammar focussed) learning conditions. This points to a need not only to *renorm* current aptitude tests (as suggested by Sparks & Ganschow, 2001) but to *reconceptualise* our aptitude constructs in line with evidence of the ID measures facilitating learning under a wider variety of instructional conditions than originally considered in the development of such tests.

As evidence for this — although not included in LABJ, or the MLAT — the present study has also shown that a measure of IDs in *working memory* does predict successful incidental learning. Overall, only WM correlates significantly and positively with the immediate and delayed listening GJ scores, and approaches significance for delayed production. These findings therefore contradict claims by Reber and Krashen described in the introduction to this paper, that implicit/incidental learning is insensitive to individual differences, and offer some support for the claims of the Fundamental Similarity Hypothesis, that L2 learning under any condition of exposure will be sensitive to IDs in cognitive abilities and resources, where these are relevant to the processing demands of the particular learning task or condition.

These results, then, strongly suggest that working memory capacity may be a particularly relevant component of the 'aptitude complex' for incidental learning (as proposed in Chapter 6, this volume). However, the results also show that working memory capacity alone cannot be equated with aptitude for incidental learning (see Miyake & Friedman, 1998), and it may be that, as noted in my introduction, speed of WM (not measured in the present study, though see e.g., Salthouse, 1996; Stankov, 1999) may also be influential on successful incidental L2 learning, along with other cognitive abilities that contribute to 'noticing', rehearsal, and further analysis of input. Further research will be necessary to specify the extent of the contribution of these aspects of individual differences to L2 learning, as well as the contribution of other cognitive ID variables that supplement working memory processes during adult incidental SLA.

Note

* I gratefully acknowledge the help and comments of the following: for comments on noun incorporation and learning, Julia Herschensohn (University of Washington), Usha Lakshmanan (University of Southern Illinois, Carbondale), William O' Grady (University of Hawaii), David Pesetsky (MIT), Andrew Radford (University of Essex), Don Smith and Minako Tani (Aoyama Gakuin University); for help with the reliability estimates Steve Ross (Kwansei Gakuin University), Bill Bonk (Kanda University) and Nick Jungheim (Aoyama Gakuin University); for comments on the effect size calculations John Norris (University of Hawaii) and Lourdes Ortega (University of Georgia); for permission to use the Language Aptitude Battery for the Japanese Miyuki Sasaki (Nagoya Gakuin University) and Charles Stansfield, *Second Language Testing, Inc;* for help translating and coding the questionnaire responses Shuichi Nobe and Mayumi Okada (Aoyama Gakuin University); for advice on the working memory test Mark Sawyer (Kwansei Gakuin University); Mariko Kotani (Aoyama Gakuin University) and Robert DeKeyser (University of Pittsburgh) for comments on the final paper, and Ryoichi Kurosaki (Meiji University), Kaoru Ochiai and

Mayumi Okada (Aoyama Gakuin University), and Keita Kikuchi (University of Hawaii) for help with the data collection and entry. I also am grateful to the Aoyama Gakuin Soken Research Institute, for supporting the Language and Comprehension research project that this study was part of.

Appendix A

Explicit learning series solution problems (from Reber et al., 1991)

Alphabetic series	Next letter choice		
ABCBCDCDE_	D*	or	C
ABBBBBCBBD_	B*	or	C
ABABBACBAD-	A	or	B*
AABABC_	B	or	A*
ABCDABCA_	D	or	B*
ABCDBCCDEC_	D*	or	B

Nonalphabetic series			
CDEADCA_	E*	or	D
CDAADCFBEE_	F	or	B*
ABCDEDEC_	B	or	A*
AEFEFAFAE_	A*	or	E
DDEFDEEFDE_	E	or	F*
AFDDAFFDA_	A*	or	F

* = correct choice

Appendix B

Artificial grammar (from Abrams & Reber, 1989) and implicit learning
training set sequences (from Knowlton & Squire, 1996)

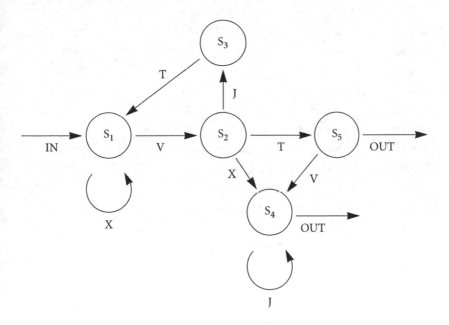

Training items

XXVT	VXJJJJ	XXVJ	XXXVTV
XXVXJJ	XVT	VTVJ	XVXJJ
VXJJ	XXXVT	VJTVX	VT
XVJTVJ	VJ	XXXVTV	VJTVXJ
XXVXJ	XVXJJJ	XXVJ	XXXVX
XVX	VJTVTV	VJTVX	VJTXVJ
			XVXJ
			XXXXVX

Appendix C

Samoan words and English/Japanese translation equivalents learned in the incidental learning vocabulary memorization phase

Samoan	English	Japanese
le tama	boy	男の子
le teine	girl	女の子
le taavale	car	車
le lupe	dove	ハト
le mago	mango	マンゴ
le televise	television	テレビ
le vaa	boat	ボート
le paka	park	公園
le pia	beer	ビール
le tusi	book	本
le fale	house	家
le ogaumu	oven	オーブン
le nofoe	chair	イス
le laulau	table	テーブル
le moa	chicken	ニワトリ
ave	drive	運転する
fana	shoot	撃つ
ai	eat	食べる
inu	drink	飲む
faitau	read	読む
fau	build	建てる
matamata	watch	見る
malaga	travel	旅行する
taalo	play	遊ぶ
tao	roast	焼く
nofo	sit	坐る

CHAPTER 11

Aptitude-exposure interaction effects on Wh-movement violation detection by pre-and-post-critical period Japanese bilinguals[*]

Steven Ross, Naoko Yoshinaga, Miyuki Sasaki

Kwansei Gakuin University / Hirosaki Gakuin University / Nagoya Gakuin University

Introduction

Research on apparently exceptional adult second language acquirers has indicated that there may be factors other than transfer and age of acquisition affecting acquisition of both peripheral and core aspects of a second language grammar. The influence of such individual difference factors has not been extensively examined against a second language acquisition (SLA) theory using the critical period as a developmental benchmark. This study examines Japanese learners' intuition about violations of *that*-trace effect and the subjacency principle. Subjects represent three different samples of critical period-sensitive language learning experience profiles: a) extensive naturalistic exposure to English in childhood; b)teenage SLA through immersion; and c) foreign language learning exclusively. Measures of *that*-trace and subjacency violation grammaticality judgements are regressed on language learning aptitude and pre-and-post critical period language acquisition experience profiles in order to test the hypothesis that individual difference factors interact with pre-and-post-critical period language acquisition experience. Results suggest that individual differences in aptitude interact in subtle ways with learning experience to influence post-critical period SLA.

Theoretical background

Recent work in second language acquisition has begun to explore variation in the post-critical period acquisition of near native-like competence in both peripheral and core grammar domains. Following early claims of complete inaccessibility to Universal Grammar for post-critical period second language learners (Birdsong, 1999; Bley-Vroman, 1989; Schachter, 1989, 1990) recent research suggests that there may be factors which may serve to compensate for post-critical period learners' diminished access to language specific aspects of second language morphosyntax (DeKeyser, 2000; Harley & Hart, 1997, this volume; Newport, 1990) and possibly even Universal Grammar-dependent phenomena (Ioup, Houstagui, El Tigi, & Moselle, 1994; White and Genesee, 1996). Exceptional language learner characteristics (Novoa, Fein & Obler, 1988; Smith & Tsimpli, 1995) are potentially akin to the kinds of individual differences phenomena Bley-Vroman (1990) hypothesized to motivate adult 'problem solving' processes that come into play in post-critical period SLA.

Just as extensive exposure to any natural language during childhood leads to virtual homogeneity in native competence, exposure to a second language in the post-critical period results in a veritable bell curve. Some complex of social, psychological and cognitive processes apparently serves to create variance in proficiency among adults (Skehan, 1989, 1998a, this volume) to such a degree that the usual picture of adult second language learning is one more obvious for its shortcomings than for its successes.

Recent research has begun to explore cognitive factors that may generate the variance in language acquisition outcomes for adults. How deeply individual difference factors can go to account for apparent anomalous cases of post-critical period SLA have yet, however, to be identified.

Aptitude research

Second language learning aptitude (henceforth, aptitude) is traditionally defined as the ability to succeed in learning a foreign language given adequate instruction and/or experience. Ever since Carroll and Sapon's (1959) pioneering development of the Modern Language Aptitude Test (MLAT), research related to aptitude has continued to support four hypotheses: (1) aptitude is typically stable, and unsusceptible to short-term training (e.g., Carroll, 1981; Politzer & Weiss, 1969; Skehan, 1989, but see also Nayak, Hansen, Krueger, & McLaughlin, 1990; McLaughlin, 1990, 1995, reporting that multilingual experiences may enhance the learners' readiness to learn a new language); (2) aptitude consists of several mutually distinct cognitive abilities (e.g., phonemic coding ability, grammatical sensitivity, rote learning ability for foreign language materials, and inductive language learning ability proposed by Carroll, 1981, 1985, 1991; see also the three factor model proposed by Skehan, 1998a, this volume); (3) aptitude is at least partially independent of other cognitive abilities such as general intelligence (e.g., Gardner & Lambert, 1965, 1972; Ganschow, Sparks, & Javorsky, 1998; Robinson, this volume; Sasaki, 1996; Sternberg, this volume; Wesche, Edwards, & Wells, 1982), and (4) aptitude generally has higher and more consistent correlations with second language (L2) proficiency, whether it is acquired formally or informally, than have other individual difference variables such as cognitive styles and personality (e.g., Ehrman & Oxford, 1995; Reves, 1982; Skehan, 1989, 1998a).

The relationship between L2 proficiency and aptitude was first investigated through validation studies of existing aptitude batteries (Carroll, 1958, 1979, 1981; Carroll & Sapon, 1959; Pimsleur, 1966b). Aptitude batteries such as the MLAT and the Pimsleur Language Aptitude Battery (PLAB) correlated moderately (generally between $r = .2$ and $.6$) with subsequent proficiency tests and final foreign language grades. With homogeneous sample populations, the correlation sometimes went up as high as $r = .7$ (Carroll & Sapon, 1959). However, such validation studies were typically conducted in the psychometric/structuralist tradition, and "researchers in this area have not been excessively influenced by other developments in second language acquisition and learning" (Skehan, 1998a, p. 186).

Skehan's studies in the 80's were among the first to introduce acquisition and learning perspectives into aptitude research. For example, Skehan (1980) focused on memory, one aspect of multidimensional aptitude, and looked at the correlation between the test scores of various memory tests and other measures of English-speaking adults' success in learning Arabic. Skehan reported that tests for "response integration" (memory for unknown language structures) and "memory for text" predicted the participants' language learning success better than those for other types of memory. Subsequently, Skehan (1986a) analyzed the same data, and found two different types of successful language learners: One was the relatively young group that depended more on their memory, and the other was the relatively older group that depended more on their analytic abilities (see also Wesche, 1981 for similar findings).

Later in the 80's, Skehan (1986a, 1986b, 1989) further investigated "the origin of aptitude" (1989, p.194) issue by examining the relationship among three latent traits: first language (L1) development, aptitude, and foreign language achievement. English speaking children's L1 development was measured by such indicators as mean length of utterance and sentence structure complexity when they were three to four years old. Later, when they entered secondary school (ages 13 to 14), their aptitude and foreign language success were measured. Skehan (1989) reported significantly high positive correlations (above $r= .4$) between some of the L1 indices and those of later aptitude. In fact, these figures were generally higher than the correlations between first language measures and foreign language achievement measures. Based on these results, Skehan posited a latent trait of "pre-programmed autonomous language learning ability" (Skehan, 1989, p. 33) underlying both first language development and second language learning aptitude.

In their analysis of individual differences in French proficiency, Harley and Hart (1997, this volume) identified two patterns of language learning aptitude that correlated differently with proficiency outcomes. Harley and Hart compared the relationship between three different measures of aptitude (associative memory, memory for text, and analytical ability) and various L2 proficiency measures among learners starting to learn French before and after adolescence (early and late immersion students respectively). Harley and Hart first found that the early immersion students' scores on three aptitude subtests were not significantly higher than those of the late immersion students, which contradicts the findings of some previous research (e.g., McLaughlin, 1990) that aptitude can be developed through language learning experiences. Furthermore, Harley and Hart reported that early immersion students' L2 learning success tended to be associated with the memory measures (especially the memory for text measure) whereas late immersion students' L2 learning success was associated with the analytical ability. Of interest was the distinction between pre-critical period learners' 'verbal memory' aptitude scores and post-critical period learners' 'language analysis' aptitude scores, which were correlated with several measures of French proficiency development. These differences between the two profiles of learners are of particular relevance to the present study because they suggest the possibility of an aptitude by experience interaction.

The potential influence of experience interacting with aptitude is also seen in research undertaken by DeKeyser (2000), who found evidence corroborating the Harley and Hart observation that language learning aptitude interacts with initial exposure to a second language. DeKeyser, in replicating Johnson and Newport's (1989, 1990) studies using grammaticality judgments, observed that adults' ability to perform 'language analysis' correlates with English proficiency for Hungarian-Americans, whose exposure to English began in the post-critical period. The correlation between language analysis and proficiency was seen to diminish into insignificance for those subjects whose acquisition began early, presumably before the critical period, relative to the robust correlation between language analysis and proficiency among adults. For peripheral aspects of English and French grammars at least, these two studies suggest that individual differences in language learning aptitude influence child and adult language learning success in different ways. It appears that child second language acquirers might not need aptitude for success, possibly because of the immutable influence of Universal Grammar. If neurological maturation leads to the eventual atrophy of language learning, individual differences among adults may reflect variation in neurological organization (Eubank & Gregg, 1999; Smith & Tsimpli, 1995), or possibly the emergent influence of other cognitive factors such as language learning aptitude.

To date, few studies have found instances of post-critical period SLA resembling native-like competence (Birdsong, 1992; Coppieters, 1987; Ioup, et al. 1994). When such cases are observed, transfer of first language parameters has been the preferred explanation (see White, 1996 for a review) In examining near-native intuition by adults without a specific consideration of transfer, White and Genesee (1996) interviewed adults who apparently had achieved near native-like performance. The object of their interest was to determine if such adults could demonstrate native-like competence in detecting 'strong' island violations — extraction out of complex noun phrases, relative clauses, adjuncts, and subjects in the process of *wh*-question formation. White and Genesee concluded that indeed there was a consistent pattern of 'no difference' between their near-native subjects and the native controls, and more significantly, that there was no effect for age of acquisition (cf. Eubank & Gregg, 1999).

White and Genesee's study suggests that even post-critical period second language learners "can achieve native-like competence with respect to constraints of UG, provided care is taken to ensure native-like proficiency" (1996, p.251). Of interest to SLA research is how such learners *get* native-like proficiency — given the widespread observation that the vast majority of adults come nowhere close to native-like L2 competence or performance.

It now appears that cognitive accounts of individual differences consistently show effects for formal learning and language-specific aspects of morphosyntax. The extent to which these individual differences interact with pre-

and-post critical period second language acquisition experience profiles sets a new research agenda. In order to examine this interaction, we operationalize grammar analysis aptitude, which we assume to approximate Bley-Vroman's (1990) notion of 'problem solving' ability in adult learners.

Wh-movement phenomena

This section describes the subjacency condition and the empty category principle (ECP), which are considered to be the constraints relevant to the formation of *wh*-questions, following the traditional principles-and-parameter approach[1]. We will use a pre-minimalist version of syntactic theory (i.e., the government-and-binding theory) since it is widely known and is easily accessed in the literature. The main focus is on three constructions, which are of interest in the present study: constructions with subjacency violations involving *wh*-extraction out of relative clauses and out of adjunct clauses, and a construction with an ECP violation involving the *that*-trace effect, which will be clarified in what follows. We briefly discuss these principles in relation to the SLA research on UG accessibility issues.

The subjacency condition and the empty category principle

In English, *wh*-questions are formed with the *wh*-word moved to the sentence initial position regardless of its underlying position, as *what* in *What did John eat?* In the tradition of generative grammar, such *wh*-words are considered to be extracted from their underlining position to the sentence initial position, leaving their trace behind (see e.g., Haegeman, 1994, pp. 371–372).

English *wh*-question formation involving the extraction of *wh*-words out of clauses, shown in (1a) and adjunct clauses shown in (1b) are not permitted, leading to unacceptability of the sentences (see e.g., Chomsky, 1986, p.34 & p.31).

(1)   a.   *What did Kate like the story that described_?
       b.   *Who did Mary see the doctor after the rock hit_?

In sentence (1a), *what* originates in the position of the direct object of the verb *described*, which is in the clause modifying the noun *story*; in sentence (1b) *who* originates in the position of the direct object of the verb *hit*, which is in an adjunct clause beginning with *after*.

The subjacency condition rules out those structures. In the *Barriers* framework (Chomsky, 1986, p.30), this is explained in terms of the notion of barriers; the movement of *wh*-words over more than one barrier leads to unacceptability by native speakers of English. The extraction of the *wh*-word in both structures illustrated in (1) involves more than one barrier, violating the subjacency condition[2].

Wh-questions such as in (2a), where the *wh*-word originates in subject position in the embedded clause, are often considered to be ungrammatical unless the complementizer *that* is deleted. The comparable grammatical sentence without *that* is shown in (2b).

(2)   a.   *What did Mary think that broke the window?
       b.   What did Mary think broke the window?

This phenomenon, known as the *that*-trace effect (see e.g., Haegeman, 1994, pp.398–399), is accounted for by the empty category principle (ECP, Chomsky, 1986, pp.47–48). The ECP rules out sentences with empty categories (such as traces of *wh*-words) from being properly governed; the existence of the complementizer '*that*' prevents the trace of *wh*-word in subject position in a sentence like (2a) from being properly governed, hence violating the ECP (e.g., Chomsky, 1986; Lasnik & Saito, 1984).

UG principles and studies of UG access

The analysis of UG principles like the subjacency condition and the ECP in the performance of learners whose native language lacks overt *wh*-movement comparable to English has been an important tool in the issue of the access to UG (see e.g., Bley-Vroman, Felix, & Ioup, 1988; Schachter, 1989, 1990). As Herschensohn (1999) points out, even though linguistic theory has changed in recent years, variance in judgement of subjacency violations has not adequately been explained and thus remains a viable object of study.

If learners of English whose native language lacks syntactic *wh*-movement (such as Korean or Japanese) show knowledge of the subjacency condition in judging English *wh*-question sentences, their knowledge is not directly attributable to transfer from their L1; neither is it likely to be available from L2 input (e.g., Bley-Vroman et al., 1988, p.5; see White, 1989, p.74; 1992, pp.448–49).

The prevailing interpretation is that input-independent and transfer-independent accurate judgements about UG principles indicates continued access to those principles (see e.g., Martohardjono & Gair, 1993; White, 1989). If, on the other hand, learners fail to show the knowledge of such UG principles, it can be taken to suggest no more access to UG; however, it has also been claimed that inaccurate judgements do not necessarily show inaccessibility to UG principles (White,1989; Martohardjono & Gair, 1993).

White (1992, p.448) warns that it is very difficult to find transfer-independent interlanguage syntax (e.g., subjacency operates in L2 but not in L1), referring to the possibility that learners may make use of L1 knowledge of subjacency which constrains movement of other structures in their L1. If such knowledge is transferable, it should help learners to accurately reject relevant violations.

It has been reported that second language learners are somewhat less accurate than native speakers in rejecting ungrammatical sentences involving *wh*-movement (White, 1992, p.449). In Schachter (1989), for example, many subjects, especially Korean learners of English, did not perform well on detecting subjacency violations (Schachter, 1989, p.85). Bley-Vroman et al.'s results showed that Korean learners of English performed better than chance, but they performed well below native speaker norms (Bley-Vroman et al., 1988, p.27).

Second language acquisition researchers who support the continuity hypothesis (access to UG) attempt to account for the phenomenon that learners do not perform like native speakers by arguing that the learners may analyze sentences differently from native speakers, and that inaccuracy of the learners does not necessarily mean that they do not have access to UG (Martohardjono & Gair, 1993; White, 1992; cf. Yusa, 1999). For example, White (1992) claims that Korean or Japanese learners who accept English sentences with subjacency violations analyze those English sentences as involving no movement, since such an analysis is possible in the learners' L1; thus subjacency is not relevant and they are not violating principles of UG.

As for the ECP, it is considered possible in the principle-and-parameter model (pre-minimalist program model) that *wh*-words move at the level of Logical Form (LF) in languages such as Japanese and Korean which do not have syntactic *wh*-movement. This type of movement in LF is subject to the ECP; that is, the ECP is used in those languages (White, 1989, p.74; Yusa, 1999, p.291). White notes that the ECP is used in Korean, but not for syntactic *wh*-movement. White further notes that learners could detect ECP violations via knowledge of their native language, although Bley-Vroman et al. (1988) did not find strong evidence of it.

White and Genesee (1996, p.245) report that judgements on *that*-trace effect among their pilot native speakers of English were not consistent. They attributed this fact to the claim that there may be dialectal variations for *that*-trace effects (see Rizzi, 1990, p.53).

Japanese phenomena

Unlike English, Japanese lacks overt *wh*-movement. *Wh*-phrases can remain in their underlying positions. The assumption, however, that Japanese completely lacks syntactic *wh*-movement has been questioned. Japanese may have other types of overt movement subject to the subjacency condition, which may undermine the claim of complete non-transferability from Japanese.

For example, Grewendorf (1996, pp.727–728) cites Watanabe's null operator movement in Japanese and Saito's claim that scrambling out of relative clauses and adjunct clauses is subject to the subjacency condition.

Watanabe (1992) claims that a null *wh*-operator associated with the *wh*-phrase, which is phonetically unrealized, moves at overt syntax (S-structure). His claim is based on the observation that sentences such as (3a), where a direct object *wh*-phrase is in a *wh*-island, are marginally unacceptable. Sentences such as (3a) are therefore sensitive to the subjacency condition (Watanabe, 1992, pp.257–8).

(3) a. (?)John-wa [Mary-ga nani-o katta ka dooka] shiritagatte iru no?
John-Top Mary-Nom what-Acc bought whether know-want Q
'What does John want to know whether Mary bought?'

b. John-wa [nani-o katta hito]-o sagashiteiru no?
John-Top what-Acc bought person-acc looking-for Q
'What is John looking for the person who bought?'
(Watanabe, 1992, p.257; 3a is Watanabe's (5b) and 3b is his (5a))

Watanabe (1992), however, also notes that unlike sentence (3a), which involves a *wh*-island, sentence (3b), where the *wh*-word *nani-o* inside of the relative clause, is grammatical. He follows the pied-piping analysis that Nishigauchi (1986, 1990) proposed to account for this (see also Groat & O'Neil, 1996). Setting aside the technical details here, this pied-piping operation is done at LF, and might not be transferred to incorrectly lead Japanese learners to judge English *wh*-questions involving extraction out of a relative clause as acceptable.

If Watanabe's claim is correct, it implies that syntactic *wh*-movement sensitive to the subjacency condition exists in Japanese. It follows that Japanese learners of English may be able to apply their L1 knowledge to detect the ungrammaticality of such sentences if they "are at least familiar with the fact that overt *wh*-movement is constrained in some way" (Grewendorf, 1996, p.727).

Another possible source of positive transfer from Japanese discussed in the literature is the fact that Japanese has an overt movement — scrambling. Saito (1992, p.72) notes that the sentence in (4), in which a *wh*-phrase is scrambled out of a relative clause, is a case of subjacency violation[3].

> (4)   ?*Dono hon -o$_i$ [Hanako-wa [NP t_i kaita hito] -ni atta] no
>   which book-Acc   -Top   wrote person-to met Q
>   'Which book$_i$, [Hanako met the person who wrote t_i]'
>   (Saito, 1992, p.72, Saito's (6))

According to Saito (1985), scrambling out of adjunct clauses leads to unacceptable sentences, as shown in (5).

> (5)   ??Sono hon-o$_i$ John-ga [Mary-ga t_i yomioete kara] dekaketa (koto)
>   that book-acc   -nom   -nom finish-reading after went-out fact
>   (John went out after Mary finished reading that book)
>   (Saito, 1985, p.247, Saito's (147a))

Thus if these analyses are correct, it can be predicted that Japanese learners of English may correctly reject ungrammatical English sentences involving *wh*-movement out of relative clauses and adjunct clauses owing to L1 transfer. However, Grewendorf (1996, p.728) argues that if UG is accessible, L2 learners should be as successful as native speakers of English in rejecting *wh*-movement violations. He notes also that this is usually not the case.

White (1992) contends that even if scrambling of *wh*-phrases occurs in Japanese, the scrambling itself is subjected to a subjacency constraint[4], and therefore cannot be used explain L2 subjacency violations. Although not much research addresses *that*-trace effect influences from Japanese, research on Korean suggests that cross-linguistic influences should be similar.

In sum, if these claims and observations are correct, knowledge of Japanese may help Japanese learners of English to accurately reject English sentences involving subjacency and ECP violations. Our goal is to evaluate learners' L1 knowledge effects in light of the differential exposure to English before and after the critical period before modeling the influences of language learning aptitude. We take up this stage-wise comparison in the remainder of the paper.

To the extent that L1 transfer affects the learners' performance, it should apply consistently to all of the Japanese participants in our study. Variability in performance differences among the participants should be attributable to three competing, and potentially interacting, sources: 1) L1 influences; 2) exposure to English during and after the critical period; 3) individual differences in aptitude for language analysis.

Method

Participants

As a preliminary step in designing the present study, a pilot study was conducted in the first of a four-year data gathering project. The pilot phase involved 75 Japanese university students who took all of the aptitude tests and a pilot grammaticality judgment task. From observed correlations between aptitude, group membership, and subjacency violation grammaticality judgements, effect sizes likely to be observed in a larger study were generated. The pilot study coefficients of determination (R^2s) were used as input into a statistical power simulation (Cohen, 1988; Cohen & Cohen, 1983). A power analysis provides parameter estimates for adequate sampling given a set of projected effect sizes. Since a non-rejection of the null hypothesis for the effect of aptitude on UG principles will lead to a substantive theory-based interpretation, it is essential that any insignificant effect size be interpreted as correctly indicating a true null hypothesis for the population. The power analysis simulation (Cohen & Bornstien, 1990) in this phase of the study indicated a minimum sample of 115 subjects in order to maintain a statistical power of .80. This became the sampling goal in the second year of the study.

One hundred twenty-nine Japanese university students participated in the main study. All students were between the ages of 18 and 21. As a proficiency baseline for comparing the groups, the Test of English as a Foreign Language (TOEFL) was used. In addition, an English language learning/exposure survey was conducted in order to provide data about individual differences in exposure to English. Membership in one of the three groups (levels of the independent variable) was determined by age of initial exposure to English, and length of residence overseas.

A control group of 17 native speakers of English was also formed. This group provided a baseline comparison for grammaticality judgements used as the criterion variables in the study.

Dependent variables

The criterion test in the study, the Wh-Movement Violation Survey, (WHVS) was devised to present subjects sentences manifesting three types of *wh*-movement in English. Different types of extractions were included in order to create violations and well-formed sentences. The subjects' task was to rate the degree of naturalness of each sentence.
Example:

What did Kate like the story that described?

-3   -2   -1   0   1   2   3

not   perfectly
natural   natural

The Wh-Movement Violation Survey consisted of 24 items. Twelve of the items constituted violations. Four were *that*-trace effect violations, four were movement out of relative clauses, and four were movement out of adjunct islands. The other 12 control items were well-formed examples of *wh*-movement in English. The survey was given to four groups; participants who had acquired English pre-critical period during residence overseas, a group who had acquired English through overseas immersion post-critical period, a post-critical period foreign language learner group who had never left Japan, and a group of native English speaker controls.

Operationalizing the Critical Period

Several putative critical periods have been used in SLA research, ranging from 7 through 16 years of age. In the present study, the cut-off age for operationalizing 'Child SLA' was set at the threshold age of puberty (less than age 12). As these participants had begun acquiring English well prior to the onset of maturation, we assume that they were the most influenced by UG principles. If a participant had lived in childhood in a country where English was the dominant language, or had attended an English-medium elementary school longer than three years before the age of twelve, he/she was classified as a child second language acquirer. Members of the Child SLA group had in general lived with their parents, who were posted on extensive overseas assignments with Japanese corporations.

Participants who were first exposed to English in adolescence, 'Teen SLA', we expect to have been comparatively less influenced by UG. The Teen SLA classification was made if a participant had resided in an English-dominant country after the age of 12 for at least two years before returning to Japan at the age of 18 to attend college. This group had a shorter period of naturalistic exposure to English than the Child SLA group members.

For a third group who began learning English formally in middle school we anticipated the least relative influence by UG principles. The 'Teen FLL' classification was made if participants had never resided in an English-dominant country after the age of twelve or if they had never attended an English-medium international school in Japan. Members of this group had exposure to six years of English instruction beginning in junior high school. They were also enrolled in a teacher-certification program, and thus might be considered more highly motivated than average undergraduates. Few members of this group reported exposure to English outside of Japan, usually exposure through short-term summer vacations.

Table 1. Exposure group means

Group	N	TOEFL (SD)	Length of Residence
Child SLA/1	34	583 (36)	8.1
Teen SLA/2	38	548 (32)	3.2
Teen FLL/3	57	511 (43)	0.4

Table 1 provides the mean profile of English proficiency (TOEFL) and length of residence (LOR) overseas in years for each of the three groups participating in the study. At the time of the study all of the participants were between the ages of 18 and 21 years old.

The Child SLA group stands out in its pattern of exposure to English, with an average of 8 years of overseas residence. The mean TOEFL for this group is perhaps lower than what might be expected from an average of eight years of exposure. Since TOEFL content samples academic English, and many of the Child SLA group members had returned to Japan at junior or senior high school age, their TOEFL scores belie the near native-like fluency and accent that many of these students demonstrate in face to face interviews. The Teen SLA group do not have the same native-like fluency of the Child SLA group, mainly because they have developed their English proficiency in the context of immersion in junior or senior high school contexts. The Teen FLL group achieved a TOEFL score that is above the current national average ($t = 2.69$, $p < .01$), which includes both overseas and non-immersion exposure to English Japanese learners (ETS, 1997), a fact which may indicate keenness and strong motivation to get certification as future teachers, as well as exceptional talent in learning English as a foreign language.

Aptitude measurements

In addition to Test of English as a Foreign Language, the Japanese participants in this study took two aptitude tests in multiple choice format, which facilitated dichotomous (right/wrong) scoring and item analyses. The tests used were the MLAT — Modern Language Aptitude Test (Carroll & Sapon, 1959) Part 4–the Words in Sentences subtest, which was given in English. A Japanese-medium aptitude test was also given, the LABJ — Language Aptitude Battery for Japanese Part 2–the Artificial Language Analysis subtest (Sasaki, 1991, 1996). The Words in Sentences subtest of the MLAT was used as an index of learners' sensitivity to the semantic and syntactic roles that different constituents play in sentences. Example:

> The player hit   *the ball*   with a bat.
> *The man   left   his hat   on   the bench*
>   a   b   c   d   e

Here the task is to locate the semantic role in the test sentence that matches *the ball* in the cue sentence.

The rationale for using English as the medium of testing on one of the aptitude tests was to provide a possible counterbalance to the Japanese-medium aptitude measure used in the study. This decision was based on the possibility that some of the undergraduates who had acquired English as children could in fact be more literate in English than they would be in Japanese.

The LABJ was designed for adult Japanese language learners and has produced reliable data in Sasaki (1991, 1996). LABJ3 (artificial language) was designed to measure inductive language learning ability. It was based on a translation of PLAB-Part 4, where the examinees were given a gloss and two sentence structures of an unknown language as follows:

> gade   father, a father
> shi   horse, a horse
> gade shir le   Father sees a horse
> gade shir la   Father saw a horse
> be   carries

After having studied the gloss and samples, the participants in the next 15 items had to choose a correct sentence in the artificial language correspond-ing to a target English sentence (e.g. "Father carries a horse"). For LABJ3, all glosses and sentences of the unknown language were changed into *katakana* (see Sasaki, 1991 for details). Other than the orthographic change, the method was the same as that used in PLAB-Part 4.

The use of two language analysis aptitude measures allows for a validity check relative to the participants' English language proficiency. Since English and Japanese-medium measures of aptitude are used, the effect of language-of-measurement can be assessed through correlational evidence. If the lan-guage-of-measurement creates an artefact, we would expect to find that lan-guage analysis aptitude measured via English would be more correlated with English proficiency than it would be with a Japanese-medium measure of aptitude. If the construct of aptitude is here language-of-measurement inde-pendent, we would expect that the two aptitude measures correlate with each other more than they would correlate with English proficiency. This issue is examined with the use of principal axis factor analysis below.

Reliability and validity evidence

The three tests used in the study were subjected to internal consistency relia-bility estimates (Kuder-Richardson 20 or Cronbach's alpha). All tests were Rasch-analyzed for fit and transformed onto a logit scale so as to provide a common metric. Table 2 provides a sketch of the internal consistency esti-mates for the tests used in the study.

Table 2. Internal consistency reliability estimates

Test	Code	Language	Reliability	Items
Words in sent.	MLAT4	English	.84	45
Artificial gram.	LABJ3	Japanese	.84	15
Wh-Movement				
Violation survey	WHVS	English	.83	24

In order to avoid a confound between ability and aptitude, the construct of aptitude as it is operationalized in this study must be distinct from the con-struct of proficiency. Given the fact that the data here were collected cross-sec-tionally *ex-post facto*, there is a possibility that aptitude could correlate with proficiency in an ambiguous manner. That is, proficiency could be the cumu-lative *result* of individual differences in earlier as well as current aptitude states. Conversely, the construct of aptitude could be the consequence of individual differences in second language acquisition experience. Zero-order correlations between proficiency and aptitude (cf. Harley & Hart, 1997; DeKeyser, 2000) are often not straight forwardly interpretable for this reason. In order to avoid this type of potential conundrum, an exploratory factor analysis was conducted on the two aptitude measures and the three subtests which make up the TOEFL battery.

The factor analysis takes the matrix of correlations and searches for clusters of measures that are relatively interrelated. These are extracted and their communalities are estimated. Since the battery comprises five measures, we anticipate at least two factors if the three TOEFL proficiency measures indicate 'proficiency' and the two measures of aptitude covary to cluster into an 'aptitude' dimension.

Principal Axis Factor Analysis was used with an extraction criterion set at greater than 10% of the variance. Two factors were thus extracted as they accounted for 44 and 19 percent of the variance, respectively. Since all of the measured variables in some way assess language knowledge and would lead to correlated latent factors, an oblique rotation method was selected. Table 3 lists the factor loadings for the five measures.

Table 3. Factor loadings

Measure	PROFICIENCY	APTITUDE
TOEFL LC	0.737	-0.402
TOEFL ST	0.917	0.053
TOEFL RC	0.836	-0.071
LABJ3	-0.090	0.449
MLAT4	0.001	0.833

The exploratory factor analysis of the proficiency and aptitude measures suggests that they are distinct, but correlated latent constructs. The three measures of English language proficiency — TOEFL listening comprehension (LC), TOEFL grammar and vocabulary (ST), and TOEFL reading comprehension (RC) — all load highly on the proficiency factor. The two measures of aptitude, LABJ3 and MLAT4, show very small loadings on the proficiency factor. Although their loadings on the aptitude factor are not symmetric, they still suggest that aptitude and proficiency are distinct constructs.

Analyses of main effects

If complete access to UG principles governing *wh*-movement diminishes after the onset of puberty, there should be a distinct disadvantage for acquirers with exposure to English beginning in their teens. Two types of exposure are included in this study; exposure in an immersion environment (Child and Teen SLA), and exposure in a foreign language environment only (Teen FLL). We begin with global analyses of differences between the three groups on *that*-trace effect and subjacency violations compared with identification of well-formed *wh*-questions in English. We will then progress to differences in the type of violations before examining the effects of aptitude and its interaction with exposure.

The first test of the effects of critical period begins with a global classification of the 24 WHVS items into the 12 items that constitute violations of *that*-trace effect or subjacency with the other 12 that were well-formed examples of *wh*-movement in English. To this end, the ratings of grammaticality given by all of the Japanese participants were subjected to multivariate analysis of variance. Here, the two dependent variables are the sum of all well-formed items (ALLOK) and the sum of the twelve items that involve a violation of *that*-trace effect or subjacency (ALLVIO).

Table 4. MANOVA for effects of Critical Period on grammaticality judgements

UNIVARIATE F TESTS

VARIABLE	SS	DF	MS	F	P
ALLOK	4.006	2	2.003	1.948	0.147
ERROR	116.169	113	1.028		
ALLVIO	1.440	2	0.720	0.876	0.419
ERROR	92.873	113	0.822		

MULTIVARIATE TEST STATISTICS

WILKS' LAMBDA =   0.917
F-STATISTIC =   2.471   DF = 4, 224   PROB = 0.045

The main effect for the critical period (Table 4) is not large enough to suggest that the foreign language learners differ from the Teen SLA acquirers or the Child SLA acquirers in accepting the well-formed *wh*-questions. The test of violations likewise suggests that no group differences exist. This observation might at first glance be taken to support the 'full access' position (Epstein, Flynn & Martohardjono, 1996). At this stage such an interpretation is not warranted, since we have not yet compared the Child SLA intuitions to a native speaker benchmark on the same items. Further, since there are different types of violations embedded in the 12 item index of *wh*-movement violation examples, there remains the possibility that group differences are hidden.

In order to examine this possibility, a second between-groups analysis is performed. In this phase, the means of the summed scores for all well-formed items and the means of the summed items containing a violation of the *that*-trace effect or subjacency principles are tested after entering aptitude covariates into the model. Thereafter, the means of each of the three *wh*-movement violation types are tested. Table 5 shows the main effects analysis for well-formed items.

Table 5. Multiple ANCOVA for effects of aptitude on well-formed items

ANALYSIS OF COVARIANCE

SOURCE	SS	DF	MS	F	P
GROUP	5.092	2	2.546	2.506	0.087
MLAT4	0.142	1	0.142	0.139	0.710
LABJ3	0.000	1	0.000	0.000	0.992
APT	0.151	1	0.151	0.149	0.700
ERROR	105.664	104	1.016		

The influence of aptitude on the judgement of well-formed sentences appears to be negligible. There remains a slight trend ($p=.087$) favoring the Child SLA group in their mean recognition of the lack of any type of violation in the twelve well-formed sentences on the WHVS (Figure 1). However, these Japanese learners of English as a whole falter in their recognition of well-formed sentences (cf. White & Genesee, 1996). The tendency is to opt for the mid point of the Likert scale in the judgement process.

The situation changes when we consider the influence of the aptitude covariates on the summed ratings of *that*-trace effect and subjacency violations. Here, as the bottom portion of Figure 1 indicates, all of the Japanese groups tend in varying degrees to reject sentences containing violations. They do so, however, with less accuracy than does the native speaker control group.

When the aptitude covariates are entered into the model (Table 6), there is a clear effect of LABJ3 and the factor score APT, suggesting that rejections of sentences containing violations may be influenced by individual differences in aptitude for language analysis. The trend that indicated an advantage for the Child SLA group disappears entirely ($p=.617$).

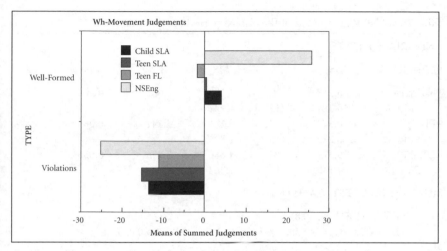

Figure 1. *Wh*-movement judgements for each group

Table 6. Multiple ANCOVA for effects of aptitude on violations

ANALYSIS OF COVARIANCE

SOURCE	SS	DF	MS	F	P
GROUP	0.746	2	0.373	0.485	0.617
MLAT4	1.897	1	1.897	2.466	0.119
LABJ3	5.907	1	5.907	7.679	0.007
APT	6.430	1	6.430	8.359	0.005
ERROR	79.998	104	0.769		

Thus far we have observed that there is an effect for aptitude for language analysis that neutralizes the effect of exposure to English in childhood. The criterion variables have been the sum of well-formed item types and the sum of items containing violations of the *that*-trace effect or subjacency. In order to sort out specific effects, we now turn to testing the effects of aptitude and exposure on individual types of violations. We begin with a preliminary analysis to test the effect of exposure on violation types independently of aptitude. Here we of course omit the native speaker control group. Table 7 shows the effect of exposure grouping on each type of violation.

The groups do not appear to differ on their ratings of *that*-trace effect violations, but begin to separate progressively more on relative clause extractions and extractions out of adjunct islands. Raw score means (Figure 2) suggest that there are differential rejection rates for the three types of violations, with

Table 7. MANOVA for effects of the critical period on violation types

UNIVARIATE F TESTS

VARIABLE	SS	DF	MS	F	P
That-trace	6.217	2	3.108	1.601	0.206
ERROR	219.384	113	1.941		
RELCL	10.372	2	5.186	2.841	0.063
ERROR	206.272	113	1.825		
ADJISLE	9.372	2	4.686	3.435	0.036
ERROR	154.148	113	1.364		

MULTIVARIATE TEST STATISTICS

WILKS' LAMBDA = 0.877
F-STATISTIC = 2.500   DF = 6, 222   PROB = 0.023

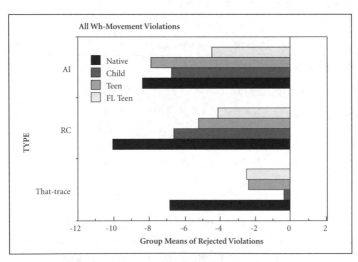

Figure 2. *Wh*-movement violations for each group

the *that*-trace effect being the least recognizable as a violation. We might infer at this point that there are only weak effects for post-critical period differences on the violation detection rates examined. We note that while the three groups differ among each other, they tend to differ in their judgements of grammaticality from the native speaker group on judgements of the *that*-trace effect violations and relative clause extraction, but less so on judgements of extractions from adjunct islands. At this stage, since the effects of aptitude have not yet been modeled, there remains the possibility that groups may differ in more complex ways if individual difference factors work differentially *within* the three exposure profile groups.

Aptitude-exposure interactions

A notable phenomenon among proficiency, aptitude, and *wh*-movement tests in this study is the difference in between-group means, which are related to differences in exposure to English in childhood. The aptitude score mean differences in fact rival the mean differences seen in the ratings of *wh*-movement violations, suggesting that there may well be some other set of factors covarying with subjects' intuitions about grammaticality. As noted earlier, recent research has suggested that there may be other influences on post-critical period acquisition (Ioup, et al., 1994; White & Genesee, 1996). The question of interest here is whether individual differences in aptitude interact with the *that*-trace effect or subjacency domains.

Prior to assessing the influence of language learning aptitude measures on *wh*-movement phenomena, it is necessary to establish the extent of between-group differences on the two measures of aptitude. Here again, a multivariate analysis of variance is used.

Table 8. MANOVA effects for aptitude measures

UNIVARIATE F TESTS

VARIABLE	SS	DF	MS	F	P
Artificial Grammar/LABJ3	7.662	2	3.831	3.921	0.023
ERROR	110.410	113	0.977		
Words in Sentences/MLAT4	26.013	2	13.006	19.657	0.000
ERROR	74.766	113	0.662		

MULTIVARIATE TEST STATISTICS

WILKS' LAMBDA = 0.732
F-STATISTIC = 9.449   DF = 4, 224   PROB = 0.000

Significant main effects in Table 8 can be observed for both Artificial Grammar/LABJ3 and Words in Sentences/MLAT4. Of particular importance is the fact that both of these measures were designed to assess aptitude for the construct of language analysis. Figure 3 plots the group means for the *wh*-movement measures and the aptitude measures. The measures here are factor scores derived from a factor analysis of the three *wh*-movement measures and the two aptitude measures. The resulting loadings were rotated orthogonally providing factor scores, which have been standardized (z scores) so as to show relative group mean outcomes on the grammaticality judgments and aptitude scores on a common scale.

The group factor score means strongly suggest that, in contrast with the age-related effects for *wh*-movement assessment, the advantage here goes to the foreign language learners. Two interpretations to account for why the foreign language learners obtained such relatively high aptitude scores come to mind: 1) the non-random sample of students comes from a teacher certification course which may tend to attract relatively 'talented' foreign language learners; 2) there is a 'transfer of training' from extensive form-focused instruction given in the current Japanese high school curriculum. Many students become familiar with the meta-language of English grammar before actually acquiring much tangible language proficiency. It is of interest to note that the majority of the Child SLA and Teen SLA groups did not graduate from high school in Japan, and in general tend to be relatively unfamiliar with metalinguistic terminology or methods of grammar analysis. The second of these interpretations is at variance with early research on aptitude which has asserted that language learning aptitude is not subject to amelioration through training or experience (see Skehan, 1998a for a review, and Sternberg, this volume for arguments and evidence in support of the view that aptitude *is* trainable and learnable).

The observed difference between Child SLA naturalistic acquirers and foreign language learners is striking. It may be taken as complementary evidence for what Harley and Hart (1997) and DeKeyser (2000) observed as near-zero correlations between their youngest second language acquirers relative to robust correlations between aptitude and proficiency among the older learners. In the present study, product-moment correlations between MLAT4, LABJ3 and TOEFL were -.151 and -.186 among the SLA Child group, and .411 and .195 among the Foreign Language Teens. The question we must turn to now is whether individual differences in aptitude influence the critical period-constrained grammaticality judgments of *wh*-movement phenomena.

In order to test the influence of the three aptitude measures (Words in Sentences/MLAT4, Artificial Grammar/LABJ3 and the factor scores APT) on subjects' relative ability to detect the three types of *wh*-movement violations, the general linear model (Tabachnick & Fidell, 1996) was used employing the two aptitude measures and the aptitude factor score as covariates and group codes as the independent variable. The three separate dependent variables in the analysis were the *that*-trace effect, relative clause extraction, and adjunct island extraction subscores from the grammaticality judgment (WHVS) test. Here, the initial null hypothesis of interest is that the covariates (aptitude) will have no significant influence on the grammaticality judgments independently of the group codes, which, we hypothesize, encode the critical period effect. The multivariate main effect observed in Table 9 suggests that exposure profile effects remain even after we partial out the influence of the aptitude measures. The three types of *wh*-movement violations show varying effects related to the critical period, however. In order to examine the influence of aptitude

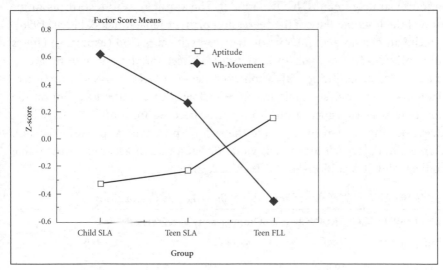

Figure 3. Aptitude and *Wh*-movement factor scores

Table 9. MANCOVA effects for exposure controlling for aptitude

UNIVARIATE F TESTS

VARIABLE	SS	DF	MS	F	P
That-Trace	4.608	2	2.304	1.167	0.315
ERROR	219.223	111	1.975		
RELCL	14.635	2	7.317	4.061	0.020
ERROR	199.984	111	1.802		
ADJISLE	12.810	2	6.405	4.720	0.011
ERROR	150.622	111	1.357		

MULTIVARIATE TEST STATISTICS

WILKS' LAMBDA = 0.856
F-STATISTIC = 2.927   DF = 6, 218   PROB = 0.009

on *that*-trace and subjacency violation detection independently, we need to test for interactions between aptitude and exposure to English. The interaction analysis permits a diagnosis of differential influence of aptitude on the grammaticality judgement process. It tests whether learners with relatively high language analysis aptitude (primarily FLL group members) do better in rejecting *wh*-movement violations independently of their status as members of the post-critical period exposure group.

The first step in this process is to examine each type of *wh*-movement violation separately in an ANCOVA model. The aim here is to test the assumption of the homogeneity of the regression planes (Tabachnick & Fidell, 1996), which will diagnose an interaction between critical period (exposure) effects and aptitude. In the event of a significant effect for the aptitude by group interaction, we continue with a Johnson-Neyman (JN) analysis of the interaction. The JN analysis (Huitema, 1980) allows us to locate the point on the covariate scale at which group differences become insignificant. That is, it diagnoses the amount of aptitude that allows post-critical period Teen FLL learners to detect *wh*-movement violations at a rate of accuracy comparable to the Child SLA subjects or the Teen SLA subjects.

Table 10. ANCOVA effects of aptitude on *that*-trace effect violations

ANALYSIS OF COVARIANCE/Test of homogeneity of regression slopes

SOURCE	SS	DF	MS	F	P
GROUP	19.950	2	9.975	5.511	0.005
MLAT4	0.859	1	0.859	0.475	0.492
GROUP*MLAT4	20.291	2	10.146	5.606	0.005
ERROR	199.091	110	1.810		

ADJUSTED LEAST SQUARES MEANS

	ADJ. LS MEAN	SE	N
Child SLA	-0.140	0.323	29
Teen SLA-	0.561	0.247	31
Teen FLL-	0.876	0.208	56

That-trace effect analysis

The first analysis is of the *that*-trace effect violations. It is noted that the three groups did not differ on their judgement of the *that*-trace effect violations at the outset. The present analysis tests the possibility that group differences are obscured by differences in aptitude. If this hypothesis is correct, there will be a significant interaction between group membership and aptitude. As can be seen in Table 10, MLAT4 interacts with exposure, and in doing so reveals group differences in accuracy that were hidden earlier.

The scores adjusted for differences on the covariate (MLAT4) indicate that the Teen FLL group, which has the largest mean aptitude as measured by MLAT Words in Sentences, is most likely to reject the *that*-trace effect violation. The Child SLA group in general was the least keen to reject *that*-trace effect violations.

It appears that the *that*-trace effect is a 'weak' violation, which tends to be variable among native speakers of English (cf. Rizzi, 1990; White & Genesee, 1996), as indicated in Figure 2. While the Teen FLL participants with high aptitude rejected the violations of *that*-trace effect with the greatest relative accuracy, they are still dramatically different from the rejection rates of native speakers of English.

The Johnson-Neyman analysis indicates that Teen FLL participants with a logit of aptitude reaching 1.06 or larger will not differ significantly ($p < .05$) from the Child SLA subjects. It appears then, that once aptitude interacts with exposure to English, group differences do not reach significance using Bonferroni post-hoc criteria. Given the group means on aptitude (Appendix A), we estimate that about 60% of the Teen FLL learners reach the 'no difference' zone compared with the Child SLA group. We can infer then that aptitude allows these post-critical period foreign language teen acquirers to not differ from the average judgements of pre-critical period subjects. Still, when contrasted to the native speaker reference group, it appears that the three Japanese groups are equally unsure about the ungrammaticality of *that*-trace effect violations — all groups differ from the native speaker reference group on post-hoc tests. It would appear that neither exposure nor aptitude influences the acquisition of the *that*-trace effect for these learners of English.

Extraction out of Relative Clauses

Three measures of aptitude for grammatical analysis were used as covariates. Two, MLAT4 and LABJ3, were direct measures. The third measure was the aptitude factor score derived for each individual. Of the three aptitude measures, the factor score (APT) showed the largest covariance with the judgements of the grammaticality of the *wh*-movements from the relative clause position. It is therefore tested here for its interaction with group membership.

The test of homogeneity of regression slopes for relative clause extractions reveals that although aptitude (APT) shows a trend toward influencing judgements of grammaticality, it does not significantly interact with group membership.

Table 11. ANCOVA effects of aptitude on relative clause extractions

ANALYSIS OF COVARIANCE

SOURCE	SS	DF	MS	F	P
GROUP	11.120	2	5.560	3.042	0.052
APT	5.394	1	5.394	2.951	0.089
APT*GROUP	1.921	2	0.960	0.525	0.593
ERROR	190.112	104	1.828		

ADJUSTED LEAST SQUARES MEANS

	ADJ. LS MEAN	SE	N
ChildSLA	-1.771	0.283	25
TeenSLA	-1.384	0.263	29
TeenFLL	-0.960	0.190	56

Table 12. ANCOVA effects of aptitude on adjunct island extractions

ANALYSIS OF COVARIANCE

SOURCE	SS	DF	MS	F	P
GROUP	14.441	2	7.220	5.088	0.007
LABJ3	0.831	1	0.831	0.585	0.445
LABJ3*GROUP	7.095	2	3.547	2.499	0.086
ERROR	212.880	150	1.419		

ADJUSTED LEAST SQUARES MEANS

	ADJ. LS MEAN	SE	N
ChildSLA	-1.653	0.217	32
TeenSLA	-1.948	0.202	37
TeenFLL	-1.047	0.133	56

The group means, once slightly adjusted for differences in aptitude, show that the child SLA learners are most inclined to reject violations of subjacency when the movement is out of a relative clause. This finding generally conforms to the predictions made by the Critical Period Hypothesis among the exposure profiles. Figure 2 indicates that the mean rejection rate for the Child SLA group approximates the mean observed for the native speaker reference group ($p =.099$). It appears here that aptitude has no influence on learners' detection of subjacency violations when the movement is out of relative clauses. Further, the argument that Japanese learners in general transfer a movement constraint from their L1 is not supported. However, there remains a significant difference between the native reference group and the post-critical period Teen SLA and Teen FLL groups (see Figure 2).

Adjunct island extractions

The analysis of differences in the judgements of the grammaticality of movement out of adjunct islands reveals a pattern different from the previous analyses. Here, neither the SLA Child group nor the Teen SLA group differ significantly from the native speaker reference group in rejecting subjacency violations when movement is out of adjunct islands. The question of interest here is whether the higher aptitude of the Teen FLL group interacts in a manner that decreases the between group differences.

The analysis of the interaction between exposure to English and aptitude indicates that there is a nearly significant effect. There is no significant main effect for aptitude directly on rejection of adjunct island extraction.

The Johnson-Neyman analysis conducted on the near-significant interaction ($p=.086$) indicates that Teen FLL group members with a LABJ3 logit score of >2.57 would not differ significantly from the Child SLA group with respect to the mean adjunct island rejection rate. Fifty-three percent of the foreign language learners meet this criterion with logit-scaled LABJ3 scores larger than 2.57, suggesting there is considerable influence of aptitude serving to compensate for a lack of exposure to English in childhood for these teen foreign language learners in recognizing subjacency condition violations involving adjunct island extractions.

Summary of results

Table 13 summarizes the main effects of the critical period, aptitude, and their interaction on the three types of *wh*-movement violations examined in this study. In the table, brackets [ ] denote ranges of significant post hoc differences among the exposure groupings relative to the native English speaker reference group, (NES). Groups outside of the brackets are significantly different ($p < .10$) from the native speaker reference group, while groups inside do not differ from each other once the influence of aptitude is modeled. Parentheses ( ) denote ranges of 'no difference' based on the Johnson-Neyman analyses. The percentage figure next to TFLL, the Teen foreign language group, indicates the percentage of that group with the amount of compensatory aptitude that, once modeled, results in no significant difference from the Child SLA (pre-critical period) group.

While there is an interaction between exposure to English before and after the end of the critical period and aptitude on the *that*-trace effect violations, even with the compensatory effect of aptitude, there is still a large difference between the native English reference group and all of these Japanese learners of English. Here, aptitude interacts with exposure, the result of which qualifies 60% of the foreign language learners as 'no different' from the Child SLA group in rejection rates of *that*-trace effect violations. Yet none of the Japanese groups approximates the rejection rate of the native English speakers.

Table 13. Summary of main effects ($p < .10$)and interactions

Test	Critical period		Aptitude	Interaction
That-Trace Effect	Yes NES	[(CSLA	No TSLA	Yes TFLL60%)]
Relative Clause	Yes [NES	CSLA]	Yes TSLA	No TFLL
Adjunct Island	Yes [NES	(CSLA	No TSLA]	Yes TFLL53%)

On the extraction from relative clause violations, there were main effects for the critical period influences and for aptitude. Here, the Child SLA group was nearest to the native English reference group mean ($p = .099$). Although there was a weak main effect for aptitude, it showed no interaction with group membership, obviating a need for the Johnson-Neyman analysis.

The adjunct island violation main effects analysis revealed that both the Child SLA and Teen SLA groups differed from the Teen FLL group as a whole, but did not differ from the native English reference group. Though not significantly different, the means of the Teen SLA group are in fact closer to the NES group than are the Child SLA group means. This result in particular suggests that some violations of *wh*-movement are detectable even for post-critical period acquirers, provided there has been exposure through immersion. Here again, aptitude interacts with exposure. The Johnson-Neyman analysis indicates that about half of the Teen FLL learners, those with the highest aptitude scores, are no different from the Child SLA group in rejecting these extractions from adjunct islands. We can infer also that the main effect result (done prior to the Johnson-Neyman analysis) is attributable to the Teen FLL with the least aptitude.

Conclusions

The first generalization to be made about the results of these analyses is that the effect of exposure before and after the critical period appears more complex than originally thought. The between-group differences, based on the age-of-acquisition grouping factor alone, indicate that the three groups are not equal in their accuracy in detecting violations of subjacency when extractions are from relative clauses or adjunct islands. Since all subjects are Japanese, transfer can be ruled out as a source of this difference, since rejection rates apparently vary with length of exposure to English. Moreover, among these Japanese groups, it appears that an interaction of aptitude and exposure induces a convergence effect that allows slightly more than half of the Teen FLL group members to approximate the rejection rates of the Child SLA and Teen SLA groups on the *that*-trace effect violations and extraction from adjunct islands type of violation.

If UG had been accessible to the SLA teens and FLL teens through their knowledge of Japanese, no main effects for exposure or aptitude would be expected. Knowledge of Japanese would be a sufficient basis for rejecting *wh*-movement violations in English. This was not the case.

As an alternative to a partial access mediated-by-exposure interpretation, we have provided empirical evidence that individual differences in language learning aptitude — particularly aptitude for language analysis — possibly indicate a factor that compensates for some learners' relatively late and infrequent access to English. Our findings support the notion of differential parameter resetting for post-critical period learners with high levels of metalinguistic awareness or aptitude for language analysis.

The effects of aptitude for language analysis are our approximation to Bley-Vroman's hypothesis (1989) that adult (post-critical period) problem solving — composed of cognitive processes such as analogical reasoning, distributional analysis, and hypothesis testing, is an important influence on post-critical period SLA. Whether language analysis, as we have operationalized it, conforms to Bley-Vroman's notion of 'problem solving traits' is a matter for further empirical exploration. Future studies of language learning aptitude need to be conducted longitudinally in order to examine whether the early emergence of individual differences endures across different profiles of exposure to an L2 in second and foreign language contexts.

We can surmise that a plausible picture of post-critical period SLA is a composite of varying influences which are likely to conform to both biological (critical period and possibly aptitude) and experiential (naturalistic exposure and formal learning) factors. As maturation-sensitive UG attenuates with age, differences in aptitude gradually emerge and interact with exposure to create variation in post-critical period SLA. The end result is the emergence of individual differences in peripheral *and* core grammar knowledge. We represent this notion in Figure 4. Here, darker shades indicate stronger influences relative to lighter shades.

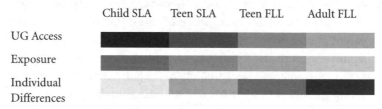

Figure 4. Maturational and experiential influences on SLA/FLL

The invariant influence on child second language acquisition, UG, (darkest cell) diminishes with maturation but interacts with exposure. Children in an SLA context have full access to UG and rich exposure (relatively dark cells) to positive evidence, but show the smallest variation (lightest shade) in individual differences (McLaughlin, 1985). Late critical period and early post-critical period teens show incipient maturation effects. Teens in an SLA context also have relatively robust exposure profiles, usually with access to both naturalistic exposure and formal language instruction. SLA teens, we surmise, will start to show the earliest emergence of individual differences in aptitude and metalinguistic awareness.

The situation for foreign language learners shows a dramatic difference. Teenage exposure to foreign language instruction is typically input-weak, based largely on deductive learning, and occurs near the end of the critical period. Individual differences here emerge to interact with the limited exposure, which cumulatively leads to variance in acquisition. The weakest possible SLA profile in this scheme is that of the mature adult in a foreign language context, where diminished access to UG (other than that which is potentially transferable from L1) compounded with the weakest form of exposure (usually infrequent lessons), the end result is most dramatically different from target language norms. In the adult SLA profile, we assume that individual differences emerge as the greatest relative influence on variation in the acquisition of core and peripheral aspects of a second language grammar.

Finally, we have not addressed the possibility that what we have labeled 'aptitude' may be the *result* of extensive deductive learning experiences. Research on aptitude has largely operated under the assumption that it is immutable, though very little longitudinal research on language learning aptitude (cf. Skehan, 1986a, 1986b) has been undertaken. Skehan for instance infers that language learning aptitude, especially aptitude for verbal memory, may not be amenable to instruction. Our study cannot evaluate this interpretation, since our measures of aptitude were related to the construct of inductive language analysis. The results of this study do not necessarily support an interpretation of inductive language analysis ability being invariant over time. A plausible interpretation is that the teenage foreign language learners in this study appear to have relatively high aptitude because they have transferred extensive training in formal deductive grammar analysis to the grammaticality judgment tasks. The research agenda on the Critical Period in SLA needs to augment the growing body of work done on UG-based constraints with longitudinal studies of emergent aptitude after puberty in order to assess its role. SLA research needs, in short, to explore how 'exceptional' post-critical period second language learners ever manage to beat the odds.

Notes

* We would like to thank Kevin Gregg and an anonymous reviewer for comments on an earlier draft of the paper.

1. It should be noted that some scholars argue such constraints are not relevant to the *wh*-question formations such as *wh*-movements out of relative clauses (Deane, 1992).

2. In earlier work, the notion of bounding nodes is used. The subjacency condition holds that any movement crossing more than one bounding node (IP and NP in English) is blocked (Chomsky, 1977). Although Chomsky (1986, p.31) earlier posits that extraction out of an adjunct island involves crossing two barriers, in his later analysis (1986, p.66), this was reanalyzed when the moved element is an NP (e.g., *who*) as in:

a. he is the person who [IP they left [before speaking to *t*]] (before meeting *t*)

In this initial analysis, the matrix IP and the adjunct CP are the two barriers between *who* and its trace. However, in a later analysis, *who* adjoins to the *before*-phrase. This results in the movement of *who* out of the adjunct in (a) not crossing any barriers.

Lasnik and Saito (1992, p.91) say a sentence such as (b) "has the status of a weak Subjacency violation" .

b. [Which linguist]$_i$[IP did you [VP write your thesis] [after you consultedt_i]

In studies of second language acquisition, Martohardjono (1993, cited in Schwartz and Sprouse 2000, pp.176–177), White and Genesee (1996), and Shimizu (1994), treat these adjunct islands as strong violations.

3. Haig (2000) argues that subjacency does not constrain syntactic movements such as scrambling in Japanese. Rather, pragmatic constraints account for the unacceptable sentences that appear to violate subjacency.

4. Shimizu (1994) translated both English declaratives and interrogatives into Japanese in order to examine the status of Japanese sentences when *wh*-phrases are fronted, possibly by scrambling. He found that combined mean judgements of the translated sentences did not differ significantly from native English speaker judgements.

5. MANCOVA and ANCOVA impose a number of assumptions: normal distributions of covariates and the dependent variable; homogeneous regression slopes; reliability of covariates > .80; linearity as evidenced by predicted values of Y' plotted against residuals after adjusting for the effects of covariates. All of these assumptions were met in this data.

Appendix A

The following results are for:
  Child SLA Group

Total observations:	34		
	LABJ3	MLAT4	APT
N OF CASES	32	31	25
MEAN	2.306	0.286	-0.221
VARIANCE	1.646	0.792	1.029
STANDARD DEV	1.283	0.890	1.014

The following results are for:
  Teen SLA Group

Total observations:	38		
	LABJ3	MLAT4	APT
N OF CASES	37	32	29
MEAN	2.347	0.875	-0.213
VARIANCE	1.085	0.674	0.971
STANDARD DEV	1.041	0.821	0.985

The following results are for:
  Teen FLL Group

Total observations:	57		
	LABJ3	MLAT4	APT
N OF CASES	57	57	56
MEAN	2.838	1.504	0.379
VARIANCE	0.577	0.603	0.846
STANDARD DEV	0.760	0.777	0.920

CHAPTER 12

Age, aptitude, and second language learning on a bilingual exchange[*]

Birgit Harley and Doug Hart

Ontario Institute for Studies in Education / University of Toronto

Introduction

The study presented in this paper examines the relative importance of memory ability and analytical language ability for second language (L2) learning in a natural environment. The participants in this research are secondary school students of French as a second language who, in the context of a bilingual exchange, each spend three months living with a French-speaking family in the Province of Quebec. The study follows from previous research conducted in French immersion classrooms at the secondary school level (Harley & Hart, 1997), where different aspects of language aptitude were found to be associated with L2 outcomes depending on whether students had begun early immersion in grade 1 or late immersion in grade 7. In late immersion, analytical language ability was predictive of L2 outcomes, whereas in early immersion, a measure of memory was a better predictor. These findings are in line with the argument, originally put forward by Lenneberg (1967), that age of initial L2 exposure determines the language learning process, with later learners using a more analytical approach to the L2.

However, an alternative interpretation cannot be ruled out: The differences we found between early and late immersion may also have been prompted by contextual factors, with the classroom learning context in late immersion arguably more formal than that in early immersion. In the present study, by extending our research to learners in a natural L2 environment, we hope to clarify the relative importance of age of initial exposure and learning context as factors affecting students' learning orientation. If age of initial intensive exposure is a prime factor, we would expect the pattern of aptitude-L2 proficiency relationships found for late immersion students to apply to the adolescent bilingual exchange students in the present study as well. Alternatively, if learning context is a more important consideration, the aptitude-proficiency relationships among the bilingual exchange students could be more similar to that found for early immersion students whose classroom learning context has arguably been more natural and informal than that of the late immersion students.

Theoretical background

The issues outlined above should be seen in the broader context of prior research and theory concerning individual differences in L2 learning: in particular, research on age effects, the role of language aptitude, and individual differences in cognitive style. In this section we provide a brief review of some relevant studies, followed by a summary of the research we conducted in the context of early and late immersion.

Age effects

The effect of age on second language learning is a controversial issue at the heart of ongoing debates about the relative contribution of maturational versus environmental, and universal versus individual, factors in language acquisition. Despite an enormous body of research, answers to key questions have remained elusive. Opinions are still divided, for example, on the much-studied question of whether there is an innately predetermined critical period for language acquisition that ends around the age of puberty (for discussion, see Birdsong, 1999; Harley & Wang, 1997; Singleton, 1995; and Ross, Yoshinaga & Sasaki, this volume). Empirical study of this issue has most often consisted of measuring the relative success of learners whose initial exposure to the target language began at different ages. Although a pattern of declining ultimate attainment has been found in association with increasing age of L2 onset, researchers disagree on how to interpret this research (see e.g. Bialystok & Hakuta, 1994; Johnson & Newport, 1989), and particularly the fact that, in some studies, adults have attained a level of L2 performance that appears indistinguishable from that of native L2 speakers (e.g., Birdsong, 1992; Ioup, Boustagui, El Tigi, & Moselle, 1994; White & Genesee, 1996).

Approaching the age issue from a different perspective, we note that from the outset, the critical period hypothesis has had a process-oriented dimension which has so far received much less research attention. According to

Lenneberg (1967), the L2 acquisition process in children contrasts with that of older learners, and this contrast serves as evidence in support of a critical period for language acquisition. Specifically, he maintained that children learn a second language intuitively without conscious effort, whereas postpubertal learners approach language learning more intellectually as an arduous task that demands the application of study techniques. Later proponents of similar process-oriented dichotomies in the second language domain (e.g., Felix, 1985; Krashen, 1981; Schwartz, 1993) have argued that an intellectual, problem-solving approach to the language, seen as characteristic of adults, is less useful, if not positively harmful, to eventual L2 success. This negative view of the value of problem-solving abilities for language acquisition does not sit well with the results of language aptitude research which has typically found analytical language ability to be positively associated with L2 outcomes (see below). It is quite possible, however, that this analytical ability is more closely associated with L2 outcomes in adolescent and adult L2 learners than in those who are first exposed to the L2 as children. This is what our earlier research in the immersion classroom context, and a recent study among Hungarian immigrants in the United States (DeKeyser, 2000), would suggest. Whether analytical language ability is as strongly implicated in the L2 learning of adolescents in a natural environment as it appears to be in classroom L2 learning is a key question we go on to explore in the present study.

Language aptitude research
In classroom learning contexts, overall measures of language aptitude such as the Modern Language Aptitude Test (MLAT) (Carroll & Sapon, 1959) and the Language Aptitude Battery (LAB) (Pimsleur, 1966b) are widely recognized as being among the strongest predictors of second language outcomes in adolescent and adult L2 learners (for review see, e.g., Ehrman & Oxford, 1995; Gardner & McIntyre, 1992; Skehan, 1989, this volume; Sternberg, this volume). These test batteries consist of several subtests designed to cover a number of relatively independent cognitive abilities. Carroll (1981), for example, describes language aptitude (defined as 'the individual's initial state of readiness and capacity for learning a foreign language and probable facility in doing so' (p. 86)), as a composite of at least four abilities: phonetic coding ability, grammatical sensitivity, rote-learning ability, and inductive language learning ability, with auditory ability and further aspects of memory also seen as relevant (Carroll, 1993; Skehan, this volume). This multi-componential view of language aptitude begs the question, central to the present study, of whether

specific component abilities are more or less involved in language learning success for different learners and/or under different learning conditions.

Wesche (1981) was the first to give credence to the idea that individuals differ not just in overall aptitude scores but in their aptitude profiles, with different strengths and weaknesses on the various component abilities. She also observed that enhanced satisfaction and L2 outcomes can result from matching individuals with instructional approaches that make the most of their aptitudinal strengths. Wesche's research was conducted among adults taking language courses required for bilingually designated positions in the Canadian Public Service. In a different adult context (the intensive L2 training of army personnel), Skehan (1986a) identified a similar set of 'learner types' based on their language aptitude subscores. Of these, two types of learners who did equally well on a communicative L2 test appeared to Skehan particularly interesting and in accord with Wesche's findings. He elaborates as follows:

> One successful group was characterized as young, having good memories, but with grammatical sensitivity only slightly above average. The other was considerably older, fairly average in memory, but much higher in grammatical sensitivity. The first successful group achieved its success through greater reliance on memory, which was probably used to assimilate large amounts of material without much analysis. The other group achieved success through more impressive language-analytic abilities and the capacity to organize and structure material.(Skehan, 1989, p. 36)

Skehan went on to suggest that these two learner types represent 'two different orientations to language development' (Skehan, 1989, p. 37, and this volume), with the memory orientation consistent with observations to the effect that neither language learners nor mature native speakers necessarily analyse the language they are using, but may instead rely on memorized chunks. Our research in the immersion and bilingual exchange contexts builds on Skehan's proposal of two different orientations to language development, probing further to see how these proposed orientations are affected by age of initial L2 exposure and learning context.

With respect to the issue of learning context, there is good evidence that overall language aptitude is relevant to learning success under a variety of classroom conditions. Ehrman and Oxford, for example, studied the correlates of language learning success among adults receiving intensive language training at the U.S. Department of State, and found overall scores on the MLAT to be just as predictive of success in a communicatively-oriented program as in a past program involving audiolingual training. Their results thus support Carroll and Sapon's (1959) suggestion that the MLAT taps 'learning abilities that are independent of [teaching] methodology'(Ehrman & Oxford, 1995, p.77).

Others have argued that language aptitude is relevant for learning success not only in the context of communicative language instruction but in non-classroom L2 learning contexts as well. In Gardner's socio-educational model (Gardner, 1985; Gardner & McIntyre, 1992; MacIntyre, this volume), language aptitude is seen to have a direct influence on L2 learning in a formal classroom context, and a secondary, indirect influence in informal contexts since 'the voluntary nature of these contexts is such that individuals may avoid them if they wish' (Gardner & McIntyre, 1992, p. 215). Skehan (1998a, this volume), on the other hand, has suggested that language aptitude is likely to be even more important in informal contexts than in formal ones, because in informal contexts it is up to the learner, without the assistance of linguistically organized input, to 'bring structure to unstructured material' (p. 197).

Two studies (DeKeyser, 2000; Reves, 1982) provide some empirical support for the view that language aptitude is relevant for L2 learning by adolescents and adults in a natural L2 context. In one study conducted in Israel, Reves (1982) compared the impact of various individual factors, including language aptitude, on the learning by Arabic-speaking high school students of Hebrew as a second language (largely outside the classroom) and English as a foreign language (primarily in the classroom). Reves found some of her aptitude measures (in Arabic) to be roughly equivalent predictors of L2 proficiency in both contexts, although overall, the aptitude measures predicted the English language outcomes better than the Hebrew ones (Reves, 1982, p. 64). An interesting detail from the perspective of the present research is that a measure of language aptitude consisting of an Arabic adaptation of the MLAT Words in Sentences subtest correlated positively with English outcomes but not with Hebrew ones. Since this MLAT subtest requires the testee to analyze the syntactic role of highlighted sentence constituents, this finding suggests a greater role for analytical language ability in the more formal classroom learning context than in the natural L2 environment.[1] In the other study, conducted with Hungarian immigrants in the United States, DeKeyser (2000) found relatively high analytical ability to be characteristic of those adult arrivals who achieved near-native scores on a grammaticality judgment test in English. In contrast, analytical ability was unrelated to achievement among those who had arrived in the U.S. as children, virtually all of whom achieved a native or near-native level of success on the grammaticality judgment test.

Cognitive abilities

Some interesting parallels to Skehan's proposed two orientations to language development can be seen in the more general psychological domain. In a review of the literature on cognitive styles, for example, Riding and Cheema (1991) identified a major bipolar dimension on which individuals are seen to habitually differ in their approach to processing information. The authors labelled this dimension 'wholist — analytic', and argued that it underlies a number of other bipolar cognitive style and strategy distinctions in the literature. That there may nonetheless be age-related and contextual factors involved in the way that a learning task is approached is suggested by developmental psychologists Kemler, Nelson and Smith (1989). They argued that a holistic mode of processing information is characteristic of children but continues to be available to adults when circumstances do not encourage recourse to their 'normally deliberate, resource-intensive, problem-solving bent'. This view suggests that, at least beyond childhood, mode of processing is not a fixed characteristic of the individual but may vary in keeping with the context. In the present study, we explore the related idea of whether adolescents' L2 learning that occurs in the informal learning context of the bilingual exchange is more closely associated with memory ability than in the classroom context of a late immersion program. In examining the interaction between individual differences in aptitude and learning conditions, we are taking a step in the direction of the interactionist research approach advocated by Robinson (Chapter 6, this volume). In a hierarchical model including a wide range of first- and second-order cognitive abilities, he argues that these can be grouped into different aptitude complexes that interact with learning conditions in influencing the second language outcomes of post-critical period learners.

The immersion study

Our recent study in French immersion classrooms (Harley & Hart, 1997) was designed to investigate the issue of age differences in language learning orientation by examining how memory and analytical language abilities related to L2 outcomes in classroom learners whose intensive exposure to French had begun at different ages. The participants in that research were 65 early and late French immersion students in a Southern Ontario school board who at the time of the study had all reached grade 11. Thirty-six of them had started early immersion in grade 1 and 29 had started late immersion in grade 7. Based on the predictions of Lenneberg and others, we hypothesized that there would be a positive correlation between memory ability and language learning outcomes for the early immersion students, while for the late immersion students, a positive relationship would be found instead between analytical language ability and L2 outcomes. Two memory measures, administered in English, were used in the study. One was the MLAT-IV Word Pairs subtest (Carroll & Sapon, 1959), included as a measure of associative memory; the other was an adapted version of a subtest from Wechsler's (1972) Memory Scale, given as a measure of memory for text. Analytical language ability was measured by the Language Analysis subtest from Pimsleur's (1966b) Language Aptitude Battery. L2 proficiency measures included tests of vocabulary recognition, listening and reading comprehension, and oral and written production in French. The results of the study supported the hypothesis. When we correlated these grade 11 immersion students' scores on memory and analytical language ability with their French proficiency scores, we found a different pattern of relationships for the early and later learners (see Table 1). For the early immersion group, almost all the statistically significant correlations were between memory and French proficiency measures, whereas for late immersion, almost all the significant correlations were between analytical language ability and French proficiency. Regression analyses indicated that memory for text was the prime predictor of the L2 outcomes in early immersion, and that language analysis was the sole predictor of L2 outcomes in late immersion. In short, the results in the immersion context provided support for the view that initial age of intensive L2 exposure has a significant impact on language learning orientation.

Table 1. Pearson correlations of language aptitude with French proficiency measures: early and late immersion students

Language aptitude	Associative memory		Memory for text		Language analysis	
French proficiency	corr.	n	corr.	n	corr.	n
Early immersion						
Vocabulary recognition	.37*	36	.53**	36		36
Listening comprehension	.49*	36	.50**	36	.48**	36
Cloze			.40*	36		36
Late immersion						
Vocabulary recognition					.41*	29
Cloze					.41*	29
Written task fulfillment					.43*	29
Written accuracy	.39*	29			.44*	29

*p < .05, **p < .01

Statistical correlations, however, are not proof of cause and effect, and in our interpretation of the findings we noted the possibility that different learning contexts in early and late immersion could have influenced the results, rather than age of initial intensive exposure *per se*. Instruction in early immersion may over the years have been more oriented to holistic memory-based learning, and in late immersion more oriented to language analysis. An observational study in early and late immersion programs in another school board had in fact documented a more analytical instructional approach in late immersion (Dicks, 1992) and a more experiential one in early immersion. This raised the issue of whether, when second language learning takes place outside the L2 classroom context, adolescents would, like the early immersion students, rely on a less resource-intensive, memory-based learning approach. As a follow-up to the study in immersion, therefore, we decided to embark on the present study to try and sort out the question of whether age or learning context has more bearing on students' language learning orientation.

Method

Participants

The new study was conducted among secondary school students whose first intensive exposure to the L2 took place outside a second language classroom setting. The initial sample consisted of 31 English-speaking Ontario students in grades 10 and 11 who had opted to take part in a provincially sponsored bilingual exchange with French-speaking students in Quebec (see Table 2 for sample details).[2] These English-speaking students went to stay for three months with a French-speaking family in the Province of Quebec, in which they were 'twinned' with a French-speaking peer. The participants were all enrolled in regular 'core' French programs in their Ontario home schools. There were 24 girls and 7 boys in the sample, representing a larger proportion of girls than in the prior immersion study where the female:male ratio was approximately 3:2 in both early and late immersion. The bilingual exchange students came from 26 different schools around Ontario, and the majority had been in core French programs since grade 4 or earlier. None of them had been in a French immersion program at any stage, and none had been on more than a brief tourist visit to a French-speaking area. The 3-month exchange visit to Quebec thus represented their first intensive natural exposure to the second language. In Quebec, they attended school in French along with their twin, but received no formal instruction in French as a second language.

With the co-operation of the organization responsible for the bilingual exchange program, we were able to test these students (with their consent and that of their parents) as they gathered in the City of Ottawa on two occasions: first on their way to Quebec and then on their way home after the three-month visit was over. Students were each offered $30 for participating in the study, in recognition that the testing sessions curtailed the social events they would otherwise have been attending in Ottawa with their peers. Following their return to school in Ontario, each student then did an individual oral test in French, administered by a bilingual exchange co-ordinator or French L2 teacher at their respective schools.

Table 2. Bilingual exchange sample: core French students

	%
Current grade	
grade 10	45
grade 11	55
Starting grade for core French	
K-grade 3	40
grade 4	53
after grade 4	7
Gender	
female	77
male	23
N^1	31

1. Total number of respondents to the questionnaire. Not all students responded to each question.

Tests and questionnaires

Background questionnaire An initial background questionnaire about prior language experience was first mailed to potential participants' homes in order to screen out those who had been, or still were, enrolled in French immersion programs, or had otherwise had major prior exposure to French. The great majority of eligible students agreed to participate in the study.

Language aptitude measures Two tests were chosen to measure memory and analytical aspects of language learning aptitude respectively: a measure of memory for text and a measure of analytical language ability. These tests were administered as the exchange students set out for their three-month visit to Quebec. The same tests, described below, had been used in the preceding study with immersion students and had proved to be significant predictors of scores on various L2 proficiency measures. A third test, Carroll and Sapon's Word Pairs subtest (1959) that had been included in the immersion study as a measure of associative memory, was not administered to the bilingual exchange students, since a correlational analysis in the earlier research (see Harley & Hart, 1997, p. 391) had shown scores on this test to be significantly associated with scores on language analysis but not with scores on memory for text, raising doubts about the distinctiveness of the Word Pairs test as a measure of memory. A further reason for its omission from the present research was that Word Pairs did not serve in the immersion study as a significant predictor in regression analyses of French L2 proficiency scores.

The memory for text measure, based on a subtest in Wechsler's Memory Scale (1972), had been adapted for group administration and to suit a Canadian context. It required students to listen to two brief news items recorded in English on audiotape. After each one, they had three minutes to write down everything they could recall of the brief narrative they had just heard. Each narrative was deemed to consist of 24 'information bits' and a student's written version was scored for the number of bits the student had been able to recall of the original. The student's final memory score was then the average of his or her scores on the two narratives.

The measure of analytical language ability was the subtest entitled 'Language Analysis' from Pimsleur's Language Aptitude Battery (1966b). In this test, the student is given a small set of sentences in an unknown language with English translations. Based on this information, from which the patterns of the language can be inferred, the student has to answer 15 multiple choice items. Each item consists of a sentence in English and four renditions in the foreign language, only one of which is a correct translation of the English sentence. Students had 10 minutes in which to complete this test.

L2 proficiency measures The French language tests used in this study had previously been developed in the Modern Language Centre at the Ontario Institute for Studies in Education. As in the previous immersion study, they were designed to measure several dimensions of French language proficiency, including vocabulary recognition, listening and reading comprehension, and oral and written production. Apart from the vocabulary recognition test which had previously been administered in the study of early and late immersion, the proficiency tests in this study were different in content from those used in the earlier study, in keeping with the fact that the core French students had overall had much less exposure to French. The tests were nonetheless of the same form as in the preceding study and were designed to assess the same dimensions of proficiency in French.

Two of the French proficiency tests — a measure of vocabulary recognition and one of listening comprehension — were given both as pretests before the exchange visit and as posttests after the three months were over. The measure of vocabulary recognition, based on Meara (1994) was the same as in the prior immersion study. It was a brief test consisting of a written list of 100 French words and pseudowords. Of these, 66 were real words and 34 were pseudowords that followed the orthographical conventions of French. The students' task was to cross out any words that they did not know well enough to say what they mean. In order not to have students abandon the task when confronted with many words they could not know, they were warned in the instructions that some of the words in the test were not real words. A scoring formula was used that credited students for each real word recognized and penalized them for guessing — i.e. when students failed to cross out pseudowords for which they could not possibly have known the meaning. All students were able to complete this test within a 5-minute period. Listening comprehension in French was measured by a test in which students listened to extracts from a tape-recorded interview with French-speaking peers in Montreal. There were 11 multiple choice comprehension questions based on the content of the interview. In scoring, a point was awarded for each question correctly answered.

Other proficiency tests were given at the end of the exchange visit as posttests only. A cloze test developed in the Modern Language Centre, and previously used with immersion students at the grade 8 level (Lapkin, Hart, & Swain, 1991), was based on a text in French about supernatural creatures. It consisted of six short paragraphs with three accompanying illustrations. This test was used to measure reading comprehension in French. Students had 20 minutes to respond to the 26 test items, i.e. 26 gaps in the text that had to be filled with one-word responses. An exact method of scoring was employed whereby students had to reproduce the original missing word in order to receive a point for an item.

Following the cloze test, students were given 10 minutes to write an answer in French to a question related to the reading passage. This writing task was scored on several dimensions: for 'task fulfillment' on a three-point scale (whether the question was in fact answered), number of non-homopho-nous errors (i.e. counting only those errors that sounded erroneous when read aloud), quality of language, and total number of words produced. The nonhomophonous error measure was controlled for length of composition, by taking into account only the first 35 words in each student's writing. This reflected the approximate minimum length of composition produced. The quality of language measure was a four-point rating scale (4= high, 1=low) based on the entire composition and designed to capture what students could do in French, rather than focus on what they were doing wrong. In their qual-ity ratings, scorers took account of the following: any correct use of plural verbs and/or verb forms other than present indicative, accurate gender/num-ber agreement in nominal phrases, use of contractions *du/au/aux*, use of *que* as a subordinator, *beaucoup de*, varied sentence structure, good range of vocabulary (beyond that provided in instructions). In the immersion study a different method of scoring language quality had been used: a simple count of error-free T-units produced. This scoring method was not feasible in the pre-sent study since the bilingual exchange students produced very few T-units that were totally free of error.

All the tests mentioned so far were administered as group tests in Ottawa. In addition, once students had returned to their regular schools, they were given an individual sentence repetition task based on a radio weather bulletin. The student first had an opportunity to read the script, which was then removed. The bulletin was subsequently heard on tape in its entirety, followed by a sentence-by-sentence presentation. The student's task was to repeat each of the 13 sentences one by one after it was heard. The student's responses were also tape-recorded. This kind of elicited imitation task involves several dimen-sions of language proficiency including both listening comprehension and oral production. After a student was tested, the test tape was mailed to us in Toronto and assigned scores of three kinds: one for exact repetition, another for semantically equivalent repetition, and a third for repetition of selected features. For the exact score, a student was awarded one point for a sentence where the exact wording was repeated. For the equivalent score, one point was given for a sentence where the meaning was conveyed even if some words were changed or missing. The features score focused on accurate reproduction of 12 selected syntactic, discursive, and phonological features of the sentences.

Post-questionnaire Finally, at the end of the group post-testing session, we administered a brief questionnaire asking students to indicate on a series of five-point scales how much, on a typical day in the past month, they had inter-acted in French with various categories of interlocutors (teachers at school, classmates at school, the French-speaking twin, the twin's parents, and friends outside school), how much progress they had made over the three months in French listening, speaking, reading, and writing, and how often they perceived themselves as having approached the learning of French in Quebec (a) by deliberately paying attention to specific aspects of the language, or (b) by absorbing the language without deliberately analyzing it. A final question asked which of a number of settings during the exchange was most important, and second most important, for the student's learning of French: in class at school, talking with friends, talking with the French-speaking twin, talking with the twin's family, watching TV, or reading books and magazines.

Results

During the course of the three-month stay in Quebec, one student returned home early. Two more students' return flights did not arrive in Ottawa early enough for them to participate in the group post-testing. For most of the analyses reported in this section, therefore, the final sample was 28. Four students did not take the individual oral test in French after returning to their home schools, resulting in a final sample for the oral testing of 27.[3]

Wherever test scores required judgment on the part of the rater, a second rater rescored a subsample of one third of the tests to verify consistency with the first rater. Raters included native speakers of English for the memory for text measure and a native French speaker and advanced L2 speakers of French for relevant L2 proficiency measures. Inter-rater reliability was found to be sat-isfactory (see Table 3). On each measure, two raters were typically either in full agreement or diverged only slightly in their scores. Where appropriate to the structure of the tests (that is, where tests consisted of multiple items, scored alike), statistical measures of reliability were calculated. These were satisfacto-ry for language analysis and vocabulary recognition pre- and post-tests (see Table 3). The alpha for the French listening comprehension test was quite low, however. Four of the multiple-choice items contributing poorly to overall reli-ability were removed, leaving a final listening test of 7 items to be included in further analyses. As Table 3 shows, reliability remained relatively weak at .45 for the pretest and .56 for the post-test. Almost all students made good progress in listening, with low-scoring students typically making greater gains from pre- to post-test than students who were higher to begin with. This is reflected in a low, nonsignificant Pearson correlation of .25 between pre- and post-listening test scores. Post-test scores on listening comprehension were skewed towards the upper end of the scale (see Figure 1 for relevant bar graph). A better distribution of scores was obtained on the vocabulary recognition measure that was also administered as a pre- and post-test (see bar graph in Figure 2). On this measure, the correlation between pre- and post-test scores was significant ($r = .62$, $p<.01$), indicating a tendency for the exchange students to make a similar amount of gain in French vocabulary during their stay in Quebec regardless of how well they scored on the pre-test.

Three tests in the present study were identical to those previously given to immersion students: the two language aptitude measures and the vocabulary recognition test. Average scores of the exchange students on the vocabulary

Table 3. Summary of reliability and inter-rater agreement

Self-reported learning strategies	Reliability (Alpha)		Inter-rater agreement (correlations)	
	Alpha	n	corr.	n
Language aptitude				
Memory for text[1]			.74	10
Language analysis	.72	31		
French proficiency				
Vocabulary recognition (pretest)				
real words (66)	.83	31		
imaginary words (34)	.84	31		
Vocabulary recognition (post-test)				
real word (66)	.88	28		
imaginary words (34)	.82	28		
Listening comprehension (pretest)	.45	31		
Listening comprehension (post-test)	.56	28		
Open writing task				
Task fulfillment[1]			.76	10
Non-homophonous error count[2]			.78	10
Quality of writing[1]			.72	10
Word count[2]			1.00	10
Sentence repetition task				
Repetition-exact[2]			.97	10
Repetition-equivalent[2]			.93	10
Features score[2]			.87	10

1. Kendall's *tau*.
2. Pearson's correlation.

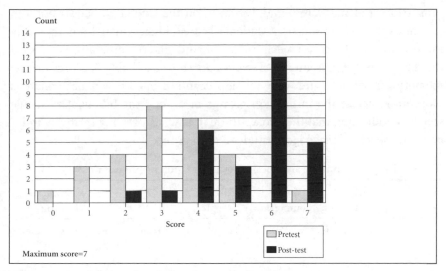

Figure 1. Distribution of pretest and post-test listening scores

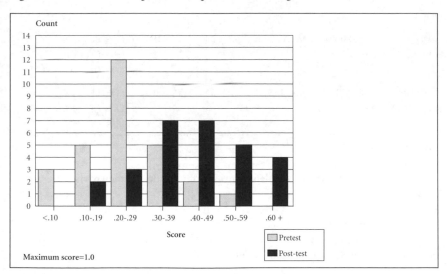

Figure 2. Distribution of pretest and post-test vocabulary scores

post-test were significantly lower than for the two immersion groups in the previous study, as would be expected given their much shorter period of intensive exposure to French. On the memory for text measure, the bilingual exchange students' scores were consistent with those obtained by early and late immersion students in the previous study, indicating that the groups were comparable in memory ability. Significant differences in favour of the late immersion students were found, however, on the language analysis test. On this measure, late immersion students scored higher than both the early immersion and the core French exchange students. (Comparative scores on the three tests are presented in Table 4). As shown in Table 5, scores on the memory for text measure were not significantly related to language analysis scores in either of the immersion groups or among the bilingual exchange students, indicating that the two aptitude tests were assessing relatively independent aspects of language aptitude in each group.

Table 4. Language aptitude and vocabulary recognition by program

	Early immersion			Late immersion			Core French			F-ratio	Paired comparisons	t-test[d]	Significance level of: Tukey
	M	SD	n	M	SD	n	M	SD	n				
Memory for text[a]	11.2	3.7	36	12.8	2.5	29	11.8	2.5	31	.131			
Language analysis[b]	7.4	3.0	36	9.1	3.7	29	6.8	3.1	31	.023	EI vs. LI	.039	NS
											EI vs. CF	NS	NS
											LI vs. CF	.008	.022
Vocabulary recognition [c]	0.66	0.12	36	0.44	0.13	29	0.42	0.14	28	.000	EI vs. LI	.000	.000
											EI vs. CF	.000	.000
											LI vs. CF.	NS	NS

a Maximum score = 24
b Maximum score = 15
c Maximum = 1; for core French students, the post-test results are shown
d two-tailed
Legend: EI — early immersion
          LI — late immersion
          CF — core French
          NS — not statistically significant ($p > .05$)

Table 5. Pearson correlations among language aptitude measures by group

	Language analysis / Memory for text[1]	n
Early immersion	.21	36
Late immersion	.32	29
Core French exchange students	.30	31

1. No correlations are statistically significant ($p>.05$)

The various French proficiency measures, and the tests on which they are based, are described in an earlier section of this paper. Table 6 presents all the French proficiency scores of the exchange students, including pre- and post-test scores for vocabulary recognition, and listening comprehension (reduced to seven items in the final form of the test). This table makes clear that on both these tests the students generally made substantial progress during their three-month stay, a finding that tallies with an earlier evaluation of the bilingual exchange program (Lapkin, Hart, & Swain, 1995). Differences between pre- and post-test scores are statistically significant for both measures. It may be noted that on the sentence repetition task the 'repetition exact' score is very low — an average of 1.19 out of a maximum of 10–indicating that exact repetition is very difficult to achieve. Similarly low scores have been typical in past administrations of this test to other student groups (Lapkin, Hart, & Swain, 1991). Pearson correlations among the various proficiency measures are displayed in Table 7. Among the findings shown on this table is that cloze

Table 6. French proficiency scores for core French exchange students

	Core French		
	M	**SD**	**n**
Vocabulary recognition (pre-test)[a]	0.25	0.12	28
Vocabulary recognition (post-test)[a]	0.42	0.14	28
Listening comprehension (pre-test)[b]	3.21	1.52	28
Listening comprehension (post-test)[b]	5.39	1.31	28
Cloze[c]	9.21	5.22	28
Open writing task			
Task fulfillment[d]	1.86	0.71	28
Non-homophonous error count	1.64	1.42	28
Quality of writing[e]	2.18	1.02	28
Word count	72.04	24.60	28
Sentence repetition task			
repetition-exact[f]	1.19	2.22	27
repetition-equivalent[g]	5.52	3.58	27
features score[h]	8.67	5.18	27

a. Maximum = 1; excludes students not completing the post-test.
b. Maximum = 7; excludes students not completing the post-test.
c. Maximum = 26.
d. Maximum = 3.
e. Maximum = 4.
f. Maximum = 10.
g. Maximum = 13.
h. Maximum = 21.

scores and quality of writing scores are positively related to each other and to scores on most other French proficiency measures, with the exception of listening comprehension and two of the writing measures — task fulfillment[4] and nonhomophonous error count. In short, these findings indicate that students who performed well on one L2 proficiency test tended also to perform well on others. The lack of correlation with the listening test may have been due to the fact that most students made substantial gains such that a large proportion are at or near the top of the range.

Table 7. Pearson correlations among French proficiency measures: core French exchange students, full sample

	Vocab Pre	Vocab Post	Listen Pre	Listen Post	Cloze	Tasks fulfill	Error count	Quality of writing	Word count	Repeat exact	Repeat equiv
Vocabulary recognition (post-test)	.62**										
Listening comprehension (pre-test)	.21	.19									
Listening comprehension (post-test)	.20	.17	.25								
Cloze	.59**	.70**	.28	.33							
Open writing task											
Task fulfillment	-.28	-.27	-.28	.02	-.10						
Non-homophonous error count	.30	.14	-.32	.08	-.00	-.05					
Quality of writing	.52**	.56**	.36	.31	.81**	-.02	.15				
Word count	.27	.30	.04	.32	.52**	.35	.19	.68**			
Sentence repetition task											
Repetition-exact	.28	.28	.49*	.07	.50**	-.12	-.04	.41*	.06		
Repetition-equivalent	.32	.36	.48*	.07	.57**	-.03	-.03	.48*	.27	.85**	
Features score	.24	.34	.43*	.15	.63**	-.09	-.03	.56**	.31	.82**	.91**

Note: Pairwise deletion of missing cases. For correlations with sentence repetition task measures and others n=25; for correlations among sentence repetition measures n=27; for correlations among all other measures, n=28.
$*p < .05, **p < .01$

Correlations between the language aptitude and French post-test scores of the exchange students provide information on the central question of the relevance of language analysis and memory for text to learning success among adolescents in this context. Table 8 shows that language analysis is positively associated with performance on the cloze test and with scores on the three oral measures. Some of these relationships should be treated with caution, however, since scatterplots revealed one very high scoring student whose exclusion from the analyses would have left only one statistically significant relationship: namely, that between language analysis and exact scores on the sentence repetition task (Pearson $r.=.47$, $p=.016$) We do not regard this student as an outlier in the analysis, however, since her scores appeared to be in line with the general trend in the data. Had the number of students been larger, we would have anticipated a more continuous distribution of scores at the higher end. However, her effect on the results clearly demands that we exercise caution in interpretation. Memory for text was significantly correlated with nonhomophonous errors in writing, indicating, surprisingly, that better scores on the memory measure were associated with a higher number of errors. This relationship held when the high-scoring student was removed. No significant aptitude-proficiency relationships were added when the post-test measures of vocabulary recognition and listening comprehension were controlled for scores on the respective pre-tests.

A multivariate multiple regression analysis was conducted of the relationship of memory for text and language analysis to the set of proficiency measures. The results indicate a near-significant result for language analysis (Wilk's lambda, $F=2.334$, $p=.077$). However, memory for text shows no significant association with the set of proficiency measures (Wilk's lambda, $F=.799$, p=.633). These whole-model results are consistent with the interpretation that language analysis rather than memory for text is the better predictor of differences in French proficiency. However, stepwise regression analysis reveals that this relationship is not consistent across French test measures (see Table 9). The stepwise regression produced results similar to those shown in Table 8, with language analysis a significant predictor of cloze scores and the three oral measures, and memory for text predictive of number of errors in writing. Exclusion of the high-scoring student from the regression analyses produced fewer statistically significant results: language analysis predicted only exact scores on the oral repetition task, and memory for text continued to predict errors in writing.

Table 8. Pearson correlations of language aptitude with French proficiency measures: core French exchange students

Language aptitude	Memory for text		Language analysis	
	corr.	n	corr.	n
French proficiency				
Vocabulary recognition (post-test)	.20	28	.13	28
Listening comprehension (post-test)	.25	28	.31	28
Cloze	.34	28	.39*	28
Open writing task				
Task fulfillment	-.10	28	-.25	28
Non-homophonous error count	.41*	28	-.09	28
Quality of writing	.33	28	.30	28
Word count	.32	28	.09	28
Sentence repetition task				
Repetition-exact	.14	27	.61**	27
Repetition-equivalent	.15	27	.47*	27
Features score	.12	27	.44*	27

$*p < .05$, $**p < .01$

In addition to the preceding analysis of test scores, we examined the exchange students' responses on the post-questionnaire. These responses reveal the learners' perceptions about their language use in Quebec, improvement in French language skills, and approach to language learning. Asked about their language use on a typical day during their last month in Quebec, the students reported their use of French in different contexts. With teachers and classmates at school, and with the twin's parents and friends outside school, the great majority of students reported using French 'always' or 'mostly'. With their twin, there was more variation in use, with just over a third of the students reporting always using French, about 20% using mostly French, another third using French about half the time, and one student reporting always using English.[5] When asked to rank the importance of different settings for their learning of French while on the exchange, talking with friends emerged as the favoured setting. It was ranked most important by just over half the students and as second most important by another 38%. The twin and twin's family also provided important learning contexts. For 20% of the students, talking with their twin was ranked first in importance, and for another 20% it was talking with the twin's family.

All the respondents felt that their French had improved as a result of the exchange, and especially their comprehension skills. Most improvement was

Table 9. Stepwise regression predicting exchange students' French proficiency from dimensions of language aptitude

Dependent variables (French proficiency)		Predictor	Adjusted R^2	F value	Significance level of F value
Vocabulary recognition (post-test)	Step 1	No entry			
Listening comprehension (post-test)	Step 1	No entry			
Cloze	Step 1	Language analysis	.121	4.733	.039
Written task fulfillment	Step 1	No entry			
Non-homophonous errors	Step 1	Memory for text	.133	5.156	.032
Quality of writing	Step 1	No entry			
Word count		No entry			
Sentence repetition – exact	Step 1	Language analysis	.349	14.928	.001
Sentence repetition – equivalent	Step 1	Language analysis	.191	7.121	.013
Sentence features	Step 1	Language analysis	.162	6.022	.021

Note: Probability for inclusion = .05; probability for exclusion = .10. Language aptitude variables: memory for text and language analysis.

perceived in listening: two thirds reported that their listening skills had improved a great deal, and the remainder felt they had improved quite a lot. Major improvement was also perceived in reading, with the great majority indicating that it had improved a great deal or quite a lot, and the remaining few students reporting moderate improvement. Over two thirds also saw themselves as having also improved quite a lot or a great deal in speaking, with others indicating moderate improvement, and three students perceiving just a little improvement. Writing was the skill where least improvement was perceived. Yet even here, just under half the students saw themselves as having improved a great deal or quite a lot, another third considered improvement to have been moderate, and the remaining four students reported a little improvement.

When we related students' perceptions of improvement in listening and reading to their actual improvement on the French listening comprehension and vocabulary recognition tests administered before and after the exchange, we did not find any significant correlations. Students who said, for example, that they had improved 'quite a lot' made as much progress on the tests as those who said they had improved 'a great deal'. This lack of correlation between self-perceived progress and gains on objective test scores is similar to findings of the bilingual exchange program evaluation that involved a larger sample of both core French and immersion students (Lapkin, Hart, & Swain, 1995).

When asked in the post-questionnaire how they went about learning French while in Quebec, a majority of the exchange students in the present

Table 10. Pearson correlations of exchange students' self-reported language learning styles[1] with aptitude measures and French proficiency measures

Self-reported learning styles	Absorb without analyzing		Pay attention to specific aspects	
	corr.	n	corr.	n
Language aptitude				
Memory for text	.14	28	-.12	28
Language analysis	-.12	28	-.04	28
French proficiency				
Vocabulary recognition (post-test)	.32	28	.45*	28
Listening comprehension (post-test)	-.05	28	.40*	28
Cloze	.08	28	.25	28
Open writing task				
Task fulfillment	-.12	28	-.19	28
Non-homophonous error count	.28	28	-.13	28
Quality of writing	.08	28	.32	28
Word count	.18	28	.10	28
Sentence repetition task				
Repetition-exact	-.11	26	.14	26
Repetition-equivalent	-.02	26	.21	26
Features score	-.11	26	.22	26

1. Based on the following student questionnaire items: "How did you go about learning French while you were in Quebec?
A) By deliberately paying attention to specific aspects of language, for example, grammar or vocabulary?
B) By simply absorbing the language without deliberately analyzing it?"
Full Scale: always, often, sometimes, rarely, never. Note: No student reported never using these strategies; few report using them rarely such that this category was grouped with sometimes for correlational analysis.

Note: Scales for self-reported learning strategies have been reversed such that positive relationships (more use of strategy, higher test scores) yield positive correlations.
*$p < .05$

study claimed to have deliberately paid attention to specific aspects of the language either always or often, and a majority also claimed always or often to have simply absorbed the language without deliberately analysing. These perceptions were not positively correlated, however. We found no relationship between these perceptions and their scores on the memory and language analysis tests. However, the perception of deliberately paying attention did bear a relationship to two of the L2 proficiency scores (see Table 10). Significant correlations emerged between the deliberate attention-paying orientation and scores on the vocabulary and listening comprehension post-tests. Those who saw themselves as paying greater attention to specific aspects of the language tended to do better on these tests.

In order to take account of differences in students' use of French as a factor potentially associated with the L2 proficiency results, we included two language use variables in further statistical analyses. One variable was 'language use with friends', included as the context most often considered by students to be important for their L2 learning. For this variable, given the very small numbers in the lower use of French categories, the original 5-point language use scale was consolidated into a 3-point scale: always French, mostly French, half French/half English/mostly English. The second language use variable, 'intensity of use' of French, consisted of the number of times a student indicated on the questionnaire that he or she had always used French with the five different categories of interlocutors. Table 11 shows that these two ordinal language use variables correlated significantly with a number of other measures. Use of French with friends was positively related to both of the self-perceived learning styles (paying attention to specific aspects, and absorbing without deliberately analysing), to the memory for text measure, and to scores on the vocabulary recognition post-test. Intensity of use of French correlated positively with both self-perceived learning styles, memory for text, and several French proficiency measures: the vocabulary recognition post-test, cloze, quality of writing and word count on the writing task.

A multivariate multiple regression analysis was conducted of the relationship of memory for text, language analysis and intensity of use of French to the set of proficiency measures. The results indicate a near-significant result for language analysis (Wilk's lambda, $F=2.664$, $p=.056$), whereas memory for text again shows no significant association with proficiency (Wilk's lambda, $F=.554$, $p=.821$). The intensity of use measure, while not reaching statistical significance, shows a more marked association with the set of dependent variables than does memory for text (Wilk's lambda, $F=1.781$, $p=.171$).

Table 11. Correlations of exchange students' use of French with self-reported learning styles, aptitude measures and French proficiency measures

Self-reported learning styles, aptitude and proficiency	Use of French with friends[1]		Intensity of use[2]	
	corr.	n	corr.	n
Self-reported learning strategies[3]				
Absorb without analyzing	.43*	28	.39*	28
Pay attention to specific aspects	.39*	28	.34*	28
Language aptitude[4]				
Memory for text	.42*	28	.38*	28
Language analysis	-.16	28	-.01	28
French proficiency[3]				
Vocabulary recognition (post-test)	.41*	28	.57*	28
Listening comprehension (post-test)	.17	28	.27	28
Cloze	.24	28	.57*	28
Open writing task				
Task fulfillment	-.10	28	-.09	28
Non-homophonous error count	.11	28	.14	28
Quality of writing	.33	28	.48**	28
Word count	.13	28	.41*	28
Sentence repetition task				
Repetition-exact	-.13	26	.09	26
Repetition-equivalent	.00	26	.34	26
Features score	-.07	26	.32	26

1. Students were asked if they spoke always French, mostly French, half French/half English, mostly English or always English with friends in Quebec outside school. No student indicated they always used English; mostly English and half English/half French have been grouped for analysis.
2. The intensity measure counts the number of times a student indicated they always use French with five categories of interlocutors: teachers, classmates (at school), "twin", "twin's" family, and friends (outside school). The maximum score is five.
3. Kendall's *tau B*
4. Pearson correlations
Note: Scales have been reversed such that positive relationships yield positive correlations for use of learning strategies, use of French/intensity of use to French and test scores.
*$p < .05$

The above whole-model results are again consistent with the interpretation that language analysis rather than memory for text is the better predictor of French proficiency. However, stepwise regression again reveals that this relationship is not consistent across French test measures (see Table 12).

Table 12. Stepwise regression predicting exchange students' French proficiency from dimensions of language aptitude and intensity of use of French

Dependent variables (French proficiency)		Predictor	Adjusted R^2	F value	Significance level of F value
Vocabulary recognition (post-test)	Step 1	Intensity of use	.293	12.208	.002
Listening comprehension (post-test)	Step 1	No entry			
Cloze	Step 1	Intensity of use	.299	12.524	.002
	Step 2	Language analysis	.433	11.739	.000
Written task fulfillment	Step 1	No entry			
Non-homophonous errors	Step 1	Memory for text	.133	5.156	.032
Quality of writing	Step 1	Intensity of use	.196	7.602	.011
Word count	Step 1	Intensity of use	.138	5.329	.029
Sentence repetition – exact	Step 1	Language analysis	.362	14.632	.001
Sentence repetition – equivalent	Step 1	Language analysis	.193	6.742	.016
	Step 2	Intensity of use	.332	6.953	.005
Sentence features	Step 1	Language analysis	.156	5.424	.029
	Step 2	Intensity of use	.271	5.468	.012

Note: Probability for inclusion = .05; probability for exclusion = .10. Language aptitude variables: memory for text and language analysis.

It also shows that intensity of use of French is a significant predictor for a relatively large subset of test measures (alone or in conjunction with language analysis). Compared with the previous stepwise regression analysis in which only the two aptitude measures had been entered as predictors (see Table 9), this new stepwise analysis resulted in improvement to the prediction of L2 proficiency scores. Intensity of use of French was a significant predictor of scores on the vocabulary recognition post-test, the cloze test, quality of writing, and word count on the writing task, entering each of these equations at Step 1. Language analysis was an additional predictor of cloze scores at Step 2, and continued to predict all three scores on the oral sentence repetition test, with intensity of use of French entering the equation at Step 2 for the equivalence and features scores on this oral test. Memory for text was a significant predictor of number of errors on the writing task. Omission of the high-scoring student from these analyses had the effect of reducing the predictive relevance of both intensity of use of French and language analysis. Intensity of use continued to predict vocabulary posttest and cloze test scores at step 1; language analysis continued to be a significant predictor at step 1 of exact scores on sentence repetition, became a near-significant predictor at step 2 of cloze test scores ($p=.054$), and was no longer a significant predictor of equivalent and feature scores on sentence repetition.

Discussion

Can the findings of this study be regarded as support for the hypothesis that different learning approaches lead to more successful language learning depending on the age at which intensive exposure to a second language begins? The pattern of correlations between the adolescent exchange students' French proficiency scores and their scores on the language analysis test, along with the regression analyses, suggest that analytical language ability was a factor influencing learning success in the natural context of the exchange, though not as consistently as had been found among the late immersion students in the previous study. Moreover, memory for text was not as relevant as it had been for the early immersion students. This study thus offers some support for the argument that age of initial intensive exposure is a factor affecting students' L2 learning orientation, whether inside or outside the L2 classroom environment.

In particular, it is evident from Table 8 that, for the exchange students, the strongest correlation between language aptitude and French proficiency occurred between language analysis and exact scores on oral sentence repetition. This test demands good listening comprehension as well as oral production skills, and it is in the area of listening comprehension that the exchange students reported in their post-questionnaires that they had made the most substantial progress while in Quebec. Although relative success on the multiple-choice listening comprehension test was not related to the learners' language analysis scores, it was positively related to their perceptions of how much deliberate attention they paid to specific aspects of the language. Most students also reported having made excellent progress in reading during their three-month stay. Significantly we find some relationship as well between language analysis and cloze test results and between perceptions of paying attention and vocabulary posttest scores.

It is noteworthy that both of the self-reported learning styles (absorbing without analysing and paying attention to specific aspects), even though they were statistically unrelated to each other or to scores on the objective tests of memory for text and language analysis, were significantly correlated with students' use of French during the exchange (see Table 11). It may be that reported use of either style reflected an underlying awareness of learning and willingness to use deliberate learning and communication strategies of various kinds, rather than a clear distinction between learning orientations as we had intended.

We are unable to offer any theoretically motivated explanation as to why number of errors in writing was positively correlated with performance on the memory for text measure. Note that this writing measure was not correlated with scores on any other L2 proficiency tests, nor with any other measures based on the composition task. One possibility is that, for some students, a willingness to quickly jot down one's ideas without paying attention to form was a parallel factor in both the English memory for text test and the French composition. This might have been a good strategy in the memory for text task, but in the French composition, it could have resulted in more errors. Interestingly, the memory for text measure was also positively correlated with the language use variables 'use of French with friends' and 'intensity of use' (see Table 11), suggesting that more memory-oriented students were more willing to 'plunge in' in French. This is in line with a posited association proposed in the learning style literature between a holistic orientation to learning and willingness 'to engage in communication in real-life situations' (Skehan, 1998a, p. 249).

While the results of this study provide some support for the claim that an adolescent onset to intensive language learning will be associated with a more analytical orientation to learning than learning that begins at a younger age, we have pointed out that caution is needed given the inclusion in our sample of one outstanding learner whose presence affected the significance of the relationship between language analysis and cloze test scores in particular. This learner was a consistently high performer on all measures and, most significantly, scored highest on the memory for text measure as well as on language analysis (where she achieved a perfect score). It is interesting to note that, in the literature on talented adult language learners, high memory ability has been observed in several studies to be a characteristic of such learners (e.g. Ioup, 1989; Novoa, Fein, & Obler, 1988; Schneiderman & Desmarais, 1988). The performance of this student shows that high levels of memory and analytical abilities may together be more powerful aids to language learning than either ability alone (though overall these abilities were not significantly related in our sample). It should also be noted that the finding of a more memory-oriented approach to L2 learning among early immersion students (Harley & Hart, 1997) does not mean that analytical ability is not involved in early language learning. As shown in Table 1, for example, analytical ability was significantly related to listening comprehension among the early immersion students in our previous research. Ranta (1998, see also this volume) also found a measure of analytical ability to be associated with L2 success among French-speaking grade 6 students enrolled in a communicatively-oriented intensive ESL program in Quebec.[6]

The finding that intensity of French use was a significant predictor of several of the French proficiency scores (Table 12), and that it entered the regression equation as a predictor of cloze test scores at Step 1, demoting the role of language analysis to prediction at Step 2, is interesting in light of Gardner (1985) and Gardner and McIntyre's (1992) claim that in an informal learning environment, the relationship between language aptitude and L2 outcomes is indirect, with the learner's motivation functioning as an intervening variable influencing access to the L2. In the present study, greater or lesser use of the L2 may, however, not have been an option entirely under the learners' control. Prior research in the bilingual exchange context, where diaries were kept by English-speaking students, indicates that they were sometimes frustrated 'due to francophones' wanting to practice their English or automatically switching to English in the presence of an Anglophone' (Warden, Lapkin, Swain, & Hart, 1995, p.544). As Peirce (1995) has argued, the concept of motivation with its focus on the individual alone fails to take account of the impact of day-to-day social relations with native speakers on the learner's access to interaction in the target language. The fact that there was a significant correlation of .53 between the exchange students' scores on the pretest of vocabulary and the intensity of L2 use suggests, at the same time, that having a larger vocabulary to begin with was an advantage likely to promote more second language use.

Conclusion

In sum, there are several findings in this study that provide some support for the argument that analytical language ability is more closely associated with second language outcomes when intensive exposure to the language is first experienced in adolescence. This relationship appears to hold, though not as strongly, even when exposure takes place in an environment outside the second language classroom. Given the relatively small sample in this study, and the short period of intensive language learning they experienced in the natural L2 environment, more research is now needed to determine whether these findings can be replicated among other adolescent learners under different, more prolonged learning conditions.

Notes

* This research was supported by a grant to the first author from the Social Sciences and Humanities Research Council of Canada. We are grateful to Jan Adams for her help in contacting participants and facilitating the research in various ways, to Alina MacFarlane for conducting the group testing in Ottawa, and to the exchange coordinators and teachers who administered the individual oral test to students in their home schools. Thanks also go to Marion Chang, Claude Guillemot, and Katie Rehner who helped with the scoring of tests. Sharon Lapkin provided helpful comments on an earlier draft of this paper. Finally, special thanks are due to the exchange students who kindly agreed to spend two hours of their precious time together in Ottawa being tested.

1. As one reviewer suggested, not just the difference in learning conditions, but the difference in linguistic structure between Hebrew (structurally similar to the learners' L1) and English (structurally dissimilar) may help to account for these correlational results.

2. An additional student who took part in the testing was eliminated from the sample as a non-native speaker of English who had recently arrived in Canada with her family and who was reportedly still learning English. Her introduction to French thus represented an additional experience of intensive L2 exposure, and the validity of her language aptitude scores (in English) was placed in doubt.

3. This figure includes two students who were not present for the group post-testing.

4. Note that scores on the non-linguistic task fulfillment measure are in fact unrelated to any other measures in this study.

5. The fact that the French-speaking twins had already spent three months with the English-speaking student in Ontario was presumably a factor in this finding. Some of the French-speaking students may have wanted to keep practising their English (cf. Warden, Lapkin, Swain, & Hart, 1995) making for more interaction between twins in English. The fact that use of French with twin was not ranked as first in importance by many students

may also reflect the fact that not all twins necessarily became close friends (see also Warden et al., 1995).

6. The adolescent students in the present study had been exposed to classroom learning of French since grade 4, and this classroom experience could perhaps have predisposed them to an analytical orientation towards language learning that was carried over into the natural L2 environment of the exchange. Diaries of exchange students in a previous year (Warden et al., 1995) suggest, however, that the social experience of using the second language with families and friends in Quebec was perceived as quite different from learning the language in the L2 classroom.

References

Aguiar, L., & Brady, S. (1991). Vocabulary acquisition and reading ability. *Reading and Writing, 3,* 413–425.

Aida, Y. (1994). Examination of Horwitz, Horwitz, and Cope's construct of foreign language anxiety: The case of students of Japanese. *Modern Language Journal, 78,* 155–168.

Ajzen, I. (1988). *Attitudes, personality, and behavior.* Chicago, IL: Dorsey Press.

Alanen, R. (1995). Input enhancement and rule presentation in second language acquisition. In R. Schmidt (Ed.), *Attention and awareness in foreign language learning,* (pp. 259–302). Honolulu, HI: University of Hawai'i.

Alderson, C., Clapham, C., & Steel, D. (1997). Metalinguistic knowledge, language aptitude and language proficiency. *Language Teaching Research, 1,* 93–121.

Anastasi, A., & Urbina, S. (1997). *Psychological testing* (7th ed.). UpperSaddle River, NJ: Prentice Hall.

Andersen, R. W. (1991). Developmental sequences: The emergence of aspect marking in second language acquisition. In T. Huebner & C. A. Ferguson (Eds.), *Crosscurrents in second language acquisition and linguistic theories,* (pp. 305–324). Amsterdam: Benjamins.

Anderson, M. (1992). *Intelligence and development: A cognitive theory.* Oxford: Blackwell.

Ando, J., Fukunaga, N., Kurahashi, J., Suto, T., Nakano, T., & Kage, M. (1992). A comparative study on two EFL teaching methods: The communicative and the grammatical approach. *Japanese Journal of Educational Psychology, 40,* 247–256.

Ando, S., & Hale, D. (1994). *Mainstream II* [English textbook]. Osaka: Zoshindo.

Au, S. Y. (1988). A critical appraisal of Gardner's socio-psychological theory of second-language (L2) learning. *Language Learning, 38,* 75–100.

Avons, S. E., Wragg, C. A., Cupples, W. L., & Lovegrove, W. J. (1998). Measures of phonological short-term memory and their relationship to vocabulary development. *Applied Psycholinguistics, 19,* 583–601.

Bachman, L. (1990). *Fundamental considerations in language testing.* Oxford: Oxford University Press.

Baddeley, A. D. (1986). *Working memory.* New York: Oxford University Press.

Baddeley, A. D., Gathercole, S. E., & Papagno, C. (1998). The phonological loop as a language learning device. *Psychological Review, 105,* 158–173.

Baker, M. (1988). *Incorporation: A theory of grammatical function changing.* Chicago: University of Chicago Press.

Bames, M. L., & Sternberg, R. J. (1989). Social intelligence and decoding of nonverbal cues. *Intelligence, 13,* 263–287.

Baron, J. (1985). *Rationality and intelligence.* Cambridge: Cambridge University Press.

Bar-Shalom, E., Crain, S., & Shankweiler, D. (1993). A comparison of comprehension and production abilities of good and poor readers. *Applied Psycholinguistics,14,* 197–227.

Becker, A., & Carroll, M. (1997). *The acquisition of spatial relations in second language acquisition.* Amsterdam: Benjamins.

Bialystok, E. (1987). Influences of bilingualism on metalinguistic development. *Second Language Research, 3,* 154–166.

Bialystok, E., & Hakuta, K. (1994). *In other words: The science and psychology of second-language acquisition.* New York: Basic Books.

Bialystok, E., & Ryan, E. B. (1985). A metacognitive framework for the development of first and second language skills. In D. Forrest-Pressley, G. MacKinnon, & T. Waller (Eds.), *Metacognition, cognition, and human performance, Vol 1,* (pp. 207–252). Orlando, FA: Academic Press.

Binet, A., & Simon, T. (1905). Mithodes nouvelles pour le diagnostic du niveau intellectuel des anormaux. *L'Annie Psychologique, 11,* 191–336.

Birdsong, D. (1989). *Metalinguistic performance and interlinguistic competence.* Berlin: Springer-Verlag.

Birdsong, D. (1992). Ultimate attainment in second language acquisition. *Language, 68,* 706–755.

Birdsong, D. (Ed.) (1999). *Second language acquisition and the critical period hypothesis.* Mahwah, NJ: Erlbaum.

Bishop, D. V. M. (1997). *Uncommon understanding: Development and disorders of language comprehension in children.* Hove: Psychology Press.

Bishop, D. V. M., Bishop, S. J., Bright, P., James, C., Delaney, T., & Tallal, P. (1999). Different origin of auditory and phonological processing problems in children with language impairment: Evidence from a twin study. *Journal of Speech, Language and Hearing Research, 42,* 155–168.

Blaxton, T. A. (1989). Investigating dissociations among memory measures: Support for a transfer appropriate processing framework. *Journal of Experimental Psychology: Learning, Memory and Cognition, 15,* 657–688.

Bley-Vroman, R. (1988). The fundamental character of foreign language learning. In W. Rutherford & W. Sharwood-Smith (Eds.), *Grammar and second language teaching,* (pp.19–30). New York: Newbury House.

Bley-Vroman, R. (1989). What is the logical problem of foreign language learning? In S. M. Gass & J. Schachter (Eds.), *Linguistic perspectives on second language acquisition,* (pp.41-68). Cambridge: Cambridge University Press.

Bley-Vroman, R. (1990). The logical problem of foreign language learning. *Linguistic Analysis, 20,* 3–49.

Bley-Vroman, R., Felix, S., & Ioup, G. (1988). The accessibility of universal grammar in adult language learning. *Second Language Research, 4,* 1–32.

Bloom, L., Hood, L., & Lightbown, P. (1974). Imitation in language development: If, when and why. *Cognitive Psychology, 6,* 380–420.

Bohannon, J. N., III, MacWhinney, B., & Snow, C. (1990). No negative evidence revisited: Beyond learnability or who has to prove what to whom. *Developmental Psychology, 26,* 221–226.

Bohannon, J. N., III, & Stanowicz, L. (1988). The issue of negative evidence: Adult responses to children's language errors. *Developmental Psychology, 24,* 684–689.

Bowers, P. G. (1993). Text reading and rereading — determinants of fluency beyond word recognition. *Journal of Reading Behavior, 25,* 133–153.

Braine, M. D. H. (1965). The insufficiency of a finite-state model for verbal reconstructive memory. *Psychonomic Science, 2,* 291–292.

Brand, C. (1996). *The g factor. General intelligence and its implications.* Chichester: Wiley.

Brehm, S. S., & Brehm, J. W. (1981). *Psychological reactance: A theory of freedom and control.* New York: Academic Press.

Bresnan, J. (1999). Linguistic theory at the turn of the century. *Plenary presentation 12th World Congress of Applied Linguistics, Tokyo,* 1–6 August, 1999.

Brody, N. (1989). Unconscious learning of rules: Comments on Reber's analysis of implicit learning. *Journal of Experimental Psychology: General, 11,* 236–238.

Brown, H. D. (1994). *Teaching by principles: An interactive approach to language pedagogy.* Englewood Cliffs, NJ: Prentice Hall.

Brown, J. D., Robson, G., & Rosenkjar, P. (1996). Personality, motivation, anxiety, strategies, and language proficiency of Japanese students. *University of Hawai'i Working Papers in ESL, 15,* 33–72.

Buck, R. (1984). *The communication of emotion.* New York: Guilford Press.

Butler, L., & Berry, D. (2001). Implicit memory: Intention and awareness revisited. *Trends in Cognitive Science, 5,* 192–197.

Bygate, M. (1987), *Speaking.* Oxford: Oxford University Press.

Bygate, M. (1999). Task as context for the framing, reframing and unframing of language. *System, 27,* 33–48.

Bygate, M., Skehan, P., & Swain, M. (Eds.) (2001). *Researching pedagogic tasks: Second language learning, teaching and testing.* Harlow: Longman.

Cain, K., & Oakhill, J. (in press). Reading comprehension difficulties.

Canale, M., & Swain, M. (1980). Theoretical bases of communicative approaches to second language teaching and testing. *Applied Linguistics, 1,* 1–47.

Cannon, W. B. (1932). *The wisdom of the body.* New York: W. W. Norton.

Carlisle, J. (1988). Knowledge of derivational morphology and spelling ability in fourth, sixth, and eigth graders. *Applied Psycholinguistics, 9,* 247–266.

Carr, T., & Curran, T. (1994). Cognitive factors in learning about structured sentences: Applications to syntax. *Studies in Second Language Acquisition, 16,* 205–231.

Carraher, T. N., Carraher, D. W., & Schhemann, A. D. (1987). Written and oral mathematics. *Journal for Research in Mathematics Education, 16,* 37–44.

Carroll, J. B. (1958). A factor analysis of two foreign language aptitude batteries. *Journal of General Psychology, 59,* 3–19.

Carroll, J. B. (1962). The prediction of success in intensive foreign language training. In R. Glaser. (Ed.), *Training research and education,* (pp. 87–136). New York: Wiley.

Carroll, J. B. (1967). *Modern Language Aptitude Test — Elementary.* New York: The Psychological Corporation.

Carroll J. B. (1973). Implications of aptitude test research and psycholinguistic theory for foreign language teaching. *International Journal of Psycholinguistics, 2,* 5–14.

Carroll, J. B. (1979). Psychometric approaches to the study of language abilities. In C. J. Fillmore, D. Kempler, & W-S. Y. Wang. (Eds.), *Individual differences in language ability and language behavior,* (pp. 13–51). New York: Academic Press.

Carroll, J. B. (1981). Twenty-five years of research on foreign language aptitude. In K. C. Diller (Ed.), *Individual differences and universals in language learning aptitude,* (pp. 83–118). Rowley, MA: Newbury House.

Carroll, J. B. (1985). Second-language abilities. In R. J. Sternberg (Ed.), *Human abilities: An information processing approach,* (pp. 83–101). New York: W. H. Freeman.

Carroll, J. B. (1991). Cognitive abilities in foreign language aptitude: Then and now. In T. Parry & C. Stansfield (Eds.), *Language aptitude reconsidered.* Englewood Cliffs, NJ: Prentice Hall.

Carroll, J. B. (1993). *Human cognitive abilities: A survey of factor-analytic studies.* New York: Cambridge University Press.

Carroll, J. B., & Sapon, S. M. (1959). *Modern Language Aptitude Test.* New York: The Psychological Corporation/Harcourt Brace Jovanovich.

Carroll, S. (1999).Putting 'input' in its proper place. *Second Language Research,15,* 337–388.

Carroll, S. (2001). *Input and evidence: The raw material of second language acquisition.* Amsterdam: Benjamins.

Cattell, R. B. (1971). *Abilities: Their structure, growth and action.* Boston: Houghton Nefflin.

Cattell, R. B. (1987). *Intelligence: Its structure, growth and action.* Amsterdam: North-Holland.

Ceci, S. J. (1990). *On intelligence... more or less: A bio-ecological treatise on intellectual development.* Englewood Cliffs, NJ: Prentice Hall.

Ceci, S. J. (1996). *On intelligence ... more or less* (expanded ed.). Cambridge, MA: Harvard University Press.

Ceci, S. J., & Liker, J. (1986). A day at the races: A study of IQ, expertise, and cognitive complexity. *Journal of Experimental Psychology: General, 115,* 255–266.

Ceci, S. J., & Roazzi, A. (1994). The effects of context on cognition: postcards from Brazil. In R. J. Sternberg & R. K. Wagner (Eds.), *Mind in context: Interactionist perspectives on human intelligence,* (pp. 74–101). New York: Cambridge University Press.

Chapelle, C., & Green, P. (1992). Field independence/dependence in second-language acquisition research. *Language Learning, 42,* 47–83.

Chen, H.-C., & Leung, Y.-S. (1989). Patterns of lexical processing in a non-native language. *Journal of Experimental Psychology: Learning, Memory, and Cognition, 15,* 316–325.

Cheung, H. (1996). Nonword span as a unique predictor of second-language vocabulary learning. *Developmental Psychology, 32,* 867–873.

Chomsky, N. (1977). On *wh*-movement. In P. Culicover, T. Wasow, & A. Akmajian (Eds.), *Formal syntax,* (pp. 71–132). New York: Academic Press.

Chomsky, N. (1981). *Lectures on Government and Binding.* Dordrecht: Foris.

Chomsky, N. (1986). *Barriers.* Cambridge, MA: MIT Press.

Chomsky, N. (1995). *The Minimalist Program.* Cambridge, MA: MIT Press.

Cleave, P., & Rice, M. (1997). An examination of the morpheme BE in children with specific language impairment: The role of contractibility and grammatical form class. *Journal of Speech, Language, and Hearing Research, 40,* 480–492.

Cleeremans, A. (1993). *Mechanisms of implicit learning: Connectionist models of sequence processing.* Cambridge, MA: MIT Press.

Cleeremans, A., Destrebecqz, A., & Boyer, M. (1998). Implicit and explicit learning: News from the front. *Trends in Cognitive Science, 2,* 406–416.

Clément, R. (1980). Ethnicity, contact, and communicative competence in a second language. In H. Giles, W. P. Robinson, & P. M. Smith (Eds.), *Language: Social psychological perspectives,* (pp. 147–154). Oxford: Pergamon.

Clément, R. (1986). Second language proficiency and acculturation: An investigation of the effects of language status and individual characteristics. *Journal of Language and Social Psychology, 5,* 271–290.

Clément, R., Dörnyei, Z., & Noels, K. A. (1994). Motivation, self-confidence, and group cohesion in the foreign language classroom. *Language Learning, 44,* 417–48.

Clément, R., & Gardner, R. C. (2001). Second language mastery. In H. Giles & W. P. Robinson (Eds.), *Handbook of language and social psychology* (2nd ed.), (pp. 489-504). London: Wiley.

Clément, R., Gardner, R. C., & Smythe, P. C. (1977). Motivational variables in second language acquisition: A study of Francophones learning English. *Canadian Journal of Behavioural Science, 9,* 123–133.

Clément, R., Gardner, R. C., & Smythe, P. C. (1980). Social and individual factors in second language acquisition. *Canadian Journal of Behavioural Science, 12,* 293–302.

Cohen, J. (1983). Learning disabilities and the college student: Identification and diagnosis. In M. Sugar (Ed.), *Adolescent psychiatry: Developmental and clinical studies, Vol 2,* (pp. 177–179). Chicago: University of Chicago Press.

Cohen, J. (1988). *Statistical power analysis for the behavioral sciences.* Hillsdale, NJ: Erlbaum.

Cohen, J., & Borennstein, M. (1990). *Statistical power analysis: a computer program.* Hillsdale, NJ: Erlbaum.

Cohen, J., & Cohen, P. (1983). *Applied multiple regression/correlation analysis for the behavioral sciences.* Hillsdale, NJ: Erlbaum.

Cohen, Y., & Norst, M. J. (1989). Fear, dependence, and loss of self-esteem: Affective barriers in second-language learning among adults. *RELC Journal, 20,* 61–77.

Cook, V. (1996). *Second language learning and language teaching* (2nd ed.). London: Arnold.

Coppieters, R. (1987). Competence differences between natives and near-native speakers. *Language, 63,* 544–573.

Corno, L., Cronbach, L. J., Kupermintz, H., Lohman, D. F., Mandinach, E. B., Porteus, A. W., & Talbert, J. E. (2002). *Remaking the concept of aptitude: extending the legacy of Richard E. Snow.* Mahwah, NJ: Erlbaum.

Corno, L., & Kanfer, R. (1993). The role of volition in learning and performance. *Review of Research in Education, 19,* 301–341.

Cronbach, L. J. (1975). Five decades of public controversy over mental testing. *American Psychologist, 30,* 1–14.

Cronbach, L. J. (1990). *Essentials of psychological testing,* (5th ed.). New York: Harper & Row.

Cronbach, L. J., & Snow, R. E. (1977). *Aptitude and instructional methods: A handbook for research on interactions.* New York: Irvington.

Crookes, G., & Gass, S. M. (Eds.) (1993a). *Tasks in a pedagogical context: Integrating theory and practice.* Clevedon, Avon: Multilingual Matters.

Crookes, G., & Gass, S. M. (Eds.) (1993b). *Tasks and language learning: Integrating theory and practice.* Clevedon, Avon: Multilingual Matters.

Crookes, G., & Schmidt, R. (1991). Motivation: Reopening the research agenda. *Language Learning, 41,* 469–512.

Cummins, J. (1987). Bilingualism, language proficiency, and metalinguistic development. In P. Homel, M. Palij, & D. Aaronson (Eds.), *Childhood bilingualism,* (pp. 57–73). Hillsdale, NJ: Erlbaum.

Cyr, J. J., & Brooker, B. H. (1984). Use of appropriate formulas for selecting WAIS-R short forms. *Journal of Consulting and Clinical Psychology, 52,* 903–905.

Daly, J. A. & McCroskey, J. C. (Eds.) (1984). *Avoiding communication: Shyness, reticence, and communication apprehension.* Beverly Hills, CA: Sage.

Dance, K., & Neufeld, R. W. (1988). Aptitude-treatment interaction research in the clinical setting: A review of attempts to dispel the "patient uniformity" myth. *Psychological Bulletin, 104,* 192–213.

Daneman, M., & Carpenter, P. A. (1980). Individual differences in working memory and reading. *Journal of Verbal Learning and Verbal Behaviour, 19,* 450–466.

Daneman, M., & Case, R. (1981). Syntactic form, semantic complexity, and short-term memory: Influence on children's acquisition of new linguistic structures. *Developmental Psychology, 17,* 367–378.

Davidson, J. E., & Sternberg, R. J. (1984). The role of insight in intellectual giftedness. *Gifted Child Quarterly, 28,* 58–64.

de Graaff, R. (1997a). The eXperanto experiment: Effects of explicit instruction on second language acquisition. *Studies in Second Language Acquisition 19,* 249–275.

de Graaff, R. (1997b). *Differential effects of explicit instruction on second language acquisition.* The Hague: Holland Institute of Generative Linguistics.

Deane, P. D. (1992). *Grammar in mind and brain: Explorations in cognitive syntax.* New York: Mouton de Gruyter.

Deary, I., Egan, V., Gibson, G., Austin, E., Brand, R., & Kellaghan, T. (1996). Intelligence and the differentiation hypothesis. *Intelligence, 23,* 105–132.

DeKeyser, R. M. (1995). Learning second language grammar rules: An experiment with a miniature linguistic system. *Studies in Second language Acquisition, 17,* 379–410.

DeKeyser, R. M. (1997). Beyond explicit rule learning: Automatizing second language syntax. *Studies in Second Language Acquisition, 19,* 195–221.

DeKeyser, R. M. (2000). The robustness of critical period effects in second language acquisition. *Studies in Second Language Acquisition, 22,* 499–533.

DeKeyser, R. M. (2001). Automaticity and automatization. In P. Robinson (Ed.), *Cognition and second language instruction,* (pp. 125–151). Cambridge: Cambridge University Press.

DeKeyser, R. M. (in press). Implicit and explicit learning. In C. Doughty & M. H. Long (Eds.), *Handbook of second language acquisition.* Oxford: Blackwell.

Demuth, K., & Smith, N. (1987). The foreign language requirement: An alternative program. *Foreign Language Annals, 20,* 67–77.

Dennet, D. (1983). Styles of mental representation. *Proceedings of the Aristotelian Society, May,* 213–221.

Dewaele, J-M. (in press). Psychological and sociodemographic correlates of communicative anxiety in L2 and L3 production. *International Journal of Bilingualism.*

Dewaele, J-M., & Furnham, A. (2000). Personality and speech production: A pilot study of second language learners. *Personality and Individual Differences, 28,* 355–65.

Dicks, J. (1992). Analytic and experiential features of three French immersion programs: Early, middle and late. *Canadian Modern Language Review, 49,* 37–59.

Dienes, Z. (1992). Connectionist and memory-array models of artificial grammar learning. *Cognitive Science, 16,* 41–79.

Dienes, Z., & Perner, J. (1998). A theory of implicit and explicit knowledge. *Behavioral and Brain Sciences, 22,* 735–755.

Diller, K.C. (Ed.) (1981). *Individual differences and universals in language learning aptitude.* Rowley, MA: Newbury House

Dinklage, K. (1971). Inability to learn a foreign language. In G. Blain & C. McArthur (Eds.), *Emotional problems of the student.* New York: Appleton-Century-Crofts.

Dörnyei, Z. (1994a). Motivation and motivating in the foreign language classroom. *Modern Language Journal, 78,* 273–284.

Dörnyei, Z. (1994b). Understanding L2 Motivation: On with the challenge! *Modern Language Journal, 78,* 515–523.

Dörnyei, Z. (1996). Moving language learning motivation to a larger platform for theory and practice. In Oxford, R.L. (Ed.), *Language learning motivation: Pathways to the new century,* (pp. 89–101). Honolulu, HI: University of Hawai'i Press.

Dörnyei, Z. (2000). Motivation in action: Towards a process-oriented conceptualisation of student motivation. *British Journal of Educational Psychology, 70,* 519–538.

Dörnyei, Z. (2001). *Teaching and researching motivation.* Harlow: Longman.

Dörnyei, Z., & Clément, R. (2001). Motivational characteristics of learning different target languages: Results of a nationwide survey. In Z. Dörnyei & R. Schmidt (Eds.), *Motivation and second language acquisition,* (pp. 399–432). Honolulu, HI: University of Hawai'i Press.

Dörnyei, Z., & Kormos, J. (2000). The role of individual and social variables in oral task performance. *Language Teaching Research, 4,* 275–300.

Dörnyei, Z., & Malderez, A. (1997). Group dynamics and foreign language teaching. *System, 25,* 65–81.

Dörnyei, Z., Nyilasi, E., & Clément, R. (1996). Hungarian school children's motivation to learn foreign languages: A comparison of five target languages. *Novelty, 3,* 6–16

Dörnyei, Z., & Otto, I. (1998). Motivation in action: A process model of L2 motivation. *Working Papers in Applied Linguistics (Thames Valley University, London, England), 4,* 43–69.

Dörnyei, Z., & Schmidt, R. (Eds.) (2001). *Motivation and second language acquisition.* Honolulu, HI: University of Hawai'i Press.

Doughty, C. (1991). Second language instruction does make a difference: Evidence from an empirical study of SL relativization. *Studies in Second Language Acquisition, 13,* 431–469.

Doughty, C. (2001). Cognitive underpinnings of focus on form. In P. Robinson(Ed.), *Cognition and second language instruction,* (pp. 206–257). Cambridge: Cambridge University Press.

Doughty, C., & Williams, J. (1998). Pedagogical choices in focus on form. In C. Doughty and J. Williams (Eds.), *Focus on form in classroom second language acquisition*, (pp. 197–262). New York: Cambridge University Press.

Dresher, E. (1999). Charting the learning path: Cues to parameter resetting. *Linguistic Inquiry, 30*, 27–67.

Dulany, D., Carlson, R., & G. Dewey. (1984). A case of syntactical learning and judgment: How conscious and how abstract? *Journal of Experimental Psychology: General, 13*, 541–555.

Dulany, D., Carlson, R., & G. Dewey. (1985). On consciousness in syntactic learning and judgment: A reply to Reber, Allen and Regan. *Journal of Experimental Psychology: General, 14*, 25–32.

Ehrman, M., & Oxford, R. (1995). Cognition plus: Correlates of language learning success. *Modern Language Journal, 79*, 67–89.

Ekman, P., & Davidson, R. J. (Eds.) (1994). *The nature of emotion: Fundamental questions.* New York: Oxford University Press.

Elbro, C. (1990). *Differences in dyslexia.* Copenhagen: Munksgaard.

Elliott, A. R. (1995). Foreign language phonology: field independence, attitude, and the success of formal instruction in Spanish pronunciation. *Modern Language Journal, 79*, 530–542.

Ellis, N. C. (1993). Rules and instances in foreign language learning: Interactions of explicit and implicit knowledge. *European Journal of Cognitive Psychology, 5*, 289–318.

Ellis, N. C. (Ed.) (1994). *Implicit and explicit learning of languages.* New York: Academic Press.

Ellis, N. C. (1996). Sequencing in SLA: Phonological memory, chunking, and points of order. *Studies in Second Language Acquisition, 18*, 91–126.

Ellis, N. C. (1998). Emergentism, connectionism and language learning. *Language Learning, 48*, 631–664.

Ellis, N. C. (1999). Cognitive approaches to SLA. *Annual Review of Applied Linguistics, 19*, 22–24.

Ellis, N. C. (2001). Memory for language. In P. Robinson (Ed.), *Cognition and Second Language Instruction*, (pp. 33–66). Cambridge: Cambridge University Press.

Ellis, N. C., & Schmidt, R. (1997). Morphology and longer distance dependencies: Laboratory research illuminating the A in SLA. *Studies in Second Language Acquisition, 19*, 145–171.

Ellis, N. C., & Sinclair, S. G. (1996). Working memory in the acquisition of vocabulary and syntax: Putting language in good order. *The Quarterly Journal of Experimental Psychology, 49A*, 234–250.

Ellis, N. R., & Allison, P. (1988). Memory for frequency of occurrence in retarded and non-retarded persons. *Intelligence, 12*, 61–75.

Ellis, N. R. Katz, E., & Williams, J. E. (1987). Developmental aspects of memory for spatial location. *Journal of Experimental Child Psychology, 44*, 401–412.

Ellis, R. (1991). The interaction hypothesis: A critical evaluation. In E. Sadtono (Ed.), *Language acquisition in the second/ foreign language classroom*, (pp. 179–211). Singapore: SEAMEO Regional Language Centre.

Ellis, R. (1994a). *The study of second language acquisition.* Oxford: Oxford University Press.

Ellis, R. (1994b). A theory of instructed second language acquisition. In N. C.Ellis (Ed.), *Implicit and explicit learning of languages*, (pp.79–114). London: Academic Press.

Ellis, R. (1995). Interpretation tasks for grammar teaching. *TESOL Quarterly 29*, 87–105.

Ellis, R. (2000). Task-based research and language pedagogy. *Language Teaching Research*, 4, 193–220.

Ellis, R., Tanaka, Y., & Yamazaki, A. (1994). Classroom interaction, comprehension, and the acquisition of L2 word meanings. *Language Learning, 44*, 449–491.

Engle, R. W., Tuhoski, S., Laughlin, J., & Conway, A. (1999). Working memory, short term memory and general fluid intelligence: a latent-variable approach. *Journal of Experimental Psychology: General, 128, 309–331*.

Epstein, S., (1993). Emotion and self-theory. In M. Lewis & J. M. Haviland-Jones (Eds.), *Handbook of emotions*, (pp. 313–326). New York: Guilford Press.

Epstein, S., (1994). Integration of the cognitive and psychodynamic unconscious. *American Psychologist, 49*, 709–724.

Epstein, S. D., Flynn, S., & Martohardjono, G. (1996). Second language acquisition: Theoretical and experimental issues in contemporary research. *Behavioral and Brain Sciences, 19*, 677–758.

ETS (1997). *TOEFL Test and Score Manual 1997–98*. Princeton, NJ: Educational Testing Service.

Eubank, L., & Gregg, K. R. (1999). The critical period and second language acquisition: *Divide et impera*. In D. Birdsong (Ed.), *Second language acquisition and the critical period hypothesis*. Mahwah NJ: Erlbaum.

Eysenck, M. W. (1979). Anxiety, learning and memory: A reconceptualization. *Journal of Research in Personality, 13*, 363 385.

Faerch, C., & Kasper, G. (1986). The role of comprehension in second language learning. *Applied Linguistics, 7*, 257–274.

Farrar, M. J. (1992). Negative evidence and grammatical morpheme acquisition. *Developmental Psychology, 28*, 90–98.

Feldman, J., Kerr, B., & Streissguth, A. (1995). Correlational analyses of procedural and declarative learning performance. *Intelligence 20*, 87–114.

Feldman, L. B. (Ed.) (1995). *Morphological aspects of language processing*. Hillsdale, NJ: Erlbaum.

Feldman, L. B., Fowler, A., Andjelkovic, D., & Oney, B. (in press). Morphological and phonological analysis by beginning readers: evidence from Serbo-Croatian and Turkish.

Felix, S. (1985). More evidence on competing cognitive systems. *Second Language Research, 1*, 47–72.

Ferguson, K. Scott (1996). Shortest move and object case checking. In W. Abraham, S. Epstein, H. Thrainsson & C. Jan-Wouter Zwart (Eds.), *Minimal ideas: Syntactic studies in the minimalist framework*, (pp. 97–111). Amsterdam: Benjamins.

Feuerstein, R. (1979). *The dynamic assessment of retarded performers: The learning potential assessment device theory, instruments, and techniques*. Baltimore, MD: University Park Press.

Fisher, E. (1986). Learning disability specialist looks at foreign language instruction. *Hilltop Spectrum, 4*, 1–3.

Fodor, J. (1983). *The modularity of mind: An essay on faculty psychology.* Cambridge, MA: MIT Press.

Fodor, J., & Lepore, E. (1999). Impossible words? *Linguistic Inquiry, 30,* 445–453.

Foster, P. (1998). A classroom perspective on the negotiation of meaning. *Applied Linguistics, 19,* 1–23.

Foster P. (2001). Rules and routines: A consideration of their role in the task-based language production of native and non-native speakers. In M. Bygate, P. Skehan & M. Swain (Eds.), *Researching pedagogic tasks: Second language learning, teaching, and testing.* London: Longman.

Foster, P., & Skehan, P. (1996). The influence of planning and task type on second language performance. *Studies in Second Language Acquisition, 18,* 299–324.

Fotos, S. (1993). Consciousness-raising and noticing through focus on form: Grammar task performance versus formal instruction. *Applied Linguistics, 14,* 385–407.

Fowler, A. (1988). Grammaticality judgments and reading skills in Grade 2. *Annals of Dyslexia, 38,* 73–94.

Fowler, A. (1991). How early phonological development might se the stage for phoneme awareness. In S. A. Brady & D. P. Shankweiler (Eds.), *Phonological processes in literacy: A tribute to Isabelle Liberman,* (pp. 97–117). Hillsdale, NJ: Erlbaum.

Fowler, A., & Liberman, I. Y. (1995). Morphological awareness as related to early reading and spelling ability. In L. Feldman (Ed.), *Morphological aspects of language processing,* (pp. 157–188). Hillsdale, NJ: Erlbaum.

Gajar, A. (1987). Foreign language learning disabilities: The identification of predictive and diagnostic variables. *Journal of Learning Disabilities, 20,* 327–330.

Ganschow, L., Jarovsky, J., Sparks, R. L., Skinner, S., Anderson, R., & Patton, J. (1994). Differences in language performance among high-, average-, and low-anxious college foreign language learners. *Modern Language Journal, 78,* 41–55.

Ganschow, L., Myer, B., & Roeger, K. (1989). Implications of foreign language policies and procedures for students with language learning disabilities. *Learning Disabilities Focus, 5,* 50–58.

Ganschow, L., & Sparks, R. L. (1986). Learning disabilities and foreign language difficulties: Deficit in listening skills? *Journal of Reading, Writing, and Learning Disabilities International, 2,* 116–123.

Ganschow, L., & Sparks, R. L. (1991). A screening instrument for the identification of foreign language learning problems. *Foreign Language Annals, 24,* 383–397.

Ganschow, L., & Sparks, R. L. (1993). "Foreign" language learning disabilities: issues, research, and teaching implications. In S. A. Vogel & P. B. Adelman (Eds.), *Success for college students with learning disabilities,* (pp. 282–317). New York: Springer-Verlag.

Ganschow, L., & Sparks, R. L. (1995). Effects of direct instruction in Spanish phonology on the native-language skills and foreign-language aptitude of at-risk foreign-language learners. *Journal of Learning Disabilities, 28,* 107–120.

Ganschow, L., Sparks, R. L., & Javorsky, J.(1998). Foreign language learning difficulties: An historical perspective. *Journal of Learning Disabilities, 31,* 248–258.

Ganschow, L., Sparks, R. L., Javorsky, J., Pohlman, J., & Bishop-Marbury, A. (1991). Identifying native language difficulties among foreign language learners in college: A "foreign" language learning disability? *Journal of Learning Disabilities, 24,* 530–541.

Gardner, H. (1983). *Frames of mind: The theory of multiple intelligences.* New York: Basic Books.

Gardner, H. (1993). *Multiple intelligences: The theory in practice.* New York: Basic Books.

Gardner, H. (1999). Are there additional intelligences? The case for naturalist, spiritual, and existential intelligences. In J. Kane (Ed.), *Education, information, and transformation,* (pp. 111–131). Upper Saddle River, NJ: Prentice Hall.

Gardner, H., Krechevsky, M, Sternberg, R. J., & Okagaki, L. (1994). Intelligence in context Enhancing students' practical intelligence for school. In K. McGilly (Ed.), *Classroom lessons: Integrating cognitive theory and classroom practice,* (pp. 105–127). Cambridge, MA: NET Press.

Gardner, R. C. (1980). On the validity of affective variables in second language acquisition: conceptual, contextual, and statistical considerations. *Language Learning, 30,* 255–270.

Gardner, R. C. (1985). *Social psychology and second language learning: The role of attitudes and motivation.* London:Arnold.

Gardner, R. C. (1996). Motivation and second language acquisition: perspectives. *Journal of the CAAL, 18,* 19–42.

Gardner, R. C., Lalonde, R. N., & Pierson, R. (1983). The socio-educational model of second language acquisition: An investigation using LISREL causal modeling. *Journal of Language & Social Psychology, 2,* 1–15.

Gardner, R. C., & Lambert, W. E. (1959). Motivational variables in second language acquisition. *Canadian Journal of Psychology, 13,* 266–272.

Gardner, R. C., & Lambert, W. E. (1965). Language aptitude, intelligence, and second language achievement. *Journal of Educational Psychology, 56,* 191–199.

Gardner, R. C., & Lambert, W. E. (1972). *Attitudes and motivation in second-language learning.* Rowley, MA: Newbury House.

Gardner, R. C., & Lysynchuk, L. M. (1990). The role of aptitude, attitudes, motivation, and language use on second-language acquisition and retention. *Canadian Journal of Behavioural Science, 22,* 254–270.

Gardner, R. C., & MacIntyre, P. D. (1992). A student's contribution to second language learning: Part I, Cognitive factors. *Language Teaching, 25,* 211–220.

Gardner, R. C., & MacIntyre, P. D. (1993a). A student's contribution to second language learning: Part II, Affective factors. *Language Teaching, 26,* 1–11.

Gardner, R. C., & MacIntyre, P. D. (1993b). On the measurement of affective variables in second language learning. *Language Learning, 43,* 157–194.

Gardner, R. C., Smythe, P. C., Clément, R., & Gliksman, L. (1976). Second language acquisition: A social psychological perspective. *Canadian Modern Language Review, 32,* 198–213.

Gardner, R. C., Smythe, P. C., & Lalonde, R. N. (1984). *The nature and replicability of factors in second language acquisition* (Research Bulletin No. 605). London, Canada: University of Western Ontario, Department of Psychology.

Gardner, R. C., & Tremblay, P. F. (1994). On motivation: Measurement and conceptual considerations. *Modern Language Journal, 78,* 524–527.

Gardner, R. C., Tremblay, P. F., & Masgoret, A. M. (1997). Towards a full model of second language learning: An empirical investigation. *Modern Language Journal, 81,* 344–362.

Gass, S. M. (1991). Grammar instruction, selective attention and learning processes. In R. Phillipson, E. Kellerman, L. Selinker, M.Sharwood Smith & M. Swain (Eds.), *Foreign/second language pedagogy research*, (pp.134–141). Clevedon, Avon: Multilingual Matters.

Gass, S. M. (1997). *Input, interaction, and the second language learner.* Mahwah, NJ: Erlbaum.

Gass, S. M., & Mackey, A. (2000). *Stimulated recall methodology in second language research.* Mahwah, NJ: Erlbaum.

Gass, S. M., Mackey, A., & Pica, T. (1998). The role of input and interaction in second language acquisition. Introduction to the special issue. *Modern Language Journal, 82,* 299–307.

Gass, S. M., & Selinker, L. (2001). *Second language acquisition.* Mahwah, NJ: Erlbaum.

Gass, S. M., & Varonis, E. M. (1994). Input, interaction, and second language production. *Studies in Second Language Acquisition, 16,* 283–302.

Gatbonton, E., & Segalowitz, N. (1988). Creative automatization: Principles for promoting fluency within a communicative framework. *TESOL Quarterly, 22,* 473–492.

Gathercole, S. E. (1995). Is nonword repetition a test of phonological memory or long-term knowledge? It all depends on the nonwords. *Memory & Cognition, 23,* 83–94.

Gathercole, S. E., & Baddeley, A. D. (1989a). Evaluation of the role of phonological STM in the development of vocabulary in children: a longitudinal study. *Journal of Memory and Language, 28,* 1–14.

Gathercole, S. E., & Baddeley, A. D. (1989b). The role of phonological memory in normal and disordered language development. In E. I. Lundberg & G. Lennerstrand (Eds.), *Brain and reading.* New York: Macmillan.

Gathercole, S. E., & Baddeley, A. D. (1990a). The role of phonological memory in vocabulary acquisition: A study of young children learning new names. *British Journal of Psychology, 81,* 439–454.

Gathercole, S. E., & Baddeley, A. D. (1990b). Phonological memory deficits in language disordered children: is there a causal connection? *Journal of Memory and Language, 29,* 336–360.

Gathercole, S. E., & Baddeley, A. D. (1993). *Working memory and language.* Hillsdale, NJ: Erlbaum.

Gathercole, S. E., Hitch, G. J., Service, E., & Martin, A. J. (1997). Phonological short-term memory and new word learning in children. *Developmental Psychology, 33,* 966–979.

Gathercole, S. E., & Martin, A. J. (1996). Interactive processes in phonological memory. In S. E. Gathercole (Ed.). *Models of short term memory* (pp. 73–100). Hove: Psychology Press.

Gathercole, S. E., Service, E., Hitch, G. J., Adams, A. M., & Martin, A. J. (1999). Phonological short-term memory and vocabulary development: Further evidence and the nature of the relationship. *Applied Psycholinguistics, 12,* 349–367.

Gathercole, S. E., & Thorn, A. S. C. (1998). Phonological short-term memory and foreign language learning. In A. F.Healy & L. E. Bourne (Eds.), *Foreign language learning: Psycholinguistic studies on training and retention,* (pp. 141–158). Mahwah, NJ: Erlbaum.

Gathercole, S. E., Willis, C. S., Emslie, H., & Baddeley, A. D. (1991). The influences of sylla-bles and wordlikeness on children's repetition of nonwords. *Applied Psycholinguistics*, *12*, 349–367.

Gerken, L., & Ohala, D. (2000). Language production in children. In L. R. Wheeldon (Ed.), *Aspects of language production*, (pp. 275–290). Hove: Psychology Press.

Geschwind, N. (1985). Biological foundations of reading. In F. Duffy & N. Geschwind (Eds.), *Dyslexia: A neuroscientific approach to clinical evaluation*, (pp. 197–201). Boston: Little, Brown.

Gibson, E., & Wexler, K. (1994). Triggers. *Linguistic Inquiry*, *25*, 407–444.

Giles, H., & Byrne, J. L. (1982). An intergroup approach to second language acquisition. *Journal of Multicultural and Multilingual Development*, *3*, 17–40.

Gleitman, L., & Gleitman, H. (1970). *Phrase and paraphrase*. New York: W. W. Norton.

Gleitman, L., Newport, E., & Gleitman, H. (1984). The current status of the motherese hypothesis. *Journal of Child Language*, *11*, 43–79.

Gopnik, M. (1990). Feature blindness: a case study. *Language Acquisition*, *1*, 139–164.

Gopnik, M., & Crago, M. B. (1990). Familial aggregation of a developmental language dis-order. *Cognition*, *39*, 1–50.

Gouvernement du Québec, Ministère de l'Education. (1981). *Programme d'études, pri-maire: anglais, langue seconde*. Quebec: Direction de la formation générale.

Graf, P., & Ryan, L. (1990). Transfer-appropriate processing for implicit and explicit mem-ory. *Journal of Experimental Psychology: Learning, Memory and Cognition*, *16*, 978–992.

Green, P. (1975). *The language laboratory in school: The York study*. London: Oliver and Boyd.

Greenberg, J. (Ed.) (1978). *Universals of human language, Vols. 1–4*. Stanford, CA: Stanford University Press.

Greenslade, T., Bouden, L., & Sanz, C. (1999). Attending to form and content in process-ing L2 reading texts. *Spanish Applied Linguistics*, *3*, 65–90.

Gregg, K. R. (2001). Learnability and second language acquisition theory. In P. Robinson (Ed.), *Cognition and second language instruction*, (pp. 152–181). Cambridge: Cambridge University Press.

Grewendorf, G. (1996). Does second language grow? *Behavioral and Brain Sciences*, *19*, 727–28.

Grigorenko, E. L., & Sternberg, R. J. (1998). Dynamic testing. *Psychological Bulletin*, *124*, 75–111.

Grigorenko, E. L., Sternberg, R. J., & Ehrman, M. (2000). A theory-based approach to the measurement of foreign language aptitude: The CANAL-F theory and test. *Modern Language Journal*, *84*, 390–405.

Groat, E., & O'Neil, J. (1996). Spell-out at the LF interface. In P. Epstein, H. Thrainsson, & C. J. W. Zwart (Eds.), *Minimal ideas: Syntactic studies in the minimalist framework*, (pp. 113–139). Amsterdam: Benjamins.

Grubb, J. D., Bush, A. M., & Geist, C. R. (1998). Effects of second language study of phone-mic discrimination and auditory event-related potentials in adults. *Perceptual and Motor Skills*, *87*, 447–456.

Gustaffson, J. E. (1988). Hierarchical models of the structure of cognitive abilities. In R. J. Sternberg (Ed.), *Advances in the psychology of human intelligence, Vol 4*, (pp. 35–71). Hillsdale, NJ: Erlbaum.

Gustaffson, J. E. (1999). Measuring and understanding G: Experimental and correlational approaches. In P. L. Ackerman, & P. C. Kyllonen (Eds.), *Learning and individual differences: Process, trait, and content determinants*, (pp. 275–291). Washington, DC: American Psychological Association.

Haegeman, L. (1994). *Introduction to Government & Binding theory*, 2nd ed. Oxford: Blackwell.

Haig, J. (2000). On the Semantic Nature of Subjacency in Japanese. In K. Takami, A. Kamio, & J. Whitman (Eds.), *Syntactic and functional explorations: In Honor of Susumo Kuno*, (pp.23–49). Tokyo: Kuroshio.

Hakstian, A., & Cattell, R. (1976). *The comprehensive ability battery*. Champaign, IL: IPAT.

Halford, G. (1993). *Children's understanding: The development of mental models*. Hillsdale, NJ: Erlbaum.

Harley, B., Allen, P., Cummins, J., & Swain, M. (1990). *The development of second language proficiency*. Cambridge: Cambridge University Press.

Harley, B., & Hart, D. (1997). Language aptitude and second language proficiency in classroom learners of different starting ages. *Studies in Second Language Acquisition 19*, 379–400.

Harley, B., & Wang, W. (1997). The critical period hypothesis: Where are we now? In A. M. B. de Groot & J. F. Kroll (Eds.), *Tutorials in bilingualism: Psycholinguistic perspectives*, (pp. 19–50). Hillsdale, NJ: Erlbaum.

Harrington, M. (2001). Sentence processing. In P. Robinson (Ed.), *Cognition and second language instruction* (pp. 91–124). Cambridge: Cambridge University Press.

Harrington, M., & Sawyer, M. (1992). L2 working memory capacity and L2 reading skill. *Studies in Second Language Acquisition, 14*, 25–38.

Hatch, E. (1978). Discourse analysis and second language acquisition. In E. Hatch (Ed.), *Second language acquisition: A book of readings*, (pp. 402–435). Rowley, MA: Newbury House.

Hatch, E. (1983). *Psycholinguistics: A second language perspective*. Rowley, MA: Newbury House.

Hatch, E., & Lazaraton, A. (1991). *The research manual. Design and statistics for applied linguistics*. New York: Newbury House.

Healy, A. F., & Bourne, L. E. (1998). (Eds.). *Foreign language learning: Psycholinguistic studies on training and retention*. Mahwah, NJ: Erlbaum.

Heckhausen, H. (1991). *Motivation and action*. New York: Springer.

Heckhausen, H., & Kuhl, J. (1985). From wishes to action: The dead ends and short cuts on the long way to action. In M. Frese & J. Sabini (Eds.), *Goal-directed behaviour: The concept of action in psychology*. Hillsdale, NJ: Erlbaum.

Hedlund, J., Horvath, J. A., Forsythe, G. B., Snook, S., Williams, W. M., Bullis, R. C., Dennis, M., & Sternberg, R. J. (1998). *Tacit knowledge in military leadership: Evidence of construct validity (Tech. Rep. 1080)*. Alexandria, VA: U. S. Army Research Institute for the Behavioral and Social Sciences.

Herrnstein, R. J., & Murray, C. (1994). *The bell curve*. New York: Free Press.

Herschensohn, J. (1999). *The second time around: Minimalism and L2 acquisition.* Amsterdam: Benjamins.

Holthouse, J. (1995). *Anxiety and second language learning task type.* Unpublished M. A. thesis, University of Queensland, Australia.

Home, K. M. (1971). *Differential prediction of foreign language testing.* Paper presented before the Burea of International Language Coordination, London.

Horn, J. L. (1989). Models of intelligence. In R. Linn (Ed.), *Intelligence,* (pp. 29–73). Urbana, IL: University of Illinois Press.

Horn, J. L. (1994). Theory of fluid and crystallized intelligence. In R. J. Sternberg (Ed.), *The encyclopedia of human intelligence, Vol 1,* (pp. 443–451). New York: Macmillan.

Horwitz, E. K. (1986). Preliminary evidence for the reliability and validity of a Foreign Language Anxiety Scale. *TESOL Quarterly, 20,* 559–562.

Horwitz, E. K. (1987). Linguistic and communicative competence: Reassessing foreign language aptitude. In B. Van Patten, T. Dvorak, & J. Lee (Eds.), *Foreign language learning* (pp. 146–157). Cambridge, MA: Newbury House.

Horwitz, E. K., Horwitz, M. B., Cope, J. (1986). Foreign language classroom anxiety. *Modern Language Journal, 70,* 125–132.

Huitema, B. (1980). *Analysis of covariance and alternatives.* New York: Wiley.

Hulme, C. (1981). *Reading retardation and multi-sensory teaching.* London: Routledge.

Hulstijn, J. H. (1990). Implicit and incidental second language learning: Experiments in the processing of natural and partly artificial input. In H. Dechert (Ed.), *Interlingual processing,* (pp.50–73). Tubingen: Gunter Narr.

Hulstijn, J. H. (1997). Second language acquisition research in the laboratory: Possibilities and limitations. *Studies in Second Language Acquisition, 19,* 131–144.

Hulstijn, J. H. (2001). Intentional and incidental vocabulary learning: A reappraisal of elaboration, rehearsal and automaticity. In P. Robinson (Ed.), *Cognition and second language instruction,* (pp. 256–284). Cambridge: Cambridge University Press.

Hulstijn, J. H. (in press). Incidental and intentional learning. In C. Doughty & M. H.Long (Eds.), *Handbook of second language acquisition.* Oxford: Blackwell.

Intelligence and its measurement: A symposium (1921). *Journal of Educational Psychology, 12,*

Ioup, G, Houstagui, E., El Gigi, M., & Moselle, M. (1994). Rexamining the critical period hypothesis: A case study of successful adult SLA in a naturalistic environment. *Studies in Second Language Acquisition 16,* 73–98.

Ioup, G. (1989). Immigrant children who have failed to acquire native English. In S. M. Gass, C. Madden, D. Preston, & L. Selinker (Eds.), *Variation in second language acquisition, Vol II: Psycholinguistic issues,* (pp. 106–175). Clevedon, Avon: Multilingual Matters.

Jacob, A. (1996). *Anxiety and motivation during second language task performance in Singaporean schools.* Unpublished M. A. thesis, RELC/National University of Singapore.

Jacoby, L. (1983). Remembering the data: Analyzing interactive processes in reading. *Journal of Verbal Learning and Verbal Behaviour, 22,* 485–508.

Jensen, A. R. (1998). *The g factor. The science of mental ability.* Westport, C-F: Praeger/Greenwoood.

Johnson, J.S & Newport, E. L. (1989). Critical period effects in second language learning: The influence of maturational state on the acquisition of English as a second language. *Cognitive Psychology, 21*, 60–99.

Johnson, J. S., & Newport, E. L. (1990). Critical period effects on universal properties of language: The status of subjacency in the acquisition of a second language. *Cognition, 39*, 215–258.

Jourdenais, R. (2001). Protocol analysis and second language instruction. In P. Robinson (Ed.), *Cognition and second language instruction*, (pp. 354–375). Cambridge: Cambridge University Press.

Julkunen, K. (1989). *Situation-and task-specific motivation in foreign-language learning and teaching*. Joensuu, Finland: University of Joensuu.

Julkunen, K. (2001). Situation-and task-specific motivation in foreign language learning. In Z. Dörnyei & R. Schmidt (Eds.), *Motivation and second language acquisition*, (pp. 29–41). Honolulu, HI: University of Hawai'i Press.

Kagan, J. (1989). Temperamental contributions to social behavior. *American Psychologist, 44*, 668–674.

Karmiloff-Smith, A. (1992). *Beyond modularity: A developmental perspective on cognitive science*. Bradford, MA: MIT Press.

Katz, R. (1986). Phonological deficiencies in children with reading disability: Evidence from an object naming task. *Cognition, 22*, 225–257.

Keller, J. M. (1983). Motivational design of instruction. In C. M. Reigeluth (Ed.), *Instructional design theories and models*, (pp. 386–433). Hillsdale, NJ: Erlbaum.

Kellerman, E. (1996). Age before beauty: Johnson and Newport revisited. In Eubank L., Selinker, L., & M. Sharwood-Smith (Eds.), *The current state of interlanguage*, Amsterdam: Benjamins

Kemler Nelson, D. G., & Smith, J. D. (1989). Analytic and holistic processing in reflection-impulsivity and cognitive development. In T. Globerson & T. Zelniker (Eds.), *Cognitive style and cognitive development*, (pp. 116–140). Norwood, NJ: Ablex.

Kessel, F. (1970). The role of syntax in children's comprehension from ages six to twelve. *Monographs of the Society for Research in Child Development, 35*, Serial No. 139).

Klein, W., & Purdue, C. (1992). *Utterance structure: Developing grammars again*. Amsterdam: Benjaimins.

Kline, P. (2000). *Handbook of psychological testing* (2nd ed.). London: Routledge.

Knowlton, B., & Squire, L. (1996). Artificial grammar learning depends on implicit acquisition of both abstract and exemplar-specific information. *Journal of Experimental Psychology: Learning, Memory and Cognition, 22*, 169–181.

Koch, A., & Terrell, T. (1991). Affective reactions of foreign language students to *Natural Approach* activities and teaching techniques. In E. Horwitz & D. Young (Eds.), *Language anxiety: From theory and research to classroom implications*, (pp. 109–126). Englewood Cliffs, NJ: Prentice Hall.

Krashen, S. D. (1981). Aptitude and attitude in relation to second language acquisition and learning. In K. C. Diller (Ed.), *Individual differences and universals in language learning aptitude*, (pp. 155–175). Rowley, MA: Newbury House.

Krashen, S. D. (1982). *Principles and practice in second language acquisition*. Oxford: Pergamon.

Krashen, S. D. (1984). Immersion: Why it works and what it has taught us. *Language and Society, 12* (Winter), 61–68.

Krashen, S. D. (1985). *The Input Hypothesis: Issues and implications.* Oxford: Pergamon.

Krashen, S. D. (1994). The input hypothesis and its rivals. In N. C. Ellis (Ed.), *Implicit and explicit learning of languages,* (pp.45–78). London: Academic Press.

Krashen, S. D. (1999). Seeking a role for grammar: A review of some recent studies. *Foreign Language Annals, 32,* 245–257.

Kroll, J. (1990). Recognizing words and pictures in sentence contexts: a test of lexical modularity. *Journal of Experimental Psychology: Learning, Memory, and Cognition, 16,* 747–759.

Kroll, J., & de Groot, A. M. B. (1997). Lexical and conceptual memory in the bilingual: Mapping form to meaning in two languages. In A. M. B. de Groot & J. Kroll (Eds.), *Tutorials in bilingualism: Psycholinguistic perspectives,* (pp. 169–200). Mahwah, NJ: Erlbaum.

Kroll, J., & Sholl, A. (1992). Lexical and conceptual memory in fluent and nonfluent bilinguals. In R. Harris (Ed.), *Cognitive processing in bilinguals.* Amsterdam: North Holland.

Kuhl, J. (1994a). A theory of action and state orientations. In J. Kuhl, & J. Beckmann, (Eds.), *Volition and personality: Action versus state orientation,* (pp. 9–46). Gottingen: Hogrefe & Huber.

Kuhl, J. (1994b). Action vs. state orientation: Psychometric properties of the Action Control Scale (ACS-90). In J. Kuhl & J. Beckmann (Eds.), *Volition and personality: Action versus state orientation,* (pp. 47–59). Gottingen: Hogrefe & Huber.

Kuhl, J., & Beckmann, J. (Eds.). (1994). *Volition and personality: Action versus state orientation.* Gottingen: Hogrefe & Huber.

Lalonde, R. N., & Gardner, R. C. (1984). Investigating a causal model of second language acquisition: Where does personality fit? *Canadian Journal of Behavioural Science, 16,* 224–237.

Lapkin, S., Hart, D., & Swain, M. (1991). Early and middle French immersion programs: French language outcomes. *Canadian Modern Language Review, 48,* 11–40.

Lapkin, S., Hart, D., & Swain, M. (1995). A Canadian interprovincial exchange: Evaluating the linguistic impact of a three-month stay in Quebec. In B. F. Freed (Ed.), *Second language acquisition in a study abroad context,* (pp. 67–91). Amsterdam: Benjamins.

Larsen-Freeman, D. & Long M. H. (1991). *An introduction to second language acquisition research.* London: Longman

Lasnik, H., & Saito, M. (1984). On the nature of proper government. *Linguistic Inquiry 15,* 235–288.

Lasnik, H., & Saito, M. (1992). *Move alpha: Conditions on its applications and output.* Cambridge, MA: MIT Press.

Lave, J. (1988). *Cognition in practice.* New York: Cambridge University Press.

Leeman, J. (2000). *Towards a new classification of input: An empirical study of the effects of recasts, negative evidence, and enhanced salience on L2 development.* Unpublished Ph.D. dissertation, Georgetown University, U. S. A.

Leeman, J., Artegoitia, I., Fridman, B., & Doughty, C. (1995). Integrating attention to form with meaning: Focus on form in content-based Spanish instruction. In R. Schmidt (Ed.), *Attention and awareness in foreign language learning*, (pp. 217–258). Honolulu, HI: University of Hawai'i Press.

Lefebre, R. (1984). A psychological consultation program for learning disabled adults. *Journal of College Student Personnel, 25*, 361–362.

Lenneberg, E. (1967). *Biological foundations of language*. New York: Wiley.

Leonard, L. B. (1998). *Children with specific language impairment*. Cambridge, MA: MIT Press.

Leonard, L. B. (2000). Specific language impairment across languages. In D. V. M. Bishop & L. B. Leonard (Eds.), *Speech and language: impairments in children*, (pp. 115–130). Hove: Psychology Press.

Leow, R. P. (1993). To simplify or not to simplify: A look at intake. *Studies in Second Lnguage Acquisition, 15*, 333–355.

Leow, R. P. (1997a). The effects of input enhancement and text length on adult L2 learners' comprehension and intake in second language acquisition. *Applied Language Learning, 8*, 151–182.

Leow, R. P. (1997b). Attention, awareness, and foreign language behaviour. *Language Learning, 47*, 467–505.

Leow, R. P. (1998a). Toward operationalizing the process of attention: Evidence for Tomlin and Villa's (1994) fine-grained analysis of attention. *Applied Psycholinguistics, 19*, 133–159.

Leow, R. P. (1998b). The effects of amount and type of exposure on adult learners' L2 development in SLA. *Modern Language Journal, 82*, 49–68.

Leow, R. P. (1999a). Attention, awareness, and Focus on Form research: A critical overview. In J. F. Lee & A. Valdman (Eds.), *Form and meaning: Multiple perspectives*. Boston, MA: Heinle & Heinle.

Leow, R. P. (1999b). The role of attention in second/foreign language classroom research: Methodological issues. In F. Martinez-Gil & J. Gutierrez-Rexac (Eds.), *Advances in Hispanic linguistics: Papers from the 2nd Hispanic linguistics symposium*, (pp. 60–71). Somerville, MA: Cascadilla Press.

Leow, R. P. (2000). A study of the role of awareness in foreign language behavior: Aware versus unaware learners. *Studies in Second Language Acquisition, 22*, 557–584.

Lepper, M. R., Green, D., & Nesbitt, R. E. (1973). Undermining children's intrinsic interest with extrinsic rewards: A test of the "overjustification" hypothesis. *Journal of Personality and Social Psychology, 28*, 129–137.

Lett, J. A., & O'Mara, F. E. (1990). Predictors of success in an intensive foreign language learning context: correlates of language learning at the Defense Language Institute Foreign Language Center. In T. Parry & C. W. Stansfield (Eds.), *Language aptitude reconsidered*, (pp. 222–260). Englewood Cliffs, NJ: Prentice Hall.

Levine, M. (1963). Mediating processes in humans at the outset of discrimination learning. *Psychological Review, 70*, 254–276.

Li, P., & Shirai, Y. (2000). *The acquisition of lexical and grammatical aspect*. Berlin: Mouton de Gruyter.

Liberman, I. Y., Shankweiler, D., Liberman, A. M., Fowler, C., & Fischer, F. W. (1977). Phonetic segmentation and recoding in the beginning readers. In A. S. Reber & D. Scarborough (Eds.), *Toward a psychology of reading*, (pp. 207–226). Hillsdale, NJ: Erlbaum.

Liebert, R. M., & Morris, L. W. (1967). Cognitive and emotional aspects of test anxiety: some distinctions and initial data. *Psychological Reports, 20*, 975–978.

Lightbown, P. M. (1985). Great expectations: Second-language acquisition research and classroom teaching. *Applied Linguistics, 6*, 173–189.

Lightbown, P. M., & Spada, N. (1993). *How languages are learned.* Oxford: Oxford University Press.

Lightbown, P. M., & Spada, N. (1994). An innovative program for primary ESL in Quebec. *TESOL Quarterly, 28*, 563–579.

Lightbown, P. M., & Spada, N. (1997). Learning English as a second language in a special school in Québec. *Canadian Modern Language Review, 53*, 315–355.

Lightbown, P. M., & Spada, N. (1998). Instruction, L1 influence and development in second language acquisition. *Modern Language Journal, 82*, 1–22.

Liljencrants, J., & Lindblom, B. (1972). Numerical simulation of vowel quality systems: the role of perceptual contrast. *Language, 4*, 839–862.

Loeb, D., & Leonard, L. B. (1991). Subject case marking and verb morphology in normally developing and specifically language-impaired children. *Journal of Speech and Hearing Research, 34*, 340–346.

Loman, D. (1989). Human intelligence: An introduction to advances in theory and research. *Review of Educational Research, 59*, 333–373.

Long, M. H. (1981). Input, interaction and second language. In H. Winitz (Ed.), *Native language and foreign language acquisition*, (pp. 259–278). New York: Annals of the New York Academy of Sciences.

Long, M. H. (1983a). Linguistic and conversational adjustments to non-native speakers. *Studies in Second Language Acquisition, 5*, 177–193.

Long, M. H. (1983b). Native speaker/non-native speaker conversation and the negotiation of comprehensible input. *Applied Linguistics, 4*, 126–141.

Long, M. H. (1988). Instructed interlanguage development. In J.Beebe (Ed.), *Issues in second language acquisition: Multiple perspectives*, (pp. 115–141). Rowley, MA: Newbury House.

Long, M. H. (1989). Task, group, and task-group interactions. *University of Hawai'i Working Papers in ESL, 8*, 1–25.

Long, M. H. (1990). Maturational constraints on language development. *Studies in Second Language Acquisition, 12*, 251–285.

Long, M. H. (1991). Focus on form: A design feature in language teaching methodology. In K. d. Bot, C. Kramsch, & R. Ginsberg (Eds.), *Foreign language research in cross-cultural perspective*, (pp. 39–52). Amsterdam: Benjamins.

Long, M. H. (1996). The role of the linguistic environment in second language acquisition. In W. C. Ritchie & T. K. Bhatia (Eds.), *Handbook of second language acquisition*, (pp. 413–468). New York: Academic Press.

Long, M. H., & Crookes, G. (1992). Three approaches to task-based syllabus design. *TESOL Quarterly, 26*, 27–56.

Long, M. H., & Robinson, P. (1998). Focus on form: Theory, research, practice. In C. Doughty & J. Williams, (Eds.), *Focus on form in classroom second language acquisition*, (pp.15–41). New York: Cambridge University Press.

Loschky, L. (1994). Comprehensible input and second language acquisition: What is the relationship? *Studies in Second Language Acquisition, 16*, 303–323.

Lubart, T. I., & Sternberg, R. J. (1995). An investment approach to creativity: Theory and data. In S. M. Smith, T. B. Ward, & R. A. Finke (Eds.), *The creative cognition approach.* Cambridge, MA: MIT Press.

Lukmani, Y. (1972). Motivation to learn and learning proficiency. *Language Learning, 22*, 261–272.

Lundberg, I. (1994). Reading difficulties can be predicted and prevented: A Scandinavian perspective on phonological awareness and reading. In C. Hulme & M. J. Snowling (Eds.), *Reading development and dyslexia*, (pp. 180–199). London: Whurr.

Macaruso, P. Shankweiler, D., Byrne, B., & Crain, S. (1993). Poor readers are not easy to fool: Comprehension of adjectives with exceptional control properties. *Applied Psycholinguistics, 14*, 285–298.

MacIntyre, P. D. (1999). Language anxiety: A review of the research for language teachers. In D. J. Young (Ed.), *Affect in foreign language and second language learning: A practical guide to creating a low-anxiety classroom atmosphere*, (pp. 24–45). Boston: McGraw-Hill.

MacIntyre, P. D., & Charos, C. (1996). Personality, attitudes, and affect as predictors of second language communication. *Journal of Language and Social Psychology, 15*, 3–26.

MacIntyre, P. D., Clément, R., Dörnyei, Z., & Noels, K. A. (1998). Conceptualizing willingness to communicate in a L2: A situational model of L2 confidence and affiliation. *Modern Language Journal, 82*, 545–562.

MacIntyre, P. D., & Gardner, R. C. (1989). Anxiety and second language learning: Toward a theoretical clarification. *Language Learning, 39*, 251–275.

MacIntyre, P. D., & Gardner, R. C. (1991). Methods and results in the study of anxiety in language learning: A review of the literature. *Language Learning, 41*, 85–117.

MacIntyre, P. D., & Gardner, R. C. (1994a). The effects of induced anxiety on cognitive processing in computerised vocabulary learning. *Studies in Second Language Acquisition, 16*, 1–17.

MacIntyre, P. D., & Gardner, R. C. (1994b). The subtle effects of language anxiety on cognitive processing in the second language. *Language Learning, 44*, 283–305.

MacIntyre, P. D., MacMaster, K., & Baker, S. (2001). The convergence of multiple models of motivation for second language learning: Gardner, Pintrich, Kuhl and McCroskey. In Z. Dörnyei & R. Schmidt (Eds.), *Motivation and second language acquisition*, (pp. 462–492). Honolulu, HI: University of Hawai'i Press.

MacIntyre, P. D., & Noels, K. A. (1996). Using social-psychological variables to predict the use of language learning strategies. *Foreign Language Annals, 29*, 374–386.

MacIntyre, P. D., Noels, K. A., & Clément, R. (1997). Biases in self-ratings of second language proficiency: The role of language anxiety. *Language Learning, 47*, 265–287.

Mackey, A. (1999). Input, interaction, and second language development: An empirical study of question formation in ESL. *Studies in Second Language Acquisition, 21*, 557–587.

Mackey, A. (2000). *Interactional feedback on L2 morpho-syntax: Learners' perceptions and developmental outcomes.* Paper presented at the annual meeting of American Association for Applied Linguistics, Vancouver, B. C., Canada.

Mackey, A., Gass, S. M., & McDonough, K. (2000). Do learners recognize implicit negative feedback as feedback? *Studies in Second Language Acquisition, 22,* 471–497.

Mackey, A., & Philp, J. (1998). Conversational interaction and second language development: Recasts, responses, and red herrings? *Modern Language Journal, 82,* 338–356.

MacNeilage, P. F. (1970). Motor control of serial ordering of speech. *Psychological Review, 77,* 182–196.

MacWhinney, B. (2001). The competition model: the input, the context, and the brain. In P. Robinson (Ed.), *Cognition and second language instruction,* (pp. 69–90). Cambridge: Cambridge University Press.

Martohardjono, G. (1993). *Wh-movement in the Acquisition of a second language: A cross-linguistic study of three languages with and without overt movement.* Unpublished Ph.D. dissertation, Cornell University, U. S. A.

Martohardjono, G., & Gair, J. W. (1993). Apparent UG inaccessibility in second language acquisition: Misapplied principles or principled misapplication? In F. Eckman (Ed.), *Confluence: Linguistics, L2 Acquisition, and speech pathology,* (pp. 79–103). Amsterdam: Benjamins.

Masny, D. (1987). The role of language and cognition in second language metalinguistic awareness. In J. Lantolf & A. Labarca (Eds.), *Research in second language learning: Focus on the classroom,* (pp. 59–73). Norwood, NJ: Ablex.

Masny, D., & d'Anglejan, A. (1985). Language, cognition and second language grammaticality judgements. *Journal of Psycholinguistic Research, 14,* 175–97.

Masoura, E. V., & Gathercole, S. E. (1999). Phonological short-term memory and foreign language learning. *International Journal of Psychology, 34,* 383–388.

Matsumura, K., & Nakatani, K. (1995). *Genius English Course II.* Tokyo: Taishukan.

Matthews, R. C., Buss, R. R., Stanley, W. B., Blanchard-Fields, F., Ryeul Cho, J., & B. Druhan. (1989). Role of implicit and explicit processes in learning from examples: A synergistic effect. *Journal of Experimental Psychology, Learning, Memory and Cognition, 15,* 1083–1100.

Mauro, R. (1988). Opponent processes in human emotions? An experimental investigation of hedonic contrast and affective interactions.*Motivation and Emotion, 12,* 333–351.

Maybery, M., Taylor, M., & O'Brien-Malone, A. (1995). Implicit learning: Sensitive to age but not IQ. *Australian Journal of Psychology, 47,* 8–17.

McAndrews, M. P., & M. Moscovitch. (1985). Rule-based and exemplar-based classification in artificial grammar learning. *Memory and Cognition, 13,* 469–475.

McBride-Chang, C. (1995). What is phonological awareness. *Journal of Educational Psychology, 87,* 179–192.

McCann, S., Stewin, L., & Short, R. (1991). Adapting instruction to individual differences: The fading promise of ATI research. In R. Short, L. Stewin & S. McCann (Eds.), *Educational Psychology: Canadian perspectives,* (pp. 101–119). Toronto: Pitman.

McCroskey, J. C., & Richmond, V. P. (1987). Willingness to communicate. In J. C. McCroskey & J. A. Daly (Eds.), *Personality and interpersonal communication,* (pp. 129–56). Newbury Park, CA: Sage.

McCroskey, J. C., & Richmond, V. P. (1991). Willingness to communicate: A cognitive perspective. In M. Booth-Butterfield (Ed.), *Communication, cognition and anxiety*, (pp. 19–37). Newbury Park, CA: Sage.

McDougall, S., Hulme, C., Ellis, A. W., & Monk, A. (1994). Learning to read: The role of short-term memory and phonological skills. *Journal of Experimental Child Psychology*, 58, 112–123.

McGeorge, P., Crawford, J. R., & Kelly, S. W. (1997). The relationships between psychometric intelligence and learning in an explicit and an implicit task. *Journal of Experimental Psychology: Learning, Memory and Cognition*, 23, 239–245.

McLaughlin, B. (1980). Theory and research in second language learning: An emerging paradigm. *Language Learning*, 30, 331–350.

McLaughlin, B. (1985). *Second language acquisition in childhood*. Hillsdale, NJ: Erlbaum.

McLaughlin, B. (1987). *Theories of second language acquisition*. London: Edward Arnold

McLaughlin, B. (1990). The relationship between first and second languages: Language proficiency and language aptitude. In B. Harley, P. Allen, J. Cummins, & M. Swain (Eds.), *The development of second language proficiency*, (pp. 158–174). Cambridge: Cambridge University Press.

McLaughlin, B. (1995). Aptitude from an information-processing perspective. *Language Testing 12*, 370–387.

McLaughlin, B., & Heredia, R. (1996). Information-processing approaches to second language acquisition and use. In W. C. Ritchie & T. K. Bhatia (Eds.), *Handbook of second language acquisition*, (pp. 213–228). New York: Academic Press.

McNeil, M., & Kent, R. (1990). Motoric characteristics of adult aphasic and apraxic speakers. In G. E. Hammond (Ed.), *Cerebral control of speech and limb movements*. Amsterdam: Elsevier.

Meara, P. (1994). *LLEX: Lingua vocabulary tests v 1.4*. Swansea: University of Wales, Centre for Applied Language Studies.

Meara, P., & Buxton, B. (1987). An alternative to multiple-choice vocabulary tests. *Language Testing*, 4, 142–154.

Meara, P., & Jones, G. (1989). *Eurocentres vocabulary test 10 KA*. Zurich: Eurocentres.

Meisel, J., Clahsen, H., & Pienemann, M. (1981). On determining developmental stages in natural second language acquisition. *Studies in Second Language Acquisition*, 3, 109–135.

Merickle, P. M., & E. M. Reingold. (1991). Comparing direct (Explicit). and indirect (Implicit). measures to study unconscious memory. *Journal of Experimental Psychology, Learning, Memory and Cognition*, 17, 224–233.

Messick, S. (1998). Alternative modes of assessment, uniform standards of validity. In M. D. Hak-el, (Ed.), *Beyond multiple choice: Evaluating alternatives to traditional testing for selection*, (pp. 59–74). Mahwah, NJ: Erlbaum.

Miura, A., & Oka, M. (1998). *Rapid reading Japanese: Improving reading skills of intermediate and advanced students*. Tokyo: The Japan Times Lid.

Miyake, A., & Friedman, N. (1998). Individual differences in second language proficiency: Working memory as language aptitude. In A. F.Healy & L. E. Bourne (Eds.), *Foreign language learning: Psycholinguistic studies on training and retention*, (pp. 339–364). Mahwah, NJ: Erlbaum.

Miyake, A., & Shah, P. (Eds.) (1999). *Models of working memory: Mechanisms of active maintenance and executive control.* New York: Cambridge University Press.

Morais, J., Cary, L., Alegria, J., & Bertelson, P. (1979). Does awareness of speech as a sequence of phones arise spontaneously? *Cognition, 7,* 323–331.

Naiman, N., Fröhlich, M., Stern, H.H., & Todesco, A. (1978). *The good language learner.* Toronto: OISE.

Nattinger, J.R. (1980). A lexical phrase grammar for ESL. *TESOL Quarterly, 14,* 337–344.

Nayak, N., Hansen, N., Krueger, N., & Mclaughlin, B. (1990). Language-learning strategies in monolingual and multilingual adults, *Language Learning, 40,* 221–244.

Neal, A., & Hesketh, B. (1997). Episodic knowledge and implicit learning. *Psychonomic Bulletin and Review, 4,* 24–37.

Nelson, H.E., & Warrington, E.K. (1980). An investigation of memory functions in dyslexic children. *British Journal of Psychology, 7,* 487–503.

Nelson, K. (1987). Some observations from the perspective of the rare event cognitive comparison theory of language acquisition. In K. Nelson & A. van Kleeck (Eds.), *Children's language.* Norwood, NJ: Erlbaum.

Newport, E. (1990). Maturational constaints on language learning. *Cognitive Science, 14,* 11–28.

Newport, E., Gleitman, H., & Gleitman, L. (1977). Mother, I'd rather do it myself: Some effects and non-effects of maternal speech style. In C. Snow & C. Ferguson (Eds.), *Talking to children: Language input and acquisition,* (pp.109–149). New York: Cambridge University Press.

Newstead, S. (2000). Arc there two types of thinking? *Behavioural and Brain Sciences, 23,* 690–691.

Nishigauchi, T. (1986). *Quantification in Syntax.* Unpublished Ph.D. Dissertation, University of Massachusetts, Amherst. [Cited in Wanatabe, A. (1992). Subjacency and S-structure movement of *wh*-in-situ. *Journal of East Asian Linguistics, 1,* 255–291.]

Nishigauchi, T. (1990). *Quantification in the theory of Grammar.* Kluwer: Dordrecht. [Cited in Wanatabe, A. (1992). Subjacency and S-structure movement of *wh*-in-situ. *Journal of East Asian Linguistics, 1,* 255–291.]

Niwa, Y. (2000). *Reasoning demands of L2 tasks and L2 narrative production: Effects of individual differences in working memory, intelligence and aptitude.* Unpublished M.A. dissertation, Department of English, Aoyama Gakuin University, Tokyo, Japan.

Noels, K.A., Clément, R., & Pelletier L.G. (1999). Perceptions of teachers' communicative style and students' intrinsic and extrinsic motivation. *Modern Language Journal, 83,* 23–34

Noels, K.A., Pon, G., & Clément, R. (1996). Language, identity, and adjustment. *Journal of Language & Social Psychology, 15,* 246–265.

Norris, J., & Ortega, L. (2000). Effectiveness of L2 instruction: A research synthesis and meta-analysis. *Language Learning, 50,* 417–528.

Norusis, M. (1985). *SPSS-X advanced statistics guide.* Chicago: SPSS.

Novoa, L., Fein, D., & Obler, L.K. (1988). Talent in foreign languages: A case study. In L.K. Obler & D. Fein (Eds.), *The exceptional brain: Neuropsychology of talent and special abilities,* (pp. 294–301). New York: Guilford Press.

Nunan, D. (1991). Communicative tasks and the language curriculum. *TESOL Quarterly*, *25*, 279–295.

Nunes, T. (1994). Street intelligence. In R. J. Sternberg (Ed.), *Encyclopedia of human intelligence, Vol& 2*, (pp. 1045–1049). New York: Macmillan.

Nunes, T., Schliemann, A. D., & Carraher, D. W. (1993). *Street mathematics and school mathematics*. New York: Cambridge University Press.

O' Brien-Malone, A., & Maybery, M. (1998). Implicit learning. In K. Kirsner, C. Speelman, M. Maybery, A. O' Brien-Malone, M. Anderson & C. Mcleod (Eds.), *Implicit and Explicit mental processes*, (pp. 37–56). Mahwah, NJ: Erlbaum.

Oberauer, K. (2000). Do we need two systems for reasoning?? *Behavioural and Brain Sceinces*, *23*, 692–693.

Ochs, E. (1985). Variation and error: A sociolinguistic approach to language acquisition in Samoa. In D. I. Slobin (Ed.), *The crosslinguistic study of language acquisition, Vol 1: The data*, (pp. 783–838). Hillsdale, NJ: Erlbaum.

Odell, K., McNeil, M., Rosenbek, J., & Hunter, L. (1991). Perceptual characteristics of vowel and prosody production in apraxic, apahsic, and dysarthric speakers. *Journal of Speech and Hearing Research*, *34*, 67–80.

Oetting, J., & Horohov, J. (1997). Past tense marking by children with and without specific language impairment. *Journal of Speech and Hearing Research*, *40*, 62–74.

Ohta, A. S. (2001). *Second language acquisition processes in the classroom*. Mahwah, NJ: Erlbaum.

Oliver, R. (1995). Negative feedback in child NS/NNS conversation. *Studies in Second Language Acquisition*, *18*, 459–481.

Oliver, R. (2000). Age differences in negotiation and feedback in classroom and pair work. *Language Learning*, *50*, 119–151.

Oller, J. (1981). Research on the measurement of affective variables: Some remaining questions. In R. W. Anderson (Ed.), *New dimensions in second language acquisition research*, (pp. 114–127). Rowley, MA: Newbury House.

Olson, D. (1996). Towards a psychology of literacy: On the relations between speech and writing. *Cognition*, *60*, 83–104.

Onwuegbuzie, A. J., Bailey, P., & Daley, C. E. (2000). The validation of three scales measuring anxiety at different stages of the foreign language learning process: The Input Anxiety Scale, the Processing Anxiety Scale, and the Output Anxiety Scale. *Language Learning*, *50*, 87–117.

Osaka, M., & Osaka, N. (1992). Language-independent working memory as measured by Japanese and English reading span tests. *Bulletin of the Psychonomic Society*, *30*, 287–289.

Oxford, R. L. (1994). Where are we with language learning motivation? *Modern Language Journal*, *78*, 512–514.

Oxford, R. L. (Ed.) (1996). *Language learning motivation: Pathways to the new century*. Honolulu, HI: University of Hawai'i Press.

Oxford, R. L. (Ed.) (1997). *Language learning strategies around the world*. Honolulu, HI: University of Hawai'i Press.

Oxford, R. L., & Shearin, J. (1994). Language learning motivation: Expanding the theoretical framework. *Modern Language Journal*, *78*, 12–28.

Panskepp, J. (1994). The basics of basic emotion. In P. Ekman & R. J. Davidson, (Eds.), *The nature of emotion: Fundamental questions,* (pp. 20–24). New York: Oxford University Press.

Papagno, C., Valentine, T., & Baddeley, A. (1991). Phonological short-term memory and foreign-language vocabulary learning. *Journal of Memory and Language, 30,* 331–347.

Papagno, C., & Vallar, G. (1992). Phonological short-term memory and the learning of novel words: The effect of phonological similarity and item length. *Quarterly Journal of Experimental Psychology, 44A,* 47–67.

Paradis, M. (1994). Neurolinguistic aspects of implicit and explicit memory: Implications for bilingualism and SLA. In N. C. Ellis (Ed.), *Implicit and explicit learning of languages,* (pp. 393–420). London: Academic Press.

Parkinson, B. (1995). Emotion. In B. Parkinson & A. M. Colman (Eds.), *Emotion and motivation.* London: Longman.

Parry, T. S., & Child, J. R. (1990). Preliminary investigation of the relationship between VORD, MLAT, and language proficiency. In T. Parry & C. W. Stansfield (Eds.), *Language aptitude reconsidered,* (pp. 30–66). Englewood Cliffs, NJ: Prentice Hall.

Pawley, A., & Syder, F. H. (1983). Two puzzles for linguistic theory: Nativelike selection and nativelike fluency. In J. C. Richards & R. Schmidt (Eds.), *Language and communication.* London: Longman.

Peirce, B. N. (1995). Social identity, investment, and language learning. *TESOL Quarterly, 29,* 9–31.

Pellegrino, J., & Glaser, R. (1979). Cognitive correlates and components in the analysis of individual differences. In R. J. Sternberg & D. Detterman (Eds.), *Human intelligence: perspectives on its theory and measurement,* (pp. 61–88). Norwood, NJ: Ablex.

Perdue, C. (Ed.) (1993). *Adult language acquisition: cross linguistic perspectives, Vol II: The results.* Cambridge: Cambridge University Press.

Perfetti, C., Beck, I., Bell, L., & Hughes, C. (1987). Phonemic knowledge and learning to read are reciprocal: A longitudinal study of first grade children. *Merrill-Palmer Quarterly, 33,* 283–319.

Perkins, D. N. (1995). *Outsmarting IQ: The emerging science of learnable intelligence.* New York: Free Press.

Perruchet, P., & Amorim, A. M. (1992). Conscious knowledge and changes in performance in sequence learning: Evidence against dissociation. *Journal of Experimental Psychology: Learning, Memory and Cognition, 18,* 785–800.

Perruchet, P., & Pacteau, C. (1990). Synthetic grammar learning: Implicit rule abstraction or fragmentary knowledge? *Journal of Experimental Psychology: General, 119,* 264–275.

Petersen, C. R., & Al-Haik, A. R. (1976). The development of the Defense Language Aptitude Battery (DLAB). *Educational and Psychological Measurement, 6,* 369–380.

Philp, J. (1998). *Interaction, noticing, and second language acquisition: An examination of learners' noticing of recasts in task-based interaction.* Unpublished Ph.D. dissertation, University of Tasmania, Australia.

Philp, J. (in press). Constraints on noticing the gap: Non-native speakers' noticing of recasts in NS-NNS interaction. *Studies in Second Language Acquisition, 24.*

Piaget, J. (1972). *The psychology of intelligence.* Totowa, NJ: Littlefield Adams.

Pica, T. (1994). Research on negotiation: What does it reveal about second-language learning conditions, processes, and outcomes? *Language Learning, 44,* 493–527.

Pica, T., Young, R., & Doughty, C. (1987). The impact of interaction on comprehension. *TESOL Quarterly, 21,* 737–758.

Pienemann, M. (1998). *Language processing and second language development.* Amsterdam: Benjamins.

Pienemann, M., Johnston, M., & Brindley, G. (1988). Constructing an acquisition-based procedure for second language assessment. *Studies in Second Language Acquisition, 10,* 217–243.

Pienemann, M., & Mackey, A. (1993). An empirical study of children's ESL development. In P. McKay (Ed.), *ESL development: Language and literacy in schools. Volume 2: Documents on bandscale development and language acquisition,* (pp. 115–259). Canberra: National Languages and Literacy Institute of Australia and Commonwealth of Australia.

Pimsleur, P. (1961). Predicting success in high school foreign language courses. *Educational and Psychological Measurement, 2,* 349–357.

Pimsleur, P. (1966a). Testing foreign language learning. In A. Valdman (Ed.), *Trends in language teaching,* (pp. 175–214). New York: McGraw-Hill.

Pimsleur, P. (1966b). *Pimsleur Language Aptitude Battery (PLAB).* New York: The Psychological Corporation.

Pimsleur, P. (1968). Language aptitude testing. In A. Davies (Ed.), *Language testing: A psycholinguistic approach.* Oxford University Press

Pimsleur, P., Sundland D. M., & McIntyre R. D. (1966). *Underachievement in foreign language learning.* Washington, DC: Modern Language Association

Pinker, S. (1989). *Learnability and cognition: the acquisition of argument structure.* Cambridge, MA: MIT Press.

Pintrich, P. R., Smith, D. A., Garcia, T., & McKeachie, W. J. (1991). *A manual for the use of the Motivated Strategies for Learning Questionnaire (MSLQ).* Ann Arbor, MI: University of Michigan.

Plotkin, H. (1998). *Evolution in mind: An introduction to evolutionary psychology.* Cambridge, MA: Harvard University Press.

Plough, I., & Gass, S. M. (1993). Interlocutor and task familiarity: Effects on interactional structures. In G. Crookes & S. M. Gass (Eds.), *Tasks and language learning,* Clevedon, Avon: Multilingual Matters.

Polio, C., & Gass, S. M. (1998). The role of interaction in native speaker comprehension of nonnative speaker speech. *Modern Language Journal, 82,* 308–319.

Politzer, R., & Weiss, L. (1969). *An experiment in improving achievement in foreign language learning through learning of selected skills associated with language aptitude.* Stanford University. (ERIC Document Reproduction Service, ED 046261).

Pompian, N. (1986). Like a Volvo lifted off my chest. *The Undergraduate Bulletin* (Dartmouth College), *3,* 1–2.

Posner, M., & Peterson, S. (1990). The attention system of the human brain. *Annual Review of Neuroscience, 13,* 25–42.

Price, M. L. (1991). The subjective experience of foreign language anxiety: Interviews with highly anxious students. In E. K. Horwitz & D. J.Young (Eds.), *Language anxiety: From theory and research to classroom applications*, (pp.101–108). New Jersey: Prentice Hall.

Rahimpour, M. (1997). *Task complexity and interlanguage variation.* Unpublished Ph.D. Dissertation, University of Queensland, Australia.

Rahimpour, M. (1999). Task complexity and variation in interlanguage. In N. O.Jungheim & P. Robinson (Eds.), *Pragmatics and pedagogy: Proceedings of the 3rd Pacific Second Language Research Forum, Vol 2*, (pp.115–134). Tokyo: PacSLRF.

Ranta, L. (1998). *Focus on form from the inside: The significance of grammatical sensitivity for L2 learning in communicative ESL classrooms.* Unpublished Ph.D. dissertation, Concordia University, Canada.

Ranta, L., & Derwing, T. M. (1999). *The non-analytic language learner.* Paper presented at the Second Language Research Forum, University of Minnesota, September, Minneapolis.

Reber, A. S. (1976). Implicit learning of artificial grammars: The role of instructional set. *Journal of Experimental Psychology: Human Learning and Memory, 2,* 88–94.

Reber, A. S. (1989). Implicit learning and tacit knowledge. *Journal of Experimental Psychology: General, 118,* 219–235.

Reber, A. S. (1990). On the primacy of the implicit: Comment on Perruchet and Pacteau.*Journal of Experimental Psychology: General,* 119, 340–342.

Reber, A. S. (1992). The cognitive unconscious: An evolutionary perspective. *Consciousness and Cognition, 1,* 93–133.

Reber, A. S. (1993). *Implicit learning and tacit knowledge: An essay on the cognitive unconscious.* Oxford: Clarendon Press.

Reber, A. S., & Allen, R. (1978). Analogy and abstraction strategies in synthetic grammar learning: A functionalist interpretation. *Cognition, 6,* 189–221.

Reber, A. S., & Allen, R. (2000). Individual differences in implicit learning: Implications for the evolution of consciousness. In R. Kunzendorf & B. Wallace (Eds.), *Individual differences in conscious experience,* (pp. 227–250). Amsterdam: Benjamins.

Reber, A. S., Walkenfield, F., & Hernstadt, R. (1991). Implicit and explicit learning: Individual differences and IQ. *Journal of Experimental Psychology: Learning, Memory and Cognition* 17, 888–896.

Reeve, J. M. (1992). *Understanding motivation and emotion.* Toronto: Harcourt Brace Jovanovich College.

Reeve, J. M. (1997). *Understanding motivation and emotion* (2nd ed.). Toronto: Harcourt Brace.

Reingold, E. M., & Merickle, P. M. (1988). Using direct and indirect measures to study perception without awareness. *Perception and Psychophysics, 44,* 563–575.

Reves, T. (1983). *What makes a good language learner? Personal characteristics contributing to successful language acquisition.* Unpublished Ph.D. dissertation, Hebrew University, Isreal.

Rice, M. L. (2000). Grammatical symptoms of specific language impairment. In D. V. M. Bishop & L. B. Leonard (Eds.), *Speech and language impairments in children,* (pp.17–34). Hove: Psychology Press.

Rice, M. L., & Wexler, K. (1996). Toward tense as a clinical marker of specific language impairment in English-speaking children. *Journal of Speech and Hearing Research, 39,* 1239–1257.

Riding, R., & Cheema, I. (1991). Cognitive styles-an overview and integration. *Educational Psychology, 11,* 193–215.

Rizzi, L. (1990). *Relativized minimality.* Cambridge, MA: MIT Press.

Roberts, P. (1998). Implicit knowledge and connectionism: What is the connection? In K. Kirsner, C. Speelman, M. Maybery, A. O' Brien-Malone, M. Anderson & C. Mcleod (Eds.), *Implicit and explicit mental processes,* (pp. 119–134). Mahwah, NJ: Erlbaum.

Robinson, P. (1994a). Implicit knowledge, second language learning, and syllabus construction. *TESOL Quarterly, 28,* 161–166.

Robinson, P. (1994b). Universals of word formation processes: Noun incorporation in the acquisition of Samoan as a second language. *Language Learning, 44,* 569–615.

Robinson, P. (1995a). Task complexity and second language narrative discourse. *Language Learning, 45,* 99–140.

Robinson, P. (1995b). Attention, memory and the 'noticing' hypothesis. *Language Learning 45,* 283–331.

Robinson, P. (1995c). Aptitude, awareness, and the fundamental similarity of implicit and explicit second language learning. In R. Schmidt (Ed.), *Attention and awareness in foreign language learning,* (pp. 303–357). Honolulu, HI: University of Hawai'i Press.

Robinson, P. (1996a). Learning simple and complex second language rules under implicit, incidental, rule-search and instructed conditions. *Studies in Second Language Acquisition, 18,* 27–67.

Robinson, P. (1996b). *Consciousness, rules and instructed second language acquisition.* New York: Lang.

Robinson, P. (1996c). Connecting tasks, cognition, and syllabus design. In P.Robinson (Ed.), *Task complexity and syllabus design: Data-based studies and speculations,* (pp. 1–16). Universiy of Queensland Working Papers in Language and Linguistics (Special Issue). Brisbane: CLTR.

Robinson, P. (1997a). Individual differences and the fundamental similarity of implicit and explicit adult second language learning. *Language Learning, 47,* 45–99.

Robinson, P. (1997b). Automaticity and generalizability of second language learning under implicit, incidental, enhanced and rule-search conditions. *Studies in Second Language Acquisition, 19,* 223–247.

Robinson, P. (1998). State of the Art: SLA theory and second language syllabus design. *The Language Teacher, 22,* 4, 7–13.

Robinson, P. (1999). Second language classroom research in Japan: Issues, studies, and prospects. In T.Fujimura, Y. Kato & R. Smith (Eds.), *Proceedings of the 10th IUJ Conference on second language research,* (pp. 93–116). Tokyo: International University of Japan.

Robinson, P. (2000). The Cognition Hypothesis of task-based language development and its implications. *Handbook of the 2nd Annual Conference of the Japanese Second Language Acquisition Association,* (pp. 13–16). Tokyo: Ochanomizu University.

Robinson, P. (2001a). Task complexity, task difficulty, and task production: Exploring interactions in a componential framework. *Applied Linguistics, 22,* 27–57.

Robinson, P. (2001b). Task complexity, cognitive resources, and syllabus design: A triadic framework for investigating task influences on SLA. In P. Robinson (Ed.), *Cognition and second language instruction*, (pp. 287–318). Cambridge: Cambridge University Press.

Robinson, P. (2001c). Individual differences, cognitive abilities, aptitude complexes, and learning conditions in SLA. *Second Language Research, 17*, 268–392.

Robinson, P. (2002). The Cognition Hypothesis of adult task-based learning. In J. Kim (Ed.), *Proceedings of the 5th KEES Conference*, Kwangju University: South Korea.

Robinson, P. (in press). Attention and memory in SLA. In C. Doughty & M. H. Long, (Eds.), *Handbook of second language acquisition*. Oxford: Blackwell.

Robinson, P., & Cornwell, S. (2000). The scope of this collection: Some issues in individual differences research. In S. Cornwell & P. Robinson (Eds.), *Individual differences in foreign language learning: Effects of aptitude, intelligence and motivation*, (pp.1–7). Tokyo: Aoyama Gakuin University.

Robinson, P., & Ha, M. (1993). Instance theory and second language rule learning under explicit conditions. *Studies in Second Language Acquisition, 15*, 413–438.

Robinson, P., Ting, S.C-C., & Urwin, J. (1995). Investigating second language task complexity. *RELC Journal, 26*, 62–79.

Robinson, P., & Yamaguchi, Y. (1999). *Aptitude, task feedback and generalizability of focus on form: A classroom study*. Paper presented at the 12th AILA symposium, Waseda University, Tokyo, August.

Roediger, H. L., Weldon, M. S., & Challis, B. H. (1989). Explaining dissociations between implicit and explicit measures of retention: A processing account. In H. L. Roediger & F. I. Craik (Eds.), *Varieties of memory and consciousness*. Hillsdale, NJ: Erlbaum.

Rogoff, B. (1990). *Apprenticeship in thinking. Cognitive development in social context*. New York: Oxford University Press.

Rosa, E. (1999). *A cognitive approach to task-based research: Explicitness, awareness, and L2 development*. Unpublished Ph.D. dissertation, Georgetown University, U. S. A.

Rosa, E., & O'Neill, M. (1999). Explicitness, intake, and the issue of awareness: Another piece to the puzzle. *Studies in Second Language Acquisition, 21*, 511–56.

Rosenhan, D. L., & Seligman, M. E. P. (1984). *Abnormal psychology*. New York: W. W. Norton.

Rossetti, Y., & Revonsuo, A. (Eds.)(2000). *Beyond dissociation: Interaction between dissociated implicit and explicit processes*. Amsterdam: Benjamins.

Ryan, E. B., & Ledger, G. (1984). Learning to attend to sentence structure: Links between metalinguistic development and reading. In J. Downing & R. Valtin (Eds.), *Language awareness and learning to read*, (pp. 151–171). New York: Springer-Verlag.

Saffran, J., Newport, E., & Aslin, R., Tunick, R., & Barrueco, S. (1997). Incidental language learning: listening (and learning) out of the corner of your ear. *Psychological Science, 8*, 101–195.

Sato, C. (1990). *The syntax of conversation in interlanguage development*. Tubingen: Gunter Narr.

Saito, M. (1985). *Some asymmetries in Japanese and their theoretical implications*. Unpublished Ph.D. dissertation. Massachusetts Institute of Technology, U. S. A.

Saito, M. (1992). Long distance scrambling in Japanese. *Journal of East Asian Linguistics*, 1, 69–118.

Salthouse, T. (1996). The processing-speed theory of of adult age differences in cognition. *Psychological Review*, *103*, 403–428.

Sandvik, E., Diener, E., & Larsen, R. J. (1987). The opponent-process theory and affective reactions. *Motivation and Emotion*, *9*, 407–418.

Santostefano, S. (1978). *A biodevelopmental approach to clinical child psychology.* New York: Wiley.

Sasaki, M. (1991). *Relationships among second language proficiency, foreign language aptitude, and intelligence: a structural equation modelling approach.* Unpublished Ph.D. dissertation, University of California at Los Angeles, U. S. A.

Sasaki, M. (1996). *Second language proficiency, foreign language aptitude, and intelligence.* New York: Lang.

Sawyer, M., & Ranta, L. (2001). Aptitude, individual differences and instructional design. In P. Robinson (Ed.), *Cognition and second language instruction*, (pp.319–353). Cambridge: Cambridge University Press.

Scarborough, H. (2001). Connecting early language and literacy to later reading (dis)abilities: evidence, theory, and practice. In S. Newman & D. Dickinson (Eds.), *Handbook for research in early literacy* (pp.97–110). New York: Guilford Press.

Schachter, J. (1989). Testing a proposed universal. In S. M. Gass & J.Schachter (Eds.), *Linguistic perspectives on second language acquisition*, (pp. 73–88). Cambridge: Cambridge University Press.

Schachter, J. (1990). On the issue of completeness in second language acquisition. *Second Language Research*, *6*, 934–124.

Schachter, J. (1996). Maturation and the issue of Universal Grammar in second language acquisition. In W. C. Ritchie & T. K. Bhatia (Eds.), *Handbook of second language acquisition*, (pp. 159–193). New York: Academic Press.

Schacter, J., Rounds, P., Wright, S., & Smith, T. (1996). *Comparing conditions for learning syntactic patterns: Attentional, non attentional, and aware.* Technical Report # 96–08. Eugene, OR: University of Oregon Institute of Cognitive and Decision Sciences.

Schmidt, R. (1983). Interaction, acculturation, and the acquisition of communicative competence. In N.Wolfson & E.Judd (Eds.), *Sociolinguistics and Second Language Acquisition.* Rowley, MA: Newbury House.

Schmidt, R. (1990). The role of consciousness in second language learning. *Applied Linguistics*, *11*, 127–158.

Schmidt, R. (1993). Awareness and second language acquisition. *Annual Review of Applied Linguistics*, *13*, 206–226.

Schmidt, R. (1994). Deconstructing consciousness in search of useful definitions for applied linguistics. *AILA Review*, *11*, 11–26.

Schmidt, R. (Ed.) (1995a). *Attention and awareness in foreign language learning.* Honolulu, HI: University of Hawai'i Press.

Schmidt, R. (1995b). Consciousness and foreign language learning: A tutorial on the role of attention and awareness in learning. In R. Schmidt (Ed.), *Attention and awareness in foreign language learning*, (pp. 1–63). Honolulu, HI: University of Hawai'i Press.

Schmidt, R. (1998). The centrality of attention in SLA. *University of Hawai'i Working Papers in ESL, 16,* 1–34.

Schmidt, R. (2001). Attention. In P. Robinson (Ed.), *Cognition and second language instruction,* (pp. 1–32). Cambridge: Cambridge University Press.

Schmidt, R., & Frota, S. (1986). Developing basic conversational ability in a second language: A case study of an adult learner of Portuguese. In R. Day (Ed.), *Talking to learn: Conversation in second language learning,* (pp. 237–322). Rowley, MA: Newbury House.

Schneiderman, E. I., & Desmarais, C. (1988). The talented language learner: Some preliminary findings. *Second Language Research, 4,* 91–109.

Schultz, E. E. (1983). Depth of processing by mentally retarded and MA-matched nonretarded individuals. *American Journal of Mental Deficiency, 88,* 307–313.

Schumann, J. H. (1978). The acculturation model for secondlanguage acquisition. In R. C. Gingras (Ed.), *Second language acquisition and foreign language teaching,* (pp. 27–50). Washington, DC: Center for Applied Linguistics.

Schumann, J. H. (1998). *The neurobiology of affect in language.* Oxford: Blackwell.

Schwartz, B. D. (1986). The epistemological status of second language acquisition. *Second Language Research, 2,* 121–159.

Schwartz, B. D. (1993). On explicit and negative data effecting and affecting competence and linguistic behavior. *Studies in Second Language Acquisition, 15,* 147–163.

Schwartz, B. D., & Sprouse, R. A. (1994). Word order and nominative case in non-native language acquisition: A longitudinal study of (L1 Turkish). German interlanguage. In T. Hoekstra & B. D. Schwartz (Eds.), *Language acquisition studies in generative grammar,* (pp. 317–368). Amsterdam: Benjamins.

Schwartz, B. D., & Sprouse, R. A. (2000). When syntactic theories evolve: Consequences for L2 acquisition research. In J. Archibald (Ed.), *Second language acquisition and linguistic theory.* Malden, MA: Blackwell.

Segalowitz, N. (1997). Individual differences in second language acquisition. In A. M. B. de Groot & J. F. Kroll (Eds.). *Tutorials in bilingualism: Psycholinguistic perspectives,* (pp. 85–112). Hillsdale, NJ: Erlbaum.

Segalowitz, N. (in press). Automaticity and second language acquisition. In C. Doughty and M. H. Long (Eds.), *Handbook of second language acquisition.* Oxford: Blackwell.

Segalowitz, N., & Lightbown, P. M. (1999). Psycholinguistic approaches to SLA. *Annual Review of Applied Linguistics, 19,* 43–63.

Seger, C. (1998). Multiple forms of implicit learning. In M. Stadler & P. Frensch (Eds.), *Handbook of implicit learning,* (pp. 295–322). Thousand Oaks, CA: Sage.

Seligman, M. E. P. (1975). *Helplessness: On depression, development, and death.* San Francisco: W. H. Freeman.

Servan-Schreiber, E., & Anderson, J. R. (1990). Learning artificial grammars with competitive chunking. *Journal of Experimental Psychology: Learning, Memory and Cognition, 16,* 592–608.

Service, E. (1992). Phonology, working memory, and foreign-language learning. *The Quarterly Journal of Experimental Psychology, 45A,* 21–50.

Service, E., & Kohonen, V. (1995). Is the relation between phonological memory and foreign language learning accounted for by vocabulary acquisition? *Applied Psycholinguistics, 16*, 155–172.

Shah, P., & Miyake, A. (1996). The separability of working memory resources for spatial thinking and language processing: An individual differences approach. *Journal of Experimental Psychology: General, 125*, 4–27.

Shanks, D. R., & St. John, M. F. (1994). Characteristics of dissociable human systems. *Behavioral and Brain Sciences, 17*, 367–447.

Shankweiler, D., & Crain, S. (1986). Language mechanisms and reading disorder: A modular approach. *Cognition, 24*, 139–168.

Shankweiler, D., Crain, S., Katz, L., Fowler, A. E., Liberman, A. M., Brady, S., Thornton, R., Lundquist, E., Dreyer, L., Fletcher, J. M., Stuebing, K. K., Shaywitz, S. E., & Shaywitz, B. A. (1995). Cognitive profiles of reading-disabled children: Comparison of language skills in phonology, morphology, and syntax. *Psychological Science, 6*, 149–156.

Shankweiler, D., Liberman, I. Y., Mark, L. S., Fowler, C. A., & Fischer, F. W. (1979). The speech code and learning to read. *Journal of Experimental Psychology: Human Learning and Memory, 5*, 531–545.

Sharwood Smith, M. (1994). *Second language learning: Theoretical foundations.* London: Longman.

Shimizu, T. (1994). *The Acquisition of Subjecency in Wh-movement and Topicalization by Japanese Learners of English.* Unpublished M. A. thesis, University of Hawai'i at Manoa, U. S. A.

Shinagawa, F., Kobayashi, S., Fujita, K., & Mayekawa, H. (1990). *Manual of the Japanese Wechsler Adult Intelligence Scale-Revised.* Tokyo: The Psychological Corporation.

Shook, D. J. (1994). FL/L2 reading, grammatical information, and the input-to-intake phenomenon. *Applied Language Learning, 5*, 57–93.

Simard, D., & Wong, W. (2001). Alertness, orientation and detection. *Studies in Second Language Acquisition, 23*, 103-124.

Sinclair, J.McH. (1991). *Computer, concordance, collocation.* Oxford: Oxford University Press.

Singleton, D., & Lengyel, Z. (Eds.) (1995). *The age factor in second language acquisition.* Clevedon, Avon: Multilingual Matters.

Skehan, P. (1980). Memory,language aptitude,and second language performance. *Polyglot, 2.*

Skehan, P. (1982), *Memory and motivation in language aptitude testing,* Unpublished Ph.D. thesis, University of London, U. K.

Skehan, P. (1986a). Cluster analysis and the identification of learner types. In V. Cook (Ed.), *Experimental approaches to second language learning,* (pp. 81–94).Oxford: Pergamon.

Skehan, P. (1986b). The role of foreign language aptitude in a model of school learning. *Language Testing, 3*, 188–221.

Skehan, P. (1989). *Individual differences in second language learning.* London: Arnold.

Skehan, P. (1990). The relationship between native and foreign language learning ability: Educational and linguistic factors. In H. Dechert (Ed.), *Current trends in European second language acquisition research,* (pp. 83–106). Clevedon, Avon: Multilingual Matters.

Skehan, P. (1992). Strategies in second language acquisition, *Thames Valley University Working Papers in English Language Teaching, No.1*

Skehan, P. (1998a). *A cognitive approach to language learning.* Oxford: Oxford University Press.

Skehan, P. (1998b). Task-based instruction. *Annual Review of Applied Linguistics,18*, 268–286.

Skehan, P., & Dörnyei, Z. (in press). Individual differences in second language learning. In C.Doughty & M. H. Long (Eds.), *Handbook of second language acquisition.* Oxford: Blackwell.

Skehan, P., & Foster, P. (1997). Task type and task processing conditions as influences on foreign language performance. *Language Teaching Research, 1*, 185–211.

Skehan, P., & Foster, P. (1999). The influence of task structure and processing conditions on narrative retellings. *Language Learning, 49*, 93–120.

Skehan, P., & Foster, P. (2001). Cognition and tasks. In P. Robinson (Ed.), *Cognition and second language instruction*, (pp.182–204). Cambridge: Cambridge University Press.

Slobin, D. I. (1993). Adult language acquisition: a view from child language study. In C. Perdue (Ed.), *Adult language acquisition: cross linguistic perspectives, Vol II: The results*, (pp. 239–252). Cambridge: Cambridge University Press

Smith, M., Ward, T. B., & Finke, R. A. (Eds.) (1997). *The creative cognition approach.* Cambridge, MA: MIT Press.

Smith, N., & Tsimpli, I. M. (1995). *The mind of a savant.* London: Blackwell.

Smith, S. T., Macaruso, P., Shankweiler, D., & Crain, S. (1989). Syntactic comprehension in young poor readers. *Applied Psycholinguistics, 10*, 429–454.

Snow, R. E. (1987). Aptitude complexes. In R. E. Snow & M. J. Farr (Eds.), *Aptitude, learning and instruction*, (pp. 13–59). Hillsdale, NJ: Erlbaum.

Snow, R. E. (1991). Aptitude-treatment interaction as a framework for research on individual differences in psychotherapy. *Journal of Consulting and Clinical Psychology, 59*, 205–216.

Snow, R. E. (1994). Abilities in academic tasks. In R. J. Sternberg & R. K.Wagner (Eds.), *Mind in context: Interactionist perspectives on human intelligence*, (pp. 3–37). New York: Cambridge University Press.

Snowling, M. J. (1981). Phonemic deficits in developmental dyslexia. *Psychological Research, 43*, 219–234.

Snowling, M. J., & Hulme, C. (1994). The development of phonological skills. *Philosophical Transactions of the Royal Society B, 346*, 21–28.

Snowling, M. J., Goulandris, N., Bowlby, M., & Howell, P. (1986). Segmentation and speech perception in relation to reading skill: A developmental analysis. *Journal of Experimental Psychology, 41*, 489–507.

Snowling, M. J., Wagtendonk, B. van, & Stafford, C. (1988). Object-naming deficits in developmental dyslexia. *Journal of Research in Reading, 11*, 67–85.

Solomon, R. L., & Corbit, J. D. (1973). An opponent-process theory of motivation: I. Temporal dynamics of affect. *Psychological Review, 81*, 119–145.

Solomon, R. L., & Corbit, J. D. (1974). An opponent-process theory of motivation: II. Cigarette addiction. *Journal of Abnormal Psychology, 81*, 158–171.

Solomon, R. L. (1980). The opponent-process theory of motivation: The costs of pleasure and the benefits of pain. *American Psychologist, 35*, 691–712.

Spada, N., & Fröhlich, M. (1995). *The Communicative Orientation of Language Teaching (COLT). observation scheme: Applications for research and teacher education.* Sydney: National Centre for English Language Teaching and Research (NCELTR).

Spada, N., & Lightbown, P. M. (1989). Intensive ESL programs in Quebec primary schools. *TESL Canada Journal, 7,* 11–32.

Spada, N., & Lightbown, P. M. (1993). Instruction and development of questions in L2 classrooms. *Studies in Second Language Acquisition, 15,* 205–224.

Spada, N., Ranta, L., & Lightbown, P. M. (1996). Working with teachers in second language acquisition research. In J. Schachter & S. M. Gass (Eds.), *Second language classroom research: Issues and opportunities,* (pp. 31–44). Mahwah, NJ: Erlbaum.

Sparks, R. L., & Ganschow, L. (1991). Foreign language learning differences: Affective or native language aptitude differences? *Modern Language Journal, 75,* 3–16.

Sparks, R. L., & Ganschow, L. (1993a). The impact of native language learning problems on foreign language learning: Case study illustrations of the linguistic coding deficit hypothesis. *Modern Language Journal, 77,* 58–74.

Sparks, R. L., & Ganschow, L. (1993b). Searching for the cognitive locus of foreign language learning difficulties: linking first and second language learning. *Modern Language Journal, 77,* 289–302.

Sparks, R. L., & Ganschow, L. (2001). Aptitude for learning a foreign language. *Annual Review of Applied Linguistics, 21,* 90–111.

Sparks, R. L., Ganschow, L., Artzer, M., & Patton, J. (1997). Foreign language proficiency of at-risk and not-at-risk learners over 2 years of foreign language instruction: a follow-up study. *Journal of Learning Disabilities, 30,* 92–98.

Sparks, R. L., Ganschow, L., Fluharty, K., & Little, S. (1995). An exploratory study on the effects of Latin on the native language skills and foreign language aptitude of students with and without disabilities. *The Classical Journal, 91,* 165–184.

Sparks, R. L., Ganschow, L., Javorsky, J., Pohlman, J., & Patton, J. (1992). Test comparisons among students identified as high-risk, low-risk, and learning disabled in high school foreign language courses. *Modern Language Journal, 76,* 142–159.

Sparks, R. L., Ganschow, L., & Pohlman, J. (1989). Linguistic coding deficits in foreign language learners. *Annals of Dyslexia, 39,* 179–195.

Spearman, C. E. (1904). 'General intelligence' objectively determined and measured. *American Journal of Psychology, 15,* 201–293.

Spolsky, B.(1989). *Conditions for second language learning.* Oxford:OxfordUniversity Press.

Stadler, M., & Roediger, H. (1998). The question of awareness in research on implicit learning. In M. Stadler & P. Frensch (Eds.), *Handbook of implicit learning,* (pp. 105–132). Thousand Oaks, CA: Sage.

Stankov, L. (1999). Capacity versus speed in intelligence and aging. *Australian Psychologist, 34,* 138–143.

Stanovich, K., & West, R. (2000). Individual differences in reasoning: Implications for the rationality debate. *Behavioural and Brain Sciences, 23,* 645–665.

Sternberg, R. J. (1977). *Intelligence, information processing and analogical reasoning: The componential analysis of human abilities.* Hillsdale, NJ: Erlbaum.

Sternberg, R. J. (1980). The development of linear syllogistic reasoning. *Journal of Experimental Child Psychology, 29,* 340–356.

Sternberg, R. J. (1981). Intelligence and nonentrenchment. *Journal of Educational Psychology, 73,* 1–16.

Sternberg, R. J. (1982). Natural, unnatural, and supernatural concepts. *Cognitive Psychology, 14,* 451–488

Sternberg, R. J. (1983). Components of human intelligence. *Cognition, 15,* 1–48.

Sternberg, R. J. (Ed.) (1984). *Mechanisms of cognitive development.* San Francisco, CA: Freeman.

Sternberg, R. J. (1985a). *Beyond IQ: A triarchic theory of human intelligence.* New York: Cambridge University Press.

Sternberg, R. J. (1985b). Implicit theories of intelligence, creativity, and wisdom. *Journal of Personality and Social Psychology, 49,* 607–627.

Sternberg, R. J. (1987a). Most vocabulary is learned from context. In M. G. McKeown & M. E. Curtis (Eds.), *The nature of vocabulary acquisition,* (pp. 89–105). Hillsdale, NJ: Erlbaum.

Sternberg, R. J. (1987b). The psychology of verbal comprehension. In R. Glaser (Ed.), *Advances in instructional psychology, Vol 3,* (pp. 97–151). Hillsdale, NJ: Erlbaum.

Sternberg, R. J. (1990). *Metaphors of mind: Conceptions of the nature of intelligence.* New York: Cambridge University Press.

Sternberg, R. J. (1997). *Successful intelligence.* New York: Plume.

Sternberg, R. J. (1998, Winter). "How intelligent is intelligence testing?" *Scientific American Presents, 9,* 12–17.

Sternberg, R. J. (2002). Human intelligence: A case study of how more and more research can lead us to know less and less about a psychological phenomenon, until finally we know much less than we did before we started doing research. E. Tulving (Ed.), *Memory, consciousness, and the brain: The Tallinn conference.* Philadelphia, PA: Psychology Press.

Sternberg, R. J., Castejón, I L., Prieto, M. D. & Grigorenko, E. L. (2001). Confirmatory factor analysis of the Sternberg triarchic abilities test (multiple-choice items). in a Spanish sample: An empirical test of the triarchic theory. *European Journal of Psychological Assessment.*

Sternberg, R. J., Clinkenbeard, P. R. (1995). A triarchic model of identifying, teaching, and assessing gifted children. *Roeper Review, 17,* 255–260.

Sternberg, R. J., Conway, B. E., Ketron, I L., Bernstein, M. (1981). People's conceptions of intelligence. *Journal of Personality and Social Psychology, 41,* 37–55.

Sternberg, R. J., & Detterman, D. K. (1986). *What is intelligence?* Norwood, NJ: Ablex.

Sternberg, R. J., Ferrari, M., Clinkenbeard, P., & Grigorenko, E. L. (1996). Identification, instruction, and assessment of Gifted Children: A construct validation of a Triarchic Model. *The Gifted Child Quarterly, 40,* 129.

Sternberg, R. J., & Gardner, M. K.(1983). Unities in inductive reasoning. *Journal of Experimental Psychology. General, 112,* 80–116.

Sternberg, R. J., & Gastel, J. (1989). If dancers ate their shoes: Reasoning with counterfactuals and factual premises. *Memory and Cognition, 17,* 1–10.

Sternberg, R. J., & Grigorenko, E. L. (Eds.) (1997). *Intelligence, heredity, and environment.* New York: Cambridge University Press.

Sternberg, R. J., Grigorenko, E. L., Ferrari, M., & Clinkenbeard, P. (1999). A triarchic analysis of an aptitude-treatment interaction. *European Journal of Psychological Assessment*, 15, 3–13.

Sternberg, R. J., & Lubart, T. I. (1991). An investment theoy of creativity and its development. *Human Development*, 34, 1–31.

Sternberg, R. J., & Lubart, T. I. (1995). *Defying the crowd: Cultivating creativity in a culture of conformity.* New York: Free Press.

Sternberg, R. J., & Lubart, T. I. (1996). Investing in creativity. *American Psychologist*, 51, 677–688.

Sternberg, R. J., & Nigro, G. (1980). Developmental patterns in the solution of verbal analogies. *Child Development*, 51, 27–38.

Sternberg, R. J., Nokes, K., Geissler, P. W., Prince, R., Okatcha, F., Bundy, D. A., & Grigorenko, E. L. (2001). The relationship between academic and practical intelligence: A case study in Kenya. *Intelligence*.

Sternberg, R. J., Okagaki, L., & Jackson, A. (1990). Practical intelligence for success in school. *Educational Leadership*, 48, 35–39.

Sternberg, R. J., & Powell, J. S. (1983). The development of intelligence. In J. H. Flavell & E. M. Markham (Eds.), *Handbook of child psychology, Vol 3: Cognitive development*, (pp.341–419). New York: Wiley.

Sternberg, R. J., Powell, J. S., & Kaye, D. B. (1983). Teaching vocabulary-building skills: A contextual approach. In A. C. Wilkinson (Ed.), *Classroom computers and cognitive science*, (pp. 121–143). New York: Academic Press.

Sternberg, R. J., Powell, C., McGrane, P. A., & McGregor, S. (1997). Effects of a parasitic infection on cognitive functioning. *Journal of Experimental Psychology: Applied, 3*, 67–76.

Sternberg, R. J., & Rifkin, B. (1979). The development of analogical reasoning processes. *Journal of Experimental Child Psychology, 27*, 195–232.

Sternberg, R. J., & Smith, C. (1985). Social intelligence and decoding skills in nonverbal communication. *Social Cognition, 2*, 168–192.

Sternberg, R. J., Torff, B., & Grigorenko, E. L. (1998). Teaching triarchically improves school achievement. *Journal of Educational Psychology, 90*, 374–384.

Sternberg, R. J., & Wagner, R. K. (Eds.) (1986). *Practical intelligence: Nature and origins of competence in the everyday world.* New York: Cambridge University Press.

Sternberg, R. J., & Wagner, R. K. (Eds.) (1994). *Mind in context: Interactionist perspectives on human intelligence.* New York: Cambridge University Press.

Sternberg, R. J., Wagner, R. K., & Okagaki, L. (1993). Practical intelligence: The nature and role of tacit knowledge in work and at school. In H. Reese & J. Puckett (Eds.), *Advances in lifespan development.* Hillsdale, NJ: Erlbaum.

Sternberg, R. J., Wagner, R. K., Williams, W. M., & Horvath, J. A. (1995). Testing common sense. *American Psychologist, 50*, 912–927.

Sternberg, R. J., & Williams, W. M. (1996). *How to develop student creativity.* Alexandra, VA: Association for Supervision and Curriculum Development.

Sternberg, R. J., & Williams, W. M. (1997). Does the Graduate Record Examination predict meaningful success in the graduate training of psychologists? A case study. *American Psychologist, 52*, 630–641.

Stevens, J. (1986). *Applied multivariate statistics for the social sciences.* Hillsdale, NJ: Erlbaum.

Suenaga, K., & Yamada, Y. (1995). *Unicorn English Course II.* Tokyo: Buneido.

Suzuki, N. (2002). *Individual differences and the acheivement of High School learners of English in Japan: Effects of aptitude, anxiety, motivation, personality, and learning strategies.* Unpublished M.A. dissertation, Aoyama Gakuin University, Department of English, Tokyo, Japan.

Swain, M. (1985). Communicative competence: Some roles of comprehensible input and comprehensible output in its development. In S.M. Gass & C. Madden (Eds.), *Input in Second Language Acquisition.* Rowley, MA: Newbury House

Swain, M. (1995). Three functions of output in second language learning. In G. Cook & B.Scidlehofer (Eds.), *Principle and practice in applied linguistics,* (pp.245–256). Oxford: Oxford University Press,

Swain, M., & Lapkin, S. (1998). Interaction and second language learning: Two adolescent French immersion students working together. *Modern Language Journal, 82,* 320–337.

Swain, M., & Lapkin, S. (2000). Task-based second language learning: The uses of the first language. *Language Teaching Research, 4,* 251–274.

Swan, D., & Goswami, U. (1997). Phonological awareness deficits in developmental dyslexia and the phonological representation hypothesis. *Journal of Experimental Child Psychology, 60,* 334–353.

Swanson, H. L., & Berninger, V. W. (1996). Individual differences in children's working memory and writing skill. *Journal of Experimental Child Psychology, 63,* 358–385.

Tabachnick, B., & Fidell, L. (1996). *Using multivariate statistics,*(3rd ed). New York: Harper Collins.

Tallal, P., & Piercy, M. (1973). Developmental aphasia: Impaired rate of nonverbal processing as a function of sensory modality. *Neuropsychologia, 11,* 389–398.

Tallal, P., & Piercy, M. (1975). Developmental aphasia: The perception of brief vowels and extended stop consonants. *Neuropsychologia, 13,* 517–533.

Tallal, P., & Stark, R. (1980). Speech perception of language delayed children. In G.H. Yeni-Komshian, J.F. Kavanagh, & C.A. Ferguson (Eds.), *Child phonology: Perception.* New York: Academic Press.

Tetewsky, S. J., & Sternberg, R. J. (1986). Conceptual and lexical determinants of nonentrenched thinking. *Journal of Memory and Language, 25,* 202–225.

Thorndike, R. L., Hagan, E., & Sattler, J. (1986). *The Stanford-Binet Intelligence Scale: Fourth Ed., technical manual.* Chicago: Riverside.

Tibbetts, J. (2000, June 10). Worker vindicated over bilingual test. *Edmonton Journal,* p.A3.

Ting, S.C-C. (1995). Tasks and planning time in the acquisition of Mandarin Chinese as a second language. In P. Robinson (Ed.), *Task complexity and syllabus design: Data-based studies and speculations,* (pp. 35–66). Universiy of Queensland Working Papers in Language and Linguistics (Special Issue). Brisbane: CLTR.

Tobias, S. (1979). Anxiety research in educational psychology. *Journal of Educational Psychology, 71,* 573–582.

Tobias, S. (1980). Anxiety and instruction. In I. G. Sarason (Ed.), *Test anxiety: Theory, research and applications.* Hillsdale, NJ: Erlbaum.

Tobias, S. (1986). Anxiety and cognitive processing of instruction. In R. Schwartzer, (Ed.), *Self-regulated cognition in anxiety and motivation*, (pp.101–110). New York: Academic Press.

Tomkins, S. S. (1970). Affect as the primary motivational system. In M. B. Arnold (Ed.), *Feelings and emotions*, (pp. 101–110). New York: Academic Press.

Tomlin, R., & Villa, V. (1994). Attention in cognitive science and second language acquisition. *Studies in Second Language Acquisition, 15*, 183–203.

Tremblay, P. F., & Gardner, R. C. (1995). Expanding the motivation construct in language learning. *Modern Language Journal, 79*, 505–520.

Tremblay, P. F., Goldberg, M. P., & Gardner, R. C. (1995). Trait and state motivation and the acquisition of Hebrew vocabulary. *Canadian Journal of Behavioural Science, 27*, 356–70.

Truscott, J. (1998). Noticing in second language acquisition: A critical review. *Second Language Research, 14*, 103–135.

Turner, M. L., & Engle, R. W. (1989). Is working capacity task dependent? *Journal of Memory and Language, 28*, 127–154.

Van der Lely, H. (1993). Canonical linking rules: forward vs. reverse linking in normally developing and specifically language impaired children. *Cognition, 51*, 29–72.

Van der Lely, H., & Howard, D. (1993). Children with specific language impairment: linguistic impairment or short-term memory deficit? *Journal of Speech and Hearing Research, 36*, 34–82.

Van Kleeck, A. (1982). The emergence of linguistic awareness: A cognitive framework. *Merrill-Palmer Quarterly, 28*, 237–265.

Vanezky, R. (1970). *The structure of English orthography*. The Hague: Mouton.

VanPatten, B. (1990). Attending to content and form in the input: an experiment in consciousness. *Studies in Second Language Acquisition, 12*, 287–301.

VanPatten, B. (1996). *Input processing and grammar instruction in second language acquisition*. Norwood, NJ: Ablex.

Vellutino, F. R., Pruzek, R., Steger, J. A., & Meshoulam, U. (1973). Immediate visual recall in poor readers as a function of orthographic-linguistic familiarity. *Cortex, 9*, 368–384.

Vellutino, F.R., & Scanlon, D. (1986). Linguistic coding and metalinguistic awareness: Their relationship to verbal memory and code acquisition in poor and normal readers. In D. B. Yaden & S. Templeton (Eds.), *Metalinguistic awareness in beginning literacy*, (pp. 115–141). Portsmouth, NH: Heinemann.

Velmans, M. (Ed.) (2000). *Investigating phenomenal consciousness*.Amsterdam: Benjamins.

Vogel, S. (1988). Some preliminary findings on predicting success for LD college students. In D. Knapke & C. Lendman (Eds.), *Proceedings of the 1988 AHSSPPE Conference*, (pp. 111–115). Columbus, OH: Association on Handicapped Student Service Programs in Postsecondary Education.

Vokey, J., & L. Brooks. (1992). Salience of item knowledge in learning artificial grammars. *Journal of Experimental Psychology: Learning, Memory and Cognition, 18*, 328–344.

Vygotsky, L. S. (1978). *Mind in society*. Cambridge, MA: Harvard University Press.

Wagner, R. K., & Sternberg, R. J.(1985). Practical intelligence in real-world pursuits: the role of tacit knowledge. *Journal of Personality and Social Psychology, 49*, 436–458.

Wagner-Gough, J., & Hatch, E. (1975). The importance of input data in second language acquisition studies. *Language Learning*, 25, 297–308.

Ward, J. H. (1963). Hierarchical grouping to optimize an objective function. *Journal of the American Statistical Association*, 58, 236–244.

Warden, M., Lapkin, S., Swain, M., & Hart, D. (1995). Adolescent language learners on a three-month exchange: Insights from their diaries. *Foreign Language Annals*, 28, 537–550.

Watanabe, A. (1992). Subjacency and S-structure movement of *wh*-in-situ. *Journal of East Asian Linguistics*, 1, 255–291.

Waters, G. S., & Caplan, D. (1996). The measurement of verbal working memory capacity and its relation to reading comprehension. *The Quarterly Journal of Experimental Psychology*, 49A, 51–79.

Wechsler, D. (1939). *The measurement of adult intelligence*. Baltimore: Williams & Wilkins.

Wechsler, D. (1972). *Wechsler Memory Scale, Form 1*. New York: The Psychological Corporation.

Wechsler, D. (1997). *The Wechsler Adult Intelligence Scale: Revised*. New York: The Psychological Corporation.

Wells, G. (1981). *Learning through interaction*. Cambridge: Cambridge University Press.

Wells, G. (1985). *Language development in the pre-school years*. Cambridge: Cambridge University Press.

Wells, G. (1986). Variation in child language. In P. Fletcher & M. Garman (Eds.), *Language acquisition*, (pp.109–139). Cambridge: Cambridge University Press.

Wells, W., Wesche, M. B., & Sarrazin, G. (1982). *Test d'Aptitude aux Langues Vivantes* (adapted from Carroll & Sapon, 1959). Montreal: Institute of Psychological Research.

Wesche, M. B. (1981). Language aptitude measures in streaming, matching students with methods, and diagnosis of learning problems. In K. C. Diller (Ed.), *Individual differences and universals in language learning aptitude*, (pp.119–154). Rowley, MA: Newbury House.

Wesche, M. B., Edwards, H., & Wells, W. (1982). Foreign language aptitude and intelligence. *Applied Psycholinguistics*, 3, 127–140.

White, J. (1996). *An input enhancement study with ESL children: Effects on the acquisition of possessive determiners*. Unpublished Ph.D. dissertation, McGill University, Canada.

White, J. (1998). Getting the learners' attention: A typographical input enhancement study. In C. Doughty & J. Williams (Eds.), *Focus on form in classroom second language acquisition*, (pp. 85–113). Cambridge: Cambridge University Press.

White, L. (1987). Against comprehensible input: The input hypothesis and the development of L2 competence. *Applied Linguistics*, 8, 95–110.

White, L. (1989). *Universal Grammar and second language acquisition*. Amsterdam: Benjamins.

White, L. (1991). Adverb placement in second language acquisition: Some effects of positive and negative evidence. *Second Language Research*, 7, 133–161.

White, L. (1992). Subjacency violations and empty categories in L2 acquisition. In H. Goodluck & M. Rochemont (Eds.), *Island constraints: Theory, acquisition, and processing*. Dordrecht: Kluwer.

White, L. (1996). Universal grammar and second language acquisition: Current trends and new directions. In W. C. Ritchie & T. K. Bhatia (Eds.), *Handbook of second language acquisition*, (pp. 85–120). New York: Academic Press.

White, L., & Genesee, F. (1996). How native is near-native? The issue of ultimate attainment in adult second language acquisition. *Second Language Research, 12*, 233–265.

Whittlesea, B. W. A., & Dorken, M. D. (1993). Incidentally, things in general are particularly determined: An episodic-processing account of implicit learning. *Journal of Experimental Psychology: General, 12*, 227–248.

Whittlesea, B. W. A., & Wright, R. L. (1997). Implicit (and Explicit) learning: Acting adaptively without knowing the consequences. *Journal of Experimental Psychology: Learning, Memory and Cognition, 23*, 181–200.

Williams, J. N. (1999). Memory, attention, and inductive learning. *Studies in Second Language Acquisition, 21*, 1–48.

Williams, W., Blythe, T., White, N., Li, J., Sternberg, R. J., & Gardner, H. (1996). *Practical intelligence for school.* New York: Harper Collins.

Willingham, D. (1998). Implicit learning and motor skill in older subjects: An extension of the processing speed theory. In M. Stadler & P. Frensch (Eds.), *Handbook of implicit learning*, (pp. 573–594). Thousand Oaks, CA: Sage.

Willis, J. (1996). *A framework for task-based learning.* Harlow: Longman.

Wimmer, H. (1996). The early manifestation of developmental dyslexia: Evidence from German children. *Reading and Writing, 8*, 171–188.

Wimmer, H., Myringer, H., & Landeri, K. (1998). Poor reading: A deficit in skill-automatization or a phonological deficit? *Scientific Studies of Reading, 2*, 321–340.

Windfuhr, K. (1998). *Verbal learning, phonological processing, and reading skills in normal and dyslexic reading.*Unpublished Ph.D. dissertation. University of York, U. K.

Winne, P. H., & Marx, R. W. (1989). A cognitive-processing analysis of motivation within classroom tasks. In C.Ames & R. Ames (Eds.), *Research on motivation in education, Vol& 3: Goals and cognitions*, (pp. 223–257). New York: Academic Press.

Wolf, M., & Bowers, P. G. (1999). The double deficit hypothesis for the developmental dyslexias. *Journal of Educational Psychology, 91*, 415–438.

Wynne, C. D. L. (1998). A natural history of explicit learning and memory. In K. Kirsner, C. Speelman, M. Maybery, A. O'Brien-Malone, M. Anderson & C. Mcleod (Eds.), *Implicit and explicit mental processes*, (pp. 255–269). Mahwah, NJ: Erlbaum.

Yamashiro, A., & McLaughlin, J. (2000). Relationships among attitudes, motivation, anxiety and English language proficiency in Japanese college students. In S. Cornwell & P. Robinson (Eds.), *Individual differences in foreign language learning: Effects of aptitude, intelligence and motivation*, (pp.9–28). Tokyo: Aoyama Gakuin University.

Yang, S., & Sternberg, R. J. (1997). Taiwanese Chinese people's conceptions of intelligence. *Intelligence, 25*, 21–36.

Young, D. (1986). The relationship between anxiety and foreign language oral proficiency ratings. *Foreign Language Annals, 19*, 439–445.

Yule, G., & Powers, M. (1994). Investigating the communicative outcomes of task-based interaction. *System, 22*, 81–91.

Yusa, N. (1999). Multiple specifiers and *wh*-island effect. In E. C. Klein & G. Martohardjono (Eds.), *The development of second language grammars: A generative approach*, (pp. 289–315). Amsterdam: Benjamins.

Zobl, H. (1992). Sources of linguistic knowledge and uniformity of nonnative performance. *Studies in Second Language Acquisition, 14*, 387–403.

Zobl, H. (1995). Converging evidence for the acquisition/learning distinction. *Applied Linguistics 16*, 35–57.

Index

abilities 2-7, 13-15, 18-22, 25, 28-30, 32-36, 38-42, 70, 75-77, 80-83, 95, 96, 100, 103, 106, 111, 113-132, 159, 160, 162, 165, 168, 170, 177, 186, 195, 211-219, 221, 222, 225, 227-229, 242, 254-256, 258, 260-262, 269, 303-306, 328

Ability Differentiation Hypothesis (ADH) 116, 120, 132
(see also aptitude)

achievement 14, 34, 36, 37, 39, 40, 47-50, 53, 54, 65, 72, 73, 76, 99, 117, 122, 126, 149, 155, 160, 270, 305

action control 56, 57, 139, 141, 142, 156

action motivation 57, 58, 139

additive bilingualism 58

adjunct island extraction 278, 293, 295

affective filter 63

Afrikaans 102

age 5, 8, 17-19, 24, 74, 76, 79, 81, 105, 106, 114, 117, 120, 125, 126, 132, 162, 167-169, 189, 223, 257, 267, 271, 277-279, 288, 295, 296, 301, 302, 304, 306-308, 326, 327
(see also Child SLA, critical period, Teen FLL)

Aguiar, L. 106

Aida, Y. 66

Ajzen, I. 58

Alanen, R. 183

Alderson, C. 162

analogical reasoning 24, 25, 116, 295

analogies tests 23, 24, 25, 27, 115

Anastasi, A. 36, 37

Andersen, R.W. 4

Anderson, J.R. 123, 215, 222, 255

Anderson, M. 132

Ando, J. 185, 186, 204

Ando, S. 191

anxiety 2, 5, 7-9, 21, 45, 47, 56, 61, 64-67, 99, 114, 139, 140, 147-149

appraisal 141, 142, 148, 156

aptitude 1-7, 9, 13, 14, 19-21, 26, 28, 34, 42, 46, 47, 65, 69-83, 86-93, 96-98, 100, 101, 105, 110, 111, 113, 114, 115-120, 122, 123, 125-132, 147, 159-165, 169, 170, 175, 176, 178, 179, 184, 186, 195, 205, 208, 211, 213-216, 219-222, 225, 228, 229, 237, 240-243, 251-253, 256, 258-262, 267-272, 276, 277, 280-297, 301-307, 309, 310, 314, 316, 319, 325, 326, 328, 329

Aptitude complexes 3, 100, 101, 105, 110, 111, 116, 117, 120, 125-129, 131, 222, 262, 306

Aptitude Complex Hypothesis (ACH) 100, 116, 117, 129, 306

aptitude profiles 73, 77, 115, 304

aptitude-exposure interactions 268-297

aptitude-treatment interactions 1, 34-35, 77, 115, 130-132, 160-179, 181-209, 211-264

Arabic 76, 77, 164, 269, 305

artificial grammar learning 227, 231-232, 254, 259

associative memory 71, 92, 208, 270, 307, 310
(see also memory)

attention 9, 40, 45, 53, 63, 64, 75, 78, 84, 85, 88, 91, 100, 115, 118, 124, 137, 176, 177, 182-184, 195, 206, 208, 211, 212, 215, 216, 221, 226, 227, 257, 261, 302, 313, 323, 327

attentional capacity 84, 182
attentional resources 84, 177, 182, 184
attitudes 8, 46-50, 56, 58, 63, 64, 66, 68, 99, 143, 147-151
attitudes and motivation 8, 47, 49, 50, 63
Attitudes and Motivation Test Battery (AMTB) 8, 9, 47, 48, 49, 50, 56, 68, 148 (see also Gardner's socio-educational model, motivation)
attitudes toward the learning situation 48, 49
attitudinal motivation 56, 58, 139
Au, S.Y. 50, 180, 312
audiolingualism 6, 78, 165, 215
auditory skills 73
automaticity 96, 184, 217, 223, 225
Avons, S.E. 180, 187
awareness 3, 62, 84, 85, 87, 88, 103, 107-111, 114, 127, 182-184, 188, 192, 206, 211, 212, 215-217, 222, 223, 226, 227, 229, 233-236, 240, 241, 243, 250-252, 256-261, 295, 296, 327 (see also attention, implicit learning, language-based learning diabilities)

Bachman, L. 176
Baddeley, A.D. 76, 103, 105, 106, 108, 181, 184, 185, 187, 215
Baker, M. 51, 139, 223, 224, 258
Bar-Shalom, E. 110
Baron, J. 22
barriers 272, 273, 297, 298 (see also subjacency, Universal grammar)
Becker, A. 4
Belgium 19
bell curve 268
Bialystok, E. 80, 81, 162, 178, 302
bilingualism 58, 59
Binet, A. 36, 39, 40
Birdsong, D. 4, 178, 268, 271, 302
Bishop, D.V.M. 99, 107, 109
Blaxton, T.A. 213
Bley-Vroman, R. 115, 124, 125, 213, 268, 272-274, 295, 296

(see also Fundamental Difference Hypotheisis)
Bloom, L. 203
Bohannon, J.N.III, 206, 207
bounding node 297
Bowers, P.G. 107
Brand, C. 16, 28, 35, 120
Brehm, S.S. 60
Bresnan, J. 184
Bristol Language Project 80, 161
Brody, N. 222
Brown, H.D. 168
Brown, J.D. 8
Buck, R. 62-64
Butler, L. 216
Bygate, M. 86, 133, 137, 144

Cain, K. 111
Canada 8, 66, 68, 159, 160, 163, 166, 178, 329
CANAL-F aptitude test 2, 74, 92
Canale, M. 176
Cannon, W.B. 58
Carlisle, J. 109
Carpenter, P.A. 75, 186, 187, 206
Carr, T. 206
Carraher, T.N. 16
Carroll, J.B. 3-5, 14-16, 70, 71, 73-75, 79, 80, 91, 93, 96, 97, 116, 117, 159-162, 165, 170, 195, 215, 237, 268, 269, 280, 303, 305, 307, 310
Carroll, S. 206, 121, 217
Cattell, R.B. 15, 117, 178
Ceci, S.J. 9, 16, 22, 214
central processing 5, 83, 213, 214, 217, 225, 258
Chapelle, C. 178, 179
Chen, H.C. 105
Cheung, H. 106
Child SLA 278, 279, 283, 284, 288, 290-295
Chinese 21, 42, 102
Chomsky, N. 5, 224, 257, 272, 273, 297
chunking 123

classroom learning 7, 69, 72, 124, 127, 130-132, 137, 148, 160, 214, 216, 255, 301-303, 305, 330
classroom studies 1, 2, 137-157, 159-179, 212
Cleave, P. 110
Cleeremans, A. 211, 217, 222, 261
Clément, R. 50, 57-59, 64, 66, 67, 143, 145, 146, 148
cloze tests 48
cluster analysis 76, 159, 171, 174, 175, 179
cognitive comparison 118, 119, 123
cognitive style 302, 306
Cohen , J. 98
Cohen, Y. 67
collocation 205
Communicative Orientation of Language Teaching observation scheme (COLT) 167, 168
communication apprehension 56, 145
communicative language teaching 1, 7, 83, 121, 130, 137, 159, 160-179, 214, 215
communicative tasks 9, 121, 137, 138, 139, 140, 155, 159-179, 189, 204
   (see also tasks and second language learning)
Competition Model 123
complexifying 84, 88
comprehensible input 7, 83-85, 160
comprehension 96, 98, 104, 110, 111, 126, 128, 133, 163, 164, 170, 173, 176, 177, 182, 184-186, 188, 221, 223, 233, 263, 282, 307, 310-314, 317-321, 323, 326, 328
comprehension difficulties 111
comprehension skills 111, 320
connectionsim 123
conscious learning 212
contingent speech 100, 118, 130, 132
conventional tests of intelligence 17, 20, 26, 28, 31, 35, 38
   (see also Wechsler Adult Intelligence Scale-Revised)
Cook, V. 72, 160
Coppieters, R. 271

Corno, L. 1, 113, 114, 141
counterfactuals 27
creative intelligence 26, 28, 29
critical period 4, 5, 79-83, 87, 93, 124-126, 214, 267, 268, 270-272, 276-278, 283, 286-297, 302, 303, 306
Cronbach, L.J. 1, 36, 113, 147, 148, 160, 179, 232, 239, 281
Crookes, G.V. 8, 9, 50-53, 55, 63, 68, 114, 137, 215
cross modal transfer 246, 249
cultural knowledge 16-18, 27, 30
Cummins, J. 176, 219
Cyr, J.J. 236

Daly, J.A. 66
Dance, K. 113
Daneman, M. 75, 185, 187, 206
Daneman and Carpenter's Reading Span Test 75
Davidson, J.E. 29, 64
de Graaff, R. 4, 6, 78, 79, 83, 121, 211, 219-221
Deane, P.D. 297
Deary, I. 120, 121
debilitating anxiety 66
deep semantic processing 100, 118, 120, 131
Defense Language Aptitude Battery (DLAB) 74
DeKeyser, R.M. 4, 6, 81, 83, 121-123, 125, 126, 130, 133, 211, 216, 222, 255, 262, 268, 270, 282, 288, 303, 305
Demuth, K. 98
Dennet, D. 217
depression 21, 33, 60
depth-of-processing 71
developmental level 193, 197, 199, 201-203, 205
developmental stage 194, 199
Dewaele, J-M. 148, 156
Dicks, J. 164, 308
Dienes, Z. 217
digit span 75
Dinklage, K. 97

Dörnyei, Z. 1, 7-9, 17, 52-58, 63, 68, 121, 122, 137, 138, 140, 142-148
Doughty, C. 3, 4, 6, 7, 79, 117, 118, 123, 130, 131, 182, 183, 215, 216, 229, 257
Dresher, E. 217
dual-coding 89
Dual system explanations of learning 212-213, 219-220
Dulany, D. 222
Dutch 101, 219
dynamic testing 20, 42
dyslexia 3, 75, 97-100, 104-110

early vs. late immersion 164
effect size 131, 230, 244, 245, 262, 277
Ehrman, M. 2, 20, 42, 74, 117, 159, 165, 214, 269, 303-305
Ekman, P. 64
Elbro, C. 109
Ellis, N.C. 4, 6, 115, 121, 123, 181, 184, 205, 211, 215-217, 229, 254
Ellis, N.R. 219
Ellis, R. 84, 137, 182, 184, 212,
emotion 2, 7, 9, 45, 47, 60-65, 67
emotions and attitudes 64
Empty Category Principle (ECP) 224, 258, 272, 273, 274, 276
engagement 48, 51, 72, 138, 143, 144, 146, 152
Engle, R.W. 184, 190, 191, 207
English for Specific Purposes (ESP) 72
Epstein, S. 62, 63, 283
equity theories 55
ergative markers 257
error-free T-units 312
Educational testing Service (ETS) 279
Eubank, L. 271
expectancy-value 54, 55
experimental studies 185
explicit conditions 218, 219, 259
extroversion 145
Eysenck, H. 66
facilitating anxiety 66
factor analysis 19, 33, 56, 76, 77, 171, 281, 282, 287

Faerch, C. 182
Farrar, M.J. 206
fear of assimilation 59
feedback 20, 85, 87, 91, 118, 130, 143, 170, 178, 181, 182, 184, 187-189, 192, 194, 197, 199, 201-204, 207, 208, 231, 233 (see also focus on form, recasts)
Feldman, J. 127
Feldman, L.B. 103, 109
Felix, S. 273, 303
Ferguson, K.Scott. 224, 257
Feuerstein, R. 20
fight or flight response 61
Fisher, E. 98, 208
Flemish 19
fluency 31, 86, 89, 164, 166, 279
focal attention 84, 88, 115, 124, 183, 226
focus on form (FonF) 3, 6, 7, 79, 83, 87, 113, 117, 130-132, 167, 168, 172, 175, 215, 221, 222 (see also attention, awareness, noticing)
Fodor, J. 125, 217, 224, 225
foreign language learning 3, 5, 70, 75, 80, 82-85, 99, 267
form-function mappings 4
fossilization 85, 87
Foster, P. 86, 114, 121, 137
Fotos, S. 183
Fowler, A. 105, 106, 108-110
French 8, 13, 14, 19, 21, 56, 63, 66, 102, 163-166, 168-170, 172, 173, 175, 176, 270, 271, 301, 306-330
Fundamental Difference Hypothesis (FDH) 115, 116, 124, 125, 129, 213
Fundamental Similarity Hypothesis (FSH) 115, 116, 124, 125, 127, 129, 213, 214, 221, 222, 262

g factor 35, 117-118
Gajar, A. 98
Ganschow, L. 5, 65, 74, 98-100, 103, 178, 261, 269
Gardner, H. 16, 21-23, 32, 214

Gardner, R.C. 5, 8, 9, 45-59, 63-68, 72, 77, 139, 147, 148, 269, 303, 305, 328
Gardner's socio-educational model 50, 53, 55, 56, 64, 305
Gass, S.M. 4, 97, 114, 137, 181, 182, 184, 191, 203, 204, 206
Gatbonton, E. 178
Gathercole, S.E. 76, 103, 105, 106, 108, 187, 189, 215
generalizability 228, 253, 254
Gerken, L. 103
German 101-103, 140
Geschwind, N. 98
Gibson, E. 120, 123, 217
Giles, H. 51
Gleitman, L. 162, 203
goal-setting 54
Gopnik, M. 109
Government and Binding Theory 258, 272-277
Graduate Record Examination (GRE) 38, 39
Graf, P. 213, 256
grammatical sensitivity 71, 74, 78, 82, 91, 97, 100, 117, 118, 125, 129, 131, 161, 162, 202, 215, 237, 269, 303, 304
    (see also Modern Language Aptitude Test)
grammaticality judgement test 125, 128, 243, 246, 249, 253
Green, P. 27, 28, 59, 74, 178, 179
Greenberg, J. 102
Greenslade, T. 183
Gregg, K.R. 5, 115, 271, 297
Grewendorf, G. 275, 276
Grigorenko, E. 2-5, 8, 17, 19-21, 31, 32, 34, 37, 38, 42, 65, 74, 75, 92, 95, 117, 118, 120, 187, 214
Groat, E. 275
Gustaffson, J.E. 2

Haegeman, L. 272, 273
Hakstian, A. 117
Halford, G. 122

Harley, B. 1, 3, 5, 7, 76, 117, 122, 125-127, 132, 163-166, 219, 268, 270, 282, 288, 301, 302, 306, 310, 328
Harrington, M.W. 75, 91, 92, 115, 177, 181, 184-186, 190, 191, 196, 205
Hart, D. 1, 3, 5, 7, 76, 117, 122, 125-127, 132, 163-166, 268, 270, 282, 288, 301, 306, 310, 311, 317, 322, 328, 329
Hatch, E. 182, 208
Healy, A. 184
Hebrew 77, 105, 110, 164, 305, 329
Heckhausen, H. 140
Hedlund, J. 31
Herrnstein, R.J. 35, 38, 39
Herschensohn, J. 262, 273
hidden cost of reward 59
high school students 34, 165, 305
holistic orientation to learning 327
Holthouse, J. 9
Home, K.M. 14, 18, 27, 29, 60, 125, 126, 308, 309, 313, 329
homeostasis 58, 60, 68
Horn, J.L. 15, 178
Horwitz, E.K. 66, 67, 165
Huitema, B. 290
Hulme, C. 104-106
Hulstijn, J.H. 4, 6, 121, 133, 176-178, 211, 212
Hungarian 101, 125, 144-146, 148, 271, 303, 305

immersion education 125, 126, 165, 214, 219, 301-302, 306-309
implicit conditions 78, 218, 222
implicit deductive learning 216, 217
implicit inductive learning 216, 217
implicit learning 31, 124, 127, 206, 211-214, 216-219, 222, 227-230, 232, 238-240, 242, 243, 253-255, 259, 260, 261, 265
    (see also attention, awareness, tacit knowledge)
implicit negative feedback 118, 130
    (see also focus on form, recasts)

incidental learning 1, 7, 114, 126-129, 131, 211-213, 216, 218, 219, 221-223, 228-230, 234, 238, 240-245, 249, 251, 253, 254, 256-262, 266
inductive language learning ability 71, 74, 78, 82, 97, 161, 208, 269, 280, 303 (see also the Modern Language Aptitude Test)
inductive reasoning 24, 27
information processing 4, 6, 7, 24, 83, 84, 87, 93, 114, 116, 121-124, 129, 214, 242
input 3, 5-7, 65, 72, 78, 80, 82-85, 87, 91, 100, 118, 123-126, 129, 131, 137, 160, 161, 163, 167, 176, 182, 183, 184-187, 192, 202-204, 206, 207, 212-215, 217, 220, 221, 225-227, 242, 249, 262, 273, 277, 296, 305
input flooding 7, 85, 131
input processing instruction 7, 131
Input Processing Output Anxiety Scale (IPOAS) 5, 65
inspection time 132
instructional psychology 113
instrumental motivation 8, 53
instrumental orientation 56, 143
instrumentality 52
intake 183
integrative motivation 8, 48, 54, 63, 68
integrative orientation 48, 56, 68
integrativeness 48, 49, 52, 58, 68, 147, 148, 151
intelligence 2, 3, 7, 9, 13-24, 26, 28-36, 38, 40-42, 46, 47, 76, 77, 82, 95, 97-99, 117, 118, 120, 121, 123, 127, 128, 178, 211-214, 216, 218, 229, 236, 240, 251-253, 256, 258, 259, 269
interaction 1, 2, 4-7, 13, 16, 34, 48, 62, 113, 116-118, 121, 122, 125, 129, 130, 132, 146, 153, 160, 162, 168, 178, 181, 182, 184, 186-189, 192, 204-207, 215, 216, 242, 243, 245, 246, 248, 249, 267, 270, 272, 283, 290, 291, 293-295, 306, 328, 329
interaction-driven L2 development 186

interactional feedback 181, 182, 184, 188, 189, 192, 197, 201-204
interlanguage 85, 86, 88, 89, 177, 181, 182, 184, 194, 199, 201, 203, 205, 274
intrinsic motivation 54, 59
introversion 145

Ioup, G. 268, 271, 273, 287, 302, 328
Jacob, A. 9
Jacoby, L. 256
Jamaica 40, 41
Japanese 21, 76, 77, 125, 127, 181, 186-191, 195, 207, 208, 220, 223-225, 229, 232, 234, 236, 237, 262, 266, 267, 273-281, 283, 284, 288, 291, 293-295, 298
Jensen, A.R. 2, 16, 22, 35, 117
Johnson, J.S. 81, 125, 270, 290, 291, 293-295, 302
Johnson-Neyman analysis 291, 293-295
Jourdenai, R. 121
Julkunen, K. 9, 138, 139, 148

Kagan , J. 61
Karmiloff-Smith, A. 126
Katz, R. 107, 219
Keller, J.M. 51
Kellerman, E. 80
Kenya 17-19
Kessel, F. 162
Kiswahili 101-103
Klein , W. 222
Kline , P. 236
Knowlton, B. 222, 232, 265
Koch, A. 66
Korean 273, 274, 276
Krashen, S. 7, 51, 63, 72, 83, 84, 124, 127-129, 160, 161, 163-165, 175, 176, 213, 214, 219-221, 228, 242, 254, 259, 262, 303
Kroll , J. 4, 106
Kuhl , J. 56, 57, 139, 140
Language Aptitude Battery for the Japanese (LAB)J 125, 128, 129, 208, 229, 237, 256, 259, 261, 262, 280 (see also Sasaki, M)

laboratory studies 121, 127, 211, 212, 219

Lalonde, R.N. 9, 49, 57

language analytic ability 77, 126, 159-163, 165, 166, 169, 170, 173-175, 177, 178

language anxiety 45, 47, 64-67, 149

language learning aptitude 2, 3, 5, 7, 19, 80, 117, 119, 128, 216, 240, 241, 259, 267, 268, 270, 271, 276, 287, 288, 295-297, 309

(see also aptitude)

language learning strategies 47

language level 52-54, 68

language-based learning disabilities 3, 95, 96-101, 110, 112

Lapkin, S. 137, 181, 182, 311, 317, 322, 328, 329

Larsen-Freeman, D. 84

Lasnik, H. 273, 298

latent trait 270

Latin 13, 14, 21

Lave, J. 16

learned helplessness 60

learner level 53, 54

learner types 304

learning conditions 1, 6, 113, 114, 116, 119, 121, 122, 124, 186, 211, 212, 215, 216, 254, 261, 304, 306, 329

learning from context 25

learning orientation 301, 306-308, 326

learning situation level 53, 68

Leeman, J. 183

Lefebre, R. 98

Lenneberg, E. 301, 303, 306

Leonard, L.B. 103, 109, 110

Leow, R.P. 182, 183

Lepper, M.R. 59

Lett, J.A. 14

Levine, M. 207

lexical retrieval 176, 177

lexicalised chunks 86

lexicalising 5, 89, 90

Li, P. 4, 32

Liberman, I.Y. 105, 108, 109

Lightbown, P.M. 161, 166, 167, 178, 184, 188, 193, 203, 206

Likert scale 190, 284

Liljencrants, J. 103

linguistic coding deficit hypothesis 5, 75, 99-101, 103

linguistic self-confidence 143

listening comprehension tests 176, 177

listening span 186, 187, 190, 191, 194-196, 206, 208

listening span tests 186, 190, 191, 194, 196

Loeb, D. 110

Logical Form 274

Loman, D. 178

Long, M.H. 1, 3, 4, 6, 84, 87, 114, 121, 130, 131, 137, 182-184, 188, 215, 256-258

Loschky, L. 182

Lubart. T.I. 28, 29

Lukmani, Y. 8

Lundberg, I. 108

Macaruso, P. 110

MacIntyre, P.D. 5, 8, 9, 17, 45-51, 56, 58, 63-68, 139, 145, 148, 156, 305

Mackey, A. 1, 3, 4, 7, 85, 91, 105, 118, 123, 131, 133, 181-184, 188, 189, 191, 193, 194, 203, 204, 206, 215, 229

MacNeilage, P.F. 103

MacWhinney, B. 123, 207

Markov grammar 222

Martohardjono, G. 273, 274, 283, 298

Masny, D. 162

Masoura, R. 105

Matsumura, K. 191

Matthews, R.C. 216, 227

Mauro, R. 60

Maybery, M. 211, 218

McAndrews, M.P. 222

McBride-Chang, C. 104

McCann, S. 160

McCroskey, J.C. 56, 66, 145, 146

McDougall, S. 104

McGeorge, P. 218

McLaughlin, B. 4, 8, 160, 184, 268, 270, 296

McNeil, M. 103

Meara , P. 171, 311

measures of anxiety 21, 56

measures of memory 3, 125, 166
Meisel, J. 4, 222
memorized chunks 87, 304
memory 2, 3, 7, 14, 32, 33, 35, 38, 39, 42,
      62, 71, 74-78, 82, 86, 91-93, 97, 98,
      100, 103-107, 110, 111, 115, 116, 118,
      122, 124-127, 130-132, 160, 165, 166,
      176-178, 181-188, 190, 194-199, 201-
      208, 211, 213, 215-220, 222, 226, 229,
      231, 236, 237, 241, 242, 244, 246, 249,
      251, 252, 256, 260-262, 269, 270, 297,
      301, 303, 304, 306-310, 313, 315, 316,
      319, 323, 324, 326, 327, 328
      (see also short term memory, working
      memory)
memory and noticing 100, 118, 119, 130
      201
Memory for Contingent Speech (MCS)
      100, 118, 119, 130, 132
      (see also aptitude complex hypothesis)
Memory for Contingent Text (MCT) 100,
      118, 119, 131
      (see also aptitude complex hypothesis)
memory for text 125, 269, 270, 307, 309,
      310, 313, 315, 316, 319, 323, 324, 326-
      328
Merickle, P.M. 227
Messick, S. 36
metalinguistic ability 125, 162
Metalinguistic Rule Rehearsal (MRR) 100,
      118, 119, 130, 131
      (see also aptitude complex hypothesis)
Mill Hill Vocabulary Scale 18
Minimal Link Condition 257
Minimalist Program 224, 274
Miura, A. 190
Miyake, A. 76, 181, 185-187, 190, 195, 196,
      205, 206, 215, 262
Modern Language Aptitude Test (MLAT)
      3, 6, 70, 71, 73, 74, 76, 78, 91-93, 97,
      98, 117, 125, 128, 129, 160-165, 169,
      170, 178, 215, 219-221, 229, 237, 259,
      261, 268, 269, 280, 291, 303-305, 307
      (see also Carroll, J.B., and Sapon, S.)
modularity 79, 81, 82, 93, 125, 213

Morais, J. 108
moras 189, 191
morphological awareness 103, 108, 109
motivation 2, 7-9, 29, 45-61, 63-66, 68, 96,
      97, 99, 114, 122, 137-140, 142-144,
      149, 150, 152-156, 168, 258, 280, 328
      (see also Attitudes and Motivation Test
      Battery, anxiety, willingness to com-
      municate)
motivational processing 141-144, 156
multiple aptitudes 2, 120, 130, 215-216
multiple intelligences 2, 21-22, 41, 42, 214

Naiman, N. 176, 178
native-like competence 268, 271
Nattinger, J.R. 184
Nayak, N. 268
Neal, A. 213
near-native intuition 271
need for achievement 53, 54
need theories 55
Nelson, H.E. 106
Nelson, K. 123
Newport, E. 81, 125, 203, 214, 268, 270,
      302
Newstead, S. 213
Nishigauchi, T. 275
Niwa, Y. 9, 121, 190
Noels, K. 58, 63, 67, 143, 145, 146, 148
nonword repetition 105, 108, 208
Norris, J. 131, 212, 245, 262
noticing 1, 3, 5, 6, 84, 87, 88, 90, 91, 100,
      115, 118, 120, 123, 124, 131, 132, 181-
      184, 186-188, 192, 194, 195, 196-199,
      201-203, 205-208, 213, 221, 226, 227,
      229, 262
      (see also attention, awareness, focus
      on form)
Noticing The Gap (NTG) 100, 118, 119,
      120, 123, 132
      (see also aptitude complex hypothesis)
noun incorporation 223, 224, 226, 234,
      257, 260-262
novelty 27, 28, 162
Novoa, L. 268, 328

null operator movement 275
Nunan, D. 168
Nunes, T. 16

Oberauer, K. 213
Ochs, E. 223, 257
Odell, K. 103
Oetting, J. 110
Ohta, A.S. 97
Oliver, R. 206, 207
Oller, J. 50
Olson, D. 162
Onwuegbuzie, A.J. 5
open v. closed tasks 121
operating principles 123
Opponent process theory 59, 60
orientations 9, 19, 48, 54, 63, 143, 304, 306, 327
orthography 105
Osaka, M. 128, 186, 190, 196, 205, 229, 237
overjustification effect 59
Oxford, R.L. 9, 53-55, 63, 68, 159, 165, 269, 303-305

Panskepp, J. 63
Papagno, C. 105, 185
Paradis, M. 219
Parkinson, B. 62
Parry, T.S. 14, 74
parsing mechanisms 115
path analysis 186
pattern identification 88, 118
Pawley, A. 86, 184
Peirce, B.N. 328
Pellegrino, J. 120, 123
perceived competence 56
perceptual speed 130, 132
Perdue, C. 4
Perfetti, C. 106, 108
Perkins, D.N. 22
Perruchet, P. 216, 222
persistence 51
personality 29, 31, 61, 145, 148, 149, 155, 269
Petersen, C.R. 14, 74

Philp, J. 1, 118, 181, 182, 184, 188, 189, 193, 194, 203, 206
phonemic coding ability 71, 75, 77, 78, 82, 91, 165, 176, 178, 208, 269
    (see also Modern Language Aptitude Test)
phonological awareness 107-109
phonological deficits 106, 107
phonological loop 76, 105, 106
phonological sensitivity 130
Piaget, J. 26, 55
Pica, T. 4, 182, 206
Pienemann, M. 4, 84, 188, 193, 206, 222
Pimsleur, P. 14, 73, 93, 96, 97, 126, 160, 237, 269, 303, 307, 310
Pimsleur's Language Aptitude Battery (PLAB) 73, 74, 78, 93, 97, 126, 160, 162-164, 169, 170, 178, 237, 269, 280, 281, 310
Pinker, S. 109
Pintrich, P.R. 56
planned v. unplanned tasks 121
Plotkin, H. 163
Plough, I. 114
Polio, C. 181
Polish 101
Politzer, R. 79, 268
Pompian, N. 98
positive evidence 217, 222, 223, 226, 296
positive manifold 16
Posner, M. 183
practical intelligence 21, 29-32
Price, M.L. 67
primary abilities 100, 117-119, 123
primary linguistic data 82, 87
Principles and Parameters Theory 224
problem-solving 132, 145, 146, 303, 306
processing speed 100, 118, 132, 215
proficiency measures 159, 163, 165, 170, 172, 270, 282, 307, 310, 313, 317-319, 323
property theory 115, 126, 222
psychological reactance 59
psychotherapy 113

Rahimpour, M. 114, 121

Ranta, L. 1, 3, 7, 14, 117, 121, 122, 159, 160, 163, 167, 176, 178, 179, 328

Raven Coloured Progressive Matrices Test 18

Reactance theory 60

reading 32, 58, 67, 75, 91, 95, 97-101, 104, 108, 110, 126, 128, 165, 167, 186, 189, 205, 206, 229, 237, 246, 247, 249, 259, 261, 276, 282, 307, 310, 311, 313, 321, 327

reading span 75, 91, 128, 186, 206, 229, 237, 259

reasoning 7, 15, 18, 24, 25, 27, 28, 66, 116, 132, 142, 213, 295

Reber, A.S. 124, 127, 128, 211-214, 217-220, 222, 227-232, 236-240, 242, 243, 253-255, 257-259, 261, 262, 264, 265

Reber's evolutionary theory of implicit/explicit learning 238-239

recasts 1, 3, 7, 85, 118, 123, 130-132, 181, 182, 188, 189, 194, 197, 202, 203, 206, 208, 215, 216

Reeve, J.M. 46, 55, 59, 64

regression analysis 34, 164, 319, 323, 325

reinforcement theories 55

Reingold, E.M. 227

relative clause extraction 271-277, 286, 288

representation 27, 46, 83, 84, 87, 89, 97, 107, 111, 122, 140, 187, 217, 221

restructuring 4, 91, 183

Reves, T. 77, 78, 83, 164, 269, 305

reward satisfaction 55

Rice, M.L. 110

Riding, R. 73, 87, 306

risk-taking 52

Rizzi, L. 275, 291

Roberts, P. 217

Robinson, P. 1-4, 6, 7, 9, 14, 30, 31, 75, 78, 79, 83, 85, 87, 93, 100, 113-115, 120-124, 127, 128, 130, 132, 137, 160, 165, 178, 181, 182, 184, 185, 186, 188, 190, 202, 206, 208, 211, 213-216, 220-226, 228, 229, 234, 240, 242, 254, 256-259, 261, 269, 306

Roediger, H.L. 213, 222, 227, 256

Rogoff, B. 19

role-playing 189

Rosa, E. 183

Rosenhan, D.L. 60

rule complexity 225, 259, 260

Russian 21, 40, 101, 102

Ryan, E.B. 162, 178, 213, 256

Saffran, J. 214

Saito, M. 273, 275, 276, 298

Salthouse, T. 132, 215, 262

Samoan 128, 223-225, 228, 229, 232, 233, 236, 238, 240-244, 246-248, 251, 257, 258, 260, 261, 266

Sandvik, E. 60

Santostefano, S. 115

Sapon, S.M. 3, 14, 70, 97, 117, 160, 161, 195, 215, 237, 268, 269, 280, 303, 305, 307, 310

Sasaki, M. 2, 5, 14, 26, 76, 77, 82, 83, 116, 120, 122, 123, 125, 128-130, 132, 133, 208, 229, 237, 259, 262, 267, 269, 280, 281, 302

Sato, C. 4

Sawyer, M. 14, 75, 91, 92, 122, 133, 160, 177, 181, 184-186, 190, 191, 196, 205, 262

Scarborough, H. 101

Schachter, J. 5, 268, 273, 274

Schmidt, R. 3, 6, 8, 9, 50-53, 55, 63, 68, 84, 86, 115, 118, 124, 133, 181-185, 205, 206, 213, 217, 226, 257, 261

Schmidt's Noticing Hypothesis 84, 118, 183, 184, 206, 213

Schneiderman, E.I. 328

Schultz, E.E. 219

Schumann, J.H. 9, 51, 61

Schwartz, B.D. 5, 125, 213, 223, 298, 303

scrambling 275, 276, 298

Segalowitz, N. 4, 6, 122, 176, 178, 184, 216

Seger, C. 216

selective attention 40, 182, 183

self-confidence 47, 53, 56, 57, 64, 143, 149, 151

self-report 146
Seligman, M.E.P. 60
Servan-Schreiber, E. 222
Service, E. 105, 108, 160, 165, 181, 185, 187, 304
Shah, P. 76, 187, 195, 206, 215
Shanks, D.R. 216, 222
Shankweiler, D. 105, 108-110
Sharwood Smith, M. 161
Shimizu, T. 298
Shinagawa, F. 236
Shook, D.J. 183
Shortest Move Requirement (SMR) 224, 225, 257
simple and complex recasts 206
Sinclair, J.McH. 87, 181, 185, 205
Singleton, D. 302
situational constraints 114
Skehan, P. 3-6, 9, 14, 42, 51, 65, 69, 75-77, 80, 82, 86, 92, 113, 114, 117, 120-123, 137, 161, 162, 164, 165, 171, 176, 178, 185, 186, 195, 202, 221, 268-270, 288, 297, 303-306, 327
Slobin, D.I. 4
Smith, N. 268, 271
Smith, S.T. 110
Snow, R.E. 1-3, 6, 100, 113, 114, 116-119, 121, 160, 207, 215, 222
Snowling, M.J. 104, 106, 107
social intelligence 32
Solomon, R.L. 59
Spada, N. 166, 167, 178, 188, 193, 206
Spanish 13, 14, 27, 31, 34, 78, 101
Sparks, R.L. 5, 65, 74, 75, 98-100, 103, 178, 261, 269
Spearman, C.E. 16, 231, 232, 234, 235, 238
specific language disorder 101, 108, 110
specific language impairment 3, 95, 97, 100, 103, 105, 107, 109, 110
speech perception 3, 103, 104
speech production 104, 107
speed of processing 100, 118, 132, 215-216
spelling 97, 98, 100, 170
Spolsky, B. 72
Stadler, M. 222, 227

Stankov, L. 120, 215, 262
Stanovich, K. 213
state motivation 139, 152
stepwise regression analysis 319, 325
Sternberg, R.J. 2, 3, 6, 8, 9, 13-15, 17, 19, 22, 23, 26, 29, 31, 32, 34, 36-38, 41, 42, 74, 113, 117, 120, 123, 178, 214, 269, 288, 303
Stevens, J. 173
stimulated recall 189, 191, 192, 194, 196, 197, 199, 207, 208
short term memory (STM) 105, 106, 185-187, 188, 189, 196-202, 205, 206, 208, 226
strategic competence 176, 177, 179
strategies 24, 25, 47, 53, 56, 86, 99, 141, 142, 189, 217, 255, 327
study abroad 2
subjacency 125, 267, 272-277, 283-285, 287, 290, 292, 293, 295, 297, 298
Suenaga, K. 191
Suzuki, N. 8
Swain, M. 83, 137, 176, 181, 182, 219, 311, 317, 322, 328, 329
Swanson, H.L. 190
syllables 108, 191
syllogisms 23, 24
syntactic awareness 3, 103, 110, 111
syntax vs. semantics modules 82

Tabachnick, B. 288, 290
tacit knowledge 17, 18, 30, 31, 214
Tallal, P. 103
Tanzania 19
tasks and measurement of abilities 19, 23, 29, 31, 32, 50, 51, 65, 68, 98, 105, 122, 162, 163, 170, 186, 187, 218, 225, 230, 233, 238, 240, 254, 297
tasks and second language learning 9, 113, 114, 115, 121, 129, 132, 137, 139, 140, 143, 144, 147, 148, 150, 155, 156, 165, 169, 175-178, 189, 194, 204, 205, 208, 213, 215, 216, 218
task attitudes 143, 147-151
task complexity 114, 115, 121

task conditions 222
task design 121
task difficulty 115
task engagement 138, 143, 144
task motivation 138-140, 142, 144, 152-
    156
task type 9, 114, 115, 121
Teen FLL 279, 283, 290, 291, 293-295
Teen SLA 278, 279, 283, 288, 290, 293-295
Test of English as a Foreign Language
    (TOEFL) 177, 186, 188, 277, 279, 280,
    282, 288
Tetewsky, S.J. 27
that-trace effects 275
theories of intelligence 2, 15-41, 116, 117,
    214, 215
    (see also intelligence)
Thorndike, R.L. 36
Ting, S.C-C. 121
Tobias, S. 65
Tomkins, S.S. 61
Tomlin, R. 6, 115, 182, 183, 206, 212, 226
trait motivation 156
transfer 20, 127, 176, 213, 217, 220, 224,
    230, 232-236, 238, 242, 244, 246, 249,
    256, 261, 267, 271, 273, 274, 276, 288,
    293, 295
transition theory 115
Tremblay, P.F. 8, 54-56, 63, 64, 68, 139, 148
triggering 123-125, 217, 226
Truscott, J. 182, 183, 206, 212
Turner, M.L. 190, 191, 207

ultimate attainment 81, 162, 302
unconscious learning 183
unintentional learning 254
Universal Grammar (UG) 70, 87, 93, 116,
    213, 223, 224, 225, 226, 260, 268, 271,
    272-276, 295-297
university students 13, 77, 255, 277
uptake 1, 3, 7, 85, 118, 131
USA 8, 17, 31, 32, 33, 34, 35, 36

Van der Lely, H. 109
Van Kleeck, A. 162

Vanezky, R. 101
VanPatten, B. 83, 184
Vellutino, F.R. 99, 104
verbal naming deficits 107
verbal reasoning 25
visual memory 104, 105
vocabulary recognition tests 321
Vogel, S. 98, 109
Vokey, J. 222
VORD language aptitude battery 74
Vygotsky, L. 20, 55

Wagner, R.K. 2, 9, 30, 182, 214
Wagner-Gough, J. 182
Ward, J.H. 171
Warden, M. 328-330
Watanabe, A. 275
Waters, G.S. 190, 191
Wechsler, D. 3, 36, 128, 212, 236, 307, 310
Wechsler Adult Intelligence Scale-Revised
    (WAIS-R) 3, 16, 36, 128, 212, 218, 236-
    237, 240-241, 251-252
Wells, G. 80
Wells, W, 169, 269
Welsh 185
Wesche, M. 77, 78, 120, 169, 269, 304
Western schooling 18
Wh-island 275
Wh-movement 267, 272-276, 278, 283-
    290, 293-295
Wh-phrase 275, 276
Wh-questions 193, 272, 273, 275, 283
White, J. 7, 131, 183,
White, L. 5, 167, 184, 203, 235, 268, 271,
    273, 274, 276, 284, 287, 291, 298, 302
Whittlesea, B.W.A. 213, 216, 222, 260
Williams, J.N. 3, 6, 7, 79, 124, 130, 131, 181,
    185, 211, 215, 216, 219-221, 257, 258
Williams, W. 29-32, 41
Willingham, D. 215
willingness to communicate (WTC) 17, 56,
    58, 145, 146, 148, 149, 151, 153, 154-
    156
Willis, J. 106, 137, 187
Wimmer, H. 106, 107

Windfuhr, K. 106
Winne, P.H. 137, 138, 141, 142, 144, 156
working memory (WM) 2, 3, 7, 75, 76, 91,
        105, 110, 111, 115, 116, 118, 122, 128,
        129, 131, 177, 181-187, 190, 191, 195-
        197, 198, 199-208, 211, 215, 216, 221,
        229, 237, 240-243, 251, 252, 253, 256,
        258, 259, 260- 262
        (see also memory, short term memo-
        ry)
Wolf, M. 107
Wynne, C.D.L. 218

Yamashiro, A. 8
Yang, S. 42
yes/no questions 193
York Language Aptitude Test 74
Young, D. 4, 19, 27, 64, 66, 161, 182, 269,
        304
Yule, G. 137
Yusa, N. 274

Zobl, H. 127, 219, 220, 228, 259
Zone of Proximal Development (ZPD) 20

In the series LANGUAGE LEARNING & LANGUAGE TEACHING (LL&LT) the
following titles have been published thus far, or are scheduled for publication:

1. CHUN, Dorothy M.: *Discourse Intonation in L2. From theory and research to practice.*
   2002.
2. ROBINSON, Peter (ed.): *Individual Differences and Instructed Language Learning.*
   2002.
3. PORTE, Graeme Keith: *Appraising Research in Second Language Learning. A practical approach to critical analysis of quantitative research.* 2002.
4. TRAPPES-LOMAX, Hugh and Gibson FERGUSON: *Language in Language Teacher Education.* 2002.
5. GASS, Susan, Kathleen BARDOVI-HARLIG, Sally Sieloff MAGNAN and Joel WALZ (eds.): *Pedagogical Norms for Second and Foreign Language Learning and Teaching.* 2002.
6. GRANGER, Sylviane, Joseph HUNG and Stephanie PETCH-TYSON (eds.): *Computer Learner Corpora, Second Language Acquisition and Foreign Language Teaching.* 2002.